Fireworks® MX:
A Beginner's Guide

About the Author

Kim Cavanaugh is a web design teacher for the School District of Palm Beach County in Florida as well as an adjunct professor teaching Dreamweaver and Fireworks for Palm Beach Community College. In addition to his work in the classroom, Kim is also a Master Trainer for Florida Leaders.net, training school principals each summer in the instructional uses of technology of all kinds.

As a Team Macromedia Volunteer for Fireworks, Kim frequently can be found in the Fireworks and Dreamweaver newsgroups answering questions and helping new users of Macromedia products understand how to best use the fabulous and complex tools that these products provide.

Kim got his start in the world of web design when he began developing a groundbreaking course in 1999 with the goal of teaching the three primary web-authoring titles from Macromedia—Dreamweaver, Fireworks, and Flash—to middle-school students. The lessons presented in this book are a result of his vast experience as trainer, teacher, and curriculum developer.

Kim lives in West Palm Beach with his wife and daughter and loves all things associated with life in South Florida—especially warm weather, the Miami Dolphins, inshore fishing, and Jimmy Buffett tunes.

Fireworks® MX:
A Beginner's Guide

Kim Cavanaugh

McGraw-Hill/Osborne

New York Chicago San Francisco
Lisbon London Madrid Mexico City
Milan New Delhi San Juan
Seoul Singapore Sydney Toronto

McGraw-Hill/Osborne
2600 Tenth Street
Berkeley, California 94710
U.S.A.

To arrange bulk purchase discounts for sales promotions, premiums, or fund-raisers, please contact **McGraw-Hill/Osborne** at the above address. For information on translations or book distributors outside the U.S.A., please see the International Contact Information page immediately following the index of this book.

Fireworks® MX: A Beginner's Guide

1234567890 FGR FGR 0198765432

ISBN 0-07-222367-7

Publisher   Brandon A. Nordin
Vice President & Associate Publisher   Scott Rogers
Acquisitions Editor   Jim Schachterle
Project Editor   Laura Stone
Acquisitions Coordinator   Timothy Madrid
Technical Editor   Deb Maupin
Copy Editor   Melissa Onstad
Proofreader   Susan Carlson Greene
Indexer   Claire Splan
Computer Designers   Tara Davis, Melinda Moore Lytle, Lauren McCarthy
Illustrator   Michael Mueller, Lyssa Wald
Series Design   Gary Corrigan
Cover Series Design   Dodie Shoemaker
Cover Illustration   Kevin Curry

This book was composed with Corel VENTURA™ Publisher.

R0179551 786

In memory of Randy Cavanaugh, 1953–1989.
You are still the best designer I have ever known.

Contents at a Glance

Contents

PART 1

Graphics Creation with Fireworks MX

PART 3
Appendixes

Foreword

It seems like just yesterday that we had released FreeHand 8 and invited a group of Advisory board members to come to the Digital Arts Group of Macromedia's offices to celebrate the release and brainstorm some new ideas that were being bantered about at DAG. We loaded onto a bus and were taken to the small Texas town of Ponder, known mainly as the scene of one of Bonnie and Clyde's bank robberies (also the home of the Ponder Steakhouse, where we were served the most enormous cut of beef I've ever seen on one plate).

A group of FreeHand engineers and Quality Assurance team members met that week to hash out some ideas for a new product—code-named "Monkeyboy" after the famous line uttered by a fledgling John Lithgow in the cult movie *Adventures of Buckaroo Banzai Across the 8th Dimension*—that would utilize the best of vector and bitmap technology to create graphics for the Web. Ideas were discussed for a way to use a vector editing tool to produce GIF, JPEG, and PNG files that were highly optimized for web publishing. This concept was born out of many hours of discussion with web designers who were forced to use one product to create vector artwork; another for bitmap art, where the vector art was usually converted and composited with the bitmap art; and another program to optimize the saved images. Then the HTML would have to be hand coded or developed in an HTML editor and posted to a site. This cumbersome process resulted in major frustrations for the designer when changes had to be made because this meant the whole process would have to be started over from scratch, or at least from a group of base files from which the images had been created.

Fireworks, as this new product was dubbed, would combine the core vector editing features found in FreeHand with some of the paint capabilities found in many bitmap editing programs. It would enable bitmap pixels to be rendered to vector paths, making the edit/client approval/change request/re-edit process less of a headache for all involved. We soon adapted the slogan "Always editable all the time." In addition to the hybrid vector/bitmap editing capabilities, there would also be the ability to optimize the images for web graphics, create sliced tables, enable JavaScript rollovers and image maps, and generate compact HTML along with the exported images.

Since those early days, we've listened to the ideas of our customers, advisory board, and beta testers to develop Fireworks into the product that you have today. Much of the input we get has been from reading posts on the Fireworks Online Forum, a newsgroup that has been invaluable to us in learning how our users perceive the product and how they use (and sometimes misuse) the product. This forum has developed into a diverse community of helpful individuals who have served to encourage, educate, and inform those who read or post to the forum. Many of the regulars who post there are also involved in our advisory and beta programs, helping us to shape the product into what you have before you today: Fireworks MX—an approachable, creative, and interactive application that meets all of your web and screen graphics needs in one easy-to-use package.

Kim Cavanaugh appeared on the Fireworks Online Forum shortly after the release of Fireworks 4, having just written *Dreamweaver 4 Fireworks 4 Studio: A Beginner's Guide*. Reading his posts, I detected a familiar ring that brought me back to the days when I was a teacher, poring over materials for my classes to develop year-to-year curricula, defining scope and sequence, breaking each step in the learning process down to its most simple form, and writing those never-ending daily lesson plans. Having posted over 2,100 replies and answers to questions on the Fireworks Online Forum, Kim demonstrated the ability to "put the cookies on the lowest shelf," as we used to say—making difficult concepts understandable, meeting the questioner at the appropriate level, and exhibiting patience with even the stickiest questions. This comes from Kim's experience in both developing curricula and working directly with students in the classroom.

This book will take you through Fireworks MX in a deliberate, no-nonsense way to build your knowledge and skill with the software, just as you would learn any other skill: gaining the concepts, walking through the steps to get your hands around how to do things, and then putting the theory into practice as you build on what you already know. If you are just starting out with Fireworks and need this kind of comprehensive curriculum, training, and guidance; or if you are a teacher and you need a textbook for a Fireworks course, this book is for you.

Enthusiastically,
Mark Haynes
Fireworks Product Team Liaison
Macromedia Customer Care

Acknowledgments

Until you've written your first book, it's impossible to appreciate just how many people are involved in getting a book published. I have been blessed to work with some great professionals during the production of this book, including my mentor and friend at McGraw-Hill/Osborne, Jim Schachterle, as well as the terrific team that kept things moving along and looking good—Tim Madrid, Laura Stone, Melissa Onstad, and Susan Carlson Greene. My special thanks go to the technical editor for this book, Deb Maupin, for all of her encouraging words and great suggestions.

One of the phenomenal aspects of using Macromedia products is the incredibly helpful community of designers and developers who assist users in learning the ins and outs of web design. If you haven't visited the Macromedia online forums to learn from these good people, then you're missing out on a terrific resource. So, in no particular order, thanks to the great Team Macromedia volunteers for Dreamweaver who've helped me and countless others—Murray Summers, Angela Burgalia, Patty Ayers, Laurie Casolino, Massimo Foti, Mako, Colm Gallagher, Bill Horvath, Al Sparber, John Parkhurst, Alan Ames, Shane Fowlkes, Daniel Short, and James Shook.

On the Fireworks side of things, I have to thank the wonderfully helpful and talented Linda Rathgeber for always lending a hand when it's needed. And for the others who contribute to the Fireworks forum—Lanny Chambers,

Kleanthis Economou, Joey Durham, Joyce Evans, David Anderson, Sandee Cohen, and Jeffrey Bardzell—my thanks for all you do, as well. Finally, a very enthusiastic thank you to Macromedia's own Mark Haynes for all the times that he's helped me and so many others to work through the technical and practical aspects of using Fireworks.

Finally, to the two most important people in my life—my beautiful brown-eyed girls—thank you for your love, support, and patience. To my wife Kayleen——thanks for always being there for me, even when I was a million miles away. And for the other author in the family, Katy, thank you for sharing the computer with me and for knowing when it was time for me to take a break from writing and do something more important—like spending time with my daughter.

Introduction

I must have dozens of computer books around my house. As someone who is fascinated with the possibilities of working with software, I've taught myself to use any number of computer programs over the years—from Appleworks back in the early '80s to CAD in the early '90s to my latest foray into the world of web design, beginning in 1998. Through all of those journeys, I've depended on authors who were able to explain how a program should work and open my eyes to the possibilities it provides. I've also learned a great deal about what makes a book a valuable learning aid—one that enables me to understand not only the *what* of using the software, but also the *why*. Too often, though, I've left my computer books on the shelf after I discovered that the information was not presented in the kind of detailed and thorough manner that helps me learn.

This book answers the lack of a reference on web and graphic design that builds your knowledge base slowly and sequentially, beginning with the basics, and leads you through a series of step-by-step tutorials that develop your skills and comfort level to the point that you can confidently use the software to create unique and dynamic graphics of your own. In addition, because this book is written by an actual teacher—and not someone who may be an expert on the software but knows nothing about the way that real people learn—you can be sure that the lessons and tutorials have been developed in a way that makes sense and anticipates your questions every step of the way.

Who Should Read This Book

Products from Macromedia often come with a bit of an undeserved reputation as being too difficult for the new user to master. They are production tools for professionals, so Fireworks and its sister programs for creating Internet content—Dreamweaver and Flash—can be intimidating at the beginning. With the programs' incredibly rich set of features, opening them for the first time and seeing all of their tools displayed can be a bit daunting. If you're one of those people who were put off by the interface, or if you just want to finally get over the initial learning curve and get down to work with Fireworks, then this book is for you.

Many books claim to present an approach that makes you feel like you're in a classroom, but few actually deliver on that promise. Throughout the development of this book, my approach has been to literally imagine myself in front of a classroom full of bright, motivated students (no dummies here!) who are eager to learn about Fireworks and who are excited by the possibilities that the Internet affords. You can think of this book as a combination of lectures and hands-on activities, presented in self-contained modules and projects that support new concepts and tools as they are introduced.

What This Book Covers

In Part 1 of this book, "Graphics Creation with Fireworks MX," you learn how to use the creative tools that make Fireworks the best software choice for creating eye-catching graphics intended for publication to the Web. Along with reading detailed descriptions of the user interface and the tools that Fireworks provides, you'll learn practical considerations in web design and tips and techniques for getting the most out of Fireworks.

Module 1 of this book, "An Introduction to Fireworks MX," provides you with the big picture of how the software is organized and how the different tools are accessed and put to use. This module not only provides you with an overview of Fireworks MX but also serves as a handy reference as you're working through the rest of the book.

Module 2, "Creating Original Artwork With Vectors," introduces you to the world of vector art and explains how the drawing tools in Fireworks are put to use. From simple lines to complex shapes, this module focuses on the ability to draw and compose your own original images using the powerful vector tools that Fireworks provides.

The second type of computer graphics that you can create and modify—bitmap images such as photographs and clip art—are the focus of Module 3. "Working with Bitmap Images" discusses how Fireworks enables you to select the individual objects found in these kinds of images so you can change them in limitless ways.

Text and text objects in Fireworks are the focus of Module 4, "Working with Text and Text Effects." This module teaches you how to style and format text so that your message has greater impact and more visual appeal.

Module 5 begins the examination of how Fireworks enables you to modify basic objects by changing the characteristics of strokes, fills, and effects. Fireworks MX has added significant improvements to the way these attributes are changed, and "Exploring Strokes, Fills, and Effects" enables you to put these new tools into play.

"Creating and Organizing Complex Graphics," Module 6, leads you through discussions and practical examples of how you can manipulate and organize basic graphical objects in Fireworks to create entirely new works of art.

The automation features in Firework are one of the program's real strengths, especially for designers operating in a production environment. Module 7, "Tools for Creating Consistent Content," discusses how to use these laborsaving devices to make your work easier and for creative purposes.

One of the most enjoyable and fascinating aspects of working with Fireworks is its ability to create computer animations. Module 8, "Creating Animated Files" covers the world of Fireworks animations and shows how to use the program to create simple animated sequences and more complex animations that make use of Fireworks' powerful capability to use animated Symbols.

Module 9 is reserved for discussions of some of the creative tips and techniques that make working with Fireworks so much fun and let you take your creative skills to the next level. "Creative Tips for Getting the Most Out of Fireworks" does just that—provides you with practical examples of how Fireworks can be used for the creation of eye-catching graphics as well as common tasks such as retouching photos.

Module 10 concludes the first part of the book by examining how Fireworks files are prepared for publication to the Web. The export and optimization process can often confuse new users of Fireworks; after you've completed "Optimizing and Exporting Files," you'll have all the information you need to ensure that your images are prepared so they download quickly while maintaining their quality.

Part 2 of this book, "Fireworks MX and the World Wide Web," concerns itself with how to use Fireworks in real-world applications when you want to export graphics for use on the Web and in other programs. The four modules in this section of the book prepare you to integrate your work with Dreamweaver, Flash, and other programs by providing practical examples of how Fireworks images are prepared for use in these other programs.

Module 11 discusses the most common uses of interactive images, leading you through construction of buttons and rollovers. This module, "Creating Image Maps and Buttons," shows you how to turn simple images into graphics that interact with viewers of your web pages in new and exciting ways.

In Module 12, "Creating Advanced Navigation Elements," you'll take the concepts of interactivity to the next level, learning how to produce navigation bars and how to employ one of the exciting features that Fireworks provides—pop-up menus.

Module 13, "Integrating Fireworks with Dreamweaver," brings things into focus by showing how Fireworks and Dreamweaver can be used together. From inserting simple Fireworks HTML files to editing Fireworks images from within Dreamweaver to creating a complete interface in Fireworks and exporting using the new Quick Export feature of Fireworks MX, this module takes you through several real-world examples of how to use the two programs together.

Finally, Module 14, "Integrating Fireworks with Other Applications," discusses how closely aligned Fireworks MX and Flash MX are and shows the different ways that Fireworks files can be used to enhance the capabilities of Flash. In addition, this module discusses the use of Fireworks in conjunction with its other siblings from Macromedia—FreeHand and Director—and covers the integration of Fireworks with programs from other companies such as Microsoft FrontPage and Adobe Photoshop.

Appendix B, "Working with Fireworks Extensions," introduces the fabulous new tools that Fireworks MX provides for extending the basic capabilities of the software. With user interfaces built in Flash, it is now possible to take the capabilities of Fireworks to new heights. Appendix B covers some of the extensions that are included with Fireworks MX and discusses how new extensions can be added as they become available.

How to Read This Book

Much like information you learn in a class, the modules in this book build on the knowledge you gain as you work through the exercises. For the true beginner, the best approach is to work through the modules and projects in order. That way, you gain understanding of the underlying concepts as they are applied to the Web and how Fireworks puts theory into practice. For more advanced users, the information in each module can be easily accessed as a reference guide to the primary tools and ideas covered in each. If, for instance, you only want to brush up on the new features of the software, you can read only those sections that contain the information you need.

Special Features

As with the other books in the McGraw-Hill/Osborne Beginner's Guide series, this book contains a number of special features that assist your learning. Throughout each module, you will find special Tips, Notes, and Ask the Expert sections that take you beyond simply understanding how the software works. In all of those special sections, I have tried to anticipate your questions and provide solutions to problems that often puzzle beginners. Additionally, 1-Minute Drills emphasize the important concepts covered in each section of the book, and Mastery Checks at the end of each module ensure that you understand the most important elements covered.

Almost all of the modules in this book are supported by free files that you can download from www.osborne.com or from the companion web site at www.dw-fw-beginners.com. These files contain not only Fireworks source files for use in the exercises you'll find here, but also photographs and other resources you'll need to complete the exercises. To access those files, simply navigate to the link for this book and download the free files that you will find there. The files are in the ZIP format, so you will need an unzipping utility such as WinZip for Windows or StuffIt for the Mac. The files contain clear instructions for how files are downloaded and uncompressed

You can find these exercise files, plus online resources, frequently asked questions, and a forum for making suggestions to improve this book, at my own web site—www.dw-fw-beginners.com. If you are a teacher or instructor using this book as a resource, you will also find lesson plans and ideas for using the book in your courses at this site.

Part 1

Graphics Creation with Fireworks MX

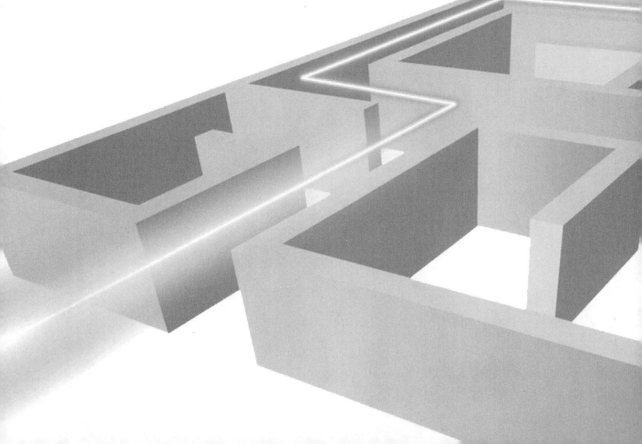

Module 1

An Introduction to Fireworks MX

The Goals of This Module

- Understand Fireworks' unique capabilities as applied to web design
- Learn the new features found in Fireworks MX
- Explore the Fireworks interface
- Understand vector and bitmap image types
- Understand the functions of Fireworks tools
- Preview Fireworks panels and tools

In these days the Internet has reached a certain level of maturity, so almost all of us expect to see visually appealing graphics that reach out from a web page and grab our attention. It's hard to believe that less than ten years ago, the Web was almost entirely text based, with little room (or need) for graphics of any kind. The Web was originally designed as a way for scientists to share data between one research facility and another; it's doubtful that the original architects of the system that would lead to the modern Internet could have envisioned what the Web would become.

Much of the credit for making the Web more visually appealing goes to those pioneers who developed software programs that would allow images to be reduced in size in such a way that they could be easily transmitted across the 'Net. Prior to the arrival of file formats that allowed for effective image compression, it was common for the World Wide Web to become the World Wide Wait. Foremost among those programs is the graphics tool developed by Macromedia—Fireworks.

The goal of this book is to teach you the many ways that Fireworks MX can be used to create visually appealing web pages while avoiding excessively large file sizes. This book introduces you to the fundamental concepts that you will need to master in order to work effectively with Fireworks, and it teaches some terrific creative techniques for using this outstanding software product along the way. From creating simple objects to working with existing images to applying sophisticated JavaScript behaviors to making animations that allow your graphics to come to life, all the tools are right at your fingertips with Fireworks. Not only is the program a powerful creative and production tool, but it also is great fun to use and surprisingly easy to learn. So, enjoy the ride, relax, and prepare to learn the power of Fireworks.

What Is Fireworks MX?

In 1998, Macromedia released the first version of a revolutionary new program known as Fireworks, creating a fundamental change in the way that web designers produced graphics for the Web. Prior to the release of Fireworks, it was a common part of a designer's work flow to bounce from program to program to produce graphics for web sites—one program in order to work with images created with bitmaps, another to do drawings, a third to produce animations, and even a fourth for optimizing images and preparing them for final inclusion in a web page. Needless to say, all that bouncing around produced some very frustrated designers. Seeing the need for one software title that would handle all of the tasks common to graphic creation and optimization specifically for use on the Web, Macromedia responded with Fireworks.

Created from the beginning as a web design tool, Fireworks has enjoyed outstanding success, and each new version of the program has grown more and more sophisticated. Now, with the release of Fireworks MX, the program has matured into an extremely robust tool for completing all of the tasks common to the design and use of graphics for the Web. The new version introduces some exciting new features and, perhaps more importantly, is now firmly entrenched as part of Macromedia's stable of web design tools, sharing a common interface with its siblings. Combined with Dreamweaver MX and the other web design titles from Macromedia, such as Flash MX, Freehand, and Director, Fireworks is now an indispensable part of working in the common Macromedia web design environment.

What Does Fireworks Do?

At its core, Fireworks is a web design tool that allows designers to produce high-quality graphics that maintain the smallest file weight possible. In addition to its basic function as a drawing program, Fireworks also includes numerous tools for generating the kinds of sophisticated graphics that today's Internet audience expects to see. From simple graphics to button rollovers to entire navigational interfaces, Fireworks places all the tools that web designers need right at their fingertips.

Drawing Tools

Fireworks makes it possible to draw, manipulate, and change almost any type of image a designer can imagine. Unique to the program is its use of vector images for the core of all the graphics it produces. Vector images are created using mathematical equations, making it exceptionally easy to modify, move, change, arrange, and composite images in almost limitless combinations. Through the use of vectors, images created in Fireworks are always editable, allowing the designer to experiment with different settings and effects to achieve just the right look for their designs. Module 2 covers Fireworks' drawing tools.

Bitmap Editing

Not every image that a designer needs is one that they produce from scratch. In addition to the original artwork that Fireworks creates, it also provides sophisticated tools for modifying images derived from clip art or photographs. Images found in the most common web formats—GIF and JPEG— can be cropped, resized, recolored, and even combined with other objects to create entirely new works of art. Module 3 discusses the tools that Fireworks provides for working with bitmap images.

Text Creation and Manipulation

As a communication medium, the Internet still depends on text for conveying ideas and information. From labels for buttons to company logos, Fireworks provides all the tools needed to work with text in exciting new ways. In addition to the simple inclusion of text as a graphic, the program makes it possible to convert text to vector-based objects, to attach text to drawings, and to modify text as you would any other drawing. Module 4 explains how Fireworks is used for creating and modifying text objects.

Vector Drawings with Bitmap Effects

Fireworks uses a unique combination of vector drawing tools with the ability to define an object in limitless ways with the application of bitmap-based fills and strokes. By using vectors to define an image's basic characteristics, the graphics produced in Fireworks can be modified at will, without losing the basic integrity of the image. Through the manipulation of the bitmap-based fills and strokes that Fireworks allows, including a new transparent gradient feature, designers can modify that basic shape into countless new creations. Module 5 teaches you how fills and strokes are applied and modified in Fireworks.

Working with Complex Images

As web pages and the Internet audience have become more sophisticated, so, too, have the images that make up a large part of those pages. Often these images require that multiple objects be combined to produce new artwork that includes photographs, text, and even interactive regions of an image. Fireworks uses several tools to make the organization of images easier for designers and allows for the inclusion of interactive regions on any image. Module 6 introduces the use of layers and web objects.

1

Production Tools

Web sites can become incredibly complex in very little time, often including thousands of images that must be created, managed, maintained, and edited. A software program designed as a production tool for web designers, Fireworks makes the type of operations essential in the world of web design—such as maintaining a consistent style throughout the site—as easy as possible. It uses tools that allow designers to save and apply their own Styles and Commands by allowing for the creation and use of repeatable symbols and now, in Fireworks MX, even allowing for the use of special commands known as extensions. Module 7 discusses the types of tools that Fireworks includes for creating consistent content.

Creating Animations

Prior to the introduction of Fireworks, designers often had to produce an image in one program and then move to a second one to create animations. Once again, Fireworks has taken the tools necessary for producing images that move, sparkle, rotate, fade, or glow, and combined them with their other production tools to make the process accessible in one package. Module 8 explains how to create and manipulate animated images.

Creative Effects

Even though Fireworks is thought of as a production tool, that doesn't mean that it lacks the ability to produce striking creative effects. From creating text that has a brushed metal look to adding 3-D fills and shadows to generating animated text that fades or even rotates around a sphere, Fireworks provides some outstanding resources for generating complex and striking visual effects. Module 9 introduces you to some tips and tricks for creating special effects with Fireworks.

Optimizing and Converting Images

Creating fascinating graphics for the Web is only the first step in the creative process. Designers must also be concerned with the speed at which their web pages will load on the viewer's computer. With Fireworks, the process of optimizing images for the most efficient download times is handled in a number of ways. Fireworks allows designers the ultimate in flexibility when balancing the often tricky process of creating images with superior quality while maintaining optimal file weight. File optimization and exporting to web-standard formats is the topic of Module 10.

Interactive Images

In addition to offering the tools for generating basic images, Fireworks also makes it possible to do all the JavaScript coding necessary for creating such interactive effects as rollovers, navigation bars, pop-up menus, and even disjointed rollovers. Once again, Fireworks excels at creating the types of interactive images that today's Internet audience has come to expect. Both Modules 11 and 12 cover the creation of interactive images in the Fireworks environment.

Integration with Dreamweaver

Fireworks' sibling program, Dreamweaver, has a well-earned reputation for allowing web designers to both design and manage their sites in a dynamic "What You See Is What You Get" (WYSIWYG) environment while providing the ultimate in design flexibility. Fireworks is the perfect companion to Dreamweaver due to the tight integration of the two programs, including a common user interface and the ability to switch seamlessly between programs to add or edit graphics. Module 13 covers the integration of Fireworks and Dreamweaver.

Integration with Other Programs

In addition to working with Dreamweaver, Fireworks also makes it possible to import files from other graphics programs, such as Adobe Photoshop and Illustrator, as well as other titles from Macromedia such as Flash and FreeHand. In addition, Fireworks makes it possible to design an image using its superior drawing tools and export the completed graphic for use in Flash. Module 14 covers the integration of Fireworks and other programs.

What's New in Fireworks MX?

Two significant changes to Fireworks make the MX version of the software worthy of the change from numbered versions to the new designation—the completely revised user interface, pictured in Figure 1-1 (which you'll learn more about in a few minutes), and the completion of the software's conversion to one compatible with Windows XP and Macintosh OS X. Macromedia did not stop there, and in Fireworks MX a number of other important changes have been made to the software.

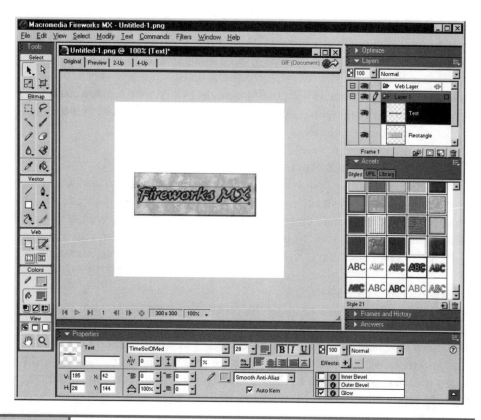

Figure 1-1 Fireworks MX features an evolutionary look to the user interface as well as compatibility with both Windows XP and Macintosh OS X.

Integrated Desktop Environment

The latest version of Fireworks features a totally reworked user interface, including both a Property Inspector for access to the most commonly applied effects and settings and a new grouping arrangement for Fireworks' panels that make it far easier to manage your work flow. In the past, Fireworks panels in particular were difficult to manage, often requiring a fair amount of moving, resizing, and juggling just to get at all the features you might need for managing an image. The new docking system greatly simplifies common tasks that require the use of panels. Coupled with the Property Inspector, a feature very familiar to users of Dreamweaver, the new interface makes significant improvements to the way that Fireworks allows images to be modified.

Enhanced User Interface

In addition to the obvious additions of the Property Inspector and the panel docking area, numerous changes have been made to other areas of the user interface in Fireworks MX. These include the ability to selectively zoom in on a portion of a document with the Magnifying Glass, the reorganization of commands in the menu bar, and enhancements to contextual menus that appear when a user right-clicks or CTRL-clicks on an object.

Tools Panel Enhancements

The tools located in the Tools panel have been reorganized to make the function of each tool easier to find and understand. Tools are now grouped by their type of operation; the groups are Select, Bitmap, Vector, Web, Color, and View. In addition, new touch-up tools, such as the Dodge, Blur, and Sharpen tools, have been added to give you greater creative control over bitmap images.

Improved Text Features

Much work has been done to make the creation of text objects in Fireworks easier and more intuitive. Text is now entered directly onto the canvas, and Fireworks now features a spell check feature as well as the ability to indent lines and more easily control the appearance of text. Additionally, Fireworks makes it easier to work with keyboard layouts other than English by offering full support for the UTF-8 character formatting encoding method.

Improved Layout Tools

Laying out complicated images in Fireworks in the past has been difficult at times, even with the enhancements to the Layers panel made in version 4. Fireworks MX makes the Layers panel more functional by allowing users to auto-scroll when selecting and moving objects in the panel. Additionally, laying out slices for creating web objects has become much easier through the use of new controls for modifying slice borders that automatically resize adjacent slices when one object is changed. Other enhancements include the ability to hold down the Spacebar while drawing an object and move it even as it is being drawn on the screen.

Improved Web Functionality

As a design tool created specifically for use with graphics intended for output to the Web, Fireworks has always excelled in creating images with web functionality. In Fireworks MX those already formidable tools are further refined, providing much greater control over the appearance of pop-up menus, the ability to export directly to Macromedia Homesite for hand-coding, and even the ability to open Fireworks source files from within Microsoft FrontPage. Other web-related improvements include an enhanced Button Editor that allows for the modification of an instance of a button without changing the source symbol, and full support for XHTML when exporting files to Dreamweaver. Fireworks is now even able to import a table created in HTML from another source, including any attached JavaScript behaviors, and reconstitute the table as a native Fireworks file.

Additional Creative Features
Much of the effort to provide new creative features centers around enhancements to the way that Fireworks users can utilize and modify gradients to create new designs. Included in these improvements are transparent gradients, new features for applying gradient masks, and the ability to apply a gradient as a fill directly from the Property Inspector.

Fireworks Extensions
One of the really exciting new features found in Fireworks is one that benefits the entire Fireworks and Macromedia community—the ability to create custom commands, known as extensions, that allows Fireworks to automatically apply effects, control appearance, and provide additional web functionality directly from within the Fireworks environment. As Fireworks MX becomes widely available, you can expect to see developers offering free and commercial extensions that will greatly expand the capabilities of this already worthy program. Figure 1-2 shows just one of the ways that this new extensibility can be applied—a custom Align panel designed within Flash that makes it easier to align objects.

Improved Bitmap Rendering
Fireworks MX features a leaner "engine" for the handling of bitmap effects and images, allowing it to open those files and apply bitmap effects in a manner that makes better use of your computer's memory.

Compatibility with Other Programs
As Macromedia continues to integrate its programs, additional functionality allows Fireworks to serve as a platform for launching and even editing graphics in other Macromedia programs. The new Quick Export button found in the

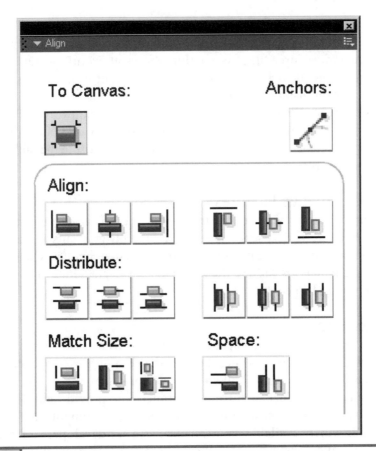

Figure 1-2 The Align panel designed by Kleanthis Economou allows users to align objects to each other or to the canvas.

document window allows users to work directly in Dreamweaver, Freehand, Flash, or Director, or to export images directly to those programs while setting the export options in one easy-to-access panel. The same functionality is provided for exporting to other programs as well, including Photoshop, Illustrator, GoLive, and FrontPage. Additionally, Fireworks will feature the ability to edit text created in Photoshop 6.

Macintosh Improvements

In addition to the incredibly gorgeous OS X interface that Fireworks has achieved, Macintosh users are now able to access recently opened documents directly from the File menu.

Tip

You'll find additional information about the new features found in Fireworks MX at the companion website for this book at www.dw-fw-beginners.com.

Working with Bitmaps and Vectors

No other graphics program takes the same approach as Fireworks does to the creation and manipulation of graphics. In Fireworks, a unique combination of the two types of graphic formats enables designers to produce images that are always editable and also easily transferred to a format suitable for the Web.

At the core of every new image created in Fireworks is a mathematical definition of the image that allows its size, orientation, and shape to be manipulated in unlimited ways. Vector images are those that use this mathematical process for defining the basic shape, position, and even color of all the images displayed on the canvas.

Fireworks performs a very interesting trick, though. On top of those mathematical vectors, it allows users to apply the second type of image created on a computer—bitmaps. Bitmaps are defined by first describing a grid and then filling that grid with color points, known as pixels, that when blended together create the kinds of images we are used to seeing on our computer screens.

The end result of this combination is the ability to create and maintain images that can be changed at any time. Buttons, for instance, can be changed from one color to another, have drop shadows applied, and even have text applied and changed at any time. As you can see in the next illustration, even simple shapes such as a line can take on various appearances when effects and other properties are applied to them.

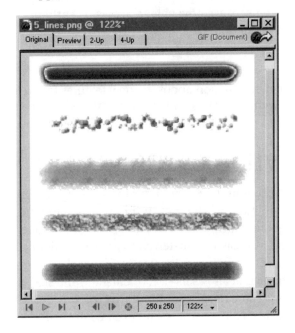

Exploring the Fireworks Interface

In Fireworks MX, the software designers at Macromedia have taken another huge step toward creating an interface that more closely aligns the different programs available in their product line. Just as in Dreamweaver MX, Fireworks uses an integrated desktop environment, seen in Figure 1-3, that allows the panels needed to apply effects or manipulate images to be opened or closed within their docking area as needed. The addition of the Property Inspector has also more closely aligned Fireworks functionality with that of its siblings, and it should be very helpful to those working with the different Macromedia products.

Note that Fireworks has no Document window present when you first open the program. Your first step, then, is to choose File | New to create a new document and follow along with the descriptions of the different features that will be summarized here. Accept the default settings for this first file and click OK to open your first file in the new working environment seen in Figure 1-3.

Main toolbar (Windows only)   Modify toolbar (Windows only)

Tools panel

Docked panel groups

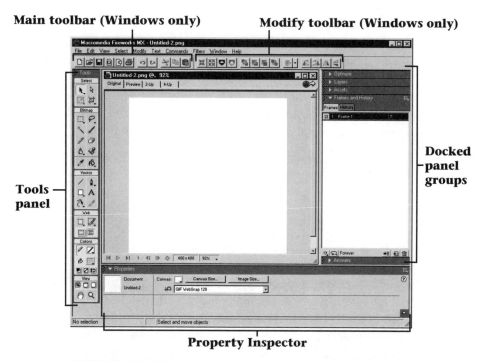

Property Inspector

Tools panel

Docked panel groups

Property Inspector

Figure 1-3   Fireworks MX now features an Integrated Desktop Environment in both Windows and Macintosh operating systems.

The Tools Panel

As in any drawing program, the tools that are used to create different objects on a canvas are at the heart of the software. Fireworks uses a special panel with an arrangement of tools, found on the left side of your screen. To save screen real estate, many of the primary tools have additional functions that are accessed by a flyout menu, represented by a small triangle to the right of the tool icon. To access the flyout menu, simply click and hold on top of the primary icon until the additional tools appear, as you see here.

Otherwise, if you have used any type of drawing or painting program in the past, you will recognize many of the icons that are located in the Tools panel. Figure 1-4 shows the Tools panel and the names of the primary tools that are found there. Note that the tools are grouped together based on how they are used and that you can float your mouse over each tool to see a label of the tool's name. Additionally, at the bottom of the panel, extra buttons have been added to allow for a quick change to how you see your document.

Note that the icons have been grouped into different categories, are separated by a gray line that divides the Tools panel, and labeled according to their function. This feature is helpful as you start working with the program and as you follow this discussion of how the different tools are put into action.

Tip

As you float your mouse over a tool in the panel, a description of its function appears next to the cursor. Once a tool is selected, you see a description of its function in the bottom of the Document window.

Selection Tools

At the top of the panel are the four icons that represent selection tools, used for choosing an object on your canvas so it can be modified, copied, deleted, or

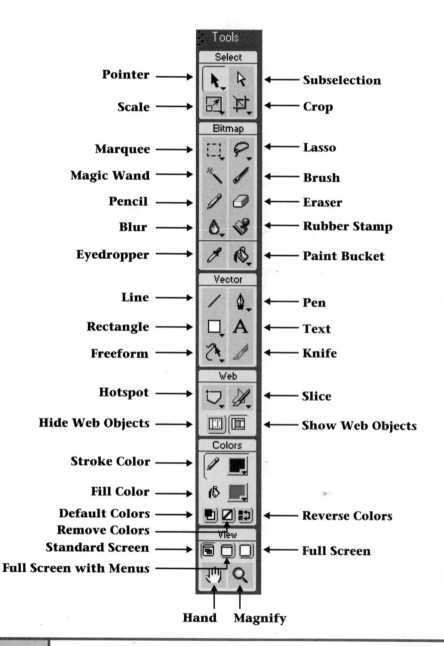

Pointer

Scale

Marquee

Magic Wand

Pencil

Blur

Eyedropper

Line

Rectangle

Freeform

Hotspot

Hide Web Objects

Stroke Color

Fill Color

Default Colors

Remove Colors

Standard Screen

Full Screen with Menus

Subselection

Crop

Lasso

Brush

Eraser

Rubber Stamp

Paint Bucket

Pen

Text

Knife

Slice

Show Web Objects

Reverse Colors

Full Screen

Hand   Magnify

Figure 1-4 Fireworks Tools panel and icons

moved. In addition to the three primary icons that are represented by default, three of these objects also have flyouts that will lead you to additional tools.

Note

As you read through this section, feel free to try the tools in the blank document you created earlier. You can also find a Fireworks PNG file for practicing in vector mode (*5_lines.png*) and a GIF file for practicing in bitmap mode (*5_lines.gif*) in the exercise files for this module at www.osborne.com or at www.dw-fw-beginners .com. Module 2 covers file formats, but for now spend some time trying out the tools as they're described.

Table 1-1 provides a summary of the primary tools available in the Select group. Those tools marked with an asterisk are available through flyouts.

Selection Tool	Appearance	Function
Pointer		Selects an entire object on the canvas so that it can be modified or moved.
Select Behind*		Selects an object that is behind another object on the canvas.
Subselection		Allows the selection of individual points along a vector path and selection of an individual item within a group.
Scale		Makes an object or a portion of an image larger or smaller, rotates it.
Skew*		Stretches or shrinks an object along a plane.
Distort*		Distorts an object by dragging handles in different ways.

Table 1-1 Selection Tools in the Fireworks Tools Panel

Selection Tool	Appearance	Function
Crop		Selects a portion of an image that will remain when the unneeded area of the image is cropped (deleted) in vector mode.
Export Area*		Chooses an area of an image for export to GIF or JPEG format.

Table 1-1	Selection Tools in the Fireworks Tools Panel *(continued)*

Bitmap Tools

Below the Select group is the Bitmap group, which consists of the primary tools for working with images created using bitmaps. Because bitmaps fundamentally differ from drawings produced in Fireworks using vector-based images, Macromedia has wisely divided these tools into their own group, including some new tools available for the first time in Fireworks MX.

Once again, flyouts (marked by an asterisk) provide access to additional tools for four of these objects. Table 1-2 summarizes the appearance and functions of the tools in the Bitmap group.

Bitmap Tool	Appearance	Function
Marquee		Selects a rectangular area in a bitmap image.
Oval Marquee*		Selects an oval area in a bitmap image.
Lasso		Selects an irregular area in a bitmap image.
Polygon Lasso*		Selects an irregular area in a bitmap image using straight lines.
Magic Wand		Automatically selects an area of a bitmap image based on similar color properties.
Brush		Draws a free-form line with attributes that can be changed in the Stroke portion of the Property Inspector.
Pencil		Draws a free-form line that is 1 pixel wide by default.
Eraser		Removes pixels from a bitmap image.
Blur		Blurs a region of a bitmap image.
Sharpen*		Sharpens a region of a bitmap image.
Dodge*		Lightens portions of a bitmap image.
Burn*		Darkens portions of a bitmap image.
Smudge*		Smudges portions of a bitmap image.
Rubber Stamp		Duplicates one area of a bitmap image onto another area.
Eyedropper		"Grabs" color from anywhere on the screen.
Paint Bucket		Fills a selected area with the color currently selected in the fill portion of the Property Inspector.
Gradient*		Fills a selected area with the gradient currently selected in the gradient portion of the Property Inspector.

Table 1-2 Bitmap Tools in the Fireworks Tools Panel

Vector Tools

Tools that enable you to create and modify vector-based objects are grouped below the Bitmap tools.

Table 1-3 summarizes these tools that are used for drawing new images and for modifying existing vectors. Notice that three of the tool icons include flyouts for accessing additional tools, listed here with asterisks.

Vector Tool	Appearance	Function
Line		Draws a straight line between two points.
Pen		Draws a series of points and connects the points with a straight or curved line.
Vector Path *		Draws a free-form vector line with attributes that can be changed in the Stroke portion of the Property Inspector.
Redraw Path *		Adds to or modifies a vector path created with any vector drawing tool.
Rectangle		Draws a rectangle with a filled center.
Rounded Rectangle*		Draws a rectangle with rounded corners.
Ellipse*		Draws a round object.
Polygon*		Draws a polygon or star based on options set for the tool.
Text		Creates an area on the document for entering text.

Table 1-3   Vector Tools in the Fireworks Tools Panel

Vector Tool	Appearance	Function
Freeform		Reshapes paths in an image by pushing or pulling the points defining the path.
Reshape Area *		Reshapes an area of an image created using vector drawing tools.
Path Scrubber–additive*		Adds additional points to a path created with a pressure-sensitive tool such as a digital tablet.
Path Scrubber–subtractive*		Removes points from a path created with a pressure-sensitive tool.
Knife		Slices a single path into two or more paths.

Table 1-3 Vector Tools in the Fireworks Tools Panel *(continued)*

Web Tools

Below the Vector tool group is a set of tools specifically designed for web-related tasks—hotspots and slices.

Hotspots are areas of an image that can have a URL assigned to them for use as links in a web page. An image that contains hotspots is known as an *image map*. While the hotspot itself is invisible to the viewer of the web page, Fireworks applies a special overlay that allows you to track and modify its location. *Slices* are used to divide a large object into multiple smaller objects that assist in creating faster downloads when inserted into a web page and which can allow special JavaScript behaviors to be attached. These tools are summarized in Table 1-4. Both have flyout options indicated by an asterisk. Two additional buttons below the primary Web tools allow you to turn off or turn on the web object overlays.

Web Tool	Appearance	Function
Hotspot		Draws a rectangular hotspot on an image.
Circular Hotspot*		Draws a circular hotspot on an image.
Polygon Hotspot*		Draws an irregularly shaped hotspot on an image.
Rectangle Slice		Divides an image into rectangular slices.
Polygon Slice*		Divides an image into irregular slices.
Hide Web Objects		Hides hotspot and slice overlays.
Show Web Objects		Shows hotspot and slice overlays.

Table 1-4   Web Tools in the Fireworks Tools Panel

Color Tools

As you would expect, Fireworks has a huge number of options available for adjusting the color and color properties of images. Still, the controls that access the color options are neatly arranged into a nice tight area of the Tools panel.

Rather than use flyout arrows, additional color options are accessed by clicking an expansion arrow that leads to dialog boxes, allowing for a number of choices in specifying stroke or fill colors. With these options, you can choose from the standard palette of web-safe colors that is presented by default, or open your system Color Chooser and use a custom color that you specify.

The most commonly used items are easily accessed from the Colors group on the Tools panel, summarized here in Table 1-5.

Color Tools	Appearance	Function
Stroke Color		Sets the colors of lines and curves (paths).
Fill Color		Sets the interior color of closed vector shapes.
Set Default Colors		Returns stroke and fill colors to their default settings; set by choosing Edit I Preferences.
No Stroke or Fill		Turns off the color in a selected stroke or fill.
Swap Colors		Swaps the color settings for stroke and fill objects.

Table 1-5 Color Tools in the Fireworks Tools Panel

View Tools

The final group of tools is used for changing how you view the image you are working with.

While they are not used for adding or changing anything in the document, you'll find these tools, summarized in Table 1-6, to be handy features when you need to change how you look at an object on your canvas.

While the possible options available on the Tools panel may seem a bit daunting, not every tool is something that you will use in everyday practice. The cleanly organized interface is something that you'll come to appreciate, though, and with practice, you will quickly find yourself confidently reaching for just the right tool when you need to get a particular job done. You'll learn how to use all of the tools in the panel during the course of this book.

1

View Tools	Appearance	Function
Standard Screen		Displays the working window in the standard mode.
Full Screen with Menus		Fills the computer monitor to its largest size. Retains the menu bar.
Full Screen		Fills the computer monitor to its largest size while hiding the menu bar.
Pan		"Grabs" the canvas and allows for its movement within the Document window.
Zoom		Changes the magnification of an image either larger or smaller.

Table 1-6   View Tools in the Fireworks Tools Panel

Ask the Expert

Question: I've used Photoshop (or FreeHand, or CorelDRAW, or Illustrator) in the past, and Fireworks doesn't seem to have as many drawing options available. Why is that?

Answer: Macromedia never set out to create the most sophisticated drawing and image-manipulation tool possible when Fireworks was designed. Remember that Fireworks has one mission—to produce the best (and smallest) images possible for use on the Web. While other programs may have some more sophisticated features available, Fireworks excels at the task it was designed to do—create and optimize graphics for use in web pages. Meanwhile, if you're more comfortable working in other drawing and painting programs, Fireworks makes it easy to import those graphics and then optimize them for the Web.

Question: Will I be able to do all of my design work in Fireworks, or will I need other programs as well?

Answer: Many professionals report that they use Fireworks without the support of any other graphics programs at all. Although it is true that Photoshop at one time was a much better tool for working with photographs, Fireworks has taken great strides in closing the gap with its competition with this release. Although you may need the advanced drawing and color support you would get from programs such as Illustrator or FreeHand if you anticipate any print work, there simply is no better production graphics tool than Fireworks if your final output is destined for the Web.

1-Minute Drill

● What tool is used for selecting objects in a document?

● How does Fireworks make it possible to access additional tools that are grouped together with a particular icon?

● What is a hotspot?

The Document Window

The Document window contains the canvas on which all work is performed in Fireworks, plus some specialized options along the bottom of the window that allow you to jump to the modification panels and change the magnification of the image. You will spend time modifying documents, canvas size, and canvas colors in succeeding modules, so Figure 1-5 just serves as an overview of the different components of the Document window.

Three components of the Document window bear emphasis at this point. Notice in Figure 1-5 that a circle with an X appears in the bottom of the window. This is your visual clue that this image is a bitmap and that Fireworks is editing in that mode.

Also notice a series of tabs across the top of the document that allow you to see different previews of how an exported document would appear when optimized and converted to a JPEG or GIF file. You learn about using these features in Module 10.

● The Pointer (selection) tool is used to select a single object on the canvas.
● Fireworks uses flyout arrows to indicate the presence of additional tools available behind the icon on the Tools panel. Clicking the flyout arrow makes the additional tools accessible.
● A hotspot is an area of an image that can have a URL assigned to it for use as a link in a web page.

Preview tabs   **Quick Export**

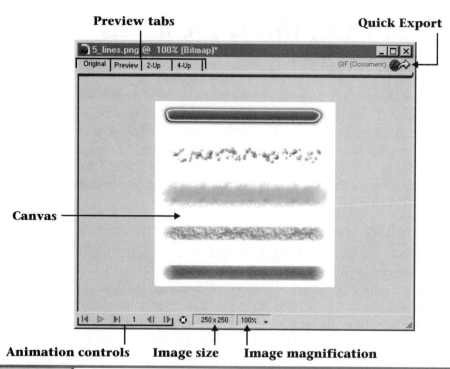

Canvas

Animation controls   **Image size**   **Image magnification**

Figure 1-5 | The Document window contains options for changing magnification
and for quick export of images for use in other programs.

Finally, the Quick Export feature found in Fireworks MX is an addition that
allows for the quick export of an image from the Fireworks working environment
to other programs. As you see here, this feature allows you to send images
quickly to other programs or even launch those programs to preview or work
with your graphic.

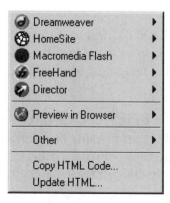

Fireworks Integrated Desktop Environment

As you saw in Figure 1-3, Fireworks now includes what Macromedia calls the "Integrated Desktop Environment," an arrangement that locks the separate elements of the program into place and allows for more efficient control of the tools that you need to modify and work with your graphics. Two improvements have significantly changed the way that work is done in the Fireworks environment, making the entire process more streamlined and logical.

Introducing the Property Inspector

One of the most exciting new features of Fireworks MX is the addition of the Property Inspector. With this new tool, many of the panels that were required in previous versions of Fireworks have been eliminated, and finding and changing image features have been made much simpler. Instead of hunting and searching for just the right panel to apply fill or stroke settings, change tool options, or apply effects to an image, all of those features and more have now been included in one easy-to-access inspector that changes based on the object selected on the canvas.

If you've used Dreamweaver in the past, the Property Inspector is nothing new; it has been present in that program since the beginning. For Fireworks users, though, the addition of the Property Inspector is a big leap forward in allowing you to quickly see the settings that are currently applied to any object and modify them as you wish.

The Property Inspector is contextual in that its appearance changes based on the object selected. Figure 1-6 shows the Property Inspector when a vector object and a text object are selected.

Because you'll be spending considerable time with the Property Inspector throughout the course of this book, and because each object selected generates its own unique look for the inspector, the features of this tool will be summarized as you put it into play during upcoming projects.

Introducing the Panel Docking Area

Probably the most frustrating part of using Fireworks in the past for many people has been the management of floating panels. As more panels needed to be accessed, it was frequently difficult to find and arrange those critical tools

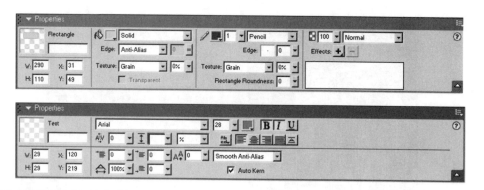

Figure 1-6 | The Property Inspector as it appears when vector objects (top) and text objects (bottom) are selected.

into just the right placement to make them easy to use. Now, in Fireworks MX, an entirely new arrangement has been devised that locks those panels into one unified section of the working environment, allowing them to open or close with the simple click of an expansion button that slides the panels into view, as seen in Figure 1-7. As with the Property Inspector, these various panels are covered as you work through the exercises in this book. For those of us who have used Fireworks in the past, this new docking environment is already greatly appreciated.

Additional Options

You have now been introduced to the three most frequently used components of the Fireworks work environment—the Tools panel, the Document window, and the Property Inspector. The great majority of your tasks will be accomplished while working between these three areas of the Fireworks interface, but, as you'd expect, a significant number of additional options are available.

The Menu Bar

Like almost every other computer application, Fireworks includes the usual menu bar across the top of your screen, with the usual array of tools—Print, Save, Save As, Copy, Cut, and Paste. Rather than go into a detailed description of the commands and options available in the menu bar, you will have the opportunity to employ these tools in upcoming exercises. A whole host of

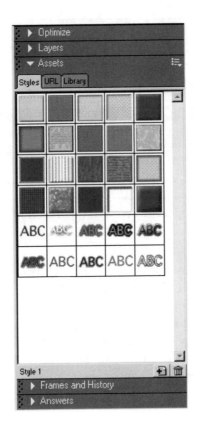
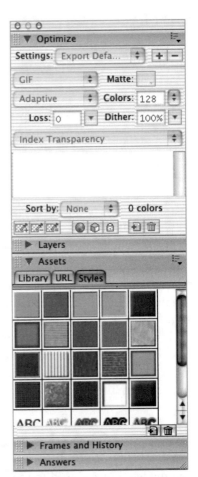

Figure 1-7 The Panel Docking Area makes access to the panels you need for applying styles, arranging objects, and applying behaviors much more efficient.

additional options are available through the menu bar that relate to the primary mission of Fireworks, creating graphics for the Web. By completing hands-on projects, you'll quickly become comfortable with these tools. Note that in Fireworks MX many of these options have been reorganized, so if you've used Fireworks in the past, it might take a little while to become comfortable with their new locations.

1

Main and Modify Toolbars (Windows Only)

In the Windows OS version of Fireworks, two toolbars are available directly below the menu bar—the Main toolbar and the Modify toolbar. The Macintosh version does not include these features. If these toolbars are not visible in your program, choose Window | Toolbars to display or hide these features.

Main toolbar   **Modify toolbar**

In the Main toolbar, you will find buttons common to most programs available in a Windows format—Open, New, Save, Print, and Undo functions can all be found in this area. On the Modify toolbar, you'll find options that are useful when working with a variety of objects on your canvas, including tools to combine (group) and arrange objects in a variety of ways.

Context Menu

As with most programs, additional options can be accessed by right-clicking (CONTROL-clicking with a Macintosh) a selected option in the Document window. Many of these features mirror those found on the menu bar and include commands to magnify, hide, arrange, animate, and convert objects on the canvas.

Whether you choose to access the commands available from the menu bar, from one of the toolbars, or from the Context menu will ultimately be based on your preferred method for working. Exercises in upcoming modules detail different choices.

1-Minute Drill

- What is the name of the work area in the Document window?
- What is the function of the tabs across the top of the Document window?
- How is the Context menu accessed?

- The work area in the Document window is known as the canvas.
- The tabs across the top of the Document window allow you to see different previews of how an exported document would appear when optimized and converted to a JPEG or GIF file.
- The Context menu is accessed by right-clicking (CONTROL-clicking with a Macintosh) a selected object in the Document window.

What to Take Away

Fireworks is the first image-creation application built from the ground up with the goal of preparing and optimizing graphics for the Web. With an impressive array of tools for creating and manipulating images and then exporting them to web-safe graphics formats, Fireworks makes it possible to create sophisticated images, all while keeping in mind the simple fact that every image needs to be as small as possible to keep download time to a minimum.

In addition to the basic drawing and optimizing tools you have been introduced to in this module, Fireworks also provides the capability to create HTML documents and images enhanced with JavaScript, as well as tools for authoring web-specific images such as animations, buttons, and drop-down menus.

Projects in upcoming modules introduce many of these advanced features as well as all of the tools you need to be a confident user of the program. Fireworks makes the life of a web designer easier by making it possible to create and optimize graphics, animations, image maps, and other images that can make your web pages more useful and interesting for your viewers. Combine its ease of use with the excellent integration Fireworks has with Dreamweaver, and you'll quickly come to appreciate why the program has become one of the favorites of web developers everywhere.

☑ *Mastery Check*

1. What is the primary function of Fireworks?

_____

_____

2. Why are files created in Fireworks exported to another image format?

_____

_____

3. How are the different tools in the Tools panel organized?

_____

_____

4. What is the primary tool used for selecting and moving objects on the canvas?

_____

_____

5. Why should caution be exercised when selecting colors from your system Color Chooser options?

_____

_____

6. What is the function of the Property Inspector?

_____

_____

7. How are panels and inspectors grouped in Fireworks MX?

_____

_____

8. Where are common commands for operations such as saving, printing, modifying, copying, and pasting found?

_____

_____

✓ Mastery Check

9. What is the purpose of "slicing" an image?

_____

_____

10. What types of commands area available through the Context Menu, accessed by right-clicking (CONTROL-clicking with a Macintosh) an object?

_____

_____

Module 2

Creating Original Artwork with Vectors

The Goals of This Module

- Understand file formats for the Web
- Explore file-management options
- Create a new Fireworks document
- Explore Fireworks' vector drawing tools
- Select and modify vector objects
- Understand the use of the Property Inspector

Fireworks is one of the few programs that allows you to switch seamlessly between the bitmap world of GIF and JPEG images, commonly used for the Web, and the world of vector-based drawing. This ability gives you the ultimate in flexibility. When you need to work with a photograph, scanned image, or clip-art file, Fireworks allows you to select sections of the image and work directly with the bitmaps that compose it. When you need to add text, create your own drawing, or even build buttons with JavaScript rollovers, it's time to crank up the vector-based drawing tools and get to work. In either mode, Fireworks provides the tools to get the job done.

The primary drawing tools are located on the Tools panel, as detailed in Module 1, but to extend the capabilities of these basic drawing tools, you will need to become much more familiar with the use of the Property Inspector and the various commands that allow for the modification of the images you create. You'll get an opportunity here to work with these powerful modification tools to create some truly awesome effects with your artwork. Again, though other drawing programs give you even greater creative control over vector-based drawings—such as Macromedia Freehand and Adobe Illustrator—the real strengths of Fireworks are its ability to work well with images that will ultimately be used on a web page and to seamlessly combine the vector and bitmap worlds of computer graphics.

Before you begin creating your first document, though, it's important that you have a basic understanding of the different image file types available for use on the Web and the appropriate use for each.

Image File Formats for the Internet

Deciding on the right kind of image to include in a web page goes beyond simply getting the best picture available and sticking it on a page—although making that choice can be a huge chore in itself. You also need to understand which types of files will be displayed properly by a viewer's browser and which types are most appropriate for the kind of image you are adding. Two file types dominate the current Internet landscape: bitmaps and vectors.

Bitmaps and Vectors— Understanding Image Types

Images can be categorized in many ways, but the most common way to think about them is in terms of how they actually are constructed. The first category of graphics is that of *bitmaps*. As the name implies, these images are created by defining a map, or grid, and then filling each of the squares created by the grid with bits of color. Bitmaps, also known as *raster* images, are the most common types of images used in all computer programs. Any time you see an image on your computer, especially if it is on the Internet, it more than likely was created by bitmaps.

The other type of image is called a *vector* image. In vector images, mathematical equations are used to describe specific points in an image, connect those points with lines known as *paths,* and then further specify the color, size, and other information that makes the image appear. Images that are created in drawing programs such as Macromedia FreeHand, Macromedia Flash, or Adobe Illustrator are vector images and most often are seen in printed artwork. Here are examples of each:

This image is of the file *ball.gif*—a bitmapped image.

This image is of the file *ball.swf*—a vector image.

In the bitmap image, you may actually be able to make out the little boxes that are filled with various shades of gray to give the illusion of shadows and light on the ball. In the vector image, there is a much smoother transition between the colors, and the image appears more natural. When the image is magnified, the difference is even more pronounced. For example, in this magnified portion of the bitmap ball, you can actually see each individual bit of the image.

If vectors are so much more efficient at producing realistic pictures, then why aren't they the type of images that you see on your computer screens and on the Internet?

The problem stems both from the competition among the software companies that produce browsers and from the competition among companies that produce the programs that generate vector-based images. Microsoft, Netscape, Adobe, and Macromedia all have a huge financial stake in gaining acceptance for their particular version of vector images. As of this date, few standards have been agreed upon. However, both of the latest versions of Netscape and Internet Explorer support the vector-based solution championed by Macromedia through their Shockwave and Flash file formats.

Additionally, the two primary bitmapped image formats still do a very good job and are universally accepted—even in the oldest versions of browsers. Although Macromedia is changing all of that with its fantastic vector-based program, Flash MX, bitmaps still rule the Internet, at least for the short term.

Bitmaps are easy to work with but have limitations inherent to the way computers display the images, so a way had to be devised to get the most out of bitmapped images while maintaining the ability to download quickly. Two bitmap file formats are most widely in use today—GIFs and JPEGs. Another format, PNG, is on the horizon, having recently gained support in the latest versions of today's browsers.

Graphics Interchange Format—GIFs

If you happened to be one of the earliest inhabitants of the Internet, then you might have connected using the CompuServe service. CompuServe was one of the first companies to realize the potential of the Web as a place the average person (as opposed to the scientists who had used it almost exclusively up to that point) might want to visit to access information. Early on, though, CompuServe decided that a purely text-based service would not be acceptable to most people. CompuServe set out to create an image format that would allow for the small file sizes needed to download quickly.

Note

The term *"file weight"* is used to describe the amount of information a file contains. For example, a file with less than 1KB of information would be considered to have a small file weight. When working on images for the Web, small file weights are critical to minimize the download time to a viewer's computer of a web page and its associated graphics.

CompuServe's solution was a format known as GIF (pronounced with a hard g as in "gift"), which stands for graphics interchange format. The GIF has been the workhorse of the Internet ever since because it allows files to be compressed for transfer without loss of quality. The primary drawback with a GIF file is its limitation to a maximum of 256 colors. In addition, the number of colors that look the same regardless of the computer and the browser being used reduce that number to 212. As a result, GIFs work best when a limited number of colors are needed and there are no fine gradations in hue and tone in the image. The following sketch of a palm tree, then, is best viewed in the GIF format.

GIFs are an excellent choice for posting images on the Web because they can be small in size but still give very good results. Other important reasons for choosing GIFs include their ability to produce transparent areas that let the rest of the web page show through them and their capacity to create small animated sequences, as you'll see when you begin working with animations in Module 8.

Joint Photographic Experts Group Format—JPEGs

Although CompuServe was the first player on the Web to develop a way to transmit images, the limitations of this format quickly became apparent when photographs were posted instead of simple drawings. Because GIFs were unable to blend colors effectively and had limitations on the number of colors available, it became apparent that another format would be necessary for those instances in which smooth transitions between colors were needed.

The JPEG (pronounced "jay peg") file format was developed as a way to address these problems. JPEGs are a great way to post pictures or other images that have subtle differences such as shadows or complex colors. For a photograph of a palm tree then, the JPEG format is the appropriate choice.

Using the JPEG format has some trade-offs, though, the biggest of which is the fact that, unlike GIF files, JPEGs lose some of their information when they are compressed. And although they do a great job of displaying photographs, they do not compress solid colors very well, do not offer the ability to do animations, and have no way to present transparent regions.

Portable Network Graphic Format—PNGs

The technology that allows GIF files to be compressed is the property of Unisys Corporation. In the mid-1990s, the company decided that it should really be paid for the work it put into making this file format possible. Early pioneers on the Internet scrambled for a free solution to this dilemma as the specter of having to pay for every image that was posted to the Web loomed on the horizon. Even though the problems associated with the possibility of having to pay a fee for each image on a web page ultimately faded away, the file format that was developed as an alternative to GIF remains today.

The portable network graphics format—or PNG (pronounced "ping")—has many of the same advantages as GIF files but avoids some of the drawbacks. Images are usually even smaller than GIFs and can display significantly more colors, all while maintaining GIFs' ability to produce transparencies and animations. As you'll see when you work with Fireworks, PNG files can even combine some of the attributes of both bitmap and vector images.

Unfortunately, the PNG file format is another victim of browser compatibility problems. Although it is supported in version 4 of most browsers (but not for the Macintosh, for instance), the PNG format has not gained wide acceptance among web designers. Perhaps it's simply a matter of users being more familiar with good old GIFs and JPEGs, but for whatever reason, PNG images are still used infrequently on the Web.

Fireworks' Native File Format—PNG

Files that you create in Fireworks use a special version of the PNG format that is different from the standard PNG format just described. Although ordinary PNG files can be read by many web browsers, the PNG files that you create when using Fireworks are not suitable for use on a web page because of the extra information that Fireworks stores along with the image as you work on a Fireworks document. As you'll learn, Fireworks maintains a library of styles and effects for each object that you create in image documents, and this extra information can create large file sizes that would lead to long download times if they were inserted on a web page. For example, the original sketch of the palm tree above is nearly 190KB in size, whereas the optimized GIF version of the same image is only 16KB. You will become quite accustomed to optimizing and exporting Fireworks files from their native PNG format to a more web-friendly version that still maintains the visual quality of the original.

File-Naming Conventions

Fireworks is a web design tool, so the standard naming rules for working on the Web apply to any files you expect to use in a web page. Here are the basic rules to follow when naming files for use on the Web and when creating Fireworks documents:

- Filenames can be as long as necessary, but spaces should not be used. However, keep your filenames just long enough so that they are descriptive.

- In place of spaces, use the underscore or dash symbol.

- Only the underscore and dash are permitted. No other special characters should be used.

- Never start a filename with a number.

- Avoid capital letters. Although in most cases this won't present a problem, there may be instances when failing to type a capital letter in a filename will cause a link to fail. It's best to be consistent and simply use all lowercase letters. By consistently avoiding capitalization when working with images that may be posted on the Web, you avoid any potential problems down the road.

- Use logic when naming files, specifying the image's appearance and function where possible. A file called *home_button.png*, for instance, will be much easier to find and work with when you need to modify it some months after its creation than a file called *image1.png*.

Managing Fireworks Files in a Web Site

Because Fireworks PNG files are significantly larger than the optimized versions of the graphics that you'll export for use in a web page, you need to give some thought to how you'll manage those original working files as you design a file structure for your site. One of the best methods is the one recommended by Murray Summers, one of the volunteers for Team Macromedia who contributes frequently to the Dreamweaver forum. In this file structure, seen in Figure 2-1,

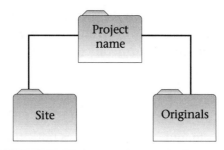

| **Figure 2-1** | Separating your working Fireworks files from those in use for your web site makes file management easier and more efficient. |

an upper-level folder is established to hold all of the information for a particular project, with two subfolders below. In this case, the folder called *Site* contains all of the optimized images and HTML files for use in a web site, and the folder called *Originals* is where all of the original Fireworks PNG files are stored. This folder might also be the place where you store photographs and other original documents that you plan to use in your site.

As you begin working with Dreamweaver or another web design software product, this separation of your working files from those in use on your site will not only make it possible to maintain those files you need for your production work in an easy-to-find location, but also make the file-management features of your web design software easier to control. This will free you from worrying about posting working files to your web server.

Now is a good time to create a site structure for the exercises you'll be completing in this book. Make a new folder somewhere handy on your hard drive and name it *Fireworks ABG*. Then create two sub-folders called *Site* and *Originals*. As you download practice files for this book from www.Osborne.com or www.dw-fw-beginners.com, be sure they go into the *Originals* folder. You learn how to optimize and export files to the Site folder as you move through upcoming modules.

Creating and Modifying Fireworks Documents

Fireworks has a number of options available for the creation of a new document right from the start of the process, as well as many ways that the work area—

called the *canvas*—can be modified once a project is underway. In this section, you will be introduced to the process of creating a new Fireworks document, see how the canvas and image can be modified, and pick up some valuable tips along the way.

Creating a New Fireworks Document

As noted in the previous module, Fireworks does not automatically open a document when the program first starts. To create a new document, choose File | New to go to the New Document dialog box, shown in Figure 2-2.

This dialog box has three purposes: to set the size of the document in width and height, to set the resolution of the document, and to establish the color of the canvas itself.

Setting Canvas Size

Width and height aren't too hard, are they? Fireworks presents this information in pixels, and because you have carefully planned your web page (right?), you know the exact size in pixels of any graphic you need for one of your pages before you design it. In the example seen in Figure 2-2, the canvas size has been set to 300 pixels wide by 300 pixels high.

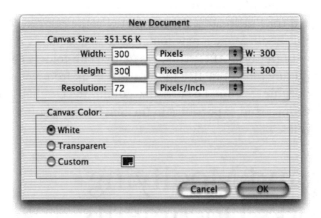

Figure 2-2 The New Document dialog box is displayed every time a new Fireworks file is created.

╋*Tip*

You may find that you get so accustomed to using Fireworks that you want to create a document for print rather than for the Web. In that case, you may set the width and height in inches or millimeters, rather than pixels, to conform to a specific paper size. To do so, click the drop-down arrow next to the unit of measurement and highlight the option you want. However, be sure to change the unit first, and then set the value; otherwise, you may get some unusual results.

Setting Resolution

Once you have determined the size of your canvas, the next step is to choose the resolution of the image in pixels per inch (ppi). *Pixels,* a word invented by combining the words *pictures* and *elements,* describes the basic unit of measurement for color in computer graphics. By default, this setting is 72 ppi, a suitable setting for an image that is to be displayed on a computer screen (almost all monitors are restricted to a resolution no higher than 96 ppi, with 72 ppi being the most common). Why pack lots of extra pixels into an image, increasing its file weight, if your viewers won't be able to see them anyway? Of course, if you are creating a document for print, you might need to experiment with this setting, but 72 ppi is just fine for the Web.

Setting Canvas Color

The final setting determines the canvas color. Again, nothing too tricky here, except the option to make the canvas transparent. To create a transparent background when the file is ultimately exported to the GIF format, you will need to begin with a transparent background at the beginning or change to a transparent background later on. Your other options are to use white or to use the Custom color button that opens the Color Chooser, shown here, to pick a custom color. Click this button to get a preview of how colors are selected in the Fireworks interface.

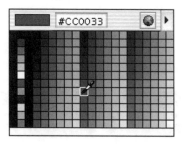

Note that as you move the pointer around the Color Chooser, the cursor changes to an eyedropper icon, representing the capability to pick up a color from the color palette. You can also pick up colors from other images active within the Fireworks window as well, a handy feature when you want to match colors in two documents.

As you pass the Eyedropper tool over the canvas, you will see a six-digit figure displayed in the top of the Color Chooser. This figure, known as the color's *hexadecimal value,* is used in HTML to specify the color used in a web page. In those instances when you need to match the colors of images and page properties, having instant access to the precise color setting is crucial. However, for this project, set your canvas to white.

Tip

Resize your window so that you have some gray area around the canvas. This "negative area" around the canvas is a tool in itself. Use it when you want to drag images off the canvas so they can be rearranged. In addition, whenever you have an object selected on the canvas, a handy way to unselect it is to click in the negative area of the Document window.

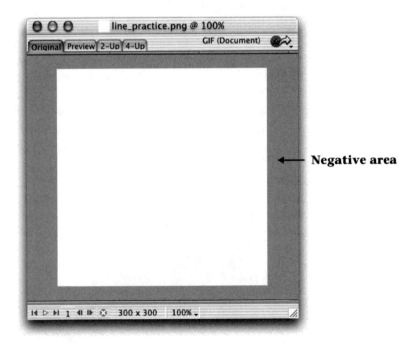

Negative area

You have now seen how easy it is to create a Fireworks document and have learned a few tips to make working with the canvas easier and more efficient. In upcoming exercises, you learn how to further modify and manipulate the canvas. For now, you can close any open documents that you may have been experimenting with as you prepare to look at some Fireworks drawing tools.

1-Minute Drill

● How are bitmap images created?

● How are vector images created?

● Which file format is most appropriate for drawings?

● Which file format is most appropriate for photographs?

Exploring Vector Drawing Tools—Lines

In vector terms, all drawings are described by the position of at least two points and by the paths that connect the points. Fireworks takes this basic concept and extends the capabilities of the program by allowing the points and paths to be described and modified in an almost limitless variety. Through the combination of various stroke, fill, and effects settings, the basic structure defined by a vector object can be fleshed out to create an entirely new graphical object.

You will recall from Module 1 that the primary tools for creating new objects on a Fireworks canvas are located under the Vector heading of the Tools panel, as shown in Figure 2-3. You can refer to Table 1-3 back in Module 1 for a summary of the vector tools you'll be using in this section.

The Line Tool

The first type of vector shape you will work with is the line, which is the simplest type of vector path because it consists of only three primary elements—a beginning

---

● Bitmaps are created by devising a grid and then filling each square of the grid with a color.
● Vector images use mathematical equations to describe the position and color of points and lines in an image.
● The GIF format is best for drawings.
● The JPEG format is best for photographs.

Figure 2-3   All vector-based drawing tools are found in the Tools panel below the Vector label.

point, an ending point, and the line that is created mathematically when the points are joined. To use the Line tool, locate its icon in the Tools panel, click the Line tool button, and move your cursor over the canvas to begin using the tool. Note as you create lines that by holding down SHIFT while dragging the cursor, you can create a perfect vertical, horizontal, or 45-degree line as you drag.

A line that you draw will appear in a light blue color with the two end points represented by small squares. This is Fireworks' way of letting you know that this line is selected. Any time you draw a new object on the canvas with a vector tool, the object remains selected until you tell Fireworks that you no longer wish to work with the object by deselecting it.

To deselect the line, switch your tool selection to the Pointer tool and click anywhere in the negative area around your canvas. The line will now appear simply as a line—1 pixel wide with a pencil-like appearance. To reselect the line, pass the Pointer tool over it. Notice that as the Pointer tool comes into contact with the line, the selection points appear and the line changes to a red color. Fireworks is letting you know that if you click your mouse button once, this is the object you will select. Click your mouse now to select the line, and it changes back to a light blue color.

Introducing the Property Inspector

It's time to take a detailed look at one of the fundamental changes in Fireworks MX, the Property Inspector, pictured in Figure 2-4.

Moving through the properties applied to this simple line provides a good introduction to the way the Property Inspector is used for inspecting and modifying objects in a Fireworks document. Start by taking a closer look at

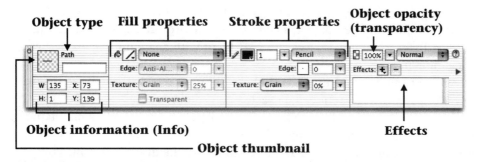

Figure 2-4   The Property Inspector summarizes information about selected objects and allows for the modification of object properties.

the Object information (Info) area, shown in the lower-left corner of the Property Inspector in Figure 2-4.

The Info area provides you with the precise location of each selected object, measured in *x* and *y* coordinates from the top-left corner of the canvas. To move an object precisely, you need only enter a new value directly into one of those fields and press ENTER/RETURN. Your object will jump to the new position as soon as the value is changed. Width and height of an object can be modified in the same way.

Modifying Stroke Properties

At the center of the Property Inspector, shown in Figure 2-5, locate the stroke properties options. In this area, you can change all of the fundamental aspects

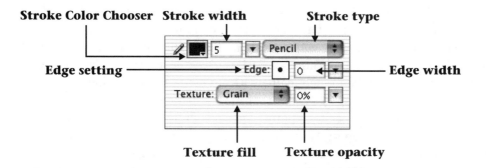

Figure 2-5   The Stroke area of the Property Inspector provides detailed information about the stroke attributes applied to an object.

of stroke properties applied not only to a line, as in this case, but also to the lines that outline a filled object, as you see in the project that concludes this module. Refer to Figure 2-5 as you experiment with changing the properties of a simple line.

As you begin to experiment with these different settings, you'll see the true power of Fireworks in action. The basic line is defined as a vector object, so its size and position on the canvas can be easily changed, all while maintaining the object's basic integrity. Meanwhile, the line can be changed in almost infinite ways by adjusting the properties applied to it. Try the different settings by changing this basic line now, modifying its stroke color, the stroke types, and the edge settings.

In the following example, the same line was duplicated by choosing Edit | Duplicate, but different stroke types were applied to each of the lines. Note that, as you apply each new style, the exact properties of the line are reflected in the Property Inspector.

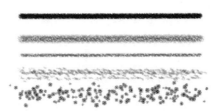

The Pen Tool

Whereas the Line tool is the most basic tool for creating an open vector path, the Pen tool may be the most advanced. The Pen tool is one of Fireworks' most versatile tools, allowing you to create both straight line segments and lines controlled through the application of *Bézier curves*. Bézier curves, based on a theory developed by the French mathematician Pierre Bézier, define curves by plotting their relationship to each other through the use of control points that define a curve as it approaches a point, and also define the properties of the curve as it leaves that point. With the Pen tool, creating Bézier curves allows you to modify curved line segments in elegant ways that might elude you if you were confined to using only arcs, which define curves in a more restrictive manner.

Although creating curved segments with the Pen tool is one of its fundamental uses, it can also create straight lines. To draw a straight line with the Pen tool, simply click anywhere on your canvas, release the mouse button, move to a new point, and click again. Using this connect-the-dots technique, you can define even complex shapes, like the dog in the following illustration, fairly easily.

Tip

Look for the small circle that appears near the base of the Pen tool icon as you near the starting point of your drawing. This is a signal that clicking again will close the shape you've created and make it possible to apply a fill.

The real power of using the Pen tool comes in its ability to create and modify Bézier curves. For a quick demonstration of how the Pen tool creates curves, follow these steps:

1. Select the Pen tool and click and drag to create a starting point for your line. Release the mouse button.

2. Next, move the Pen tool away from the original point and click and drag to designate a second control point. As you do so, you will see two *handles* appear. They are special controls that let you set the length and curve of each curved section.

3. While continuing to hold down the mouse button, move the tool. Notice that the *handles* are moving, with the line shape and direction following the settings applied with the handles.

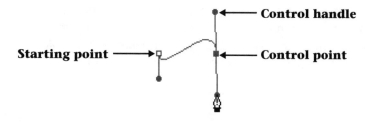

Control handle

Starting point ———▶

Control point

Bézier curves can be a bit tricky at the start, but you'll be using them in more depth in upcoming projects. For now, see if you can duplicate the heart pictured here by using the Pen tool to define the points and curves.

Tip

The Fireworks manual has a detailed section on Bézier curves and their use; it describes these powerful tools in more depth than is possible here. In addition, there is an excellent tutorial on the Web at www.freehandsource.com that describes how the tool is used in its sister program—Freehand. The techniques described there are the same as those for the Fireworks Pen tool.

The Vector Path Tool

If you have used previous versions of Fireworks you may recall that the Paintbrush tool often served two masters—working in both vector and bitmap mode depending on the type of object you were working with. In Fireworks MX, that tool has been labeled more appropriately to describe what it does—create paths by describing vectors in a free-form manner. With the Vector Path tool, creating a freehand line is a simple matter of choosing the tool (available as a fly-out option beneath the default Pen tool) and drawing your line on the canvas. Note that you may use the Stroke options of the Property Inspector to determine the exact stroke properties you want to apply before you begin drawing with this tool. Also note that, though this tool is easy to use, it is more difficult to control the appearance of curves with this tool than with the Pen tool, especially when using a mouse.

As you complete this section, take some time to experiment with the different settings available through the stroke options in the Property Inspector. Again, many of these options are explored in other projects in this book, but for now, take some time to play with the stroke types, size, and colors.

2

Exploring Vector Drawing Tools—Shapes

Shapes are created by vector paths that are closed; circles and rectangles are examples. As with the structure of lines, the initial structure of shapes is defined by vector points connected with paths. In the case of these types of objects, the path ends where it begins—creating a closed path that you can fill with colors, patterns, or gradients, all known as *fills*. As with strokes, any shape can be modified in almost limitless ways by modifying the selected fills, as demonstrated in Figure 2-6.

In Fireworks, you'll learn that one of the easiest ways to create a graphic is through vector shapes that can be combined or even used as cookie cutters to punch out one shape with another. The tools that you will explore in this

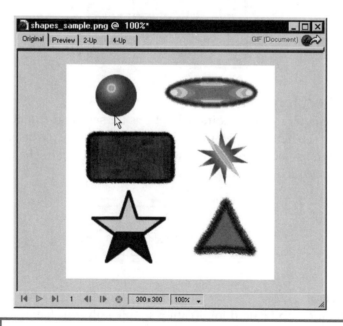

Figure 2-6 Use the Fill panel to apply different gradients, patterns, and fills to closed objects such as these basic shapes.

section are summarized below. As before, you may want to refer to Table 1-3 for a more detailed look at each of the tools and its capabilities.

Creating Basic Shapes

Drawing the basic shapes of rectangles and ellipses is a simple matter. Just drag your mouse across the canvas until the shape is the size you want. Change the fill color to a simple solid by accessing the Fill Color option at the bottom of the Tools panel or by going to the Fill properties section of the Property Inspector. When drawing these shapes, hold down SHIFT if you want to create a perfect square (Rectangle/Rounded Rectangle tools) or a perfect circle (Ellipse tool). Note that the Shape tool includes a flyout menu that allows you to choose from the Rectangle, Rounded Rectangle, Ellipse, and Polygon tools.

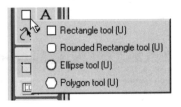

Rounded Rectangle Tool

Rounded rectangles include additional options for setting the radius of the corner, as you see here. Tucked in the bottom of the Property Inspector, under the Stroke options, locate the Rectangle Roundness setting to change the size of the radius applied to a corner when using this tool.

Polygon Tool

The Polygon tool can be used for creating simple polygon shapes based on settings accessed in the Property Inspector. To change the number of sides for a polygon, simply change the Side number by moving the value slider or typing the number directly into the field, seen here, and draw your shape onto the canvas.

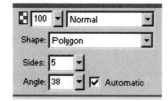

2

One of the coolest things that the Polygon tool can do is create stars. To draw a star, change the Shape category in the Property Inspector to Star and drag out your new shape onto the canvas. Note that when you leave the Automatic setting checked, as seen here, Fireworks will calculate the correct angle to create a perfectly proportioned star. Of course, you don't need to let Fireworks calculate the angle for you. You should experiment with the different settings to get a feel for the results you can achieve.

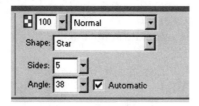

Have fun with this one. By changing the options in the Options panel for the Polygon tool, you can create some great stars with unusual attributes. When you are finished experimenting, you should be able to duplicate the stars shown here by adjusting the angle of the star and the number of points. You may note in the illustration that a star set to three points actually appears as a triangle.

Setting Fill Properties
Closed paths can be filled with colors, patterns, or gradients to create any number of effects. To create a shape with a simple solid color, set the fill color with the

options you see in this snapshot of the Fill properties area of the Property Inspector and draw your object on the canvas. You can also change the fill color of an object that is selected or set the fill color to none by accessing this option.

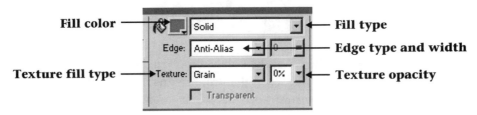

There are almost limitless possibilities for the types of fills and fill combinations that can be applied to an object, and just as with strokes, the Fill options in the Property Inspector change based on the selected category. In addition to simple solid colors, you can create fills that are composed of gradients that you can edit into entirely new color patterns and save for use with another project. Fireworks MX even makes it possible to create semitransparent gradients, as you'll learn to do in upcoming projects.

Your task as you close out this section is to experiment with the different possibilities for adjusting object fills. When you're finished, you should be able to duplicate some of the samples you saw earlier, in Figure 2-6. To access a file of this image and see which settings were used, download the file called *shapes_samples.png*, available in the Module 2 files at www.osborne.com or www.dw-fw-beginners.com.

Project 2-1: Working with Multiple Objects— Arranging, Combining, and Aligning

You have seen how easy it is to create both lines and shapes in Fireworks and have had an opportunity at least to begin experimenting with some of the possibilities that these terrific tools afford. Still, the shapes you have worked with have been relatively basic, and Fireworks is far more than a tool for creating stars, even if those stars can be pretty cool. To extend what you can do with the software, your next task is to modify multiple shapes by arranging or combining them in new ways on your canvas.

Step-by-Step

1. Create a new file by choosing File | New and set the canvas area to 300 pixels wide by 300 pixels high. Save this file as *multiples_practice.png*.

2

2. Start by creating four rectangles and placing them near the top of the canvas. You can duplicate the first rectangle by drawing it and then choosing Edit | Copy followed by Edit | Paste, or by using the keyboard shortcuts—CTRL-C to copy and CTRL-V to paste. Windows users can also access these functions on the Main toolbar. Alternately, Edit | Duplicate will automatically copy a selected object and offset it slightly from the original object. Finish by drawing a larger rectangle near the bottom of the canvas.

3. Imagine these five rectangles as cards on a table. The first card down will always be on the bottom, with succeeding cards stacked on top of it. The process of arranging objects on a canvas entails changing the order in which they are stacked. To see this in action, first drag the largest rectangle so that it overlaps the smaller ones, as shown here.

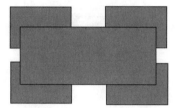

4. To change the stacking order arrangement, first select the larger rectangle by clicking it and then choose Modify | Arrange | Send To Back—moving the selection all the way to the bottom of the stack.

5. The larger rectangle now moves to the bottom of the stack, as shown here, with the smaller rectangles lying on top of it, as if you had reshuffled the cards. This process is simple and easy to learn. Experiment with the different ways that objects can be stacked higher (Bring Forward) and stacked lower (Send Backward) to gain an appreciation for how objects can be arranged on the canvas.

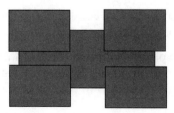

6. The next operation requires a new skill—selecting multiple objects on the canvas. Once again, this is easy to learn. First, delete all the rectangles from the previous operation by using the Pointer tool to select the object and then pressing DELETE. Now that you have a clean canvas, draw a circle and a rectangle and position the objects so they are overlapping slightly.

Tip

Remember that to easily unselect an object, just click anywhere in the negative area of the Document window.

7. To select multiple objects on the canvas, simply choose the Pointer tool and hold SHIFT while clicking on top of the rectangle and circle. Blue handles will appear on both items, indicating they have been selected, as you see here.

8. Four options are available for combining objects on the canvas, and all are accessed by choosing Modify | Combine Paths. Try the first option—Union—now, and the two shapes on the canvas will be combined into an entirely new object based on the common points they share along their outside borders.

9. Click the Undo button or choose Edit | Undo to return to the original arrangement of a separate circle and rectangle.

10. The next option to explore is Intersect. Choose Intersect from the Combine menu. In this case, only the overlapping areas created where the circle lies on top of the rectangle remain, with the rest of the shapes stripped away.

2

11. Undo the last step and choose Punch from the Combine menu. Using this command causes the object on top to work like a cookie cutter, removing the portion of the bottom object where the two objects overlap.

12. Finally, you use the Crop command when objects that have different fill and stroke characteristics are to be combined, with the area left behind taking on the attributes of the cropped object. Undo the last step. Select the rectangle, change its fill attribute, and then select the circle and set a different fill for it. Next, select both objects and choose Modify | Combine | Crop. In this example, I used a diamond fill on the rectangle and a solid fill on the circle. The shape was cropped to leave just the area on the rectangle that was covered by the circle, but the new shape kept the rectangle's fill pattern, as you see here.

Figure 2-7   Using Combine Paths commands allows you to create new objects from simple shapes.

13. Figure 2-7 displays different combinations of shapes, all made possible by using multiple objects and then combining them in new ways. See if you can duplicate these examples as you prepare to move on to a new topic.

14. There may be times when you need to align multiple objects on the canvas in nice, neat vertical or horizontal rows. To do this, you'll learn a new selection technique and then align objects on the panel using the Align commands.

15. Start by either creating a new document or deleting all the objects from the previous exercise from your existing canvas. On the canvas, draw five shapes and arrange them with the Pointer tool so that they are distributed randomly.

16. Use the Pointer tool to draw a box around all the objects on the canvas, as shown here. Release the mouse button, and—voilà!—all the objects are selected at once. This process is known as *marqueeing,* but it should not be confused with the use of the Marquee tool.

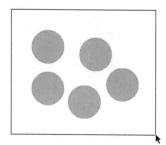

17. With all five objects selected, you can now align them in a variety of ways. Choose Modify I Align I Center Vertical, and all the objects will retain their horizontal positions but be aligned to the center of the canvas.

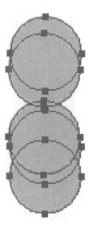

Tip

You'll achieve the best results by moving objects close to where you want their final positions to be before using the Align commands.

18. Undo that alignment and this time choose Modify | Align | Center Horizontal. All the objects will fall into alignment across the center of the canvas.

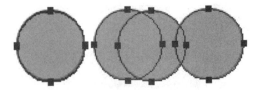

19. As you experiment with alignment options, you'll notice that the objects on the canvas are actually aligned to each other, not to the edges of the canvas as you might expect. As you finish up this project, expand on your alignment and combining skills by attempting to duplicate the friendly caterpillar that you see here.

Note

The alignment of objects on the canvas is now handled by one of the groundbreaking additions to Fireworks MX—Fireworks extensions. You can find out more about these new tools in Appendix B.

Project Summary

In this project, you have had the opportunity to complete some basic drawings and have seen how objects can be arranged and stacked on the canvas to modify basic images into new creations. You have also seen how those basic shapes can be modified to become entirely new things through the use of the Combine commands that Fireworks provides. These skills will become an important part of your Fireworks repertoire as you continue using the program, and you will return again and again to use these simple yet effective techniques for creating new graphical objects.

The Power of Transformation

Much of the work you do in Fireworks begins with the creation of very simple shapes. As you've seen already, Fireworks makes it possible to arrange and combine basic lines, rectangles, circles, and polygons into fundamentally new shapes by combining them.

This section expands on those possibilities by looking at how those basic shapes can be changed even further. Once your objects are on the canvas, Fireworks allows you to move, rotate, and resize your vector shapes in innumerable ways.

Two areas of the Fireworks interface are used for modifying and transforming vector objects—the Transform tools that you find grouped together in the Tools panel and the options listed under the Modify heading of the menu bar. You'll find as you work with Fireworks that both of these areas are necessary for changing vector shapes when you design graphics.

Transformation Tools

Three tools in the Tools panel allow for the quick transformation of selected vector objects. The functions of these tools are summarized here (as well as back in Table 1-1):

- **Scale tool**   Allows a selected object to be resized and rotated.

- **Skew tool**   Allows the corners of a selected object to be slanted.

- **Distort tool**   Allows the distortion of a selected object by moving selection handles that enclose the object.

In addition to the use of these transformation tools, objects are often changed by modifying the vector points that define the shape. Recall that vector objects are defined by the points that appear on your canvas and the paths that connect those points. Using the Subselection tool, you are able to perform point-by-point transformations of vector objects, changing their structure in fundamental ways. Using the Knife tool, you can add additional points along a path or even slice a vector shape into separate pieces.

Modifying Objects

The Modify menu contains the largest number of options for changing the basic structure, size, and appearance of selected objects in a Fireworks document. In addition to the basic transformation options for scaling, skewing, and distorting objects, the Modify menu also contains options that allow you to flip and rotate graphics, arrange them on your canvas, combine objects, or even specify precise modifications based on numeric values you enter (for rotation, scaling, and resizing of a vector shape). As you see in the upcoming project, you will frequently turn to the Modify menu when you employ the power of vectors in original artwork.

Project 2-2: Transforming Objects

The possibilities for working with vector objects in Fireworks extend well beyond the ability to simply draw objects on a canvas and even beyond the many possibilities afforded by combining shapes or modifying fills and strokes. With the tools and techniques you learn in this project, you will be able to stretch, rotate, distort, and transform objects in new ways. In addition, you also learn how a path can be transformed by using a new device, the Subselection tool, to transform individual points along a path. Once again, the possibilities are almost limitless because Fireworks provides tools that let you take basic shapes and turn them into entirely new creations.

Step-by-Step

1. Create a new document by choosing File | New and setting the document size to 300 pixels wide by 300 pixels high. Call this new file *transform_practice.png*.

2. Draw a simple rectangle and center it on your canvas. With the rectangle selected, locate the Scale, Skew, and Distort tools on the Tools panel. By default, the Scale tool is visible and the other two are available from a flyout menu.

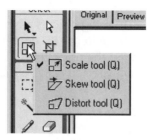

3. Select the Scale tool and try resizing the rectangle by dragging one of the handles that surround the object when this tool is selected. With the Scale tool, you can change the size of any object by changing its height or width. You can also change both at once by dragging handles from the four corners of the object.

4. Note that the cursor will change to a curved arrow when it approaches the corner of the selected object. This Free Rotate option allows you to turn any object by simply holding down the mouse button when the rotate cursor appears and turning the object as you wish.

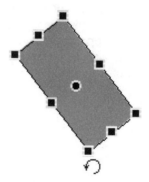

5. Skewing an object with the Skew tool transforms the path along a plane. That is, as you drag a handle, the object will be constrained by a straight line along the border. This is a great method for taking a simple rectangle or another shape and building more interesting objects.

6. The final option in the Tools panel allows any object to be twisted freely, allowing for the distortion of the object into entirely new and unusual shapes. Try this with a rectangle, a circle, or even a star.

7. Additional options for transforming objects are available from the Modify menu. For instance, to rotate an item 180 degrees, choose Modify | Transform | Rotate 180° to flip the object over. The options here are easy to understand, and you are invited to explore them on your own.

Tip

Take special note of the Numeric Transform option that lets you specify the exact height and width of an object on the canvas. This is handy if you have limited space—as almost every web page has—and you need an object to be an exact size.

8. With the Subselection tool, you are able to select an individual point along a path and then alter the appearance of the object by moving that point. That's a wordy description that cries out for an example, so to see the concept in action, start by drawing a five-pointed star on your canvas.

9. Once the star is drawn, choose the Subselection tool at the top of the Tools panel to the right of the Pointer. Notice how the handles that define the points of the star change in appearance—from solid to hollow. These hollow handles are your clue that the individual point—whether it is in a closed path such as the star or in an open path such as a line—can be moved from its location. To select an individual point on this path, click once with the Subselection tool so the point is filled. Move the individual points of the star around the canvas, and you should be able to transform your star into something like this one.

10. To create additional subselection points along a path, use the Knife tool. By choosing the Knife tool, you may slice an object into additional paths that you then can modify with the Subselection tool or Pointer tool. Simply drag the Knife tool across any path, and a new subselection point will appear

where the tool intersects the path. In this example, an ellipse has been sliced in two separate paths and then pulled apart using the Pointer tool.

Tip

Deselect an object once you've sliced it with the Knife tool by clicking on the negative area of the document window; then pass the Pointer across the new separate paths to select them.

11. To complete this brief look at the transformation capabilities of Fireworks, duplicate the book that you see here. Create two rectangles and then use the Scale, Skew, and Distort tools to create the front and back covers of the book. Create a third rectangle and scale it to the correct size to be used as the book's spine.

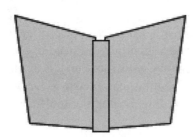

Project Summary

The power of vector objects should be more evident to you as you complete this simple project. Were you to attempt to scale, skew, or even rotate an object created with bitmaps as you have done here, the process would be much more tedious and, in some cases, nearly impossible to pull off. By using a design scheme that creates objects that can be twisted, moved, skewed, rotated, and modified in almost any way—and by making it possible to maintain full editability of all objects at all times—Fireworks has greatly reduced the amount of work required for generating fascinating and complex graphics.

1-Minute Drill

- What combination of actions allows multiple objects to be selected on the canvas?
- Which Combine command causes an object on top of another shape to cut out a section the way a cookie cutter would?
- What functions on the menu bar allow objects to be arranged on the canvas?
- What three tools are available on the Tools panel for altering the basic size and shape of an object?

Bringing Your Objects Together

Now that you've seen how easy it is to create a variety of new shapes by beginning with a basic object, you should appreciate the power of vectors. This always editable, all the time approach to computer graphics is fundamentally different from simple programs such as Microsoft Paint, and even more advanced software such as Adobe Photoshop. In those bitmap-based programs, once you've created and saved a document, the individual bits of color are locked down and cannot be changed as easily as vectors. As you see in the next module, modifying bitmap images requires that you first select an area that you wish to change before any transformation can take place.

Vector drawings, on the other hand, can be changed even after the document has been saved and reopened, whether you need to change a line or a shape or even fundamentally change the colors and effects applied to the object. As you've seen in the exercises you've completed so far, vector objects are easily modified, arranged, and combined using the tools that Fireworks provides.

Project 2-3: Combining Objects in a Fireworks Document

In the final practice exercise for this module, your task is to re-create the document you see in Figure 2-8. You'll need to use all the tools and techniques

---

- Multiple objects on the canvas can be selected by using the Pointer tool while holding down SHIFT and then clicking the objects.
- The Punch command takes an object and punches out an area beneath it that matches its shape.
- To arrange objects on the canvas, first select the objects and then choose Modify | Arrange and select one of the options.
- The three tools on the Tools panel used to alter the shape of an object are Scale, Skew, and Distort.

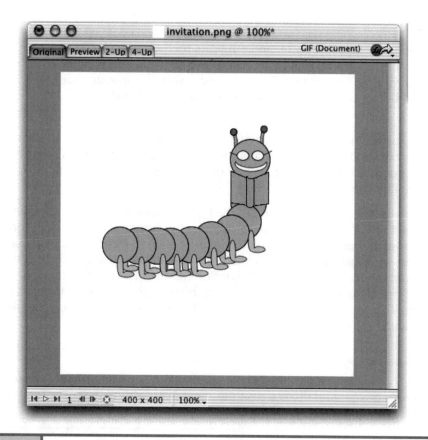

Figure 2-8   This graphic was created using the techniques you've learned in this module for combining, arranging, and transforming simple shapes.

that were covered in this module to duplicate the graphic to be used in an invitation to a special event at the (fictional) Poinciana Beach Public Library.

Step-by-Step

1. Start by creating a new document 400 pixels wide by 400 pixels high. Save the file as *invitation.png*.

2. Using the skills you have developed, create the caterpillar that you see in Figure 2-8. Start by creating a basic circle and then duplicating the object to create the body of the caterpillar.

Tip

In addition to the copy, paste, and duplicate methods discussed previously, you can also duplicate an object by holding down ALT while dragging away from the original with the Pointer tool. The object you wish to duplicate should not be selected before you begin dragging away from the original.

3. Once you have the body defined and the segments arranged, create the feet by combining two ellipses into one object. Again, duplicate as many as you need and, in order to place some of those objects behind the body, choose Modify | Arrange | Send to Back.

4. Create the antennae as you did the feet, combining two rectangles, with the top rectangle skewed at 15 degrees, by choosing Modify | Transform | Numeric Transform and using the Rotate option to move the object. Combine the rectangles with the Union command. Finish by adding a circle at the top, duplicating the antenna, and choosing Modify | Transform | Flip Horizontal to make the second antenna. As with the feet, you may want to select these new objects and use Modify | Arrange | Send to Back so they can be placed behind the caterpillar's head.

Tip

Use the Zoom tool (magnifying glass icon) to zoom in on a portion of drawing by dragging a box around the place on the canvas you wish to magnify. To return to the previous magnification, simply double-click on the Zoom tool.

5. For the caterpillar's mouth, use the Modify | Combine Paths | Punch command to punch one circle with another to make the quarter-moon shape. The glasses are simple circles with a white solid fill and lines added on the sides.

6. Finally, the book is created in the same way that you used the Skew and Scale tools in the previous project.

Project Summary

This is meant to be a fun and easy review of the skills you learned in this module. If you are having difficulty completing a particular portion of the caterpillar, review the project that covers the skills needed. In the end, your completed invitation should look at least as good as the one here, if not better!

What to Take Away

In this module, you have been introduced to many of the vector drawing tools available in Fireworks. By combining the basic shapes and lines available in the Tools panel, you can create any number of basic shapes and paths.

The real power of the software, though, lies in its ability to manipulate objects on the canvas into new and exciting graphics. By using the power to arrange, transform, combine, rotate, and distort objects, you can turn a simple series of circles into a friendly caterpillar. Combine those capabilities with the ability to modify strokes and fills and apply effects, as you learn to do in Module 5, and you quickly understand why Fireworks has become such a popular image-editing software title, particularly when creating images for the Web.

2

✓ *Mastery Check*

1. How are bitmap images created?

_____

_____

2. List three rules for naming files that will be used on the Web.

_____

_____

_____

3. What visual aid does Fireworks use to let you know that an object is available for selection?

_____

_____

4. How are vector-based drawings created?

_____

_____

5. What basic shapes can be drawn using the tools provided in the Tools panel?

_____

_____

6. What does the term "marqueeing" refer to?

_____

_____

7. Which tool is used for selecting and modifying a single point on a path?

_____

_____

☑ Mastery Check

8. How are objects freely rotated on the canvas?

_____

_____

9. How is the SHIFT key used for the selection of multiple objects on the canvas?

_____

_____

10. How is the magnification of an area of the canvas increased?

_____

_____

Module 3

Working with Bitmap Images

The Goals of This Module

- Explore bitmap selection tools
- Import bitmap images into a document
- Understand the use of Marquee and Magic Wand tools
- Explore options for edge control with bitmap images
- Use bitmap painting tools
- Combine bitmap images with vector drawings
- Create transparent image masks

As you saw in the previous module, Fireworks is an outstanding tool for creating new objects using vector-based drawing tools. However, the capabilities of this outstanding program don't stop there. In addition to giving you the ability to create new objects with vectors, Fireworks allows you to manipulate photographs, clip art, and other images in new ways, as well as to combine them with vector objects to create entirely new works of art.

In this module, you learn how to work with bitmap images—how to select areas of an image, crop an image, combine images, and import graphics from another format. All of these tasks will become a regular part of your graphics repertoire, and they serve as another good introduction to the capabilities of Fireworks.

Note

Create a new subfolder in your *Originals* folder for this module and download the images for the exercises from www.osborne.com or www.dw-fw-beginners.com.

Document Operations with Bitmap Images

Bitmap images are images that are created by defining a grid, or map, and filling the individual squares in the grid with color. Imagine taking a piece of graph paper and coloring the individual squares to create a mosaic, and you'll have the basic idea. As you learned in the last module, most images you find on the Web are in one of two bitmap formats—GIF or JPEG.

Bitmaps are more difficult to work with than vectors because those bits of color must be manipulated individually to modify an image. Vectors are modified by simply changing the mathematical calculations used to define points and paths. When working with bitmaps, then, the first task that any software must perform is the selection of the individual bits that you want to change.

Fireworks MX has greatly improved the way that these types of bitmap images can be changed by streamlining the engine that allows the program to work with bitmaps. Although you won't be able to see these improvements as they happen, the advantages for the user are a smoother handling of bitmaps, a better and faster rendering of bitmap images, and an improved use of your computer's memory—all leading to an enhanced user experience when working with bitmaps. In this first exercise, you'll have the opportunity to put these improvements into action as you learn how the program is used to select and modify bitmap images.

Simple Operations with Bitmap Images

3

You open a file in Fireworks in the same way you open any other document—choose File | Open. Fireworks will open and allow operations with a wide variety of image formats, including not only standard GIF and JPEG image types but also images created and saved in the native file formats of Photoshop, CorelDRAW, FreeHand, and Illustrator, as well as other bitmap formats such as TIF and BMP. Fireworks MX includes the capacity to open HTML files and convert them to image format.

Regardless of which file format is opened, whenever a file is opened in Fireworks, it is automatically converted to a Fireworks PNG format. To convert it back to a JPEG or GIF format, you would export the file, as you'll learn to do in Module 10. Figure 3-1 displays how a JPEG file would appear when opened in Fireworks. This file, called *rose-1.jpg,* is located in the exercise files for Module 3 if you wish to have a file to practice with.

Notice the small red circle that appears in the bottom of the Document window for the *rose_1.jpg* file in Figure 3-1 and the Bitmap label in the menu bar at the top of the Document window. These clues let you know that Fireworks is in bitmap mode. Clicking the Stop button allows you to switch back to vector mode. To return to bitmap mode, double-click the image or choose one of the Bitmap tools available from the Tools panel.

Note

If you've worked with Fireworks in the past, you may be looking for the blue and black rope border that used to appear around a Document window when you were working in bitmap mode. You can enable that option by selecting File | Preferences (Fireworks | Preferences on the Macintosh) and setting the option to "Display Striped Border" in the Editing tab.

Bitmap mode label ⟶

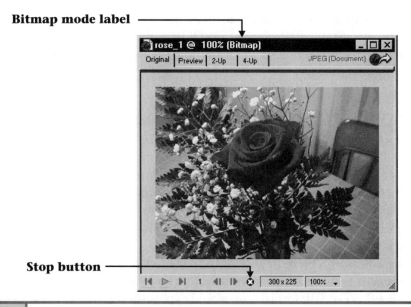

Stop button ⟶

Figure 3-1 Fireworks provides indicators in the Document window to let you know when you are working in bitmap mode.

Moving a Bitmap Image to a New Document

Often you will want to copy part of an original image to a new Fireworks document. Why? The primary reason is that, by maintaining the original document in its unmodified state, you always have the document available when you want to return to make further changes. Although Fireworks saves this image in its native file format when you choose File | Save, it's always a good idea to keep each original image in its unaltered state.

Moving a copy of a bitmap image to a new document is an incredibly easy process. Simply create a new document, select the image with the Pointer tool, and drag the image from the original document window to the new canvas. Just like that, you have a perfect copy of the original in your new document.

The second method for bringing an existing bitmap image into a Fireworks document is to use the command sequence File | Import. Fireworks will display the standard Open File dialog box for your particular system. Find the file you wish to bring into your new document and click the Open button. At that point, you will return to your Fireworks document window, where you will notice that the cursor has changed to an inverted *L* shape, signifying the upper left corner of the image to be imported. Click once, and the bitmap image will appear in your document.

Modifying Image and Canvas Sizes

In many cases, the bitmap image that you bring into Fireworks does not match your canvas size exactly. Fireworks has a great way to deal with this—just choose Modify | Canvas | Trim Canvas to have Fireworks cut the canvas size down to the smallest possible dimension.

Canvases and images can be modified once they are open by choosing other options available in the Modify menu and in the Property Inspector—Image Size, Canvas Size, and Canvas Color can all be changed at any time. To get some more practice in using the Property Inspector, start by clicking with the Pointer tool off of the picture in your practice file and note the appearance of the Property Inspector, as seen here.

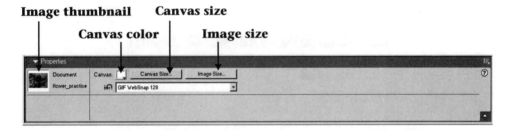

Start by clicking the Image Size button to see the available options, as shown in the following illustration.

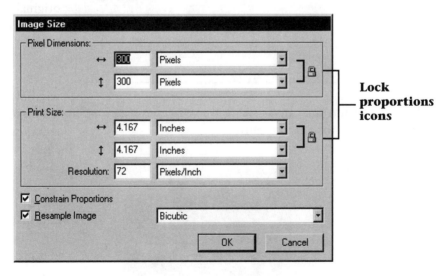

Note that the Constrain Proportions check box is checked and that lock icons appear next to the Pixel Dimensions and Print Size listings. This ensures that any change that is made to the image will keep the dimensions set to their original proportions, eliminating the distortion to the image that would occur if this option were not selected. Try changing the dimensions of the image to 200 pixels wide with the proportions constrained and then to 150 pixels wide with that option turned off. You can see how these settings affect the image. Click the Undo button twice (or choose Edit | Undo) to return the image to its original dimensions.

When the image size is changed, the entire image changes. However, what if you want to have a smaller canvas but keep the original as it is? For this operation, you would change the canvas size. Try this now by clicking the Canvas Size button in the Property Inspector and set the dimensions as you see here. Click OK when you are finished.

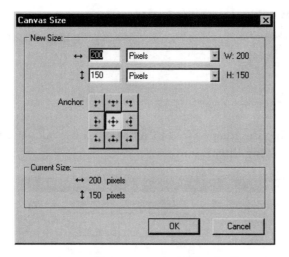

Fireworks trims the canvas size and leaves an image that has only the blossom from the rose on the canvas.

┤Tip

When an image overlaps the canvas, the area outside the canvas gets trimmed off during export but remains in the original Fireworks PNG file. You can also use the Pointer tool to move the image around on the canvas to adjust the position of your object.

Finally, you can change canvas color by selecting the Canvas Color button on the Property Inspector and setting the color you'd like to use. Note that this is the same interface used in all color-selection operations in Fireworks, and it is one that you'll return to often in upcoming practice exercises.

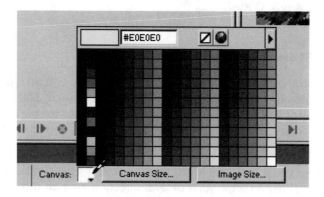

As you'd expect with a top-notch graphics program, Fireworks gives you ultimate control over the creation of image files and the canvases on which they are created. Modifying and changing canvas and image sizes is equally easy, and Fireworks makes these tasks intuitive and simple to achieve.

Project 3-1: Modifying Bitmap Images

You have now seen two ways that an image can be transformed—by changing the canvas size or by changing the image size itself. So far so good, but for this next project, your task becomes a little more difficult—and a lot more satisfying. When you use the Bitmap selection tools available in the Tools panel, the rose in your practice file will take on a life of its own as you crop the image to exclude areas that are unneeded and then modify the image in other ways as well. This is fun, so go ahead and get started.

Working in bitmap mode requires that you first select a portion of the image. Unlike when working with vectors, you can't simply use the Pointer tool to select an object on the canvas. You must first define the bitmapped area that you want to work with and then perform your operations. Luckily, there are some great tools available at the top of the Tools panel to help in this process. You may wish to return to Table 1-2 in Module 1 to see a summary of these tools and their functions.

Marquee tool ⟶   ⟵ **Lasso tool**

Magic Wand ⟶

Step-by-Step

1. Start this project by creating a new file and saving it as *flower_practice.png*. Set the canvas to a white color and make the canvas size 300 pixels wide by 300 pixels high. Choose File | Import and navigate to *rose1.jpg* (from the exercise files for this module). Click in the upper-left corner of canvas to paste a copy of the image into your new document.

2. The first tool you'll try is the Marquee tool, and it's the simplest to use. This tool creates either a rectangular or oval selection area on the image based on the option you choose from the flyout menu. Try an oval marquee first, drawing it around the rose blossom as you see here. Once an area is selected, you see the "marching ants" dashed line that dances around your selection.

Tip

Hold down SHIFT while dragging any oval tool in the Tools panel to draw a circle rather than an ellipse.

3. Now that part of the image is selected, you can create a new document that includes only the oval cutout of the rose. Fireworks has a slick method for getting this done. To see it in action, choose Edit I Copy to copy the selected area onto your computer's clipboard. As the image is copied, Fireworks automatically records the exact canvas size that is necessary to hold this image.

4. To create a new image document to hold the rose blossom, choose File I New and notice that the canvas size has already been set. Accept the default canvas size and click OK. Pasting the copy of the rose you created earlier is a simple matter of choosing Edit I Paste (or right-clicking the canvas and choosing Edit I Paste from the Context menu) and placing the copy onto the new canvas. Your finished product should appear as you see here.

5. To delete an object on the canvas, use the Pointer tool to select the entire image of the rose by clicking it and then press DELETE. You can also try moving the image around the canvas by using the Pointer tool. Notice how it snaps into place as you near the edge of the canvas. When you're finished, you can save this document or close it without saving the changes.

6. Use the Marquee tool and repeat the process covered in steps 3 and 4 to select, copy, and paste the rose blossom into a new document.

Tip

Marquee tools are great when you want to select a portion of a bitmap image in a rectangular or circular shape. To capture an irregularly shaped area, use the two Lasso tools for selecting regular- or polygon-shaped areas of the document.

7. Return to the original copy of the *rose_1.jpg* file and select the regular Lasso tool.

8. With the regular Lasso tool selected, you can draw a free-hand selection area around an object. Try it now by drawing around the outside edges of the rose blossom. Be sure that you close the circle you are drawing by returning to the starting point and overlapping the selection lines. Note that as you approach the starting point of your selection area, a small square appears underneath the Lasso tool. When you are finished, release the mouse button to stop selecting areas of the image. As you've done previously, copy the selection and paste it into a new document that you create. Your finished project should be similar to what you see here.

9. The Polygon Lasso tool is also used to select areas of an image, but rather than dragging the mouse to draw a circle, the Polygon Lasso tool is used by clicking the mouse button to define a series of points, which allows Fireworks to draw selection lines between the points. Just as with the regular Lasso tool, you should be sure to end your selection area as close to the starting point as possible and look for the small square that indicates the selection area is closed. In this illustration, you see an example of how the Polygon Lasso tool might be used to create an unusual selection area.

3

10. Next up in your bag of tricks is one of the most interesting tools available— the Magic Wand. As the name implies, it can seem a little magical at times because the effects that can be created by using this tool are often very interesting. Essentially, the Magic Wand is able to discern areas of an image based on their colors and then select those with similar colors automatically.

11. Deselect any previously selected regions of the *rose_1.jpg* image you have been working on. Remember, to deselect all regions of an image, you need only click the Stop button at the bottom of the Document window. Using any of the bitmap tools with the image automatically takes you back to bitmap editing mode.

12. Choose the Magic Wand tool and place your cursor on top of the rose blossom in the image. Click once and notice how the tool selects an irregular area that corresponds to the color of the area of the flower the tool is over when clicked. The image is magnified here for clarity.

13. Hold down SHIFT and select another area of the flower. The original selection remains while the new selection area is added. As long as you hold down SHIFT, you can move around the flower selecting multiple areas of the image. Try this now by selecting as much of the rose as possible. The result of this selection area when pasted into a new document would appear as you see here.

3

14. Changing the tolerance for color selections allows a larger area of the image to be selected. To increase the tolerance of the color settings for the Magic Wand tool, you need to access the options for the Magic Wand in the Property Inspector. Set the tolerance for the tool to a value of 60 by moving the sliding bar up or by typing 60 in the Tolerance box of the Property Inspector.

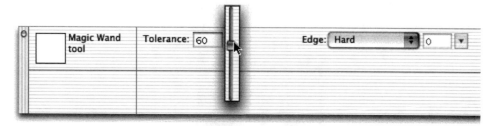

15. Return to the picture of the rose and try the Magic Wand again. Note how a much larger portion of the image is selected when the color tolerance is changed. Once again, hold down SHIFT while making your selections to add selected regions of the rose. Once the object is pasted into a new document, the difference becomes even more noticeable.

Tip

You can drag a selected object directly from the source canvas onto a new canvas by using the Pointer tool. While the original selection remains in place, a copy of the selected area will be pasted onto the other canvas.

16. Try changing the color of the canvas now by choosing Modify | Canvas Color and seeing what kinds of effects you can create just by changing the background color of the canvas that contains the rose blossom. By using the Eyedropper tool and selecting one of the colors on the rose itself, you can achieve a nice effect like the one shown here. If you wish, you can save this file or continue practicing on your own.

Project Summary

In this first exercise working with bitmap objects, you have seen how to select, delete, and modify areas of a bitmap image using the tools that Fireworks provides. The key thing to remember when working with bitmaps is that you must first select the region you want to affect and then make your modifications. Unlike vectors, which can be modified by merely changing the mathematical equations that define them, bitmaps must be dealt with on a pixel-by-pixel basis—something that Fireworks makes quite easy with the selection tools provided. In your next exercise, you will learn how to take a selected region and modify it further.

1-Minute Drill

● What is the first step necessary when working with objects in a bitmap format?

● What key should you hold down when you want to create a circle when using an Oval tool?

● How is the tolerance setting for the Magic Wand tool changed?

Controlling Edges in Bitmap Selections

Beyond simply letting you select a region of a bitmap image for the purpose of copying the selection onto another document, Fireworks tools also give you the opportunity to carefully control the output of the selection and create special effects. By using the options available in the Property Inspector for the Select tools, you can control the appearance of the edges of a selected area.

Understanding Edge Options

You have already seen how tool settings can be changed in the Property Inspector in Project 3-1 when you used it to change the Tolerance setting for the Magic Wand tool. You may have noticed that the Edge option in the same panel is set by default to "Hard." As you begin exploring these settings, it is important to remember that tool options must be set before the tool is put into use. Selection options for one of the Marquee tools appear as you see here.

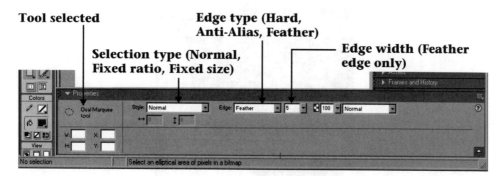

Tool selected

Edge type (Hard, Anti-Alias, Feather)

Selection type (Normal, Fixed ratio, Fixed size)

Edge width (Feather edge only)

The Hard edge setting makes a clear distinction between where a bitmap begins and where it ends. No efforts are taken to smooth the transition from the original image to the canvas where it is placed. If you magnify a selection of an

---

● When working with bitmap images, you first must select a region of the image before you can modify it.
● Holding SHIFT down while using any Oval tool lets you create a circle.
● The tolerance settings for the Magic Wand tool are found on the Property Inspector.

image captured with this setting, as has been done here, you clearly see the jagged edge created when the Edge setting is left at its default Hard option. A graphic designer would say that edges like this are suffering from the "jaggies."

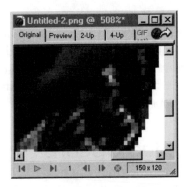

The Anti-Alias setting reduces the jaggies by softening the edges of the selected area—blending the selected area with the canvas color. With the image magnified by 400 percent, you see that the edge is softer when you use the Anti-Alias setting.

The final option for an edge setting is Feather. With the Feather option set, Fireworks creates a transition around the edges of the selection based on a width that you specify in the Property Inspector. By default, the Feather setting is set to 10 pixels in width. The effect is nice and quite easy to achieve.

Feathering edges can create some terrific results and offers limitless creative possibilities. Although feathered edges work best with the marquee tools, they

Ask the Expert

Question: Anti-aliased images seem to look much better than those created with a hard edge. Should I use anti-aliasing all the time? Why does Fireworks set a hard edge as a default?

Answer: The big issues with anti-aliasing relate to file sizes and how the Anti-Alias effect appears when an image is inserted into a web page.

Every time an image is anti-aliased (or when feathered edges are created), extra pixels are added around the outside edges of the bitmap to smooth things out. Of course, as pixels and colors are added, the file size grows larger. Part of Fireworks' mission is to keep file sizes as small as possible, so a hard edge is the default setting.

It is also important to understand how the Anti-Alias effect is achieved. Because anti-aliased and feathered edges work by mixing the colors around the selection with the colors on the canvas or the colors on any other object underneath the selected area, it is important to match the canvas color as closely as possible to the part of a web page where the image will be inserted. If, for instance, you plan on using an image on a dark blue page background, you should set the canvas color to the same dark blue color to avoid the appearance of *artifacts* around your image—small off-color pixels created when an edge mixed with the wrong color is used in anti-aliasing.

can also be employed with both the lasso tools and the Magic Wand. For example, using the Polygon Lasso tool with feathered edges rounds the edges of each selection area. However, setting a feathered edge limits the area that you may select, so using this option with lassos and the Magic Wand takes a little practice.

Project 3-2: Painting with Bitmaps

Selecting and copying portions of a bitmap image certainly allow for some great ways to control and modify the appearance of an image, but Fireworks also can paint new bitmaps onto the canvas by adding lines, shapes, or brush strokes to the image. In addition, areas of an image can be "erased" by painting pixels onto the image that match the color of the canvas. Those tools will be covered in this next exercise.

Step-by-Step

1. Once again, start by creating a new document to practice with in this project. Make the canvas size 150 pixels by 120 pixels and set the canvas color to white. Open the file *rose1.jpg* from the exercise files for this module. Select an oval portion of the rose blossom, copy it, and paste it onto the new document. Once your rose is in place, double-click the canvas to change to bitmap editing mode, looking for the Stop button and the Bitmap label in the menu bar of the document. The Bitmap tools that you'll be using in this project appear here.

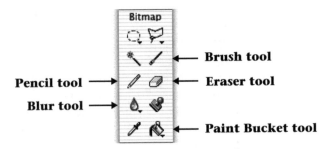

2. The first tool to try is the Pencil tool. There's nothing mysterious about this one—it simply paints a straight line of colored pixels onto the canvas. For this exercise, locate the Stroke Color settings found at the bottom of the Tools panel, as shown here. Of course, as you learned in the last module, stroke options can also be set using the Property Inspector.

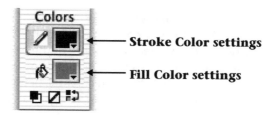

Stroke Color settings

Fill Color settings

3. Set the Line color to red and draw a box around your image by clicking and dragging the Pencil tool to create four individual lines.

Tip

Hold down SHIFT while dragging the Line tool across the image to create a straight horizontal line. Hold SHIFT down while dragging up or down to create a straight vertical line. Lines can also be created at a perfect 45-degree angle by dragging diagonally.

4. Once bitmaps are painted onto an image, they are fixed in place as part of the bitmap object and cannot be selected with the Pointer tool, as you would be able to do with a vector object. To remove these lines, or to correct lines that you don't like, you must choose Edit I Undo or use the Undo button on the toolbar (Windows only) at the top of the Fireworks window. By default, Fireworks lets you undo 20 individual actions; however, you may change the number of undo steps in the program Preferences.

5. The next tool to try is the Brush tool. As with Stroke settings for vector objects, a huge number of options are available in the Property Inspector for modifying the way that brush strokes are applied to an image. In this example, the Brush tool has been used to create a splattered texture by painting pixels onto the blank area around the picture of the rose. There are some great effects that can be achieved by using the Brush tool and its companion vector-based Vector Path tool, which you'll be working with in upcoming exercises. For now, try a few of the settings that the Brush tool affords.

6. The Eraser tool removes unwanted areas of an image by replacing existing bits of color in the bitmap with ones that match the canvas color. Although it may seem that you are removing the bits themselves by using the Eraser tool, you are in fact swapping colors within the grid defined by the bitmap region. As you see here, the Property Inspector contains options for changing the width of the area affected by the Eraser tool, the softness of the edge created when the Eraser tool is used, and the shape of the tool.

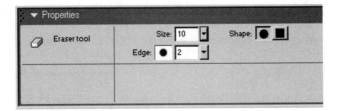

7. If your image contains an active selection area, Fireworks limits the areas you can paint to the selected region. Remember that any time you are working with a bitmap image, what you are actually doing is adding or changing colors to the bitmap grid that is defined by a selection. Anything painted outside the selection area gets trimmed away when the mouse button is released.

8. New for Fireworks MX are some tools that other graphics programs have contained for some time—the Blur, Sharpen, Dodge, Burn, and Smudge

tools. Module 1 summarizes the operation of these tools in Table 1-2, and you can take a quick look at these tools in action now. Start by selecting the Blur tool and noting how, once again, the options for this tool are set in the Property Inspector. Blurring objects on a canvas mixes the pixels in the selected area, giving them the appearance of being in the background. In the example seen here, the Blur tool has been used to de-emphasize the greenery behind the flower, making the blossom more prominent.

9. Using the Sharpen tool further accents a selected region of a bitmap image by increasing the contrast between adjacent pixels. Selecting the Sharpen tool and passing it over the rose further accents the image and makes the flower appear to pop out of the image.

10. Another photo-retouching tool in Fireworks MX is the Dodge tool. This tool makes it possible to modify images by lightening selected areas of an image. The opposite of the Dodge tool is the Burn tool, which can be used to darken areas of an image. Try both of these now and see how changing their settings in the Property Inspector changes how the effects are applied.

11. Complete your examination of these tools by trying the Smudge tool. As the name implies, this tool is used for smudging, or mixing together, pixels in a region of an image.

12. The final tool we use in this exercise is the Paint Bucket tool, which recolors a selected area of an image. Try this for yourself by selecting an area of the rose in your practice file, choosing a new color to flood the selected area with, and dropping the color onto the selection with the Paint Bucket tool.

As you can see here, combining the use of the Magic Wand and the Paint bucket tool can lead to some very interesting effects.

Project Summary

This is a great time to experiment with the different painting tools available. For instance, try using the Magic Wand to select individual rose petals in your sample file. Then use the Paint Bucket tool to change the color of the flower itself. Try adding a box to hold a caption for the picture. How about using the Eraser tool to further soften the edges of the rose so that only the outermost edges of the flower are showing? The possibilities are almost limitless, and the tools that Fireworks provides give you an incredible amount of freedom in creating your final masterpiece.

1-Minute Drill

● How does anti-aliasing affect the edge of a bitmap?

● How do you change settings for line and fill color?

● How does the Eraser tool create the effect of erasing part of an image?

● Anti-aliasing makes the edges of bitmaps appear smoother by adding additional pixels and modifying the colors along the edge so they blend more smoothly with the canvas or a background color.

● Line and fill colors can be changed by using the color settings at the bottom of the Tools panel or those found on the Property Inspector.

● The eraser works by painting an area of new pixels onto the canvas. If this is set to be transparent or if the color is the same as the canvas, the replacement colors appear to erase a part of an image.

3

The Best of Both Worlds

Fireworks is one of the few programs that allows you to work in both the world of simplified vectors and the world of more natural appearing bitmap graphics. Although other software programs may have more powerful features for working with one type of graphic or the other, only Fireworks makes it possible to work seamlessly between the two types of digital images.

In Fireworks MX these two worlds have been more closely aligned than ever. If you have used previous versions of Fireworks, you know that switching modes from vector to bitmap editing was often quite frustrating. When you needed to select pixels to work with bitmaps, you were first required to enter bitmap-editing mode to use the tools that allowed you to select and modify your pictures. If you wanted to draw an object on the same canvas, you had to remember to switch modes so that the vector tools were active.

Fireworks MX now works in what Macromedia calls a *modeless* format—switching automatically to the appropriate format based on which tool is selected. With this improvement, it is even easier than before to combine vectors and bitmaps into one image, and you can seamlessly switch to the correct editing format when you need to work with your images. As you see in the next project, combining bitmaps and vectors is another way that Fireworks excels at creating the kinds of images that lend visual impact to your web design projects.

Project 3-3: Combining Bitmap Images and Vector Objects

You have now seen how Fireworks provides tools for creating original artwork with its vector drawing tools and how bitmap images can be modified in any number of ways. In this next project, you will learn how to combine the two worlds of bitmaps and vectors to create some interesting effects. By pasting bitmap selections and working with a new technique called masking, you will be able to design some truly unique works of art.

Step-by-Step

1. Once again, start by creating a new Fireworks document with the standard practice size of 300 pixels by 300 pixels. Set your canvas color to transparent for this exercise. Note that when the canvas color is set to transparent,

Fireworks uses a gray-and-white checkerboard pattern to let you know the canvas will not be seen if the image is exported as a GIF.

2. Import a copy of *rose1.jpg* to the canvas by choosing File | Import. Using the Oval Marquee tool, select the rose from the picture. In the following examples, a Feather edge of 5 pixels has been used for the edge setting on the Marquee tool. Once you have made your selection, choose Edit | Cut to copy the area to your computer's temporary memory. With the Pointer, click the Stop button to return to vector mode and select the remaining portion of the picture. Press DELETE to remove that part of the picture, leaving a clean canvas behind.

3. Now that you have the groundwork out of the way, you can see how a picture can be combined with a vector object quite easily. Select the Oval tool from the Vector portion of the Tools panel and draw a circle. In the example here, the Stroke settings for this new object have been set in the Property Inspector to Basic, Soft Rounded line, 4 pixels wide.

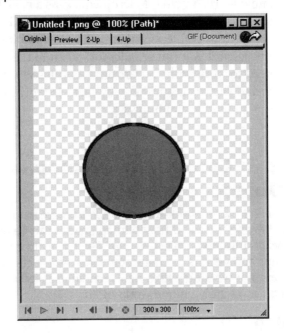

4. With your new ellipse selected, the bitmap image that you cut from this document can now be pasted inside the circle. To see this work, select the circle and choose Edit | Paste Inside. As you see here, the flower appears within the confines of the selected image.

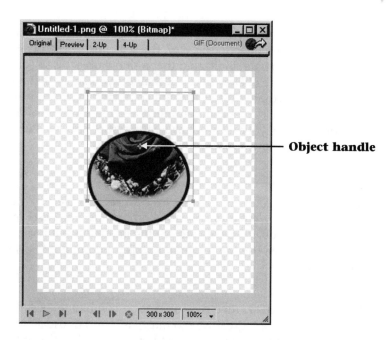

Object handle

3

5. You'll also notice that the picture isn't properly placed. To correct this, simply find the object handle, represented by four dots in a diamond shape, and, using the Pointer tool, move the selection down until it fits neatly into the circle, as you see here.

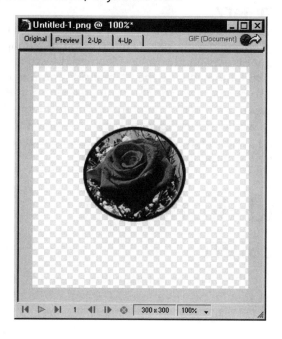

6. As you experiment with this technique, you'll notice that once two images have been combined in this way, the selection indicators for the image have changed from blue, indicating that a single object is selected, to yellow. This is a new feature of Fireworks MX that lets you know that a *mask* has been created. Masks are objects that are combined in such a way that one portion of an image obscures another, much as a mask you wear at a costume ball might obscure your eyes but allow the rest of your face to be seen. Module 6 teaches you more about working with masks.

Tip

Position the image you wish to paste inside a vector object in the approximate location where you want it to appear before you use the Paste Inside command. This ensures that you will be able to see the image once it is masked by the vector object. You can then use the selection handle to do minor fine-tuning of the image's position.

7. With Fireworks, creating new objects by combining existing images with vector objects is a great way to make new and unusual objects. Figure 3-2 shows you just a few examples of how vector objects can be combined with bitmap images for some great effects. You'll find this image, named *combine_sample.png* available for download at www.osborne.com or www.dw-fw-beginners.com.

Project Summary

In this exercise, you have used one of the most powerful and unique features of Fireworks—the ability to jump between the world of bitmap images and the world of vector objects—and you have learned how to create your first mask. In addition to letting you use the Paste Inside command, Fireworks also makes it possible to overlay a vector object on an image and then combine the two graphics to create a different type of mask. This technique is an especially important one for web designers to learn because it allows the blending of images by creating a special type of mask known as a transparency mask. You discover transparency masks in your next exercise.

Vectors and Bitmaps in Web Design

As you work through the exercises in this module, you may appreciate the creative possibilities that Fireworks affords. The real world of web design

Figure 3-2   Combining bitmap selections with vector objects can make for some very interesting effects.

frequently requires composite images like those you discovered in the last project. Consider a web site for a small resort, for example. The owner of the site may wish to display photos of the resort's rooms, swimming pool, and other amenities, but may also need to design a logo, buttons for the web page, and text that describes the hotel. Fireworks easily handles all of those tasks with its unique ability to work seamlessly with bitmaps and vector graphics.

Having a sound understanding of the basic principles of design, such as alignment, contrast, and color theory, will go a long way to producing the kinds of images and page design that are both visually appealing and have the impact on your Internet audience that you desire. Although this book focuses on a powerful software program for creating graphics for use on the Web, you should continue your education by gaining an understanding of the basics of graphic design. Whether you examine some of the books that focus on design for the Web or take a course in graphic design, the time you spend gaining a grounding in these principles will serve you well in the future as you continue to work in the world of web design.

Project 3-4: Combining Selection and Painting Tools

You have now seen some of the capabilities that Fireworks bitmap tools provide. From selecting different regions of a photograph to changing edge selections to drawing new objects onto a canvas, the tools that Fireworks provides allow you to really get your creative juices flowing. In the final project for this module, your task is to use all of those tools in combination to create a virtual postcard for the fictional town of Poinciana Beach. This postcard is something that you could offer to visitors to e-mail to their friends, for instance, or that you could even use as an image map navigation element for a web page. Whatever its use, your first task is to create a collage of images for the postcard itself.

Step-by-Step

1. Start by creating a new document 400 pixels wide by 250 pixels high with the canvas color set to white. Name the file *postcard.png*, accepting the Fireworks file format default.

2. Figure 3-3 shows how your completed project should appear when you are done. Notice that this postcard is simply a series of images that have been cropped in different ways and placed on the canvas.

3. To create your own postcard, find the following JPEG and GIF images in the Exercises folder for this module: *boat_1.jpg, cityhall_1.jpg, beach_1.jpg, golfers_1.jpg, hotel_1.jpg, poinciana_1.jpg,* and *curvedtext.gif.* These are the source files for your postcard.

4. Decide which of the images you want to use on your postcard after you've looked at the available photos. Crop each of the photos and paste a copy of each onto the new canvas. The final image you should use is the *curvedtext.gif* file; allow it to lie on top of the photo collage.

5. The original photographs that were cropped and resized for the images you used above are also located in the Exercises folder, with names such as *boat_2.jpg, cityhall_2.jpg,* and so on. Try opening these files, changing the size of the images to fit on your new canvas, and cropping them in different ways.

3

Figure 3-3 Create a virtual postcard by cropping photographs and arranging them on a canvas.

Project Summary

When you are finished with this exercise, you should have created at least two original postcards from the photographs supplied and gained some valuable skills along the way. In upcoming projects, you will learn how to modify images in the same way that the samples provided for you have been changed. Fireworks has a terrific set of tools for working with bitmap images, and as you complete future exercises you will learn how to use them to create striking visual effects of your own.

What to Take Away

The bitmap editing tools provided in Fireworks give you outstanding control over the appearance of images that might be captured in a photograph or pulled from a clip-art collection, the Web, or a scanned image. You have seen how to use Fireworks tools to select, copy, and resize an image, as well as how to paint new pixels onto a bitmap image using the Shape, Brush, and Line tools. Fireworks allows you to create entirely new versions of these types of images and to manipulate images in a bitmap format in ways that you will come to appreciate more and more as you become comfortable with the program.

☑ Mastery Check

1. What three settings do you determine each time a new Fireworks file is created?

_____

_____

2. What is the purpose of having a negative area around the edges of a canvas in a Fireworks Document window?

_____

_____

3. What options are available for edge settings when using bitmap selection tools?

_____

_____

4. How does anti-aliasing affect the edge of a bitmap?

_____

_____

5. How does the Eraser tool create the effect of erasing part of an image?

_____

_____

6. How can bitmap lines, shapes, or brush strokes be removed from a bitmap image?

_____

_____

7. Which bitmap painting tool provides the greatest flexibility for adding colored lines and shapes to an image?

_____

_____

☑ Mastery Check

8. What new photo retouching tools have been added in Fireworks MX?

_____

_____

9. What is a mask?

_____

_____

10. What special color does Fireworks use to mark a selected area when a
mask is applied?

_____

_____

3

Module 4

Working with Text and Text Effects

The Goals of This Module

- Understand the use of text as images
- Explore the Fireworks Text Editor panel
- Modify text for size, orientation, stroke, and fill characteristics
- Understand how text styles are created and saved
- Convert text into vector objects
- Work with text as vectors
- Attach text to a vector path

Text that is displayed in a web browser using standard HTML can be extremely limiting. Because of cross-browser and cross-platform issues, the number of fonts that a browser will reliably display is confined to a very narrow selection of only five families of fonts. Once you've made the decision to move beyond those standard fonts, you are going to need to turn your text into a graphical object that escapes those limitations and opens up a world of possibilities that standard HTML does not afford.

This does not mean that all of the text for your web pages should be graphics. When compared to HTML text, graphic text generates more file weight and therefore can significantly slow the loading of a web page. It would be great if you could simply use a graphics program such as Fireworks to enter all the text on a page and publish it as is. The problem becomes a matter of just how long you want your audience to wait to see your page. A page that is composed of 20 lines of HTML text will load very quickly, but one that contains the same amount of information converted into a graphic will slowly (very slowly) load onto the viewer's screen. In addition, search engines often overlook pages that rely too heavily on graphics rather than text. After all, because most search engines scan the text to determine how a page is to be categorized, if your page contains one image after another, even if those images contain text, the search engines will find nothing to index and may pass completely over your page or your entire site.

However, the use of text as graphics—especially the types of dynamic graphics that can be created with Fireworks—can still significantly add to the impact of a page. Whether you are designing a logo that becomes a common element throughout the entire web site or are simply making eye-catching buttons that include text, Fireworks puts tools at your disposal that are often found only in sophisticated desktop publishing programs. These tools can significantly improve your ability to communicate with your Internet audience.

Working with Text in Fireworks MX

Fireworks has many of the same attributes that more expensive (and more powerful) graphics programs use when working with text. Although graphic designers might lean toward Fireworks' sister program, FreeHand, or toward other programs such as Adobe Illustrator when they want to do advanced operations with text graphics, Fireworks contains many of the same features and still has a distinct edge when the text will be displayed on a web page. Before working with Fireworks' text tools, take a few minutes to understand some of the terminology that is associated with text and look at the new features now included in Fireworks MX.

Text Terminology

4

Typography, or the process (some would say art) of using type in a document, has a history dating back to the very invention of the printing press by Johannes Gutenberg in the mid-1400s. Almost continually since that time, type has been revised and modified to meet the needs of printers, publishers, and readers. That trend continues today on the World Wide Web as the producers of browsers and web designers themselves develop more efficient means of displaying high-impact text.

Text styles are known as *fonts,* and the term is often used interchangeably with the term *typeface.* Either term simply describes the style of the text. Fonts are divided into two broad categories—*serif* and *sans serif.* A serif is the little stroke that decorates some letters, as in this example:

Palatino is a serif font.

A sans-serif font is one that literally is without (sans) the extra decoration, as you see here:

Arial is a sans-serif font.

Additionally, text is also defined in terms of the amount of horizontal space it uses, and it falls into two categories—*proportional* and *monospaced.*

Proportional text is a font style that uses only the amount of space necessary for each character to display properly. For example, the capital letter *W* is allowed more space than the lowercase letter *i.* Proportional fonts are generally preferred because they are easier to read and because more characters can be displayed in the same physical space.

Monospaced type, on the other hand, allocates exactly the same amount of space to each character, regardless of how wide the character actually is. In this example, you see both categories:

Proportional—Long ago, in a galaxy far, far away...

```
Monospaced—Long ago, in a galaxy far, far away...
```

The choice of font styles has as great an impact on the overall design of a web page and web site as the choice of color scheme. Consistency is the key. If you choose a font such as Times New Roman for labels in a series of buttons and then switch to Arial for other graphics in the site, your viewers may be confused by the change and think that they have wandered off your site into unknown territory. In addition, because fonts also have an impact on the feel of your page, you must carefully consider your choice of fonts early in the design process. As with all decisions related to the Web, consider your intended audience and the style that will appeal to them the most.

New Text Tools in Fireworks MX

Fireworks MX introduced some significant improvements to the way text is entered and manipulated in the program. These features are new for the latest edition of Fireworks:

- You may enter text directly onto the canvas. Previous versions of Fireworks required opening a special editor where you entered text in a separate panel, modified the font formatting, and then, when the editor was closed, updated your document. Fireworks MX now makes it possible to type directly onto the canvas at the point where you want the text inserted. Although you can still open the Text Editor if you prefer to work in that environment, entering text directly onto the canvas is a much easier process.

- The Property Inspector is now used in place of the Text Editor for styling and formatting text. Once the Text tool is selected, the Property Inspector displays the text-formatting options available for choosing fonts, setting font sizes and colors, and modifying font properties. Once text has been entered, additional formatting options for setting the stroke and adding effects become available in the Property Inspector.

4

- Additional formatting tools are now available for text, including the ability to set indents for paragraph formatting and to control line spacing between lines of text.

- Fireworks MX now contains a spell check feature.

- Additional controls are now available for text that is attached to a vector path. You learn how to attach text to a vector path later in this module.

Taken together, these new features add to what was already an impressive array of tools for working with text. Considering all the other things that Fireworks does so well, the addition of sophisticated tools for manipulating text—tools that are usually found in programs costing much more—makes Fireworks an incredible value.

Project 4-1: Entering Text in a Fireworks Document

The process of entering text in a Fireworks document is relatively straightforward. Select the Text tool, set the font properties, and begin typing! However, with a powerful software tool such as this, there are some twists and turns along the way that reflect the depth of the program and the way that text can be modified in countless ways to attain the look and impact you desire. Perhaps the best way to get comfortable with the text tools in Fireworks is to put some of those options into practice, as you'll do in this first project.

Step-by-Step

1. Create a new Fireworks file by selecting File | New. Make the new canvas size 300 pixels wide by 300 pixels high, with a white canvas color, and save the file as *text_practice.png*. Once your file is saved, locate the Text tool on the Tools panel—represented by the capital letter *A*—and select it.

2. Text that is entered in a Fireworks document resides in a rectangular area called a text box. When you see the cursor appear as a horizontal *H*, click once and the text box will appear on the canvas. As you'll see in a moment, the initial size of the text box is not important because it automatically resizes to fit the text that is entered. For now, simply choose the Text tool and click anywhere on the canvas to create this first text box.

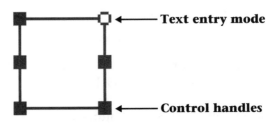

3. Note the control handles for resizing the text box that appear once you click on the canvas. You might want to think of the text box as a separate canvas atop your original document. Text boxes can be dragged around the screen or resized as you need. Take special note of the unfilled box in the upper right-hand corner of the text box. When this box is unfilled, you are in text entry mode, which allows you to click inside the box to add or modify text. This box is closed by clicking off the text box on another part of the canvas (then Fireworks knows that your text entry is complete). The unfilled control handle in the upper right corner can also be double-clicked to collapse the text box around the text—reducing the field to its smallest possible size. Try this now by typing in some text and resizing the text box. Switch to the Pointer tool, select the text box, and move the text to a new area of the canvas. Once selected, text can also be positioned using the arrow keys on the keyboard.

Note

Previous versions of Fireworks required the use of a special Text Editor in which all text was entered and modified. If you've used Fireworks in the past, you may find that it is more comfortable for you to use the Text Editor to enter and modify your text. That option is still available in Fireworks MX by selecting Text I Editor or by right-clicking (CTRL-clicking for a Macintosh) the text box on the canvas and choosing Editor from the contextual menu.

4. Once a text box is created, the text options in the Property Inspector become active, and you see the many options that Fireworks allows for the creation and modification of text. Now you can choose from a wide range of font types, sizes, colors, and other options. To acquaint yourself with the features of the Text area of the Property Inspector, refer to Figure 4-1.

5. Many people like to set the font type, size, and color before they begin typing text onto the canvas. However, it is equally easy to select text inside the text box

and then apply changes. Fireworks uses vector graphics for the creation of text objects, so text can be changed at any time. In fact, modifying text is so easy that you need only select the text box itself, and not the letters within the box, to make your modifications. For now, type **A sample of text** in the work area without changing any of the font options.

6. Click the down arrow next to the font type to access the fonts that are available in Fireworks. As you can see in Figure 4-2, the number of font types available matches all the fonts installed on your computer. To choose a font, just click the font name; the text on the canvas converts to the new type. You'll also notice that the text box automatically changes its size to fit the selected font. Experiment with a few different font types now before moving on.

7. Font size is set in much the same way that you have changed options previously. You can either type a value directly in the size box or use the slider to make the font larger or smaller to fit your needs. Notice again that as the changes are applied, Fireworks automatically applies the new value to the text on the canvas, and changes the size of the text box to accept the new setting. The slider allows you to select sizes between 8 and 96 points, but you can also enter values manually into the size box—up to 400 points if you need text that large.

Note

Fonts are set in points the same way that you set font sizes in a word processor.

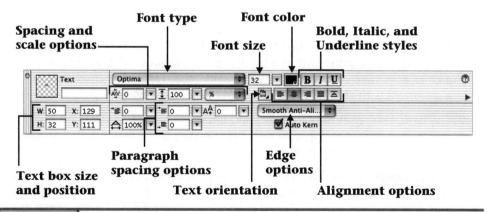

Figure 4-1   Text properties are set using the Property Inspector in Fireworks MX.

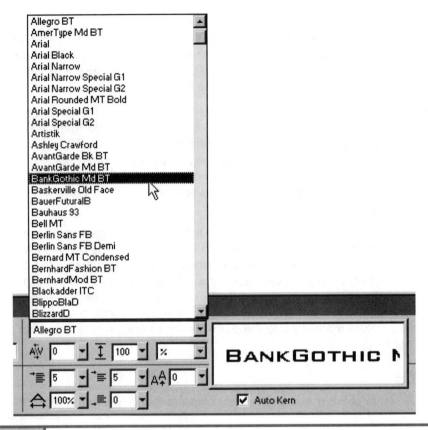

Figure 4-2   Fonts are set in the font type area, with Fireworks providing a preview of how the font appears.

8. Clicking the Color button brings up the familiar Macromedia interface for choosing colors, along with the Eyedropper tool that can be used to select a color anywhere within the Fireworks work area. Take a few moments to experiment with changing the color of your selected text.

9. The basic text styles of bold, italic, and underline are set by selecting text and then clicking the appropriate button. Again, this is very similar to what you can do in a word processor.

10. Text is aligned within the text box by using the alignment buttons on the right side of the Property Inspector. In addition to the basic alignments of left, center, and right, text can also be aligned proportionally (justified) or even stretched. Figure 4-3 shows how these settings affect text. Try typing a few lines of text and experimenting with the alignment features by clicking the different alignment buttons. Just as with any word processor, pressing ENTER/RETURN creates a new line for text that you enter.

Figure 4-3   Text can be aligned left, centered, right, justified, or stretched.

11. Note that for both the justified alignment option and the stretched alignment, the text stretches to fill the text box. Adjust the size of the text box with the Pointer tool, and the text grows or shrinks to fit the box. When the justified option is chosen, the space between letters changes; with the stretched setting, the text itself stretches to fill the box.

12. Text orientation can be set in one of four ways—either to flow from left to right or right to left when arranged horizontally, as well as when arranged vertically. To see these options, select the text box and click the small button below the font size field in the Property Inspector, seen here, to access those choices. Note that as the orientation of the text is changed from horizontal to vertical, the appearance of the buttons that control text alignment change as well.

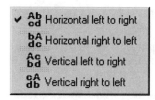

13. In addition to the basic features of entering text and formatting the font type, size, color, alignment, orientation, and style, Fireworks also includes sophisticated tools for modifying character and line spacing and how the text is arranged on the canvas. Horizontal scale, for instance, enables you to change the width of fonts to make the individual letters either narrower or wider than the standard 100 percent size. Other options in this area of the Text Editor include *kerning*, which lets you change spacing between characters; *baseline shift*, which lets you set text that falls above or below the lower border of the text box; and *leading*, which lets you adjust the amount of space between lines of text. With your sample text selected, try some of these different settings either by using the slider or by entering numbers directly into the value area for each option. You will get additional practice later on, but be sure that you familiarize yourself with the following options and their functions.

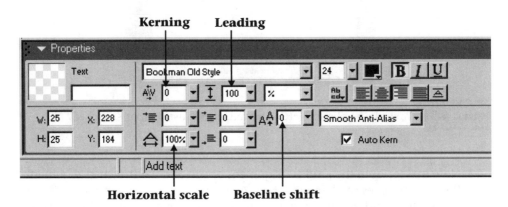

14. Paragraph-spacing controls are another interesting new feature of Fireworks MX. Located as you see here on the Property Inspector, they can be used for adding blank spaces—based either on percentage or pixels—to lines of text either before or after a break inserted using ENTER/RETURN.

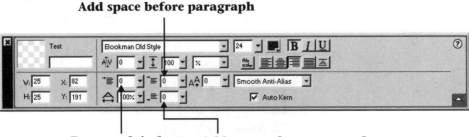

15. The final option to discuss before you move on to more advanced modification tools is the option for adjusting the anti-aliasing level, found just below the alignment options. Anti-aliasing controls the appearance of edges by mixing pixels along the border of an image. As you see here, the default setting is smooth anti-alias. However, depending on the size and type of the font you are using, you may need to change this setting to get better results. Small fonts in particular should be rendered without any anti-aliasing for the best results.

16. To conclude this project, take some time and try typing your name into the Text Editor and experimenting with the different settings. Press ENTER to create a new line for your last name. You should quickly come to appreciate the wide variety of options that Fireworks allows you to access directly in the Property Inspector. Once you are done, click OK to accept any changes you've made and close the Text Editor. You can save this file for further practice if you like or discard it when you are finished.

Project Summary

Fireworks text tools allow you to use any fonts installed on your computer to enter text directly onto your document's canvas. With the array of options for setting font styles, sizes, colors, and formatting, the possibilities for generating eye-catching graphical text are unlimited. In this first project, you have seen how text is entered on the canvas and how basic formatting is achieved.

Understanding Text Properties

Fireworks uses vectors for creating text, just as it does with other objects that you draw on your canvas. Therefore, the text objects you create are always editable and can be modified with many of the same effects, stroke, and fill settings that you have experimented with in previous modules. In essence, the Text tools create the "bones" of your text, and you "flesh out" the text by draping bitmaps colors, special effects, and stroke properties onto that basic structure. In this project, you will have the opportunity to see some of those tools in action.

As varied as the options are for entering text and modifying it with the Property Inspector, you have barely scratched the surface of what Fireworks enables you to do with text. Many of the same options that you experimented with when working with vector objects (such as shadows, glows, strokes, and fills) are available when working with text. By making these choices available, Fireworks lets you create unique, high-impact graphics for use on a web page or even in a printed document. In addition, once Live Effects are created for text, they can be saved as a new Style, allowing you to design with the type of consistency that is important when working on the Web. As you begin working with text styles, keep in mind that your goal when creating graphical text is twofold—to create text that is visually interesting *while* remaining perfectly readable. Although it may be tempting to generate fabulous looking text in Fireworks, if that same text is difficult for your web page viewer to read, then you have failed to achieve one of your primary goals. As you begin exploring the use of text as graphics, keep the following tips in mind:

- Many studies confirm that a sans-serif font is more readable when seen on a computer monitor.

- Applying stroke settings to small font sizes can detract from the appearance and readability of text. Use strokes with small fonts sparingly.

- Small fonts should not use anti-alias edge settings. For fonts smaller than 12 points, a hard edge generally results in more readable text.

- Font styles can convey their own mood and style. Serif fonts such as Times New Roman are considered more business-like, whereas sans-serif fonts such as Verdana appear more casual. Add in the wide variety of decorative fonts that are available—such as First Grader, MS Comic Sans, or Ghouly—and the simple choice of fonts can help you set the mood for your graphics (or can detract if the wrong font is chosen).

- Be consistent in how fonts are styled and sized. If you look at web pages with clean and stylish designs, you'll notice that most limit the number of font sizes and font styles to no more than two of each.

- As you create the text boxes in your documents, limit the number of words in one line to no more than eight to twelve. A line of text that is longer than twelve words becomes difficult to read.

Project 4-2: Modifying Text Properties

As with other vector objects, modifications to text are applied using the Property Inspector. In this next project you will see how strokes, fills, effects, and other attributes can be applied to text with the fabulous new interface that Fireworks MX provides. Although previous versions of Fireworks required the use of separate floating panels for making these changes, the new procedures that rely on the Property Inspector make the process much more efficient and easy to access. In this exercise you learn how to use the Property Inspector to make changes to the basic appearance of your text.

Step-by-Step

1. Create a new 300 pixel by 300 pixel document with a white canvas. Save this file as *effects_practice.png*.

2. Create a new text box by selecting the Text tool and clicking the canvas. In the Property Inspector, choose a font of your liking and set the font size to approximately 40 points. Type the words **Text Effects**.

Note

Fireworks remembers the last settings that you applied to text, so you may need to adjust the text alignment and orientation settings in the Property Inspector.

3. When text is first entered into a document, there is no stroke setting applied. Individual letters are filled with a solid color. The first change you will make to this new block of text, then, is to apply a stroke setting by accessing the Stroke options in the Property Inspector. Once you have entered your text, choose the Pointer tool and select the text box. Note that the additional options for setting stroke properties and effects appear in the Property Inspector when a text box is selected, as you see here. The red line through the Color Selection button indicates that no stroke setting is applied—this is the Fireworks default.

Stroke options

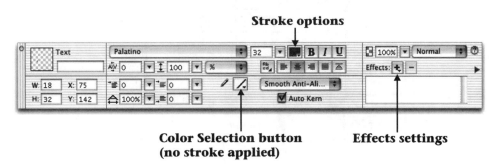

Color Selection button
(no stroke applied)

Effects settings

4. Begin by clicking the Color Selection button and using the Eyedropper tool to choose an outline color for your text from the standard Color Chooser interface. Once you select a color, a stroke property of 1-Pixel Soft will be applied to each letter in the color you have chosen, as you see in this example.

5. Using the Fill Color option button on the Property Inspector, set the fill color to none by finding the button in the upper right-hand corner of the Color Chooser. You will have lettering that only contains the outline, as you see here. Any time you see a square with a red slash mark through it, the option color or choice is set to none.

6. The same huge variety of strokes that can be applied to vector drawings can be applied to text objects. Modifying the stroke of text needs to be done with some care, though. With large text like the sample you are working on now, strokes can look great; however, with smaller fonts the stroke can quickly overwhelm the fill on the text—making it effectively unreadable. Select the text box you are working on and reset the font size to see how the readability of smaller text sizes are affected by strokes.

7. Clicking the Stroke Options button found in the Color Chooser accesses the additional stroke settings that you may apply to your text. A small window, seen next, opens when that button is selected.

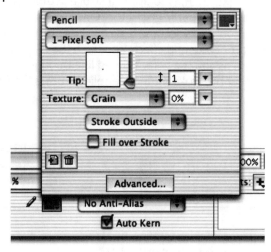

With it you can change the stroke settings for a text object in all of the same ways that stroke options can be changed for other drawings.

8. In general, the larger the text, the more pronounced impact a custom stroke will have on the appearance of your text. Try experimenting with some of the different stroke settings to see which types of strokes work best with your text. Remember that the text box must be selected before a new stroke effect can be applied. You may also want to take a sneak peek at the Stroke option settings covered in Module 5. With just a little experimentation, you should be able to produce effects similar to those you see in Figure 4-4.

9. Fills in text objects are modified in the same way that strokes are changed. By default, Fireworks always makes the fill of a text object a solid color as set in the Property Inspector. However, just as with strokes, fills can be modified

4

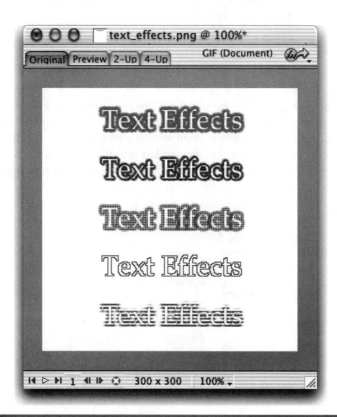

Figure 4-4 Modifying stroke properties allows some unusual effects to be achieved.

and applied by using the Fill Options button found when the Fill Color button is selected. Once again, as you see next, a small window opens when the button is selected, allowing you to access the full spectrum of fill options available for all Fireworks vector objects. As with stroke settings, you may wish to look at Module 5 to see how some of these options can be modified to create unusual effects with your text.

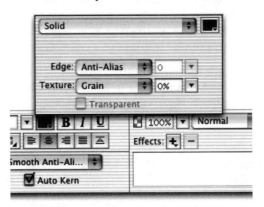

10. Effects for text are added by selecting the plus-sign button in the Effects area of the Property Inspector. As with other interface elements in Fireworks MX, selecting this button opens a small window where effects can be applied to your text, as you see here. As with strokes and fills, these options are discussed in greater detail in Module 5. For now, have a look at some popular effects applied to text.

11. One of the most common effects applied to text is the drop-shadow effect that creates the illusion that the text is floating above the canvas. With the text box selected, choose the Shadow and Glow category from the Effects window and select the Drop Shadow setting. Accept the defaults, and your final results should appear as you see here.

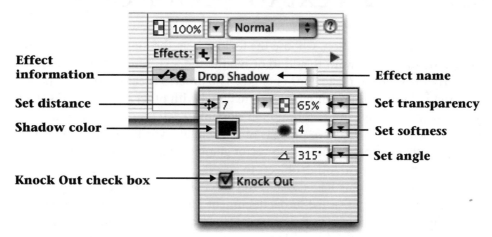

4

12. To modify the effect settings that you've applied, click the Information icon, represented by the lower case letter *i* found in the Effects panel portion of the Property Inspector. Another window opens that allows you to change the color of the shadow, set its width and transparency, and determine the angle applied from the object to the shadow. One additional option available is to create a knock-out with the shadow by selecting that check box.

Effect information —————— **Effect name**

Set distance —————— **Set transparency**

Shadow color —————— **Set softness**

—————— **Set angle**

Knock Out check box ——————

13. To complete this exploration of text effects, try some of the other settings to see what you can achieve. Module 5 covers these options in more detail, but as you experiment with text fills, strokes, and effects, you should be able to appreciate some of the possibilities that Fireworks affords you.

Project Summary

In this exercise, you have been introduced to a few of the ways that text can be modified once it has been placed into a Fireworks document. As your skills with the program progress, you'll come to appreciate how easy and intuitive the interface has become and how most modifications to text are just a few clicks away.

1-Minute Drill

● What should you consider before deciding to use text as a graphic on a web page?

● What is the primary tool for modifying text in Fireworks MX?

● What basic text styles can be applied with the Property Inspector?

Converting Text to Vector Objects

As you have seen, the entry and modification of text in Fireworks is a fairly straightforward proposition. Choose the text tool; set the font properties; enter your text; and, if you want to add to or modify the text, return directly to the Property Inspector to make your changes. The process is easy and to the point.

Fireworks does so much more with text and with other vector objects that you may miss out on some of the other possibilities if you don't take time to explore them. In the final two projects of this module, you'll have the opportunity to work with text that is converted to vector graphics and see how Fireworks allows you to combine text with other objects to generate even more interesting effects.

Programs less sophisticated than Fireworks often convert text to a graphic image as soon as it is inserted into a document. Fireworks, on the other hand, keeps the text as an editable vector object. This feature allows you to go back and forth between the Text Editor and the canvas, apply different fonts and font styles, use the spell check feature, and make other corrections as necessary. However, if you have finalized some text in Fireworks and want to play with the text graphically, you can choose to convert your editable text objects to graphical vector objects.

● Always consider whether you could achieve the same impact on your page by using much smaller HTML text as opposed to graphical text. Does the impact justify the added file size?

● The Property Inspector is the primary tool for entering and modifying text in Fireworks.

● Bold, italic, and underline styles can be applied to text in the Property Inspector.

┤Caution

Just be sure that you are completely satisfied with your text before you convert it to vector paths, as this process is irreversible. Although you can continue to manipulate the vector-based graphic, you will not be able to go back into the Text Editor later and make changes to the actual text content.

Converting text to vector objects gives you the freedom to edit the actual shape of the text, as an image. In this exercise, you'll explore how to convert text objects into vector objects, how to combine text with other vectors and bitmaps, and the possibilities that these techniques afford.

Project 4-3: Working with Vectors, Paths, and Text

As a sophisticated graphics-creation tool, Fireworks can go far beyond the effects you have created to this point. Although the different effects, fills, and strokes you have used have allowed you to create some unique text effects, the ability to convert text into a vector object and to arrange text to follow a vector-based path extends your capabilities. Add the ability to combine text objects with either vector objects or bitmaps and you'll soon find that working in Fireworks is not only very productive but lots of fun as well.

Step-by-Step

1. Create a new 300 pixel by 300 pixel document with a white canvas. Save this file as *vector_practice.png*.

2. Select the Text tool from the Tools panel and type the letters **A B C** onto the canvas. Choose a font of your liking and set the size of the font to 40 points or greater.

3. The next procedure will convert your editable text to graphical objects. It is very important that you are sure everything (including the spelling) is as it should be before you convert a text object to a vector path. If you wish to return the text to its editable state, you need to select Edit | Undo until you see the text box reappear.

4. Select the text object on the canvas and choose Text | Convert To Paths to change the letters from text objects to vectors. Though you might expect something dramatic to happen, you'll only notice that the selection area

changes from a rectangle to four square handles that appear around what used to be the text box.

← **Resize handles**

5. The handles indicate that the object is a grouped set of vector objects. A quick glance at the Property Inspector confirms this; you will see the object label Group (3), indicating that three individual objects are grouped together into one graphic. To see how this grouping can be used to your advantage, try using the Pointer tool to grab one of the resizing handles and change the size of the text. As the grouped area grows larger or smaller, the letters, now vectors, resize as you see here.

Tip

Use the command Edit | Duplicate to create an exact copy of the grouped letters and try resizing the separate objects as you see in the example above. The duplicate command is also available via a keyboard shortcut—CTRL-ALT-D (Windows) or CTRL-CMD-D (Macintosh).

6. Not only can text be repositioned and resized as a grouped object, but individual letters can be converted to vector graphics as well. With a grouped set of text selected, choose Modify | Ungroup. As you see here, the text is now three vector objects and they display the separate control points that define their shapes.

← **Vector control points**

7. What's really special about converting text to vector-based paths is that they can be modified with some of the tools that you used in Module 2. Choose the Subselection tool from the Tools panel and click one of the letters. You will see it light up with paths that can be moved, modified, and twisted into entirely new letters.

8. With the Subselection tool, you can modify any point along the path that defines the object. For instance, the letters in the following example can be changed into some dramatic new forms simply by pulling points away from the letter. Alternatively, you may use the Freeform tool to pull groups of points away from the path to create objects that only retain the hint that they were once letters. Once text is converted to a path, you have complete control over its ultimate form and position on the canvas. Just remember that the process of converting text to paths is irreversible; once you convert text, you are no longer able to edit it.

9. One of the most common techniques used with text that has been converted to a vector shape is that of combining the text object with another vector shape. To see this technique, draw a simple rectangle onto the canvas and add some text to the document. In this example, the letters **A B C** are being used again.

Tip

You'll recall from Module 2 that objects assume a stacking order as you add them to a canvas, as if you were stacking cards on a table. For this technique, you need to create the rectangle first, followed by the text. If the stacking order is incorrect, you can restack the text by choosing Modify | Arrange | Bring to Front.

10. With the text box selected, choose Text | Convert to Paths to change the text to a grouped object. Move the grouped object on top of the rectangle without ungrouping. Once the text is in place, choose Modify | Ungroup.

11. Now that the text is in position, each individual letter can be used to punch a hole in the underlying rectangle. Select all the letters and the rectangle by using the SHIFT-click technique, or simply use the Pointer tool to draw a box around all the objects, a technique known as marqueeing.

12. With all the objects selected, punch letters through the rectangle by choosing Modify | Combine Paths | Punch. As each command is executed, one letter is punched through the object. In this case, the command was done three times to punch all three letters.

13. Your new creation is a vector object, so you have the full range of options for setting stroke and fill properties. In this example, the object has been given a soft line stroke with a width of 3 pixels.

14. The punch command can also be used to punch another object through a letter. Try this by typing a capital A and converting it to a vector path. Then create a star using the Polygon tool set for that shape and position the star above the letter. Once again, choose Modify | Combine Paths | Punch to achieve the effect you see here.

15. As you wrap up this exercise in the use of text as a vector object, take some time to explore the various options that combining and modifying text affords you. By converting text to vector objects, you can create entirely new works of art, suitable for use in creating logos, adding dramatic flair to your web graphics, or simply turning the mundane into the fantastic.

Project Summary

In this exercise, you have learned how to convert text into vector objects, ungroup grouped text to allow for the manipulation of individual letters, and combine graphical objects that begin as text with other vector shapes to create unique objects. Fireworks offers so many opportunities for turning simple text into new creations (in the same clean interface that has become the hallmark of Macromedia products) that you will undoubtedly find yourself turning to these tools again and again.

Combining Text with Vectors

You have now seen many of the common ways to enter and format text in Fireworks. From letting you simply choose a font to letting you convert text into vector objects, Fireworks provides many ways to manipulate and transform text to produce some very interesting effects. In this final project, you will explore one additional technique—attaching text to vector paths, allowing you to determine not only the size and position, but the direction and shape it takes.

Remember from Module 2 that a path is a series of points that are connected by lines. All objects created with vectors have paths that define their boundaries, and Fireworks gives you the capability to attach text along these defining outlines.

There are many creative possibilities, including the common technique of attaching text to a circular path to arrange text in a round pattern.

Fireworks MX includes some new tools that allow you to further refine your text once it has been attached to a path. You can fine-tune the appearance by modifying how the text is anchored to the path—skewing or slanting the text in new ways.

As always, the power of vectors lies in the ability to change the size, shape, or location of any object that exists in your Fireworks document. Combine these two types of objects—text and paths—and some very interesting possibilities emerge from the union.

Project 4-4: Attaching Text to a Path

Considering the number of things that you might conceivably want to create with Fireworks' text tools—from logos to buttons to other types of eye-catching graphics—it's no surprise that the software contains so many ways to get the job done. In this final exercise in working with text, you will learn how to attach text to any vector path that you create. From simple lines to curves to curved text combined with a graphic, which you see in Figure 4-5, all of the tools for arranging text in unusual ways are right at your fingertips in Fireworks MX.

Figure 4-5 Text can be attached to circular paths to create logos, buttons, and other objects.

Step-by-Step

1. Start by creating a new document that is 300 pixels by 300 pixels and has a white canvas. Save this new file as *path_practice.png*.

2. To begin understanding how text is attached to a path, use the Pen tool to create a bell-shaped curve.

3. With the Pen tool selected, click and drag a control point on the left side of the canvas. Release the mouse button and then click and drag a second point near the top of the canvas. As you drag, pull the control handle to the right to define the first curved segment, as you see here. Finish by clicking and dragging again on the right side of the canvas to complete a bell-shaped curve. Remember that the Subselection tool allows you to go back to this shape for further changes.

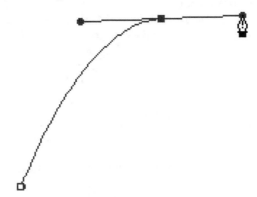

4. Using the Text tool, type in the text **A Bell-Shaped Curve** anywhere on your canvas. The size of the font should be around 25 points.

5. Once your text is in place, marquee the curve and the text so that both are selected. Finally, choose the command Text | Attach to Path to see your letters attach themselves to this simple shape, as you see here. Note that as your text attaches to a path, any stroke or fill attributes that were assigned to the path disappear, leaving only the vector structure.

6. Even though this text has been changed into a new shape, it still remains completely editable. Try editing it by selecting the text and changing the font size, or even the font type, in the Property Inspector. With Fireworks' use of vectors, you never lose the ability to edit your text, even when it has been attached to a path and arranged in new ways.

Note

Although you still retain editability of text as long as it is contained by a text box, text can be converted to individual graphic objects by converting the text object to a vector object as you learned in Project 4-3.

7. With your text selected, choose Text | Orientation. Note that although the default setting is Rotate Around Path, you can also set the text to Vertical, Skew Vertical, or Skew Horizontal. Figure 4-6 demonstrates how the text you just entered appears after being resized and set with those options.

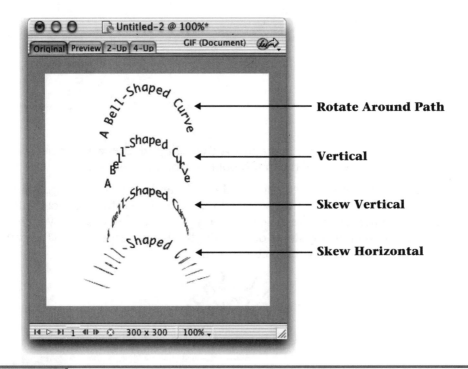

Figure 4-6 Text attached to a path can have its orientation modified by applying the settings you see here.

8. You can attach any text on your canvas to any vector shape, including a line segment, as you have just done—a polygon, a circle, or even a star. Because both the text and the shape it is attached to are vectors, you can modify or even remove the union of the two as you wish. To remove text from a path, simply select Text | Detach from Path, and your text will return to its familiar rectangular text box.

9. To complete this exercise, you will use one of the most common techniques of attaching text to a path—creating text attached to a circular path, as in Figure 4-5. To begin, either clear your canvas or begin a new document with a canvas size of 300 pixels by 300 pixels.

10. Begin by creating a circle. Select the Ellipse tool and, while holding down SHIFT, drag out a circle approximately half the size of your canvas. Don't worry about any stroke or fill settings at this point because all you need is the vector shape itself.

11. In order to attach the text in the proper orientation, you must create two half-circles. If you attach text to an ellipse, as you see here, the text flows around the circle beginning at the upper left corner. As it reaches the bottom, the text loses its proper orientation.

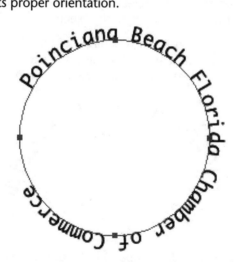

12. To split the vector shape, select the Knife tool from the Tools panel and slice the circle in half by dragging a line across its center, as shown. Once the circle is "cut" in two, deselect the object by clicking in the negative area of the canvas and then use the Pointer tool to drag the circle apart. When you are finished, you should have two half-circles.

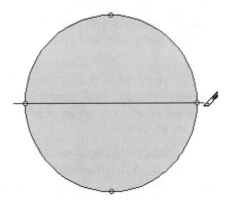

13. Select the Text tool and place a text box above the upper half of the circle. Type the text **Poinciana Beach Florida** and set the font size to no greater than 18 points. To attach the text to the path of the upper half-circle, you need to hold down SHIFT while selecting both the half-circle and the text box or use the Pointer tool to marquee both objects.

14. Finally, select Text | Attach To Path to have the text drape across the top of the circle. Once text is attached to the path, the stroke and fill associated with the path are removed, leaving only the text arranged in a half circle.

15. If you duplicate the preceding steps with the bottom half of the circle, the results are not as you might expect. Paths are originally created in a clockwise direction, so Fireworks continues to arrange the text the same way. This causes the text to display upside down, as in the earlier example.

4

16. To achieve the proper effect, you must flip over the half-circle at the bottom of the logo before you attach the text to it. This is a simple matter of selecting the lower half-circle and then choosing Modify | Transform | Flip Horizontal to turn the object over on its side. There is little visible evidence of this step, but by flipping the half-circle, you have rearranged the beginning point of the path and are ready for your second line of text. Type the text **Chamber of Commerce**, select the text and the lower half-circle, and once again choose Text | Attach to Path. As you see here, this extra step orients your text correctly.

17. You'll also note that this text is inside the vector path, whereas the initial text was placed on the outside. To adjust this positioning, open the Text editor by choosing Text | Editor. Create the adjustment by modifying the text's position in relation to the baseline, or the vector path it is attached to. In the Text Editor, locate the Baseline Shift setting, shown here, and adjust the number to approximately 80% of your font size. In this example, a font size of 18 points is used, so the Baseline Shift has been set to –14.

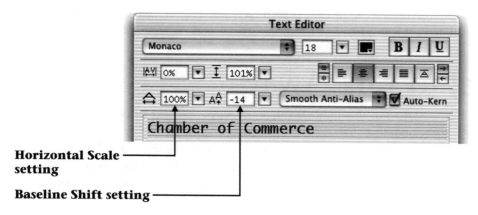

Horizontal Scale setting

Baseline Shift setting

⊣*Note*

You may find that you need to continue making small adjustments in the positioning of your text in order to get the exact look you are after. Often, when working with text on a circular path, this involves adjusting the Horizontal Scale setting, which you can find in both the Text Editor and the Property Inspector.

18. To finish the project and complete this preliminary logo, draw a second circle on the canvas and use the Modify | Arrange command to stack the circle and the text objects in the proper order. You may also want to use the Scale tool to adjust the size of the curved text so that it fits and aligns properly within the circle. The possibilities are extensive, and with some fine-tuning you can easily create a logo or a button with text attached to any object.

Project Summary

This project has demonstrated the power of Fireworks to attach text to various vector shapes. Fireworks employs vectors for the creation of text, so you can change text characteristics at any time; you can change font types and sizes, apply stroke and fill properties, and arrange text along a curve or even a circular area.

1-Minute Drill

● What happens to the editability of text when it is converted to a vector-based path?

● Which kinds of paths can you attach text to?

● Which objects on the canvas must be selected before you can attach text to a path?

What to Take Away

You have learned in this module the many ways that text can be entered into a Fireworks document. The Text tool and the Property Inspector allow you to enter text, modify it, and apply font styles, sizes, and colors to it. You can do all of this while keeping the text editable so that you can return again and again to perform other modifications as necessary. All text in a Fireworks document

---

● Text that is converted to paths can no longer be edited with the Property Inspector or Text Editor.
● Text can be attached to any vector-based path, including rectangles, ellipses, lines, and curves.
● Both the text box and the path must be selected to attach the text to a path.

exists as an editable text object unless it is converted to a vector object, so you can repeatedly modify the text by using the Text Editor even after applying strokes, fills, and effects.

You have also learned that text can be converted to noneditable vector objects, which makes it possible to manipulate the text at any point along the path that defines the image. Text that is converted to a vector object can also be combined with other vector objects to create entirely new graphics.

Finally, you saw how text can be attached to a path to create logos and other interesting effects when you want to move beyond the limitations of horizontally or vertically arranged text. In all, Fireworks provides some outstanding tools to ensure that your text-based graphics for the Web have the readability and impact you desire.

4

✓ Mastery Check

1. What is the major advantage to using text that is converted to graphical images?

   _____

   _____

2. What is the major disadvantage to using text that is converted to graphical images?

   _____

   _____

3. What font types are available for use in Fireworks?

   _____

   _____

4. What is the difference between proportional and monospaced fonts?

   _____

   _____

5. How are stroke options applied to text?

   _____

   _____

6. How are effects options applied to text?

   _____

   _____

7. Can text that has been converted to a path be edited? Can font types text be changed once text is converted to a path?

   _____

   _____

☑ Mastery Check

8. What step must you take to use text that has been converted to a vector object in combination with other vector shapes, as in punching letters through another object?

_____

_____

9. What kinds of shapes can you attach text to?

_____

_____

10. How can you modify the orientation of text after it has been attached to a path?

_____

_____

4

Module 5

Exploring Strokes, Fills, and Effects

The Goals of This Module

- Explore the Fireworks interface for applying strokes, fills, and effects
- Understand the use of the Property Inspector for applying strokes, fills, and effects
- Examine options for strokes applied to vector paths and shapes
- Understand the use of textures and patterns
- Examine the new gradient tools in Fireworks MX
- Apply Live Effects to graphical objects
- Understand the use of filters
- Use Styles to apply stroke, fill, and effects settings
- Save custom Styles

Previous modules of this book teach how to work with the three primary graphical objects commonly used with Fireworks—vector objects, bitmap objects, and text. Perhaps you have taken a few minutes to explore the various stroke and fill properties along the way and have seen a few of the things that Fireworks makes possible in changing the basic properties of the objects you have created. In this module, you take a much more detailed look at those options and have the opportunity to see just how easily you can modify even simple strokes and shapes to give them an entirely new appearance.

The tools that Fireworks MX provides are organized around the same interface you have worked in already, using the Property Inspector as a kind of central command. In addition to working extensively with the Property Inspector, in this module you'll work for the first time with some of the panels that extend the organization and control you have over your graphics.

Understanding Strokes and Fills

As previous modules show, stroke and fill properties applied to vector objects can be modified easily in the Fireworks interface. In Fireworks MX, all of these changes are made in one central location—the Property Inspector. Draw a stroke with the Line, Pen, or Vector Path tools, and the options for changing stroke settings become available. Create a shape with the Rectangle, Rounded Rectangle, Ellipse, or Polygon tool, or a closed path with one of the tools mentioned above, and both stroke and fill properties may be modified. As Module 4 teaches, you can also modify strokes and fills when you insert text.

Vector paths, such as the ones just described, are composed of two key elements—the points that describe the path and the lines that connect the points. Two types of paths can be created. An open path, one for which the beginning and end points do not coincide, can have only stroke properties applied. A *closed* path, or a path with beginning and end points at the same location on the canvas, can have both strokes and fills applied.

Module 2 discusses how Fireworks uses a unique approach to apply these properties to objects that you create. The vector paths that define an object provide the structure for the object's location, size, and shape. By applying stokes, fills, and effects, you can lay a coating of bitmaps on top of the basic structure that enables you to modify the form in innumerable ways. The genius of Fireworks is that it enables you to modify an object's basic structure and change the properties of the image at any time. If you think of your vector objects as mannequins that you can dress any way you like and change any time you want, you'll understand how the properties explored in this module work. Figure 5-1 shows some ways you can use effects to modify a simple vector object like a star.

Create a new document to practice with for this next section. Use a white canvas color and set the canvas size at 300 pixels by 300 pixels.

Exploring Stroke and Fill Settings in the Property Inspector

As you have seen, the interface for modifying both strokes and fills is found in the Property Inspector. Fireworks MX dramatically simplifies the process of accessing stroke and fill properties, enabling you to modify these settings in

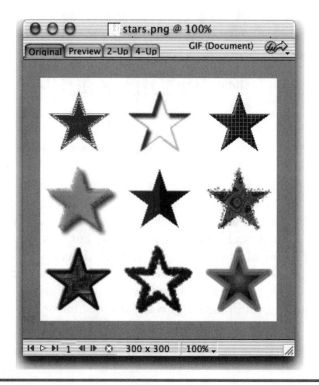

Figure 5-1   Applying various strokes, fills, and effects enables you to change the appearance of basic shapes in countless ways.

one convenient location. Previous versions of Fireworks required opening two separate panels to do the work that is now handled by the Property Inspector.

Examining Stroke Properties

The Property Inspector contains settings for strokes that appear automatically when you create a vector object, as shown in the following illustration. For a simple line drawn with the Line tool, Fireworks applies the default setting of a stroke 1 pixel wide with a soft edge. These settings appear any time you use the Line, Pen, or Vector Path tools or whenever you draw a rectangle, rounded rectangle, ellipse, or polygon with their respective tools. In addition, as Module 4 discusses, you can apply stroke properties to text objects once you enter text onto the canvas.

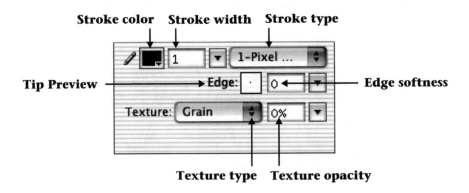

Fireworks provides so many possible combinations of colors, stroke types, and even stroke textures that it can be difficult to know where to begin. Furthermore, the choices are contextual—changing as you apply new choices— so the range of options can be downright dizzying. For now, your task is to gain an understanding of where the tools are located. As you move through succeeding projects in this and subsequent modules, you will return to the strokes settings to see their practical application. If you haven't done so already, draw a simple line on your practice canvas with the Line or Pen tool.

Note

Although stroke properties can also be accessed by selecting the Stroke Color option button in the Tools panel, this discussion will focus on the use of the Property Inspector as the command center for applying and modifying strokes. The Property Inspector is part of the common interface between the new MX family of Macromedia products, so you need to be very familiar with it.

Applying Stroke Colors   As with other color settings, stroke colors are applied with the common Macromedia interface, featuring a series of color swatches, as you see in the following illustration. The Eyedropper tool enables you to choose any color available from the color swatches, pick up a color from any object in the Fireworks window, or even set no stroke color at all. Additionally, you can set further options through the flyout menu by clicking the arrow in the upper-right corner of the Color Chooser window. Note one important option available for setting colors in the Color Chooser—the setting that forces a color to "snap" to its nearest web-safe equivalent color. Activating this option ensures that colors you select will appear the same regardless of the browser or operating system that your Internet audience uses when viewing your web graphics. As with other color selections, you need only pass the Eyedropper over the color swatches to see the color previewed in the upper-left corner of the Color Chooser.

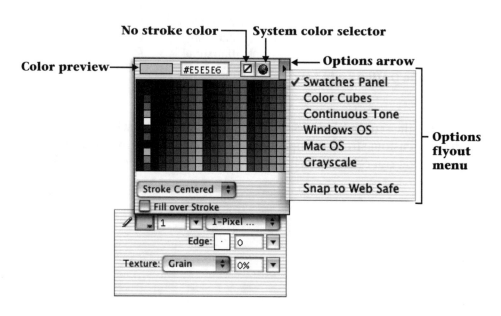

Setting Stroke Types   Stroke types are set by choosing from the options available in the drop-down menu. As you see in the following illustration, additional options are available for each category of stroke type. Everything from a basic airbrush-type stroke to a stroke with a yarn texture is available through this interface. To gain a little practice and learn how these strokes are applied and how they look, take a few minutes to draw additional lines and apply different stroke types to your lines. At the very least, you should check out some of the strokes with the more interesting names. Try Viscous Alien Paint and 3D Glow in the Unnatural category; Wet in the Calligraphy category; and Confetti, Dots, and Fur in the Random section. As you will see, there are a huge number of choices (forty-eight, to be exact). With so many choices available, it is easy to appreciate how these settings can be applied to create some fascinating visual effects.

None   100%

Pencil   ▶
Basic   ▶
Air Brush   ▶
Calligraphy   ▶
Charcoal   ▶
Crayon   ▶
Felt Tip   ▶
Oil   ▶
Watercolor   ▶
Random   ▶
Unnatural   ▶

Open Stroke Options window ⟶ Stroke Options...

Clicking the setting labeled Stroke Options opens a new window where you can define a custom stroke. By opening yet another window for advanced stroke properties, you can control precisely the way that these new custom strokes are defined. By clicking the Add Stroke Style button, you can name and generate a new stroke style based on options you specify.

Save custom stroke ———

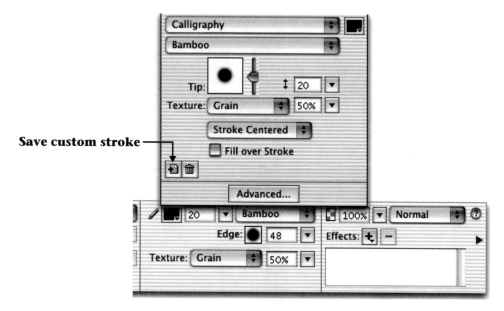

5

Applying Textures to Strokes   Stroke styles provide a wide range of options for changing the appearance of the edges of vector graphics, but the fun doesn't stop there. In addition, you can use textures to further modify your strokes. From Burlap to Wood, Fireworks contains a huge number of textures that can be applied and customized to meet your needs.

Using textures is a two-step process. First, from the options available through the Texture drop-down menu, seen here, choose the texture that you want to apply to your stroke. Note that Fireworks will display a preview of the texture's appearance as you roll your cursor over each name.

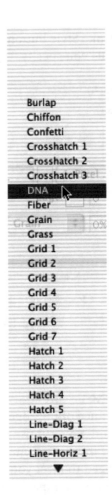

Second, once a texture is selected, use the opacity setting to determine how much of the texture appears in the stroke. A setting of 0 percent shows none of the texture, and a setting of 100 percent allows all of the texture to appear. In the following example, you can see the effect that opacity settings have on textures applied to basic airbrush style lines. Much in the same way that a textured paintbrush or roller alters the appearance of paint, texture settings vary the appearance of a stroke.

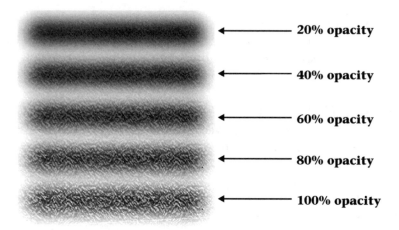

5

Modifying Tip Softness   The Edge softness setting in the Property Inspector changes the appearance of the tip of the tool applying the stroke or modifies the softness and shape of a stroke that has already been created. You can modify the relative hardness of a stroke's edges, creating brush strokes that are softer or harder as you move away from the center of the stroke. Using this setting is similar to choosing a paintbrush that has harder or softer bristles. With one of your practice lines selected, try out these settings by moving the Edge Softness slider up or down. Note that softness does not apply to every stroke type. However, with those that have a semi-opaque setting—as you see here, where a basic airbrush stroke has been applied—modifying the stroke softness enables you to further refine the edges of your graphics.

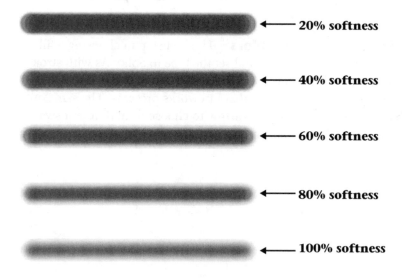

To conclude this discussion of strokes and their properties, take a few minutes to experiment with the tools that have been described here. Try out various stroke types and textures, noting how the changes that you apply in the Property Inspector affect the appearance of the strokes on your objects.

Examining Fill Properties

Fill settings are applied to closed vector shapes such as rectangles, ellipses, and polygons. They are also applied to shapes that you define by using one of the other vector drawing tools, such as the Pen or Vector Path tool. Just as with strokes, the primary tools for applying and modifying properties for fills are found in the Property Inspector. Take a few minutes to acquaint yourself with the location of the tools in the following illustration. Draw a closed vector shape on your practice canvas so that you can experiment with the settings discussed.

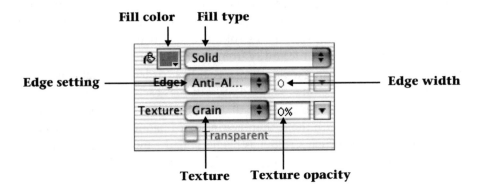

Applying Solid Stroke Colors   The first step in choosing a fill is to select the drop-down Fill type menu, and set the type to Solid. As with strokes, solid fill colors are applied through the Color Chooser, using the Eyedropper to select a color from the palette of choices that Fireworks presents. The same options are available when using the Options arrow to choose from different swatch settings, or opening your system color options and selecting from the choices presented there. You select a color with the Eyedropper; you can even use that tool to pick up a color from any object in an active Fireworks window—a particularly handy option if you want to match colors of two objects.

Understanding the Web Dither Option   Note the third option available in the fill types—Web Dither. *Dithering* is a process in which colors are mixed together to enable colors that aren't web-safe to appear correctly on a viewer's computer. Remember that one of the primary considerations in web design is the fact that you cannot know how viewers' monitors have been set. They may view your page with just the basic 256 colors that represent the lowest setting possible or may have their monitors set for millions of colors with 24-bit color depth. Dithering mixes web-safe colors together to achieve an approximation of the color that you apply as a fill. If you are using custom colors, such as a pastel shade that does not exist in the web-safe palette, dithering enables you to achieve the closest approximation of that color regardless of the viewer's monitor setting.

Applying Patterns to Fills   Fireworks ships with a huge variety of fill patterns that can be applied for some fascinating results. With 46 standard patterns and the ability to modify those patterns and add custom patterns to the available selections, you can get some really interesting fills for your graphics. As you see here, selecting the Pattern option brings up a small window listing the pattern applied. Because the listing is alphabetical, by default the Berber pattern will appear first. Note also that when a pattern is selected, the Fill Color button will change to show a small preview of the selection. Once you have applied a pattern, select the button to reopen the Pattern Options window.

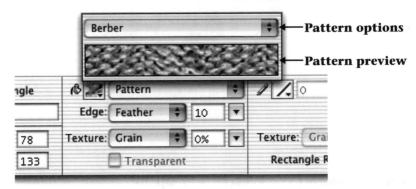

Patterns are selected by clicking the drop-down arrow to open the full range of pattern listings. As you see in the following illustration, the choices are extensive. Fireworks provides a preview as you roll your mouse pointer over each choice. For a demonstration of how you can modify patterns further, set the pattern for your object to Smear 3.

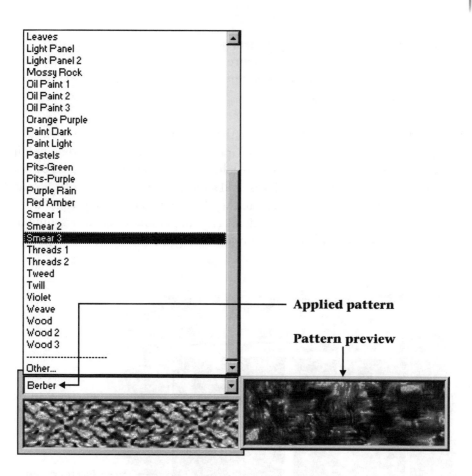

Once a pattern is applied as a fill, you will see the selection handles that Fireworks provides for the further modification of the pattern. As cool as it is to use a pattern as a fill, the possibilities are even more numerous because of the ways you can modify a pattern by changing the way you apply it. As shown in Figure 5-2, you can alter the pattern by choosing the pattern center handle. Patterns can be rotated using one of the square handles, or compressed by moving the pattern handles closer to the center. Experiment with this feature to see its true power. Following the examples in Figure 5-2, use the Pointer tool to adjust the center, angle, and width of the pattern you have applied to the shape on your practice document.

Working with Gradients   One of the most powerful features for creating terrific-looking graphics is gradient fills. Gradients are created by blending multiple colors. With gradients, it is possible to achieve effects such as the glass buttons you will build later in this module, as well as realistic looking metallic text and 3-D spherical objects. Gradients create the illusion of light playing across a surface. Understanding the use of gradients is an important aspect of learning how to use Fireworks to its full capacity for generating effects that go far beyond

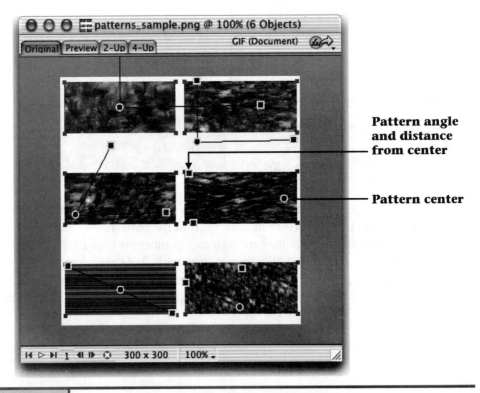

Figure 5-2   Patterns can be modified by changing the location of the pattern's center or by adjusting the pattern's rotation or width.

simple graphics. You'll use this valuable tool to achieve a depth and feel in your graphics that is not possible with just simple solid colors.

Fireworks MX has added another important improvement in this area. In addition to applying gradients, as you'll learn to do in a moment, you also can modify gradients. This enables you to further fine-tune a graphic so that parts of the gradient are transparent. With this new capability, you can combine and composite images with transparent gradients for the kinds of fascinating effects that you see in Figure 5-3.

Apply gradients as fills by selecting the various gradient patterns found in the lower part of the Fill types drop-down menu. As you see in the following

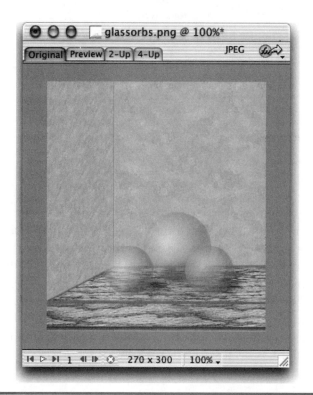

Figure 5-3   Combining patterns and transparent gradients enables you to create realistic looking graphics that simulate three-dimensional objects.

illustration, Fireworks contains presets for gradients ranging from Linear to Folds, with each option applying the gradient in different patterns. With one of the practice objects on your canvas selected, try this by applying one of the gradient presets.

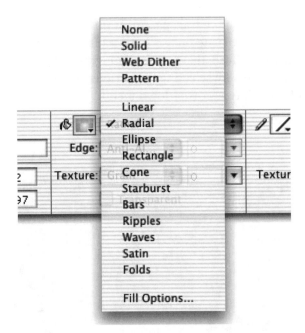

As you apply various gradients, you will see the different ways that preset patterns affect the interplay between the colors to create the desired effect. Linear gradients, for instance, produce a mixture of colors along a straight line, but radial gradients do so in a circular pattern. Take a few minutes to try each gradient type to get a feel for the way that Fireworks assigns these colors.

Once a gradient is applied, you can access the options to use a preset color scheme or to modify the gradient. Just click on the Fill Color button to open the gradient options that you see displayed next. In this example, the Emerald Green preset color has been selected from the Preset drop-down menu.

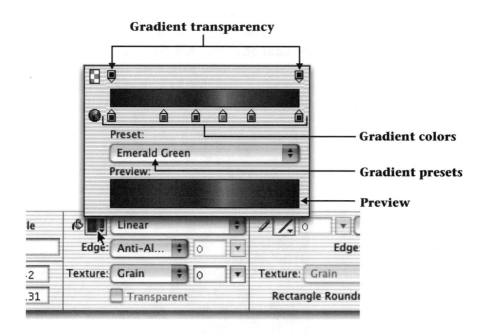

5

Use the sliders at the top of the gradient window to adjust the transparency of one side of the gradient fill. In the following example, the opacity of the left side of the gradient has been set to zero, which would allow 100 percent of an underlying object to appear through the fill. Note the checkerboard pattern that shows through the gradient, indicating that the fill is transparent.

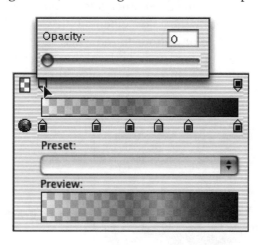

When a gradient is applied to a fill, you see the same handles for positioning and modifying the gradient that you see when you work with patterned fills. Using the handles, you can modify the location of the gradient's center by moving the round handle; or, you can rotate, skew, or modify the distance from center that the gradient is applied by using the square handles. As in the following example, objects that have the same gradient applied can take on dramatically different characteristics if you modify how the gradient is positioned.

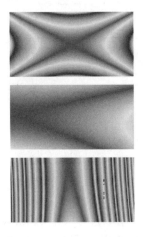

Finally, with the Gradient Fills option window open, you can also add or delete colors from any gradient pattern. Note that as you move your mouse pointer over the area below the gradient in the options window, a small plus sign appears next to the arrow. Click once to add another color point on the gradient and then click the new point to modify the color. Opening the Color Chooser gives you access to the full range of color options found when setting any color option in Fireworks. Some of these options include the ability to set gradients in preset color blends that simulate metallic colors, such as Silver and Copper.

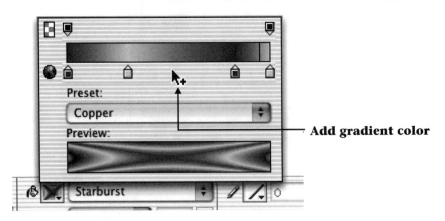

Add gradient color

To remove a color from the gradient blend, simply drag the color pointer off the scale. Additionally, gradients can create a two-tone fill when the sliders are directly atop each other. With the option to add, remove, or relocate the colors mixed into your gradient, you have the ultimate control over how the colors are mixed and applied to your objects.

Stroke and Fill Summary

As you conclude this rather lengthy look at the interface for applying strokes and fills, you should have a solid appreciation for just how varied (and, at times, complex), working with these two graphics attributes can be. Fireworks MX has taken great strides forward with the introduction of the new Property Inspector—making these fundamental properties of objects much easier to apply and modify. However, learning how to effectively apply them, how to achieve the results you want from the many possible choices, and how to most effectively use these tools to enhance your work flow and the appearance of your Web graphics will take a fair amount of practice. The rest of the projects and exercises in this module teach you how strokes and fills can be used for particular effects, and you will pick up some tips for their use along the way.

1-Minute Drill

● Where can you find the options for applying stroke and fill settings?

● How do you adjust the appearance of patterns and gradients?

● What new feature has been added to Fireworks MX for modifying gradients?

Project 5-1: Using Strokes and Fills for Three-Dimensional Effects

Now that you have had an opportunity to locate and practice with the tools for modifying strokes and fills, this next project gives you some practical experience in using those tools. You may want to turn back to look at Figure 5-3, as this project will take you through the process of creating a graphical image that simulates three spherical glass orbs resting on a tabletop.

● Options for applying and modifying strokes and fills are both found in the Property Inspector.

● You can modify patterns and gradients by moving the round handle that defines the center of the effect and by repositioning the square handles that indicate the effect's length and angle as measured from the center point.

● Fireworks MX features an option to change the transparency of a gradient fill.

Step-by-Step

1. Begin by creating a new canvas with a white background. Make the canvas size 300 pixels by 300 pixels. Save this file and name it *glass_orbs.png.*

2. Using the Rectangle tool, draw a rectangle that covers the left third of the canvas from top to bottom. Set the fill for this object as a Pattern, choosing a type that will simulate wallpaper on the wall behind the table. In the example, "Impressionist-Green" has been chosen. Using the object transparency slider in the Property Inspector, as you see here, the intensity of the color has been muted by reducing the opacity to 50 percent.

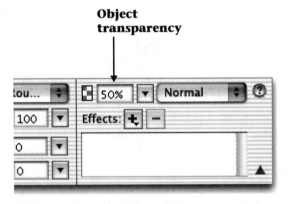

3. Using the pattern adjustment handles, change the direction of the handles on the rectangle to the left so that the direction of the pattern is skewed slightly upward. This will help create the illusion of a room in three dimensions.

4. Draw another rectangle that takes up the remaining portion of the canvas. Apply the same pattern that you used above to finish the "walls" in this room.

5. With the walls in place, it's time to draw the tabletop, starting its front edge. Again, using the Rectangle tool, draw a rectangle approximately 30 pixels high that stretches all the way across the canvas from left to right. In this rectangle, set the fill to the Wood pattern and apply a Basic stroke with the soft rounded brush style. Set the stroke width to 2 pixels and, using the Eyedropper, select one of the brown shades from the Wood fill pattern in the rectangle. This rectangle now represents the front edge of the table.

6. To create the tabletop, draw another rectangle approximately 90 pixels high directly above the table edge. Note that this rectangle will assume the same fill and stroke characteristics of the object previously drawn.

7. To get the tabletop into the correct perspective, use the Distort tool to drop the upper corners toward the bottom of the canvas so that the upper-left corner aligns with the "wall" corner and is parallel to the bottom of the canvas. Set the upper-right corner so that it is also parallel with the canvas's bottom edge, as seen here. Note that as the rectangle is distorted, the pattern is distorted as well.

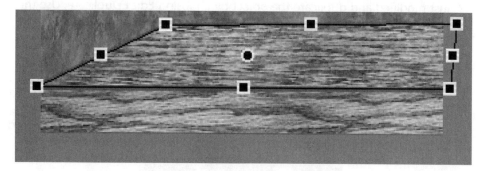

8. Now that the stage is set, it's time to add the glass orbs to the picture. Begin by drawing a simple circle, holding down SHIFT while dragging to create a perfect circle. This first circle should be approximately 80 pixels in diameter.

9. Change the fill on this circle to a radial gradient with no stroke applied. To achieve the glass look, open the Gradient Options window by clicking the color fill swatch and change the gradient fill colors so that one is white and the other is a bluish-green color. Finally, set the transparency for each gradient color to approximately 50 percent.

10. In order to achieve the correct placement of the light on this object, use the Pointer tool to move the gradient's round center handle to the upper left quadrant of the sphere. When finished, you should have a realistic looking glass orb, as you see here.

11. To create the smaller orbs seen in Figure 5-3, simply select the circle that you just modified and duplicate the object by choosing Edit | Duplicate. Use the Scale tool to change the size of each new orb you create and position those objects on your tabletop.

12. The final step to giving these objects some definition is to create an ellipse with a semitransparent gradient to act as the shadow for each. Again, draw an ellipse and, using the Scale tool, flatten the circle so that it is approximately half as tall as it is wide. Apply a linear gradient. In the example seen here, a black-and-white preset gradient has been modified so that it is darker toward the lower-left corner. The transparency for each color has been set at 50 percent.

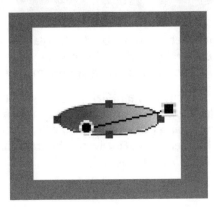

┼*Tip*

You can set up a separate canvas for creating objects that you want to use in your final composition. The ellipses used for the shadows, for instance, can be drawn on a new canvas and then dragged onto the final canvas once their properties have been set.

13. To complete this project, use the command Modify | Arrange | Send Backward to position the shadows behind the glass orbs. Position them so that the darkest area of the gradient is directly under the orbs. Once again, use the Scale tool to change the size of each of these shadows to match the size of the orb, and, when you are finished, you should have a great looking graphic that matches or improves upon the one in Figure 5-3.

Project Summary

In this practical application of the stroke and fill properties available in Fireworks MX, you have had the opportunity to see how these settings can be modified to achieve some simple yet effective techniques. By combining the various fill types such as patterns and gradients, you can create some very interesting images. With careful study of the way that gradients are applied to simulate the effect of light shining on objects, you can even simulate the depth inherent in three-dimensional objects.

Applying Live Effects and Filters in Fireworks MX

With the somewhat dizzying array of patterns, strokes, gradients, and textures that you can apply to vector objects that you create in Fireworks, it might seem that the program already provides enough options to make your graphics come to life. Still, some particular image effects remain that, when applied, can further define and improve your graphics, coaxing even more life out of them and extending your capabilities as a graphic artist.

As with strokes and fills, Live Effects, as Macromedia calls these tools, are applied to a vector base. Remember the metaphor of the mannequin from a previous discussion: Taking a basic form, you apply strokes and fills to clothe the form in new ways. Live Effects take that approach a step further, now enabling you to add jewelry and other accessories to the basic form that the vector object creates. These effects are "live" in that they take place as they are applied and, unlike some other graphic programs, do not require the modification of the underlying structure of the object itself. In Fireworks, all images that you draw are editable at any time; you may apply bevels, glows, blurs, and other effects that you explore here.

Filters are used to modify the appearance of bitmap objects and, as with effects, can be used to change the basic structure of an existing image, adjusting its color properties as well as making the image sharper or blurrier. In addition to the filters that come with Fireworks, you can purchase third-party filters that apply additional special effects.

Exploring the Effects Interface

You have undoubtedly noticed the Effects section of the Property Inspector either as you have been working with the objects that you draw or in Module 4 when you worked with text. The Effects area becomes active any time you select an object on the canvas that can have effects applied. This includes both open and closed vector paths as well as text. Note that when bitmap objects are on the canvas, the entire bitmap region can have an effect applied, but the bitmap object itself cannot.

As you can see in Figure 5-4, the settings for Live Effects are applied through the now-familiar Property Inspector interface. Like stroke types, effects are

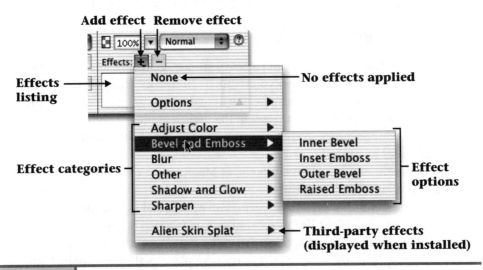

Figure 5-4 Live Effects are organized by category into the type of function they perform.

organized into a series of categories that describe their basic functions. As with strokes, each category contains additional settings that can be applied and modified, as needed.

As effects are applied to an object, they are added to the effects listing area of the Property Inspector. This area serves as a handy reference for seeing which effects you have applied. Also, by clicking the settings icon, represented by the lowercase letter *i*, you can access the available settings for any effect. As you see in the following illustration, you have ultimate control over the appearance of your applied effects, as with all graphics that you create in Fireworks.

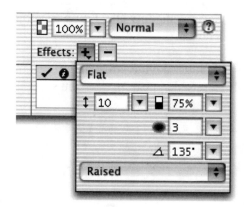

In addition to applying and modifying effects, you can also save effects and use them over and over again. Once you create a range of effects, you can save each effect as a Style by accessing the Effects options. The use of styles can be a significant time-saver when you're working on multiple objects for a web site. You will learn how to apply and save Styles in the last section of this module.

Note

Although there are many sophisticated effects that can be used for finely adjusting the look of your graphics, the discussion here will focus on those most commonly used for Web graphics.

Creating Bevel and Emboss Effects

One of the most common techniques used in web graphics is the application of a bevel effect to an object to make it look like a raised button. As you saw in Figure 5-4, the Bevel and Emboss category contains settings to apply a wide range of these kinds of effects. You will find yourself using these effects repeatedly, so take a few minutes now to create an ellipse or some text on your practice canvas using these effects to modify the appearance of common graphics. The effects in the Bevel and Emboss category include

- **Inner Bevel**   Creates the appearance of a raised bevel within the confines of the object.

- **Inset Emboss**   Creates the appearance that the object has been embossed into the canvas by generating a shadow effect.

- **Outer Bevel**   Creates a border around an object with a sloped appearance.

- **Raised Emboss**   Places a shadow effect onto the object to create the effect that it is above the canvas.

Each of these effects includes a wide range of options. Inner bevels, for instance, can be set with a raised appearance, as you see in Figure 5-5, or can be

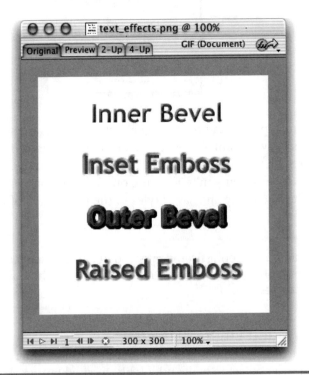

| **Figure 5-5** | The Bevel and Emboss category of effects contains four basic types of effects that can be modified and customized as you wish. |

set to appear highlighted, inset, or inverted. In addition, the pattern of each bevel can be modified to create a flat, smooth, sloped, framed, ringed, or ruffled appearance.

If those options aren't enough, you can change the bevel width, contrast, softness, and even the angle that the effect takes in relation to the object by accessing the effect information button on the Property Inspector. As you see here, the number of possible effects just for a simple bevel can be quite extensive, and you can expect to spend a little time in getting acquainted with how they affect the appearance of your images.

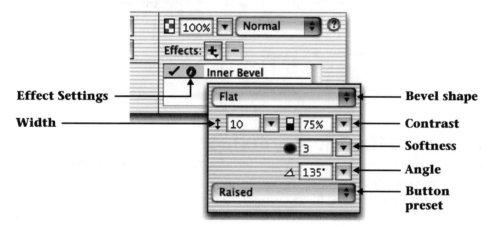

Creating Drop Shadows

The second most common category of effects is the Shadow and Glow settings. In this area, you find options to apply a drop shadow, a glow, an inner glow, and an inner shadow. Much as with bevel effects, each of these settings gives objects more depth and definition and can be used in combination with other effects to make your graphics appear to float above the page.

As you see in the following illustration, the interface for applying a setting for a drop shadow is very similar to the one for applying a bevel. Just choose the distance that the shadow is placed from the object and choose the color, opacity, softness, and angle, and you have a great effect. Alternatively, leave the default setting as it is, and, in most cases, you'll be pleased with the results.

Note the option to use the drop shadow as a knock-out. With this option selected, only the shadow remains visible; the object that it is applied to will disappear from the canvas. Of course, these are vector objects, so the graphic still exists and can be recalled by deleting the drop shadow setting from the list in the Property Inspector or removing the knock-out option.

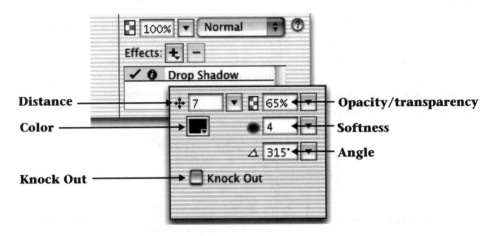

Exploring the Filters Interface

Filters behave somewhat similarly to effects in that they change a basic image to create special visual impact.

However, because using filters changes the pixels that compose bitmap graphics such as JPEG and GIF files, the effects applied are not reversible. Once you save a file that uses filters, it is changed forever.

Filters are familiar tools for users of Photoshop and other bitmap editors. Some filters created by other companies generate special effects that are beyond the realm of what Fireworks can do. Fireworks MX comes with a sample of the Alien Skin plug-in filter, called Splat, which enables you to modify bitmapped clip art to create a torn edge effect, among others. The full version of the software plug-in has much greater capabilities, and combined with other products can create effects for fire, lightning, and a host of other effects that can be applied to a bitmap object.

Unlike Live Effects, the settings for Filters are found in the Menu bar. To access the different categories of filters, including settings to adjust colors, blur and sharpen an image, and convert colors to transparencies, you must choose the Filters menu and select from the options there. Remember that because you are working with bitmaps, the first thing you must do before applying a filter is to select the bitmaps you want to modify with the Marquee, Lasso, or Magic Wand tools. Once again, using filters requires some practice and a little time spent applying various settings to your images.

1-Minute Drill

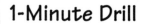

- What types of objects can you apply Live Effects to?
- How are effects added to or removed from an object?
- How do Live Effects and filters differ?

Project 5-2: Creating a Glass Button

Now that you have a basic understanding of how effects are applied to images, it's time to put that knowledge into play by creating one of the most requested image effects at the Fireworks newsgroup—the glass button. Popularized by Apple Computer as it introduced its new OS X operating system, and used extensively in that environment, these buttons have a look and feel that have captured people's imaginations. Armed with what you know about fills, gradients, and effects, you're ready to make some of your own!

5

Step-by-Step

1. Begin once again with a 300 pixel by 300 pixel document with a white canvas. Name your file *glass_button.png*.

2. Using the Rounded Rectangle tool, draw a button onto the canvas approximately 140 pixels wide by 40 pixels high in the center of the canvas. Note that you should set the corner roundness to 100 in the Property Inspector to get completely elliptical corners on your rectangle. Set the fill color to a light blue.

3. The first effect to apply to this object is a bevel. With the rectangle selected, use the drop-down arrow in the Effects area of the Property Inspector to apply an inner bevel. With the Bevel Options window open,

---

- You can apply Live Effects to open or closed vector paths or to text objects.
- The Property Inspector contains an Effects area in which effects are added by clicking the plus sign or removed by selecting the minus sign.
- Live Effects are applied to vector-based objects, and filters are used with bitmap images.

set the bevel to a smooth setting, retaining the default width of 10 pixels, as you see here.

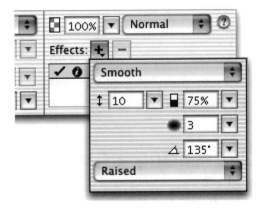

4. This button is actually composed of a number of pieces, so you'll use the Duplicate command to generate some exact copies of the button at this point. Simply choose Edit | Duplicate two times and move the copies away from the original to have some working room.

5. With the Knife tool, slice the first duplicate along the top third of the rectangle as you see here. Use the Pointer to separate the two halves of the rectangle and delete the bottom portion.

6. Because this is a duplicate that has the same effects applied as the original, return to the Effects area of the Property Inspector and remove the bevel effect from the rectangle section you have kept. Select the effect by name and click the minus sign to remove the effect.

7. You will now use the Brightness/Contrast effect to give this section a deeper color. Click the plus sign to add an effect and choose Adjust Color | Brightness/Contrast. In the window that appears, set the Brightness level to -100 and the Contrast to zero. Your slice should now be a deeper shade of blue than the original. Using the Pointer tool, position this section at the top of the original rectangle, as shown here.

8. Now, to fuzz this section up a bit and to make it appear to merge with the underlying rectangle, add another effect by clicking the plus sign. This time, choose Blur I Gaussian Blur, which will apply a mathematical formula to blur this section. A blur radius of 3.2 should be just about perfect. Set the radius and click OK to accept the change.

9. Once again, use one of the duplicate buttons to create one more lighting effect. This time, select the Duplicate button and, using the Scale tool, change the height of the rectangle to approximately 10 pixels. Note that you could also perform this operation in the Info area of the Property Inspector. Position this object at the top of the original rectangle, directly above the section you put into place in Step 7. Once it is in position, change the color of the section to a solid white fill.

10. Your button will be complete with just a bit more Gaussian Blur added to this new section. Once again, select the object and click the plus sign in the Property Inspector. As you did before, choose Blur I Gaussian Blur and adjust the setting to achieve an effect similar to the one you see here.

11. To complete this project, you need only add the appropriate label for your new glass button. In this example, an Inner Bevel effect has been applied to the text and the color has been set to black. As you can see, creating a glass button is as easy as creating the separate pieces of a puzzle and putting them

5

together. Apply some simple effects, and your image springs to life. Be sure to save this file before you move on.

Project Summary

In this project, you have seen just one example of how settings for Live Effects can be applied to simple shapes to give images depth and create the illusion that they occupy three dimensions. Although this example uses a color scheme similar to the buttons found in Apple's OS X interface, colors other than those used here would work just as well. In addition, more depth can be attained by setting the fill of the primary rectangle to a linear gradient and adjusting the transparency and direction of the fill to give the image added definition. The choices are up to you; as you move through similar exercises in upcoming projects, you will continue to appreciate how easy it is to achieve these types of effects in Fireworks.

?Ask the Expert

Question: Where can I find out more about the creative use of strokes, fills, and effects? Are there tutorials online that will show me examples of how these kinds of Fireworks tools can be used?

Answer: There are a number of creative professionals who have devoted their time and energy to developing web sites related to Fireworks and the ways that this fabulous program can be used. Here are some of my favorites:

● Playing with Fire (www.playingwithfire.com) Developed by Linda Rathgeber, this site has been demonstrating the creative use of Fireworks longer than any other and offers some great tips on color, effects, and the use of Fireworks tools to create striking visual results.

● EpaperPress (www.epaperpress.com/fireworks) Thomas Niemann's site has a number of very thorough tutorials on the use of transparencies and masking.

- **CBT Cafe** (www.cbtcafe.com/fireworks)   Short and to the point describes the tutorials that David Anderson features at his site. An extensive listing of special visual tips and tricks in both HTML and QuickTime movie format are featured.

- **Escogitando** (www.escogitando.it/en/en.html)   Available in English, Italian, and Spanish, this site from Japi Honoo features a number of great tutorials on creative tricks for making the most of Fireworks.

- **Ultraweaver** (www.ultraweaver.com)   Be sure to check the downloads section at Joey Durham's site, where you can find source Fireworks files annotated by their creators demonstrating some of the ways the program can be used to achieve visual impact.

5

Styling with Styles

Styles are special saved settings that Fireworks maintains or that you create. They have the capability of saving strokes, effects, colors, and other attributes and they can then be applied repeatedly as new objects are created. They are important labor-saving devices and can assist greatly in maintaining a consistent look to the graphics you use throughout your web site. In this final section of the module, you will be introduced to the way that styles are applied to objects and will learn how you can create your own style to apply to buttons or other objects as you work in Fireworks MX.

Introducing the Styles Panel

Up until now, all of your work in Fireworks has been done in the Tools panel and the Property Inspector, with occasional forays to the Menu bar to perform some simple operations. It is now time to have your first look at one of the biggest improvements in Fireworks MX—the docking area for the panels you will use to work with your graphics.

Prior to the release of Fireworks MX, the panels that were used for special operations could be very difficult to work with. They employed a free-floating format, so it was all too common to find a panel hidden behind another, obscuring your canvas, or just too far away from the other panels to make using these tools as easy as it could be. With the new docking style found in the MX family of products, panels used for accessing Styles, Behaviors, Layers, and Frames, among others, are just a click away as you expand or collapse them to meet your needs.

Figure 5-6 displays the Styles panel; in it you can see the standard preset styles that ship with Fireworks. Note also that additional options are available by selecting the Options flyout menu in this and all other panels. To open the panel, you need only click the arrow in the upper left-hand corner. To hide the panel, click the same arrow to collapse it. This is an elegant and effective solution to the panel clutter that used to plague Fireworks.

Understanding Styles

Styles are used to record one of two types of object properties—fills, colors, strokes, and stroke colors as applied to objects; or fonts, font sizes, font styles, and other text properties when applied to text objects. As nice as the existing presets are on their own, the true power of Styles becomes evident when you begin making your own, based on the settings that you define.

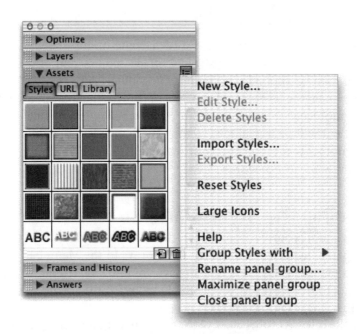

| **Figure 5-6** | Options for applying Styles are available in the Styles panel in the new panel docking area. |

To see how Styles are applied, draw an object on a practice canvas and click the button for the Style you want to try. Automatically, all of the properties associated with the Style are applied to the object. As you see in the following illustration, when you apply different styles to duplicate objects, they can take on entirely different appearances. If you choose to use the Styles that are included with Fireworks, you need only choose the look you want in the Styles panel, and your object will take on the attributes specified.

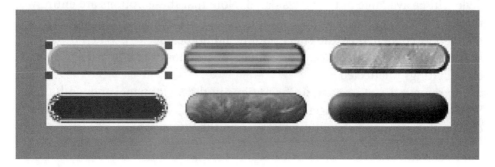

Creating Custom Styles

Creating your own Styles can go a long way toward simplifying the day-to-day work of creating web graphics. Rather than having to specify fill colors, effects, and other settings for your graphics over and over, Styles enable you to apply your saved settings at will. Your saved Styles are always available when you are working in Fireworks, so you can create multiple styles for all of your web projects. In the example you see here, the beginning of the glass button you created in Project 5-2 is seen. The colors have been set, a semitransparent linear gradient has been applied and rotated into position, and the same smooth bevel setting used previously has been applied. Try this for yourself now, choosing any color and effect settings you wish to see duplicated.

From the flyout options in the Styles panel, choose the option to define a new style. Once you have done so, you will see the dialog box that appears in Figure 5-7. Note the preview of the applied style that is shown in the upper left corner of the dialog box.

In this example, the style captures the gradient fill type, the colors selected, the stroke (or lack of stroke) and the effect that is applied to any object selected on the canvas. You need only give the Style a name and click OK, and your new Style will be available in the Styles panel. Note that these options are entirely up to you. If the Style you wish to save only includes a specific drop-shadow effect that you've created, only the effect option should be checked. When the Style is applied to an object, those categories that you've chosen will be used, leaving other settings unaffected.

To remove a Style, return to the options in the Styles panel and, with the Style you wish to delete selected, choose Delete Style. After you confirm your choice, the custom Style will disappear from the Styles panel.

What to Take Away

In this module, you have seen how Fireworks uses its unique combination of vector structure combined with bitmap fills, strokes, and effects to generate graphics that have depth, style, and character. With the tools that Fireworks

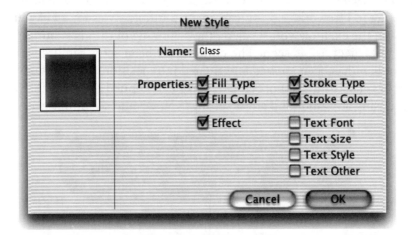

Figure 5-7 The New Style dialog box enables you to save effects, colors, and other settings for use with other objects.

provides, you have learned how simple graphical objects and text can be transformed in almost countless ways to achieve the look you are after.

With strokes, you have seen how to outline objects by choosing stroke colors, and you have learned the many stroke options that Fireworks provides. Everything from a simple pencil-like stroke to brush strokes composed of textured patterns can be applied to your images. With fills, you now have an understanding of the ways that Fireworks applies properties to closed vector paths, enabling you to fill objects with everything from simple colors to transparent gradients that allow for the simulation of objects in three dimensions.

Finally, you have seen how to apply Live Effects to objects to give them further definition and to generate special visual interest in your graphics. You have learned about using bevels, shadows, and blurs to accomplish some of the more common tricks of the web graphics trade. And, as you have worked through the explanations and exercises in this module, you should have gained an appreciation for the new interface that Fireworks MX uses to make possible these types of modifications to your graphics.

5

✔ *Mastery Check*

1. Define open and closed vector paths.

_____

_____

2. What unique approach does Fireworks use for the application of strokes, fills, and effects?

_____

_____

3. What does the "Snap to Web Safe" option accomplish?

_____

_____

☑ Mastery Check

4. How do you access and modify settings for an applied effect?

_____

_____

5. How do inner bevels and outer bevels differ?

_____

_____

6. How are filter options accessed?

_____

_____

7. Where are third-party filters found once they are installed in Fireworks?

_____

_____

8. What are Styles?

_____

_____

9. What kinds of settings can be saved as Styles when used with vector objects?

_____

_____

10. What kinds of settings can be saved as Styles when used with text?

_____

_____

Module 6

Creating and Organizing Complex Graphics

The Goals of This Module

- Understand how objects are grouped in a Fireworks document
- Combine vectors and bitmaps with the Group function
- Use mask groups to create transparent fade effects
- Understand how mask groups can achieve special image effects
- Explore the use of masks for cropping images
- Understand how layers are used for organizing complex images
- Use layers for bitmap and vector editing
- Create and manage complex graphics for use on the Web

Fireworks' capabilities as a bitmap-editing and vector-drawing program extend beyond the simple creation and manipulation of single objects. You have already combined some images you have created; the sophisticated features of Fireworks enable you to group, arrange, and create different interactions between objects in ways that not many programs offer. In addition, Fireworks is unique because it maintains the editability of objects during the design process so that you can add, delete, arrange, and ultimately combine objects to create a final integrated graphics file for publication to the Web. The main goal of the program is to provide unique, high-impact images suitable for use in web pages. This module shows how Fireworks significantly extends your creative freedom through the use of groups, masks, layers, styles, and libraries.

The new integrated panel docking area makes accessing and modifying complex graphics with the important organizational tool of the Layers panel much more efficient. The examination of the Styles panel in Module 5 was brief; this module spends significantly more time with the Layers panel. You will learn how essential it is to the organization and optimization of your graphics.

Understanding Groups and Layers

As you continue to build your skills in the use of Fireworks, you will find that your graphics become increasingly complex. Previous exercises have shown how you can combine, arrange, duplicate, paste, and manipulate objects in a variety of ways to achieve some very interesting image effects. However, as those graphics become more complicated, the ability to work with individual objects becomes more difficult. Fireworks provides two basic ways of dealing with complex images: groups and layers.

Organizing with Groups

Grouped objects can be compared to six individual cans of soda joined together by a plastic holder. Once joined together, the individual cans become one singular unit—a six-pack. Groups are created in the same way when individual objects on the canvas are joined together so that effects and other operations can be made on the group as a whole. Module 2 shows how to create a caterpillar from a number of objects that are arranged on the canvas but are independent of each other. Had that same graphic been grouped, however, the effects you see in Figure 6-1 could have been applied to the grouped image. Grouping objects is essential to turning simple objects into complex graphics.

Organizing with Layers

Layers, on the other hand, are used for organizing your images as if you were placing them on separate transparent sheets above the canvas, as you see in Figure 6-2. Fireworks enables you to create multiple layers for information so that you can build highly complex graphics while still making the task of working with individual objects manageable. Layers can be combined and rearranged in a multitude of ways to give you even more flexibility in creating graphics for use on the Web or in print. In addition, Fireworks contains a special layer that can hold web-specific instructions for creating hotspots or slices that act as links when viewed in a browser. These *web objects*, or HTML and JavaScript instructions embedded in your image, make possible the types of image rollovers and other effects that you will learn about in the second part of this book.

6

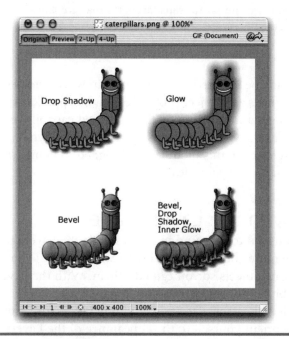

Figure 6-1   Grouping objects enables you to apply different Live Effects or Xtras to several objects that form a graphic.

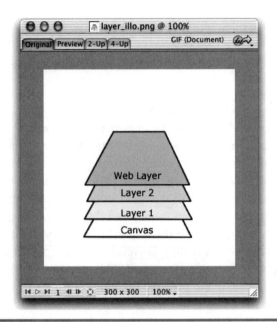

Figure 6-2 Layers are similar to transparencies that are stacked on top of the document's canvas.

You may already be satisfied with the way Fireworks creates images and the many ways that effects and object properties can be applied to them. However, until you understand and can employ the advanced capabilities made possible with groups and layers, you will not discover the really dynamic features of the program. The exercises in this module are designed to familiarize you with some of these advanced capabilities.

Working with the Layers Panel

One of the most useful tools found in Fireworks is the Layers panel. As your graphics become more complex, one of the real challenges you will face is the task of selecting objects so you can edit them. With the Layers panel, you can locate thumbnails of every object contained in your document. This allows you to select those objects easily and quickly. Before moving on, take a few minutes to orient yourself to the appearance of the Layers panel and its primary tools as detailed in Figure 6-3, which shows both Macintosh (top) and Windows (bottom) formats.

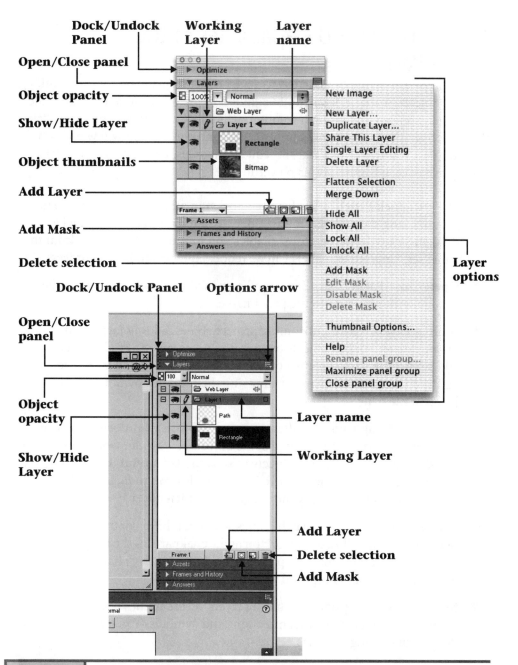

6

Figure 6-3 The Layers panel displays thumbnails for each object on your canvas, enabling you to select and modify them more easily.

Components and Capabilities of the Layers Panel

As you can see in Figure 6-3, the Layers panel contains many options for working with the objects in your document. In addition to the tools contained within the panel itself, you can find more in a pop-up window that appears when you click the Options button in the panel's upper right-hand corner. You will work with some of these features in this and subsequent modules. For now, here is a brief description of each feature of this powerful tool.

- **Dock/Undock Panel** This feature appears in all panels of the new panel group. Using the grabber in the upper left-hand corner of the panel and dragging away from the group enables you to remove each panel from the panel set. Ungrouped panels can be redocked by reversing the process.

- **Open/Close Panel** All panels can be opened or closed by clicking the triangular button next to the panel name.

- **Adding Layers** As an upcoming project shows, adding layers and organizing an image's objects can greatly increase your productivity and add some interesting creative twists. In addition to adding layers, you can also reposition entire layers by dragging them up or down in the stack listed in the panel.

- **Showing/Hiding Layers** Often as you work with your document, you will want to turn off the view of some objects so you can work more closely with others. Placing objects in separate layers and then turning on or off the view of one or more layers enables you to focus on the individual components of your image more efficiently.

- **Locking Layers** There may be times when you have completed a portion of a graphic but still need to work on additional parts of the image. Locking a layer that contains finished products ensures that any changes you make will not affect your completed work.

- **Sharing Layers (Options)** Sharing layers across frames is an important technique for working with animations and symbols. You learn how this is done in upcoming modules.

Although in many instances you may create simple graphics and won't need the Layers panel, as your skills with Fireworks increase, so too will your dependence on the Layers panel for selecting, modifying, moving, and organizing the individual objects that make up your document. As you complete the projects in this module, you will appreciate the things that the Layers panel enables you to do.

Project 6-1: Basic Grouping Operations

Grouping objects is the process of combining and locking separate objects into a single graphical object. Once grouped, these objects can have Live Effects applied and can be modified in ways not possible when the objects remain separate from each other. As the saying goes, the whole is greater than the sum of the parts, and this is certainly true of grouped objects.

Note

You can download practice files for this module either at www.osborne.com or at www.dw-fw-beginners.com.

Step-by-Step

1. To begin understanding groups, create a new file that is 300 pixels wide by 300 pixels high with a white canvas. Name this file *group_practice.png*.

2. Draw a rectangle in the middle of the canvas and insert a text box into the rectangle that contains the words **Grouped Images**.

3. The rectangle and the text box are two separate elements of this single image. You can group the two objects by holding down SHIFT while using the Pointer tool to select both items or by marqueeing the objects (drawing a selection area around both objects with the Pointer tool). You can also choose Select | Select All to select all of the objects on a canvas at once.

4. Once you select the objects, you can find the command to group the objects in the Modify menu. Choose Modify | Group to combine the two separate objects into a single graphical object. When the grouping is completed, handles appear in the four corners of the area bounded by the rectangle—the same kind of handles you see when working with grouped text. Deselect the grouped object by clicking in the negative area of the Document window and then try reselecting it using the Pointer tool. Grouped objects

are always denoted by the four handles that you see in the following illustration and by the lack of the selection outline that's visible when you work with single objects.

Selection handles

5. Grouped objects can be ungrouped at any time. In this case, you would have to ungroup the text box from the rectangle if you needed to modify the text. To ungroup an object, select the group and choose Modify | Ungroup, and the objects return to their separate states.

6. Objects that are grouped can be modified in a variety of ways. For instance, the Skew tool can be used to give this graphic the appearance that it is receding into the distance. Notice how the skew effect is applied to both the rectangle and the text at the same time and in the same proportions. Try this now with your document by combining the Scale and Skew tools to nudge the object into place so that it duplicates this example.

7. The final practical exercise for this project is to open the file named *caterpillar.png*, located in the exercise files for this module. Note that as you marquee each caterpillar, Fireworks provides you with the information that the image is composed of 37 separate objects. This practice file contains a duplicate of the image shown in Figure 6-1. Practice grouping and ungrouping the caterpillars and applying the Live Effects shown in Figure 6-1. For an object like this, use the marqueeing technique to select all the separate objects that make the image of each caterpillar.

8. Continue practicing grouping and ungrouping objects. You can save or discard this practice file when you have finished.

Project Summary

As you have seen in this brief exercise, grouping images that began as individual objects enables you to perform operations as if images had always been one coherent whole. By grouping text and vector objects with each other, you can change their size and color, apply effects, and modify other basic properties of the individual objects to attain the look you want. Another grouping operation involves creating masks with bitmap images, which you explore in the next project.

1-Minute Drill

- What is the primary function of the Layers panel?
- What are the two basic ways that separate objects can be organized?
- Define grouping.

6

Using Masks to Create Transparent Images

You can create a special type of group by instructing Fireworks to use one object in a group to mask, or partially hide, another object in a group. You may have seen this effect when letters appear as if they have been cut out of a photograph, or you may have seen pictures that fade from opaque to transparent. Module 3 shows you how to use a mask to paste a bitmap image inside a vector shape.

With the masking tools that Fireworks provides, you can create sophisticated masks that cause images to become partially transparent and fade from fully opaque to fully transparent in whatever shape and pattern you desire. Fireworks makes this a very simple task, and the steps to get it done are both easy and fun.

- The Layers panel is used for organizing and selecting objects in a Fireworks document.
- Objects can be combined as groups or organized into separate layers.
- Grouping is the process of combining multiple objects into a single object.

Figure 6-4 Combining objects with transparent masks applied enables you to create seamless collages

The process of creating a mask using images is similar to the way that you combine images using the paste inside technique from Module 3, in which a picture was pasted inside shapes. Objects are created on a canvas and then arranged and combined in such a way that the object on top controls the appearance of the object underneath it. One of the most common masks is a transparent mask that uses a linear gradient to fade an image from opaque to transparent, as you will do in the following project. By applying this technique to a series of images, you can create collages from your pictures that fade into each other, as you see here.

Project 6-2: Creating Transparent Masks

Using vector images as masks puts some terrific creative tools at your disposal. When you place a mask above an image, it partially obscures the underlying object so that you can create a mask effect that fades an image from opaque to transparent, and you can also change how a gradient is applied to the masking object. By gaining an understanding of how masking objects are created and modified, as you'll learn in this project, you'll be adding another significant technique to your Fireworks bag of tricks.

Step-by-Step

1. Create a new file that is 300 pixels wide by 300 pixels high with a transparent canvas. Save this file and name it *mask_image.png*.

2. Start by importing the beach scene found in the exercise files for this module at www.osborne.com or at www.dw-fw-beginners.com. Choose File I Import, locate the file called *beach_scene.jpg*, and import the image into your blank document. Your cursor turns to an inverted *L*, as you see in the following illustration. Place it in the upper left-hand corner of the document and click once to import the JPEG image. Use the Pointer tool to position the picture on your canvas.

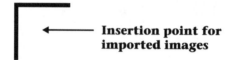

Insertion point for
imported images

6

Tip

As you work through this exercise, open the Layers panel and watch as thumbnail images are created when you import or add objects to your document.

3. Using the Rectangle tool, draw a rectangle that completely covers the picture. This object will act as the mask for the underlying image. Begin creating your mask by changing the fill for this rectangle from a solid color to a linear gradient. In the Property Inspector, change the fill type from Solid to Linear, as seen here.

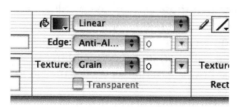

4. If you changed the color or layout of the gradients previously, Fireworks may use those settings when the linear gradient fill is chosen. To change to a preset gradient, as you need to do in this case, click on the Color button and change the gradient to the Black, White gradient preset you see in this illustration.

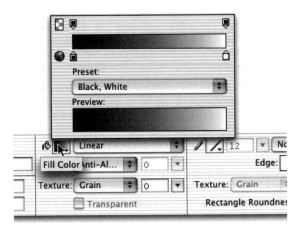

Note

The process of creating a transparent mask in Fireworks MX differs from that in previous versions of the software. If you have created transparent masks in Fireworks before this current release, the following steps may seem backwards to you.

5. With your rectangle in place and the gradient applied, it is time to see how the grouping of the two objects on your canvas creates a transparent mask. To apply the mask and see the transparency effect, select both objects (Select I Select All) and choose Modify I Mask I Group as Mask. When the mask has been applied, note that those areas of the picture covered by the white portions of your image are opaque, and those covered by the black area are transparent. The grayscale gradations from white to black in the gradient create a very subtle transition from opaque to transparent. In this portion of the image, you see how the mask creates the transition from left to right.

6. To ungroup the two objects so that you can modify how the gradient is applied, choose Edit | Undo Group. Once you have done so, you will return to your previous arrangement of having two separate objects on the canvas.

Tip

Although you can disable a mask by choosing Modify | Mask | Disable Mask, doing so deletes the masking object from the canvas.

7. As you saw in previous modules, gradients can be modified in many ways once they have been applied. In this next step, your task is to change the way that the gradient is applied to see how the application of the mask can generate different results. Select the rectangle and note the appearance of the gradient selection handles, which you see here.

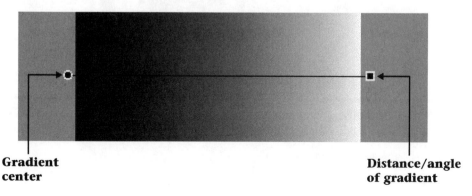

Gradient center

Distance/angle of gradient

6

8. Changing the appearance of the mask involves moving the gradient's center and changing its angle. Using the Pointer tool, adjust the gradient's center and angle by dragging the handles to new locations on your canvas. Remember that in Fireworks MX, those areas covered by the lightest portion of the gradient are opaque and those covered by the darkest portion of the gradient are transparent. By experimenting with the application of the gradient and repeating the steps of choosing both objects and applying the Modify | Group | Mask as Group command, you should be able to duplicate the effects seen in Figure 6-5.

9. As you would expect, masking can be done not only with rectangles and linear gradients (as you have done here) but also with any vector shape that you create and with any of the gradient fills available in the fill portion of the Property Inspector. Try this by ungrouping the mask group that you've

Figure 6-5   Modifying the center, angle, and distance of a gradient fill enables you to modify an applied mask in a variety of ways.

created. Select Edit | Undo Group, delete the rectangle, and draw a new shape onto your canvas. Try an ellipse, a polygon, and a star; experiment with the different types of gradients that Fireworks provides. You'll quickly come to appreciate the fascinating possibilities that grouping with grayscale masks provides.

Project Summary

In this exercise, you have seen how special groups, known as masks, can be created to enable you to change an object so that it fades from opaque to transparent. You have determined the direction and angle of the fading effect by applying gradients to an object and then using that object to mask an underlying image. The effects can be truly fascinating and are especially critical when you wish to perform the common task of fading one image into another.

Advanced Masking Techniques

6

In the previous exercise, you saw how to use a grayscale gradient to apply a transparency effect that fades an image along a path you determine. If you wondered at the time whether it was possible to use this technique for other image effects, then you were thinking along the right track. You can not only create fades by applying gradients, but also achieve some really interesting image effects by combining patterns, textures, edge options, and strokes to the objects that you will use to mask underlying images.

As you work with masks, remember that the lightest portion of any masking object that will be used for the mask will appear opaque, and that as the object becomes progressively darker, it will become more transparent. As you consider what types of masks to apply to an image, the challenge is to visualize how this interplay between light and dark areas of the masking object will interact with the image once the mask is created. Luckily you are using vector images for your masks (not more destructive methods that actually alter the image as the mask is applied), so you need only disable the mask when you want to delete a mask, try a different fill, or even change the shape of the masking object. Unlike a program such as Photoshop, which uses bitmaps for masking, your original picture is never disturbed. Once again, the advantages of vector graphics are ably employed by Fireworks.

Project 6-3: Masking with Fills and Strokes

Fireworks masks are powerful creative tools that make this program stand out from its competitors. With the versatility of vector graphics, you will be able to apply masks in a variety of ways to create striking visual effects. Vector graphics are the primary vehicle for creating your masks, so you will find the process of applying and modifying masking objects to be very easy. As you move through the steps in this module you will find that through the careful creation of masking objects and the application of a few simple techniques, even a beginner can make graphics that are truly unique.

Although it would take an entirely separate book to detail every option, this project will introduce you to just a few of the possibilities that the use of masks affords you. It will be up to you to use your own creativity to take the application of masks to the next level.

Step-by-Step

1. Once again, begin this project by creating a new document that is 300 pixels by 300 pixels and set the canvas color to white. Name and save your file as *fill_masks.png*.

2. You will find a series of small 150 pixel by 150 pixel JPEG images in the exercise files for this module. Import one of the images now by choosing File | Import and navigating to the exercise folder that you have saved. In this case, the file called *coconuts.jpg* (shown here) has been selected. As you have done previously, click once when you see the inverted *L* appear on your canvas. Use the Pointer tool to position this small picture.

―――Tip ―――――――――――――――――――

Be sure you have the Layers panel open while completing this exercise. Note how Fireworks creates thumbnail images in the panel as you import pictures and draw on the canvas.

3. Use the Ellipse tool to draw an ellipse over part of the picture and set the fill color to solid white. In the example for this project, the ellipse was drawn above the coconuts in the picture.

4. For this first effect, use the Property Inspector to change the edge options for the ellipse to Feather and set the width of the feathered edge to 20 pixels. When you are finished, your ellipse should appear as you see here.

5. With a feathered edge like the one you've applied here, the picture of the coconuts will be cut out of the background and fade outward to the edges of your feathered ellipse. To complete the mask, select both objects and choose Modify | Mask | Group as Mask as you have done previously, and your finished product will look like the next example.

6. Textured fills that are applied to a masking object can also be used to create some interesting effects. Import a second image from the exercise files and place it on your canvas. For this example, the file called *dolphins.jpg* has been used. Draw an object over the picture as you have done previously.

7. Using the Property Inspector, change the color of the fill to solid black and choose a texture. Note that the textures are listed in black and white and that those textures that have the greatest amount of white enable more of your masked image to appear. In the following illustration, the texture has been set to Waffle, and the texture opacity has been set to 100 percent.

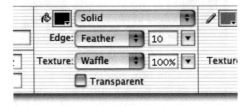

8. As you apply the mask using the now-familiar sequence of selecting both objects and choosing Modify | Mask | Group as Mask, you will see that the texture appears as an integral part of the image, generating a very interesting effect. Practice on your own with this technique; choose Edit | Undo Group and modify and change the applied texture to see some of the possible ways that combining textures can create unusual masks.

9. In the same way that you can use textures for masking effects, you can apply patterns to fills. For this technique to be effective, you need to choose light-colored patterns so that the masked object is visible through the transparent mask. In this example, the picture named *egret.jpg* has been imported to the document, a rounded rectangle with a Colored Glass setting has been chosen, and the mask has been applied. Once again, take some time to experiment with the different ways that this type of masking can be done.

10. Finally, you can apply stroke settings to objects to further refine the appearance of a masked object. Import another picture to your canvas and draw an object above the picture to be used as a mask. In the example used here, the image named *pelican.jpg* has been imported and a rounded rectangle has been drawn above the picture. Change the fill of the object to solid white.

11. With the huge variety of strokes that can be applied to the object you have just drawn, you can easily generate picture-frame effects by applying a stroke and masking the object, as done previously. To duplicate this example, set the fill edge to a feathered setting of 5 pixels and apply a medium gray stroke to the object. Finish by changing the stroke type to the Random setting of Dots, and change the stroke width to 1 pixel. You can further refine the stroke by changing the tip softness. In the following illustration, the tip softness has been changed to a softness setting of 15.

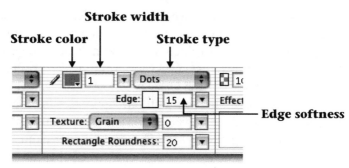

12. Now that you have applied the stroke settings to the masking object, finish by applying the mask. As you see in this illustration, using stroke settings can further add to your masking effects.

Project Summary

In this project, you have seen how masks can generate some highly creative effects for your images. Again, the many ways that Fireworks enables you to apply masks could fill an entire book; however, after completing this exercise, you should have an appreciation for the ways you can combine vector objects with bitmap images to make truly unique images.

Using Masks to Crop Images

You have seen how to use masked groups of images to take an existing image and create transparent fades and how to apply textures and patterns to masks. Although these techniques are certainly important additions to your Fireworks bag of tricks, one additional skill still needs to be developed—using masks to crop an image.

You've already seen how to use the Bitmap selection tools provided by Fireworks to crop images by selecting an area of a picture, copying the selection area, and pasting it into a new document. You may be wondering why you would need to learn how to use masks for cropping. The primary reason is that it takes advantage of one of Fireworks' most powerful features—the ability to use vector objects in combination with bitmap images in an unlimited fashion. Cropping an image is a destructive process in that it removes unwanted portions of a picture by removing pixels. Masking, on the other hand, combines one object with another. An image you have masked can be changed at any time.

When you use masks, you do not destroy the original image; you modify it by hiding portions through the magic of masking. The original image always exists, and you can reverse the process at any time because of the use of vectors.

In addition to maintaining editability, vector drawing tools are much more refined than the selecting and cropping tools that Fireworks provides. As a result, when you attempt to do fine work in cropping an image, you will find that turning to the vector drawing tools to draw a mask above an image is much more efficient than cropping the image and removing unwanted portions.

Project 6-4: Cropping with Masks

Using vector shapes to remove unwanted portions of an image is a fundamental technique in Fireworks. In this project you will get some additional experience using the Pen tool and see how a vector shape may be used to hide portions of picture.

The Pen tool is your precision instrument when it comes to drawing shapes. Although the creation and modification of control points that are connected by paths does take some practice, the time spent in learning how to construct these complex vector shapes with the Pen tool is an important skill. As you'll see here, by generating points that can be moved or modified at will, you can very precisely control the shape of a masking vector object and more carefully crop a portion of an image.

6

Step-by-Step

1. For this exercise, you will open one of the images found in the exercise files for this module and apply a mask. Locate and open the file called *fisherman1.jpg*. For purposes of this exercise, zoom in on this image to magnify it by 200 percent by selecting View | Zoom In or by changing the magnification setting at the bottom of the Document window.

Tip

As with the other exercises in this module, note how the Layers panel records and displays the actions you take in this project.

2. Your task here is to hide the background of this image by creating a mask that shows the fisherman but obscures the rest of the picture. To do this, you'll return to the Pen tool to create your mask. Select the Pen tool and move the tool to the top of the man's cap to begin drawing your mask.

3. You'll recall that the Pen tool enables you to create two types of control points: fixed points that anchor a position on the canvas or curved control points that you can modify by moving the handles that appear when you drag the tool across the canvas. In this exercise, you want to create handles that can be curved later on. As you select each point, be sure to drag the tool until the Bézier curve handles appear, as you see here.

4. Using the Pen tool takes some getting used to, but it is such an essential tool that the time spent in getting accustomed to the way it draws objects is well worth it. In this case, continue clicking and dragging to define the location of each control point on your masking shape and note the position of the control handles. By moving the Pen slightly, you will be able to get a feel for how the position of the control handles affects the curve you are defining. Control handles that are parallel to the line connect in a straight line. Moving the Pen so that the handles are perpendicular creates a curve on a right angle. Remember the sequence to control this process: click to define the point's location and then drag to define the shape of the curve that connects the point to the previously drawn point

5. As you move around the man's body and prepare to close the shape, look for the special symbol that appears below the Pen as you approach the beginning point of your shape. As you see here, when Fireworks places a small circle below the Pen, you can click to add an end point and close the shape.

6. With the Pen tool, you can add or delete control points around the perimeter of your shape to more carefully control the shape's position, location, and size. In this illustration, you see the symbol that enables you to add a new control point to an existing path: the plus sign that appears below the Pen when you float the tool over the path. Add at least one additional control point to the shape now.

7. In the same way that you can add points to the path, you can delete them. Look for the inverted *V* that appears as you float the Pen tool near a control point; the *V* enables you to select the point. Once you select the point, a minus sign appears when you float above the point with the tool, as you see here. The minus sign indicates that clicking the tool will remove the point. Practice this technique by removing at least one point.

8. By using the Subselection tool (the white arrow in the Tools panel), you can easily move or reshape points along a path created with the Pen tool by dragging the control handles of the Bézier curve. Again, this gives you a great deal of freedom in creating a complex mask shape such as this because you can modify individual points at any time.

9. With the power of the Pen tool, you can draw a very complex vector path to be used for a mask that closely matches any shape. As you finish using the Pen tool to draw this mask, you should be able to closely follow the shape of the fisherman in the image to generate the mask that you need to remove the background. Your finished product should appear as you see next, with the fill color set to white so that the entire image will be opaque.

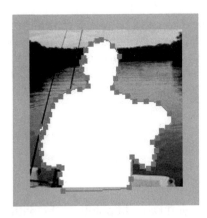

10. Completing the mask involves applying the now-familiar sequence of selecting both the picture and the shape and choosing Modify | Mask | Group as Mask to mask out the background of the image. Your finished product should appear as you see here, with the background completely removed and only the handsome fisherman and his catch remaining in your picture.

Note

Remember that Fireworks displays a checkerboard pattern to indicate a transparent canvas.

11. Final fine-tuning can be applied to this mask by choosing Edit | Undo to remove the mask grouping and then changing the edge options for the shape. As you have seen previously, changing from an anti-aliased edge to a feathered edge can produce a transparent effect around the edges of the mask. Alternatively, by setting the Feather value to a small number such as

2 pixels, you can create a nicely eased edge that enables you to blend an image such as this into other images. As you complete this project, be sure to save your file because you'll be using it again in the concluding project for this module.

Project Summary

Masking images with complex paths enables you to do some very sophisticated cropping while maintaining the integrity of the original image. In this exercise, you have removed the background of a picture, but you could return the image to its original state by deleting the masking shape or disabling the mask entirely. This feature by itself makes the use of masks such as this a valuable technique. Add on the greater control that the Pen tool affords when creating masks, and masking with vector shapes becomes an incredibly valuable tool for editing your images.

1-Minute Drill

- Define masking.
- How do the color properties of an image used as a mask affect transparency when the mask is applied?
- What is the primary advantage for using the Pen tool to create a masking object?

Organizing Objects with the Layers Panel

In the four projects of this module, you have seen how Fireworks enables you to use a combination of images to create groups that take on characteristics entirely different from the original versions. The tools and techniques you have explored are important for your success not only as a designer of graphical objects but as a web designer, as well. The final Fireworks tool to explore here is the use of layers.

- Masking is the process of using one image to partially hide an underlying graphical object.
- In Fireworks MX, lighter colors allow more of the underlying object to appear more opaque, and darker colors cause areas of greater transparency when a mask is applied.
- With the Pen tool, individual control points along a path can be added, deleted, moved, or modified at any time.

Layers are used to organize your images as if you were placing them on separate transparent sheets above the canvas. When you are working with highly complex images, layers become an important tool for not only organizing your individual objects, but also locking areas of an image to prevent you from inadvertently modifying a completed portion of your graphic.

Layers can be combined and rearranged in a multitude of ways to give you even more flexibility in creating graphics for use on the Web or in print. The primary tool for working with layers is the Layers panel. The Layers panel will display all of the individual layers assigned to an image and assist you in moving and selecting objects within your image. Note as you work in Fireworks that a small thumbnail of each object in your document will appear in the Layers panel with a pencil icon next to an image that you are working on. This simple visual representation can be extremely valuable as your images become more complex and selecting objects becomes more challenging. In addition to these techniques, the basic functions of the Layers panel include:

● **Arranging objects** Individual objects can be stacked higher or lower by dragging them by name up or down in the stack of objects on the canvas. Remember that objects on the canvas are arranged like cards stacked on a table—those higher in the stacking order obscure those beneath them.

● **Arranging layers** Entire layers can be moved by dragging the layer by name in the panel. As with individual objects, layers at the top of the stack obscure those beneath them.

● **Deleting objects** Selecting either an object or layer by name enables you to remove the item from your document by clicking the trash can icon at the lower right of the Layers panel.

The final exercise in this module will give you valuable practice in using the Layers panel and demonstrate some of the important organizational capabilities of this valuable tool.

Project 6-5: Controlling Complex Images with the Layers Panel

This final project builds on the techniques you've used and gives you a thorough grounding in how the Layers panel helps manage your images and improves your workflow. From the techniques you have learned, you will construct a complex image that might be used for the home page of a web site developed for a small resort in the fictional town of Poinciana Beach. Your prior work has dealt primarily with the simple grouping of objects; in this project, you will use multiple images to construct an eye-catching image for publication to the Web. The finished product that you'll create can be seen in Figure 6-6.

Step-by-Step

1. This new document will be slightly larger than the ones you've created previously because it will be the dominant image on your imaginary web page. Begin by creating a document 500 pixels wide by 500 pixels high, with the canvas color set to white. Name and save the file as *pbresort_main*.

2. Open the Layers panel and orient yourself to the main tools that you will use in this exercise. As you see in the following illustration, the Layers panel contains a number of key features that enable you to effectively manage a

6

Figure 6-6   Combining images using Fireworks' tools enables you to create highly complex images for use on the Web.

complicated image like the one you are about to create. You may also want to refer back to Figure 6-3 for more detailed information about this panel.

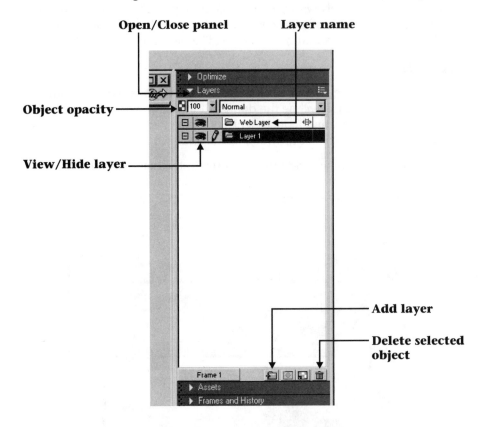

Open/Close panel   **Layer name**

Object opacity

View/Hide layer

Add layer

Delete selected object

3. To begin this project, draw a rectangle that covers the entire canvas. Remember that you can use the Info area of the Property Inspector to set the exact size for an object and position it precisely in the upper left-hand corner by setting both the X and Y coordinates to zero. Apply a fill or pattern to the rectangle and, because this image acts as a kind of stationery, use the transparency slider in the Layers panel or the Property Inspector to reduce the opacity of the object so that only a textured background remains. Note the first thumbnail that appears in the Layers panel for this new object.

4. To create a border for the image, select the rectangle and choose Edit | Clone. This places an exact duplicate of the first object in the same position on the canvas. Set the fill for this rectangle to none. For the example shown in Figure 6-6, a stroke type of Oil I Strands was used, with the width of the stroke set to 8 pixels, and a smooth Inner Bevel I Inset was applied as an effect. Remember that as you create objects, Fireworks applies the last settings you used. In addition to changing the fills, stroke, and effects for this object, you need to adjust the transparency as well.

5. You have created the background for your image. It will lie beneath all of the other objects you add to the image, so you want to ensure that these objects stay in place and are not inadvertently moved or deleted as you continue your work. To do this, start by naming the Layer where the objects are contained. To name a layer, double-click the layer's name in the panel and, in the pop-up window that you see here, type **Background** to name the layer. You will find that naming layers greatly assists you in finding elements as you continue to build a graphic such as this.

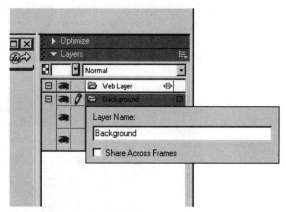

6. To lock the layer and prevent further work on this now-completed part of your image, simply click the Pencil icon to the left of the layer name. When the Lock icon replaces the pencil, as illustrated here, you know that this layer is safe from editing until you decide to unlock the layer to do additional editing.

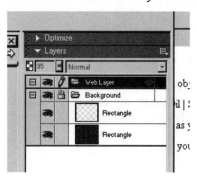

7. You'll note that, as you locked the layer, the Pencil icon shifted to the Web layer—the special layer that rests at the top of your layer structure and contains HTML and JavaScript commands. The image you are trying to create requires more graphical objects, though, so you must add an additional layer. Do so by clicking the New/Duplicate Layer icon and changing the default Layer 1 name to **Header.**

8. The Header layer will contain the logo for the resort. To create the logo, draw a rectangle, apply a textured fill, and add the text **Poinciana Beach Resort**. Once you have those objects looking as you'd like, you can use a new technique to select them prior to grouping. In the Layers panel, simply select the rectangle by its name and hold down SHIFT to add the text to your selection. When selected, the objects will be highlighted, as you see in the following illustration. Once you have both items selected, choose Modify | Group to group them together. Then use the Skew or Distort tool to generate the slanting look to the text and rectangle. Note that once objects are grouped, the name of the object in the Layers panel changes to indicate the grouping and the number of objects it contains.

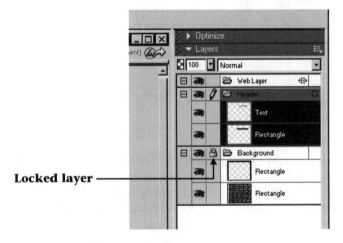

Locked layer

9. With that layer complete, it's time to lock the layer and add another. Repeat the steps from above to lock the Header layer, and add a layer called **Photos**.

10. As you'd expect, the Photo layer is the place to add masked images to create the photo collage you saw in Figure 6-6. Once again, there are a number of pictures contained in the exercise files for this module for you to choose from. Before you begin adding and masking your own, though, import the photo called *beach_scene.jpg* and place it in the upper left-hand corner of your document. Use the Pointer tool to drag the image from the corner selection handles to resize it properly.

11. With the picture in place, use the Pen tool to draw a masking vector shape above the picture. As you've done before, set the fill for this object as a linear gradient to fade the image, or use a feathered edge setting to retain more of the image's opacity. As you draw your shape, you will see an outline of the object in the Layers panel. Once you have the vector object looking as you'd like, select the objects labeled bitmap and path in the Layers panel and complete the masking process by choosing Modify I Mask I Group as Mask. Note the appearance of the group in the Layers, as seen in the illustration here.

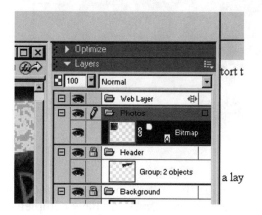

┼*Tip*

Use the Magnifying tool to zoom in on portions of your image as you work. Double-click the tool to return to the previous magnification setting.

---

12. Now that your mask is created, the Layers panel enables you to directly select the masking vector object and modify it live on the canvas. This is a terrific feature that enables you to fine-tune a mask even after you have applied it. To see this in action, click on top of the thumbnail that contains the Pen icon, and the outline of your mask appears in yellow on the screen. (In the following black-and-white illustration, the outline looks light gray.)

To modify the mask, you need only use the Pen tool or Subselection tool to move the points in your shape, to modify curves, or to add or delete points. Your ability to work directly with the masking object is yet another example of how well Fireworks does its job and how important the Layers panel can be for you to do yours.

Selection handles

13. Continue to add images from the samples provided, mask them, and position them on the canvas. Once you have completed that step, lock the Photos layer and add a new layer called **Text.** As you'd expect, this is where you should place your text.

14. Finally, add a last layer called **Buttons** and add a rectangle with text, as you see in Figure 6-6. When you are finished, your image should look at least as good as the one you've seen here, and you should have gained an appreciation for the simple, yet critical, functions that the Layers panel performs.

Project Summary

This concluding project was designed to both reinforce your skills with grouping and masking objects and enable you to see how important it is to have a tool for organizing and arranging your images. Although not every detail of the Layers panel was covered in this exercise, you should have a solid understanding of how this tool is used for organizing and protecting your work.

In addition to offering these techniques, the Layers panel enables you to organize your web objects and make changes to layers to better optimize rollover buttons and animations. You'll learn those steps in upcoming projects.

1-Minute Drill

- How can you use the Layers panel to prevent the inadvertent modification of an object?
- Why should you name layers when you're working with complex images?
- How does the Layers panel assist in the selection of objects on the canvas?

What to Take Away

6

In this module, you have seen the powerful and yet simple tools that Fireworks puts at your disposal for combining objects and for masking to create transparencies and to crop images. You have also seen how the Layers panel makes it possible to more carefully manage your images. With these tools, Fireworks enables you to take even the most mundane images and add some fascinating effects by combining fills, textures, and gradients and then applying them as masks. As your skills grow and your images become increasingly complex to take advantage of these techniques, Fireworks enables you to lock, hide, move, organize, and manage even the most complicated graphics in an easy-to-understand format.

- You can use the Layers panel to prevent the inadvertent modification of objects by placing them in a layer and then locking the layer.
- Naming layers enables you to more easily locate the objects contained in each layer for future editing.
- Objects in a document can easily be selected by simply clicking the object's name in the Layers panel.

☑ Mastery Check

1. What is the primary advantage of using vector objects for masking?

_____

_____

2. How does Fireworks list objects in the Layers panel?

_____

_____

3. What tool would you use to hide an object on the canvas?

_____

_____

4. Define grouping.

_____

_____

5. Define masking.

_____

_____

6. What is a grayscale mask?

_____

_____

7. How do the color properties of an image used as a mask affect transparency when the mask is applied?

_____

_____

8. How can you select multiple objects using the Layers panel?

_____

_____

☑ *Mastery Check*

9. How can you use the Layers panel to modify a mask after the mask has been applied?

_____

_____

10. How can you use the Layers panel for deleting objects from a document?

_____

_____

6

Module 7

Tools for Creating Consistent Content

The Goals of This Module

- Gain an understanding of the production tools that Fireworks contains
- Understand how Symbols and instances are created
- Explore the Library panel
- Use Symbols and instances for advanced image techniques
- Understand the use of the History panel
- Create and apply custom Commands
- Explore the batch process function
- Use Fireworks' Find and Replace commands

Y ou have probably realized by now that the capabilities of Fireworks as an image-editing program are vast and that with the advanced features you have seen so far, you can go well beyond creating simple buttons and optimized images for use on the Web. With the incredible number of settings and effects available when you're working with both bitmap and vector objects, as well as the sophisticated ways that those objects can be grouped, masked, and layered, you could easily get lost in the complexity of the program.

Luckily, Fireworks provides a number of ways to automate the work that you do in order to capture effects and settings so that you can use them repeatedly, saving you the effort of having to redesign every new graphic that you create. Fireworks uses a special type of image, known as a *Symbol*, as the primary vehicle for automating the creation of graphics. In addition to saving you work, using custom Symbols that you design and save for use at a later time can provide a level of consistency to your graphics that leads to a more cohesive look and feel for your web site.

As powerful and useful as Symbols are, they are not the only way to maximize your productivity. In addition, Fireworks also enables you to copy individual steps that you apply to an image and use those steps again and again, saved as Commands. This feature enables you to resize an image, set an effect, change the color of an object, and apply those same steps to any other image in your document—or to any image you create in the future. You can not only do this yourself but also take advantage of the creativity of other members of the Fireworks community who make their Commands available for download.

Finally, for those really heavy-duty production tasks such as resizing or editing a large number of graphics, Fireworks makes it possible to apply a saved Command to one or 100 images all at once. This batch processing feature, along with the powerful Find and Replace function built into Fireworks, makes this software program an incredibly powerful tool for the professional web designer or for anyone who wants to work like one.

Understanding Symbols and Instances

In Module 5, you saw how you can create Styles that save a series of effects so you can reapply them to an object in the document you are working on or to any image you create in the future. Symbols are much like Styles in that they capture the settings that have been applied to an object and save them for future use.

Unlike Styles, however, Symbols are complete graphical objects rather than simply the settings that have been applied to them. With Symbols, you create an object that then becomes part of the library for the document you are working on. Although Symbols can be exported to a special file where you can access them in the future, by default a Symbol only belongs to the document where it is created.

So, with that limitation in mind, what's the big fuss about? Why not simply create a style and apply that to separate objects as you create them?

The answer lies in the type of workflow that web designers require. Their work may, for instance, require the production of hundreds of buttons that all look alike or even simply the insertion of ten buttons into one document. Although you could certainly use styles to make that workflow easier, having complete graphical objects at your fingertips that you can use over and over again makes the prospect of creating many duplicate images a little easier to face. In addition to using Symbols to save labor, you can generate some nice effects along the way because Fireworks enables you to modify each instance of a Symbol as it appears on your canvas.

You can not only use Symbols repeatedly in a single document but also export them to a library that you define, where all of the Symbols reside. If you have a project two months from the time when you originally create a button, for instance, you need only import the Symbol from your library and you're ready to use it again.

Finally, Symbols enable you to create a single graphical object such as a button and then, when you need to change the Symbol, enable Fireworks to automatically update every copy, or *instance* of the Symbol as it appears in your document.

7

Project 7-1: Working With Symbols

If you use the other vector graphics program in the stable of Macromedia products, Flash, then you know what powerful creative tools Symbols can be. There are some fundamental differences in how the two programs use Symbols, but the concept is the same in both; Symbols are objects that can be used for the automated production of graphical objects. Even if you know nothing about Flash, you'll find that using Symbols enables you to be both more efficient and more creative as you allow Fireworks to take much of the work out of working with objects that reappear in a document.

Fireworks Symbols can be powerful tools, and in the first exercise of this module you'll learn a bit more about them as you create your first set of Symbols.

Step-by-Step

1. One of the most common types of Symbols that you will work with on the Web is the button. Used to indicate a hyperlink, the simple button is probably the most often seen type of graphic on the Internet. In this exercise, you will create some buttons for use in a web site and save them as graphical Symbols. To begin, create a 300 pixel by 300 pixel white canvas. Save this new file and name it *buttons.png*.

2. You have already spent considerable time exploring the creative possibilities of Fireworks, so the actual creation of your button images will be left to you. Just remember that buttons that are too large look amateurish. A good rule of thumb with buttons is to make them no larger than necessary to hold the text label that you intend to place on them. For the examples in this exercise, a glass button like the one you created in Module 5 will be used. Be sure not to place any text on your button. What's needed here is just the graphical object. You will add text labels later on.

3. Once your button is created and the effects you want have been applied, group the object and choose Modify I Symbol I Convert to Symbol. Once this command is executed, you will see the dialog box in Figure 7-1 appear.

4. As you can see, Symbols come in three varieties—graphical Symbols, as you'll create here, animated Symbols as you learn to create in Module 8, and button Symbols that contain web objects that allow links to be attached to them. For this simple image-type Symbol, choose the graphic type and name the Symbol as you see in Figure 7-1.

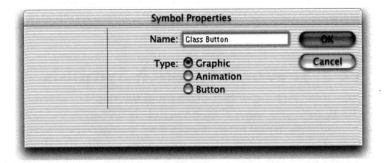

| | Figure 7-1 | The Symbol Properties dialog box is used for naming Symbols and setting basic Symbol properties. |

Tip

Use the same commonsense approach to naming your Symbols that you apply to naming files. Give each one a descriptive name that details its appearance and function so you'll be able to recognize it down the road when you want to reuse it.

5. Once an object is converted to a Symbol, Fireworks provides two indications that the Symbol has been generated: A shortcut appears in the lower left-hand corner of the object, as you see here, and a thumbnail and description of the Symbol are created in the Library panel.

6. As with the other panels that you've used to this point, the Symbols panel contains the usual options for expanding and hiding the panel and for accessing additional options, and it lists the Symbol with a thumbnail image as well as its name and type. Orient yourself to the features of the Library panel by referring to Figure 7-2.

7

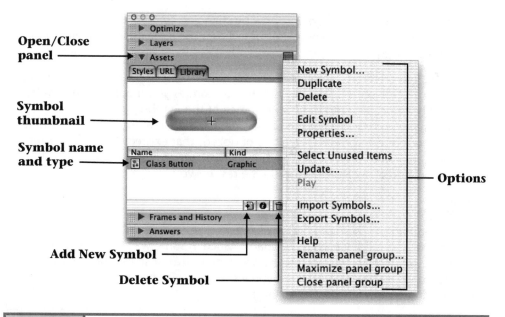

Figure 7-2 The Symbols panel contains information about each Symbol present in the document as well as enabling you to perform other operations with the Symbol.

7. To add an existing Symbol to the document, you need only drag the thumbnail of the Symbol from the Symbols panel onto the document. Remember that each duplicate of the Symbol is known as an instance. Try this now by dragging duplicates of your button graphic onto the canvas.

Tip

Fireworks provides a number of premade Symbols which you can select by choosing Edit | Libraries and making a selection from the offerings for animations, bullets, buttons, or themes.

8. To edit a Symbol, you can either double-click its thumbnail in the Library panel or open the panel options and select Edit Symbol from the options listed. In either case, once you choose to edit a Symbol, you will be taken to a special Fireworks window called the Symbol Editor. Note that the object's state as a Symbol is denoted by the presence of a crosshair that marks the center of the Symbol, as you see here.

9. Try editing your button graphic now by changing some or all of the properties of the object. You have complete control over the appearance of your graphic because the Symbol Editor has the capabilities of any Fireworks document.

10. When you are done, simply close the Symbol Editor to return to your canvas. What you will note right away is that the changes you made to your Symbol have been propagated to every instance of the Symbol, providing an automatic update to all of the objects. Imagine what a time-saver this would be if your button graphic were one of dozens that existed throughout your web site. Rather than editing each individual image, you simply change the Symbol and allow Fireworks to do the rest for you.

Note

Although editing the Symbol's fills, strokes and effects causes all instances to be updated, you can modify each individual instance in some ways. You can, for instance, resize or skew Symbol instances into new sizes or shapes or modify their opacity settings. In the next exercise, you'll see how this enables you to create some very interesting effects with your graphics.

11. Try creating a new Symbol from scratch by choosing Edit I Insert I New Symbol—a sequence that will cause the Symbol Editor to open with a blank canvas so that you can create an entirely new Symbol. Close the Symbol Editor, and a single instance of the Symbol will be placed on your canvas.

12. Because Symbols only exist in the document in which they are created, making your Symbols available to other images takes a bit of work. To export your Symbol to a custom library that you define, start by choosing Export Symbols from the options detailed in Figure 7-2.

13. Once this option is chosen, Fireworks will present you with a new dialog box in which you can select the Symbols you wish to export. In the example you see here, the initial glass button has been duplicated, renamed, and modified to contain new color schemes. You can choose to export a single Symbol or export multiple Symbols by holding down SHIFT while selecting them by name. You can also choose to export all the Symbols by using the Select All button. As you select Symbols for export, their names become highlighted.

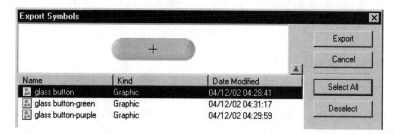

14. Once you click the Export button, you see yet another dialog box, shown in Figure 7-3, which enables you to name the file where you will store the Symbols. By default, Fireworks uses a file called *Custom Symbols.png* to store your Symbol, but you could just as easily name it yourself and change its location. What's important is to remember what you named your custom file; to retrieve your Symbols for use in another document, you will need to reverse this process to import your Symbols. For now, use the default file as a place to store this first set of Symbols.

Tip

You can also drag an instance of a Symbol from one Library panel directly onto the canvas of another open document.

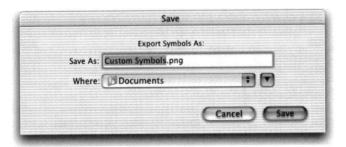

Figure 7-3   To complete the export of custom Symbols, choose a name and location for the file where you will store them.

15. To see how Symbols are imported, open a new document from the Library Panels options and choose Import Symbols. As you'll see, the process is just the opposite of the process of exporting Symbols. Choose the file where the Symbols are stored, decide which you want to import, and bring them onto your document. To use a custom Symbol once it has been imported, you need only drag an instance from the Library panel onto your canvas.

Project Summary

In this exercise, you have received your first introduction to the power of Symbols. By creating an object on your canvas and converting it to a Symbol, or by creating a new Symbol directly in the Symbol Editor, you can use the same graphic over and over again in your document. Because it is so easy to create your own custom library file containing your most commonly used Symbols, you can significantly reduce the amount of work necessary to manage your images and create a consistent look for your web site. Finally, as each Symbol is automatically linked to its parent graphic, any change you make to the original Symbol is reflected in its every instance throughout your document. This once again eliminates what would otherwise be a tedious process of opening each individual file to make the changes you need.

1-Minute Drill

● How do Styles and Symbols differ?

● Where are Symbols stored?

● How can you store Symbols for use in other documents?

● Styles are a collection of attributes that can be applied to any vector object. Symbols are complete graphical objects with all of their settings applied.

● Symbols are stored in the Library panel.

● You can export Symbols that you want to use in other documents to a custom library that you designate.

Creative Techniques with Symbols

Automating workflow is all well and good, but it's not nearly as much fun as making new images come to life. You should be able to appreciate how much time Fireworks can save you through the use of Symbols, but it's much more satisfying and enjoyable to use them for their other mission—applying special effects.

The special creative technique that you'll explore next is done through a process known as *tweening*. Tweening may sound like a silly word, but it is very descriptive of the process you are about to learn. Early in the days of movie animation, when every image was drawn by hand, the process of making animated films was both time-consuming and expensive. Those early pioneers in the field of animation decided that it would be more cost-effective to hire less experienced, and lower paid, apprentice animators to fill in the parts of the animation that only conveyed motion and did not contain the key elements of the animated sequence. These *tweeners* would draw in the simple missing parts of the animation, enabling the more experienced animators to focus their efforts on the most important scenes and sequences in the animation. Tweening became known as the process of automatically completing a graphical sequence between two key objects. If you've ever worked with Fireworks' sister programs, Flash and Director, you are intimately familiar with tweening.

The exercise you are about to complete is not an animation, but the concept is the same. Two instances of a symbol are placed on a canvas and modified, and Fireworks fills in the sequence in the number of steps you specify. With this technique, you can create graphics that simulate motion or even create three-dimensional text.

Project 7-2: Special Effects with Symbols

Fireworks enables you to use tweening for creative techniques by modifying instances of the same Symbol for position, opacity, or size. Once you have two Symbols on your canvas and have the attributes you want applied to them, you need only unleash the power of automated tweening to see your new creation take shape. In this project, you will learn how this technique can be used to create text that zooms across the canvas or has a three-dimensional appearance. These examples will use text objects, but the methods you will learn can be applied to any graphical Symbol you create.

Step-by-Step

1. Create a new Fireworks document with the standard practice size of 300 pixels by 300 pixels. Save and name this first file as *zoom_text.png*. From the Menu bar, choose Edit | Insert | New Symbol to open the Symbol Editor and create your first Symbol. Name it **Zoom** and set the Symbol type as a graphic.

2. With the Symbol Editor open, type the word **Zoom** onto the canvas in a font size of approximately 40 points. Choose a dark color for the text color and center it over the crosshair in the middle of the Symbol Editor's canvas. With your text Symbol in place, close the Symbol Editor and return to your Document window.

3. Fireworks automatically places a single instance of your Symbol onto the canvas, but, to see how tweening can be used, you will need a second instance in place. Drag another instance of your Symbol onto the canvas and place it to the right of the first, as you see here.

Zoom   Zoom

4. As noted before, Symbol instances can be modified in some ways without affecting the parent Symbol. In this case, use the Property Inspector to change the opacity of the second instance to approximately 25 percent, and use the Scale tool to reduce its size. With your two instances set as you see here, you're ready to move on to the next step.

Zoom   Zoom

5. Select both of the instances on the canvas by using the Pointer tool to marquee them and select Modify | Symbol | Tween Instances from the Menu bar. A small dialog box will appear asking you to specify the number of steps in the tweening sequence and asking whether you want each new image to go on its own frame. This can be a useful option when working with animations, but for this exercise leave that option unchecked and set the number of steps to 5, as you see here. Click OK to create your tweened image.

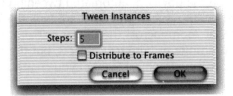

6. As you can see, every object in the document is selected once you apply the tweening to the Symbol instances. Click on the negative area around the canvas to deselect your instances, and you will see the effect displayed in this illustration. This example probably needs some fine-tuning, which you can easily do by selecting Edit | Undo Tween Instances, but the effect can also be a real eye-catcher. Continue to practice with this effect by changing the opacity and size of the instances of the text Symbol.

7. Create a second graphical text Symbol now by choosing Edit | Insert | New Symbol. In the Symbol Editor, type **3D Text,** once again using a font size of approximately 40 points. For this technique, choose a blocky font such as Tahoma or Verdana and set the stroke option to a Pencil type stroke set to 1 pixel soft, in a color darker than the fill.

8. Before dragging the second instance of this new Symbol onto the canvas, set the opacity of this first instance to approximately 20 percent. With that task complete, drag out a new instance and place it slightly to the left of the first instance. Choose both and, as you did in the previous step, choose Modify | Symbol | Tween Instances and set the number of steps to 5 to create a block of text with a three-dimensional feel, as you see here.

9. Getting the feel you want will take a little practice, but remember that to return to the state where your instances are separate objects you only need choose Edit | Undo Tween Instances to remove the tweening effect. Once that is done, experiment with the opacity and position of the instances until you are able to generate a text block that looks as though it exists in three dimensions. To complete the illusion, group the separate text objects and set a drop-shadow effect in the Property Inspector. When you are finished, you should be quite satisfied with your work.

Project Summary

The two examples you have seen here of tweening text to create special effects should give you a good feel for how this technique can be used to give your images depth and the illusion of movement. This exercise has used text to demonstrate the power of tweening Symbols, but you could just as easily apply the same technique to any graphical object that is converted to a Symbol.

You should note as you experiment with this technique that Fireworks enables you to modify an instance of a Symbol in ways other than those demonstrated here, such as applying a Live Effect. However, only size, position, and the opacity of an instance can reliably use the tweening technique. Still, this exercise should have given you an idea of the kinds of effects that tweening makes possible and hopefully sparked a bit of creativity in you to take the use of tweening Symbols further.

Automated Workflow with the History Panel and Custom Commands

Much of the work of a web designer is just that—work. Although composing images, deciding on color schemes, or getting an effect just right to capture the look you want for an image can be great fun, having to do it over and over again as you continue working on additional images can become tedious. After all, making one button can be a great creative challenge, but generating dozens more to complete all the graphical objects you might need in a typical web page can be a laborious process.

Right from the start of this book, Fireworks has been identified as a production tool for web designers. This means that the mission of the software is to reduce the number of repetitive tasks required from you as you go about the business of building your site. You have seen how Symbols can be created that assist in this tedium-busting mission. In this next exercise, you have the opportunity to become acquainted with the History panel and see how the tools it provides enable you to make the most of your time while still maintaining your creative freedom.

Fireworks records every important step you take while using the program. Along the way, those actions can be copied, duplicated, repeated, or even stored as custom Commands that you can repeat in the future. This project will take you through an introduction to the History panel and let you see a few real-world applications of this important asset, including a look at how you can save your steps as Commands for future use.

Before you begin this exercise, refer to Figure 7-4 for an introduction to the features of the History panel.

The power of the History panel can range from the simple replay of an individual step to the creation of a custom Command that replays a series of steps. You can access the History panel any time you are using Fireworks.

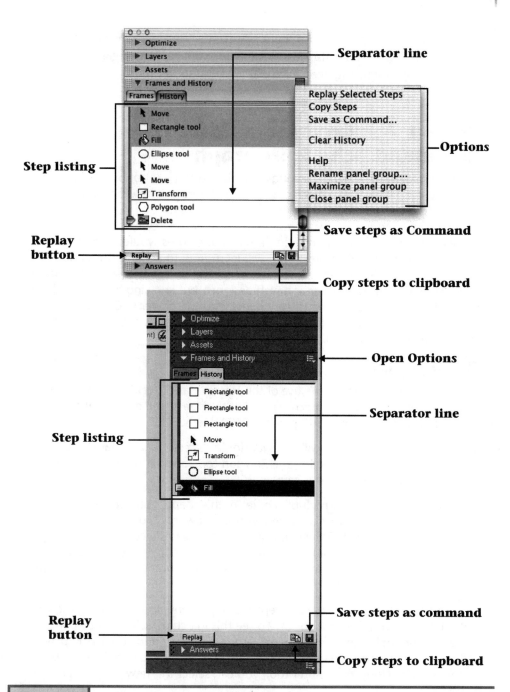

Figure 7-4 The History panel lists each step you take while working with a document and contains options for saving or replaying actions.

Although the creative possibilities that Commands afford you may not be readily evident, you can use this powerful feature for automatic generation of some incredibly complex images, as you'll learn to do in Project 7-3.

Project 7-3: Creating a Custom Command—the Spirograph

You may remember making drawings as a child using a set of plastic gears to draw circular patterns on a piece of paper. The Spirograph was great fun to use and created some cool drawings.

You could certainly draw an image like that with Fireworks, but doing so by copying, pasting, and rotating a series of ellipses would be pretty time-consuming. In this project, you will learn how to achieve the same effect automatically. You may not need to create too many images with this appearance during your career as a web designer, but knowing how this is done by combining the tools in the History panel with the power of Commands will give you a solid grounding in how these Fireworks features can be used. Just like the original Spirograph, it's lots of fun.

Step-by-Step

1. To begin understanding the use of the History panel, create a new practice document called *history_practice.png*. Set the size of the document to the standard practice size of 300 pixels by 300 pixels.

2. In this first example, you will replay a single step to create a star on your document. Begin by selecting the Polygon tool, and set the tool's shape to a star to draw a star on your canvas.

3. If you wanted to create multiple copies of this shape, you could certainly use one of the other command sequences that Fireworks provides for getting that job done, such as Edit | Duplicate (which creates a copy offset slightly from the original), or Edit | Clone (which places a copy directly on top of the original). Each of those steps would generate another star and, in many cases, meet your needs.

4. With the History panel, you can replay a step at any time, including the step that created your original object. To see this in action, select the step listed as Polygon tool in the History panel, as you see here, and click the Replay button. As you do so, a new copy of your star will be created directly above the original. Using the Pointer tool, you can select this new copy and move it

away from the original to see that in fact a new object does exist. Note also that the step labeled Play Steps is listed in the History panel. It's not a bad trick to know, but you have other options for creating copies of objects, so this isn't necessarily one that you will use very often.

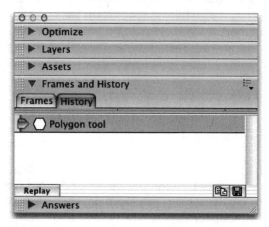

5. A more likely scenario is one that will enable you to choose a series of steps and apply those to objects on the canvas. For example, you might want to resize all of the button graphics that exist in a document to make them just a little smaller, change their color, and reduce their opacity—without having to do so manually. To see the value of an option such as this, draw a rectangle on your canvas and duplicate it a few times so that you have a series of objects arranged as you might with a navigation bar.

6. Once your new objects are on the canvas, select one of them and choose Modify | Transform | Numeric Transform. Using the Scale option available from the drop-down menu, set the scale of the object to be 75 percent, with the Scale Attributes and Constrain Proportions check boxes selected, as you see here. Click OK to apply the transformation.

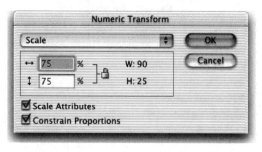

7

7. In the Fill panel, change the color of your rectangle and set the opacity of the object to a value less than 100 percent. Note that all three steps you have taken are now recorded in the History panel.

8. To apply those attributes to the other objects on your canvas, select each step in the History panel while holding down SHIFT. When all three are selected, choose one of the rectangles on your canvas and click the Replay button. As you do so, the object's attributes will be changed to match the others. Magic!—and a huge time-saver.

Tip

If you want to clear out the steps in the History panel, simply choose Clear History in the panel options.

9. So far so good, but this capability to save and replay steps can make your life as a designer even easier through the power of custom Commands, which you will learn to create now. In this example, you will create a Command that automatically duplicates a graphic and arranges it on top of the original to produce a design that you might remember from one of the fun drawing tools you used as a child. Start by creating a new 300 pixel by 300 pixel document called *spirograph.png*.

10. On your document, draw an ellipse and set the fill and stroke as you'd like. In the example that you'll see here, the ellipse has been set with a basic soft line stroke set to 4 pixels in width, with no fill. Once the object is on the canvas, select Edit | Clone to place an exact duplicate directly above the original.

11. With the duplicate ellipse selected, choose Modify | Transform | Numeric Transform to open the dialog box you see here. From the drop-down menu, choose Rotate from the options listed. Set the rotation to 15 degrees as you see in the illustration and click OK. Back on your canvas you'll note that the cloned copy of the ellipse has been rotated and you now have two ellipses in place.

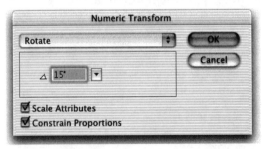

12. The trick to getting this Command saved is to select the two steps you just completed—cloning and transforming the original ellipse—and replaying

those steps to complete the image. Hold down SHIFT, select the Clone and Transform steps in the History panel, and click the Replay button until enough new objects are created to create a complete circle composed of your ellipses. Clicking the Replay button ten times should give you an image similar to the one you see here.

13. Now that you've used those commands, Fireworks actually enables you to use them in combination to create an even more complex custom Command. To create this series of steps so that you can apply it to any object, select all the steps you just completed in the History panel. Hold down SHIFT and select every step between the original Clone step and the last Play Steps command listed in the panel. Do not select the original Ellipse tool step. Figure 7-5 displays the correct selections you should make at this point.

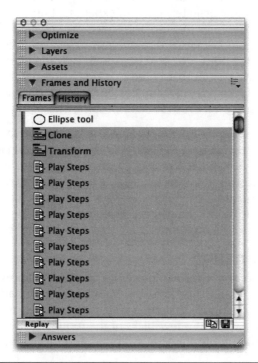

7

Figure 7-5 Fireworks enables a series of steps, even repeated steps, to be selected for use as a custom Command.

14. With the proper steps selected in the History panel, it's now time to make your custom Command. Open the Options for the History panel and select Save as Command, or click the Save as Command button in the lower right-hand corner of the panel. Once you have done so, Fireworks will display the Save Command dialog box you see here. Name this new Command **Spirograph** and click OK.

Note

If you have taken an action that cannot be combined with other steps reliably, you will see a separator line indicating that you should not attempt to play the steps together. Steps that are not seperated by this line can be combined or converted to commands.

15. Commands that you save are found in the Commands menu of the Menu bar. Open that menu now and note that the new Command you created is listed. Now, let the fun begin!

16. Draw a new object onto your canvas. You can draw any object and apply this Command, so you'll definitely want to experiment here. Once your object is in place, select Commands | Spirograph to see the power of Fireworks put into play. This command clones and rotates any object you draw, so it can be used for any number of objects to produce some really fun effects. It is much better than those plastic wheels that I used as a kid to draw designs, and equally fun. Figure 7-6 displays a few ways this custom command could be applied to ellipses, stars, and even brush strokes for some interesting effects.

17. If things have not gone as you expected, you can choose Commands | Manage Saved Commands to display a dialog box that enables you to delete or rename a Command at any time. Once you are done, you can even discard this file. Your custom Command to create a cloned copy of an original object arranged at 15-degree intervals will always be available to you now that you have saved those steps. You can even create a new spirograph effect using a different value for the rotation of your object to get different results.

Project Summary

In this exercise, you have seen some of the powerful features that Fireworks contains for making your workflow easier and have even had the opportunity to use the power of custom Commands to automatically generate some highly complex graphics with just a few clicks of the mouse. Commands are one of the most fascinating tools that Fireworks has, and this combination of drawing

Figure 7-6   Using a custom Command set to clone and rotate objects enables you to automatically create unusual shapes.

tools and the capability to replay selected steps not only makes editing your graphics easier but also can be a great deal of fun.

In addition to the Command that you have created here, you can generate Commands that mirror common tasks that may be required of you. For instance, if you find that a client doesn't like a particular font that you've chosen for your graphic, you could create a custom Command that would enable you to change the font properties of all of your text with just one or two clicks of the mouse. Alternatively, imagine that you need a Command that resizes bitmap images to a set size—and you need to apply this change constantly. With Commands, what would have once been a tedious chore of opening each image and manually resizing can be reduced to a simple set of steps that you can apply any time you need it.

In addition to making your own Commands, you can use Commands made by others. Many members of the Fireworks community make custom Commands freely available for download and use in your documents. A quick trip to the Macromedia Fireworks Support page at www.macromedia.com/support/fireworks will lead you to a listing of those sites offering Commands for download. Look for instructions as to the proper folder to save those Commands into depending on your operating system. Once the Command has been saved into the proper folder, it will be available for you to use in the same way that your new Spirograph command is available.

Finally, one of the terrific new features in Fireworks is the capability to create extensions that are quite similar to Commands but use the code engine of Flash for their creation rather than JavaScript. This is a new feature and was still being refined by the developers of these new extensions as this module was being written, so Fireworks extensions are covered in their own section, found in Appendix B.

1-Minute Drill

● What is the name for a copy of a Symbol found in a document?

● Define tweening.

● How can you create custom Commands?

Automated Workflow with Batch Processing

As a production tool, Fireworks is unmatched in its capability to automate common chores in a way that lets you spend more of your time focusing on creating graphics and less time managing them. No competing software product handles these types of automated tasks as well as Fireworks does.

● Each copy of a Symbol is referred to as an instance.
● Tweening is the process of automatically creating new instances of Symbols in the number of steps you specify.
● Custom Commands are created by selecting a series of steps found in the History panel and saving those steps with a name you specify.

In addition to converting the graphics that you use repeatedly into Symbols, using the History panel to replay steps, and harnessing the power of custom Commands, you can use Fireworks to work with groups of images through a process known as *batch processing*. In batch processing, a collection of files that you designate can be edited in any number of ways to scale, resize, optimize or modify those files as you determine. In the busy world of web design, where time is always an issue, this capability provides another extremely valuable set of functions to what is already a very powerful program.

Project 7-4: Batch Processing Files

This exercise will take you through a common task faced by web designers— resizing photographs for use in a web page. Although this exercise provides you with a good introduction to the power of batch processing, you'll note as you go along that this feature contains far too many options to cover here. However, because the interface that Fireworks uses is so intuitive, you will easily be able to apply batch processing to your own files once you've completed this introduction.

Step-by-Step

1. Batch processing is done with existing documents, so there is no need to create a file at this time. Simply open Fireworks, and you will be able to start processing your files. To make this a more realistic exercise, sample files are provided for Module 7 at www.osborne.com or www.dw-fw-beginners.com for you to practice with.

2. To begin processing your images, choose File I Batch Process. Once this command is selected, you will be presented with the dialog box that you see in Figure 7-7.

3. The first step in batch processing is locating the files you want to apply changes to. Navigate to the location where you saved the practice files for this module and change the file type to JPEG. Once the files are located, you can select them individually and click the Add button or use the Add All button to select all the files in the folder. Select all the files and note that their names appear in the selected files listing at the bottom of the dialog box. Click the Next button to move to the second dialog box in the process.

7

File listing

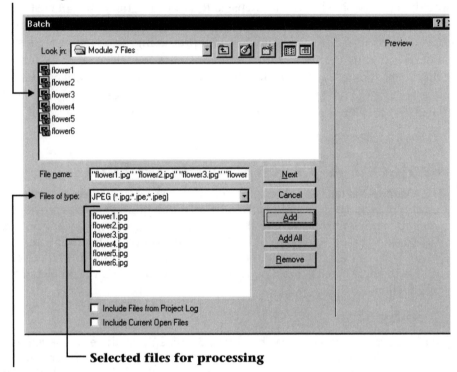

Select file type

Figure 7-7   The initial screen of the Batch Process dialog box is used to select the files to be processed.

4. As you can see in the next illustration, the second dialog box provides a number of options for editing your files. Your task here is to change the size of photographs that would be too large to fit into a web page at their current size, so the option you will be selecting will be the one you see applied here—Scale. To use this option, first select Scale in the left side of the dialog box and click the Add button. As each option is selected, the settings for that process become available in the lower portion of the dialog box.

Available processes   **Selected processes**

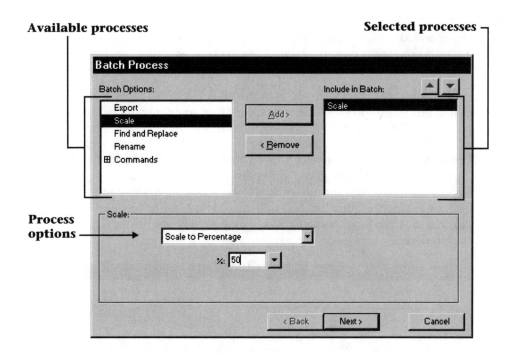

Process options

5. For the sample photographs provided, the images must be scaled to 50 percent to fit comfortably into a web page. At their current width of 1280 pixels, these pictures are simply too large to fit into most browser windows and need to be resized to make working with them easier. Using the drop-down options for the Scale process, choose Scale to Percentage and set the value to 50 percent.

6. Before moving on, take a few minutes to look at the other options available for use in batch processes. You'll note that, among other choices, you can set the optimization settings for images, rename your images, and even employ any saved Command to set a series of image modifications all at once. For instance, with batch processing you could create a custom Command that resizes your pictures to a set width and height and sets the optimization for each file all at once. Once a Command of any type is saved, it becomes available as part of the batch process Command set.

7

Note

If you have added new processes to the listing, be sure to use the Remove button before moving on. For this exercise, you will only be scaling the pictures provided.

7. With the Scale process selected, click the Next button to move to the final dialog box in this process. This final dialog box enables you to specify a location for the processed images to be stored. In this case, an empty folder is provided for your scaled-down pictures. Select the Custom Location radio button and browse to the folder called *flowers* contained within the Module 7 exercise folder. Although you could just as easily have placed your revised images into the folder they were originally located in, it's best to put them into a subfolder or other location to avoid conflicts with filenames. This illustration shows how this final dialog box should be set before you complete the process.

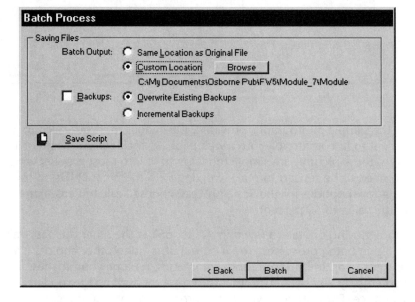

8. That's really all there is to it. Click the Batch button at the bottom of this dialog box, and Fireworks takes care of the rest—in this case scaling your original images to 50 percent of their size. Imagine if you had to do this by opening each file and editing the image manually! Instead, take a break and get a breath of fresh air. In just a few minutes, Fireworks will report that it has completed the task and you will be ready for something more interesting to do.

Project Summary

In this brief exercise, you have been introduced to the interface that Fireworks uses for its very powerful batch processing function. Although in this case the task used was a relatively simple one, it is an excellent example of the real-world capabilities of the software. If, for instance, you needed to produce a photo album from a collection of images, Fireworks would enable you to resize all of the pictures at once. If that photo album also needed thumbnail images to use as links to the full-size pictures, Fireworks could handle that task as well. In all, batch processing is an incredibly powerful tool and one that you will come to appreciate as you need to generate modified images for use in your site.

Editing Graphics with the Find and Replace Feature

The final production tool that you'll explore in this module is equally as powerful as the batch processing commands that you just learned about. With this feature, Fireworks enables you to specify a series of attributes and change them to a setting you determine. Once again, this feature makes your time spent with the program more productive and removes much of the work from making changes across a range of files.

Imagine that you are working as a web designer and that you have finalized your proposal for your first client. You're excited about all the work you've done, but unfortunately, your client isn't thrilled with just one aspect of your design— the background color you've chosen for the site. Now, because you have a huge number of buttons and other graphics that depend on that particular color, your heart sinks as you hear the client tell you that they would really rather see a darker shade of blue than the one you have chosen. Had you used another graphics program, you might be faced with many hours of opening files, selecting colors, changing colors, and saving files just to accomplish this one task. With Fireworks, however, the entire process can be automated, and you can move on to preparing a bill for your client and looking for additional work!

Find and Replace is much like batch processing in that the number of options available is extensive. As with the last project you completed, this exercise will take you through a simple real-world application of its use as a way to introduce you to the interface. In addition to the example you'll use here, in which you'll change colors, you can use this feature to make changes to font types and sizes, apply strokes to objects where none currently exist, and use special search phrases called regular expressions to change the appearance of objects based on a pattern that you specify. The options available are very powerful and, for someone involved in production work, can significantly reduce the amount of time needed to make changes throughout an entire web site.

Project 7-5: Using Find and Replace

In the world of web design, change is the one constant. Just as you think you've finally settled on a particular design decision for your site, you discover that your client doesn't (or even you don't) care for a particular shade or color combination. Even with all the automated tools for image creation that Fireworks puts at your disposal, having to change something as simple as the background colors on all your graphics would be a very tedious task if you had to do it by opening each file, making the change, saving the file, and exporting to a web format again. Find and Replace makes this a manageable task. In this exercise, you'll look at a real-world example of how a design change can be handled quickly and efficiently with this terrific feature.

Step-by-Step

1. As with batch processing, the Find and Replace feature does not require a file to be opened in order to function. Although you can use the feature with a single file, including one that is currently open in the program, for this exercise files are provided for you in the folder called *Find-Replace* located in the exercise files for this module. Open the file called *home_button.png* now.

2. To begin the process of changing a color, select Edit | Find and Replace from the Menu bar. Figure 7-8 displays the dialog box that Fireworks uses for choosing which attributes you want to find and the values you want to replace them with. This little dialog box seems rather modest, but the range of possibilities is in fact quite extensive. Before moving on, take a few minutes to orient yourself to its features.

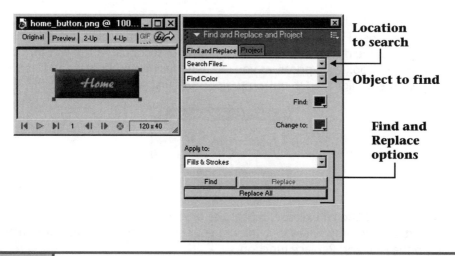

Figure 7-8   The Find and Replace dialog box enables you to choose attributes you wish to find and decide how to change them.

3. Fireworks enables you to search an individual document or a range of files that you designate. Use the drop-down menu at the top of the dialog box to set Search Files. You will be presented with a dialog box that enables you to select the files to be processed. Hold down SHIFT and select each of the files found in the sample folder for this module. Click the Done button.

4. For this exercise, the task is to change the color of both the text and the button itself. To make that change, use the drop-down menu at the top of the dialog box and select Find Color. When this option is selected, the options area will change to display two separate color buttons—one to select the color you want to find and a second to designate the color you want to replace it with.

5. With the *home_button.png* file opened, you can select the color you want to change by using the standard Eyedropper tool. Do this now by clicking the Find color button, and float the eyedropper over the button graphic in your open file.

6. Set the replacement color by clicking the Change to button and, this time, using the color palette to choose a darker shade of blue. Note that both color buttons in the panel will display your choices.

7

7. To complete the process, simply click the Replace All button at the bottom of the panel. Fireworks will open each file, change the color, close the file, and save the document, all within a matter of seconds. At the end of the process, a box will appear, as you see here, telling you how many files were processed. Click the OK button to finish this first process.

8. For one additional exercise, repeat the process to change the color of the text in your sample files to a color of your choice and finish this introduction to the Find and Replace function.

Project Summary

As with the batch processing function, using Fireworks Find and Replace feature is quite easy and incredibly powerful. Although this exercise has only scratched the surface of what the software can do to make your life as a web designer more productive, it is important that you not lose sight of all that this feature can do for you. Undoubtedly, at some point in your career as a designer, you will need to make wholesale changes to your graphics. At that point you should remember that you can save yourself hours of work by turning to Fireworks and letting it do the job for you.

1-Minute Drill

● Define batch processing.

● How can you use the Find and Replace feature?

● What feature enables you to find and replace all occurrences of the designated attributes at once?

● In batch processing, a collection of files that you designate can be edited in any number of ways to scale, resize, optimize or modify files as you choose.
● The Find and Replace feature is used by selecting the files you wish to search and then setting the parameters of the attributes you wish to change.
● To change a selected attribute in all occurrences at once, click the Replace All button.

What to Take Away

When Macromedia set out to create Fireworks, their primary goal was to produce a graphics program that took into account the needs of the professional web designer. Part of the genius of Fireworks is the automation that it provides for completing common tasks that previously required many hours of work on the part of designers. Fireworks MX has continued to build upon the success of the program not only by creating new features, such as the capability to build extensions for the software (see Appendix B), but also by refining the tools already in place to make them even more intuitive and accessible for busy designers.

In this module, you have learned how to create Symbols and export them to custom Libraries for use in other documents. You also have seen how you can employ instances of Symbols to create interesting visual effects. With the History panel and Commands, you have been able to repeat steps that you've applied to objects, and you have even learned to make your own custom Commands for use at any time. Finally, with the batch process and Find and Replace features built into Fireworks, you know how to make changes to large collections of documents to complete common tasks such as resizing pictures or replacing colors.

All of these features have one thing in common—they make your life as a designer less tedious by automating many of the common chores that face you as you continue building images for use on the Web.

7

✓ Mastery Check

1. What primary features does Fireworks contain for the creation of consistent content?

_____

_____

2. How can you access Symbols?

_____

_____

3. Are Symbols available in all Fireworks documents?

_____

_____

4. What attributes of Symbol instances can be safely tweened?

_____

_____

5. What panel tracks changes made in a Fireworks document?

_____

_____

6. How can you apply custom Commands to objects or documents?

_____

_____

7. What is the first step in applying a batch process?

_____

_____

☑ Mastery Check

8. How can you use the Find and Replace feature?

_____

_____

9. What kinds of objects can you search for using the Find and Replace feature?

_____

_____

10. How is the process of finding and replacing colors completed?

_____

_____

7

Module 8

Creating Animated Files

The Goals of This Module

- Understand the principles of animation
- Explore Fireworks' options for creating animations
- Use the Frames panel to animate files
- Create and use animated Symbols and instances
- Apply animation techniques to fine-tune an image
- Understand the use of layers in animations
- Understand proper file format settings for animated files
- Explore file optimization settings

Since 1987, animated files on the Internet have been handled by a version of the GIF format that allows a series of images to be played back in sequence. More like a miniature filmstrip than a movie, animated GIFs can create the illusion of movement or perform other animation tricks such as having objects fade in or out of an image. They are a variation of the GIF format, so these types of files have the same limitations as standard GIFs when used on the Web—colors are limited to 216 web-safe colors, and fine variations in shades and tones do not display well. Unlike other animation formats such as Flash, Director, or QuickTime, animated GIFs cannot contain sounds or provide interactivity for the viewer. Even though they have these limitations, animated GIFs are the most common files in use on the Web when the illusion of movement is needed because of one factor—they are widely supported by all common browsers, without the need for a plug-in. Fireworks provides all the tools you need to design and build animations that take full advantage of the format's possibilities and helps you to work around its limitations.

A new and very powerful feature was added to the lineup of the program's tools in a previous version of Fireworks. Animated Symbols enable you to create a miniature animation that can be used over and over as part of an animated GIF. Much like actors on a stage, these animated Symbols can perform movement and actions independently as an animation unfolds.

As you would expect when an image contains multiple graphics, file size and download time are a major issue in the creation of animated GIFs. Fireworks provides the usual tools for optimizing and exporting animated files, but it is extremely important that you consider file size at every step in creating animations. The most successful animated GIFs are those that load quickly and create the visual impact desired in the simplest manner possible. Techniques such as limiting the colors and effects used, reducing the number of graphics contained in the image, and animating carefully are all part of successfully designing animated files.

Fireworks can be used to create animations in one of two ways: either by manually creating frame-by-frame animation—creating or copying objects into different frames—or by using the tools that Fireworks provides to make animation Symbols. Frame-by-frame animation is the simpler of the two and is useful when you want to make a quick animation to use a single time. Symbols, on the other hand, are very powerful because of the way they can be combined, exported to custom libraries, and reused, but they require a little more work on the part of the designer. Ultimately, you will find yourself choosing the animation technique that fits your work style best and accomplishes your animation goals with the least amount of effort.

Simple Animations

An animation is essentially a trick; whether it's a Bugs Bunny cartoon, a full-length Disney movie, or an animated computer graphic, animations all function the same way. A series of images are placed on separate canvases, called frames, and then played back in rapid succession. Where there are differences between one frame and the next, the eye translates the change as movement, effectively tricking the mind into believing that the object has moved on the screen. Creating computer animations means designing these separate frames and then arranging them in a manner that creates this illusion.

In Fireworks, the Frames panel is the primary tool for creating, organizing, and working with frames that, when pieced together and played, make objects on the canvas appear to move. "Movement" is a relative term; although it can describe an object that actually changes its position on the canvas, it can also describe an object that changes its transparency, grows or shrinks in size, or even rotates around an axis. Animations can be powerful tools for attracting attention to an element of a web page and, if designed and optimized carefully, can add a sophisticated and exciting look. Take a few minutes to acquaint yourself with the appearance and functions found in the Frames panel, seen in Figure 8-1, before moving on to the first exercise in this module.

8

Project 8-1: Creating Frame-by-Frame Animations

Using the Frames panel for controlling your animations allows you to manage all aspects of an animated file. By selecting the frame you want to edit, you can make changes to the appearance, location, or even transparency setting of an object to give it the appearance of movement.

The Frames panel also includes important tools for the automatic creation of animations and allows you to add and delete frames, copy an existing object to a specified number of frames, and control the playback speed of your animation. In this first project, you have the opportunity to become comfortable with the Frames panel and animated files as you create some simple animations.

Step-by-Step

1. To begin understanding animations, create a new file that is 300 pixels wide by 300 pixels high with a white canvas. Name this file *frames_practice.png*. Expand the Frames panel by clicking the Open panel button in your panel set.

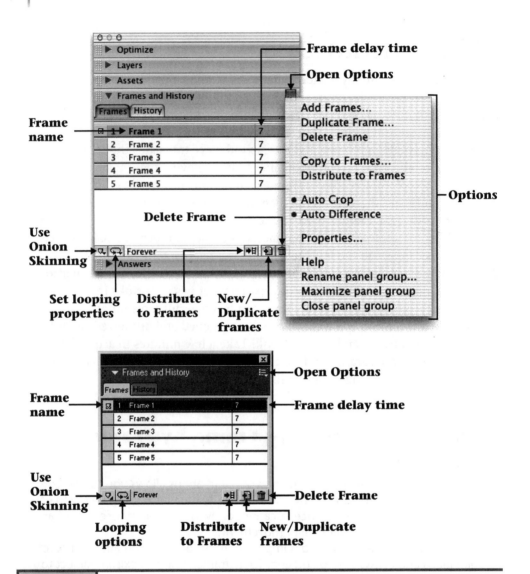

Figure 8-1 The Frames panel allows you to create, delete, organize, and apply properties to animated files. (The Macintosh format is shown at the top; the Windows format appears at the bottom.)

2. Note that, in the Frames panel, your new file has exactly one frame, called Frame 1. To create an animation, the first step is to add frames to the file.

To do this, click the expansion arrow and choose the option to Add Frames, which will open the Add Frames dialog box that you see here. Add three frames to the file after the current frame and click OK.

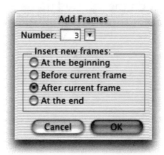

Tip

You can also add one frame at a time by clicking the Add Frame button at the bottom of the panel.

---

3. The Frames panel now contains four frames, and the process of creating your first animation can begin. Select Frame 1 by clicking its name in the Frames panel, and draw a simple vector object on your canvas, such as a circle, in the upper left-hand corner. With the circle selected, choose Edit I Copy to place a copy of the circle on your computer's clipboard.

Note

When frames are added, the first new frame in the sequence is automatically selected. Be sure that you are working in the correct frame by checking to see that it is highlighted in the Frames panel.

---

4. Next, select Frame 2 in the Frames panel and choose Edit I Paste to place a copy of the circle from Frame 1 onto the new blank canvas. Position the new circle a little lower than the first one. Complete this process by copying circles in Frames 3 and 4 as well, dropping each circle a little lower on your canvas.

5. Once you have a circle in each frame, you can use a nice feature that Fireworks provides for positioning the different objects. *Onion Skinning* will create semitransparent versions of each object in the animation sequence and allow you to position or modify them as you wish. To turn on Onion

Skinning, locate the button in the bottom of the Frames panel (labeled in Figure 8-1), click it, and select the option Show All Frames from the menu that appears. Once Onion Skinning is enabled, your image will appear as you see here, with the object on the selected frame at full opacity, and the objects on the other frames shown semitransparently.

6. Besides its use as a layout tool, Onion Skinning also allows you to work on multiple frames at once. Try this by using the pointer to move the circles into different positions on the canvas. Notice that when you work in a frame other than the one that is selected, a small blue square appears next to the name of the frame.

7. To see your animation in action, locate the Play/Stop button at the bottom of the Document window that you see illustrated here. Just like the buttons on a VCR or CD player, you can play or stop a preview of your animation by using these controls, or use them to navigate through the frames in your animation. As each frame plays in sequence, the object appears to move on the canvas, and your first animation is complete.

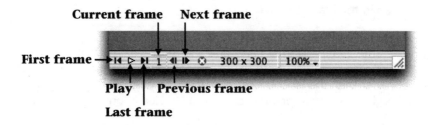

Tip

Use the 2-Up preview panel to check the file size of this simple animation and to see a preview of how it will look in the animated GIF format.

8. Fireworks has a great feature that enables you to take some of the work out of this simple animation process. Objects that are placed on a canvas can be copied automatically to your frames, effectively taking much of the effort out of creating an animated sequence. To see this feature, create a new 300 pixel by 300 pixel document and name it *frames_practice2.png.*

9. Draw an object on the canvas and choose Edit I Duplicate to place a second copy of the object on the canvas. Do not add any new frames at this time. As before, move the new object away from the original slightly so the illusion of movement can be created. Complete this process so that you have a total of four objects on your canvas arranged as you see in Figure 8-2.

Note

The Frames panel has been undocked from the panel group in this example for the sake of clarity.

10. Choose Edit I Select All so that all four objects are selected or marquee the objects with the Pointer tool and then click the Distribute To Frames button

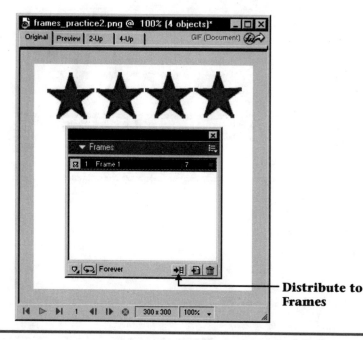

Distribute to Frames

Figure 8-2 Choosing the Distribute to Frames option automatically animates multiple objects.

at the bottom of the Frames panel. Almost magically, three frames are added to the document, and by using the Play button, you can see your new animation in action.

Note

Objects are distributed to frames in the order in which they are created. The original object will be on Frame 1, the first copy on Frame 2, the second on Frame 3, and so on.

11. Frame-by-frame animation can also be used for other techniques that add spice to an animation. To make the object in this animation appear to fade in from the background as it moves, for instance, you can manually adjust the opacity settings for objects in each frame by using the setting found in the Property Inspector, as you see here.

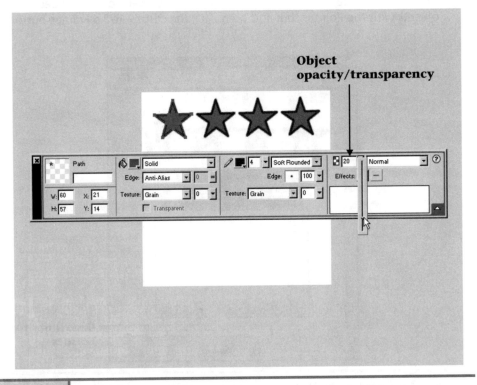

Figure 8-3 Use the opacity slider in the Property Inspector to adjust the transparency of an object.

12. To apply this technique, select Frame 1 in the Frames panel and then select the object. Adjust the opacity (transparency) setting in the Property Inspector to around 20 percent. Continue in this way, adjusting the opacity for objects in the remaining frames until you reach the last frame and the opacity setting remains at 100 percent. Play your animation, and your object will appear from out of the background of the canvas.

Tip

The file size of an animation can quickly grow quite large, so it is best to start with the smallest number of frames that you think will provide a smooth animation and then add frames as necessary.

13. This effect looks pretty good, but adding frames to the document and further adjusting the opacity settings will lead to a smoother animation. Select Frame 4 and add four additional frames to this file by clicking the expansion arrow in the Frames panel and choosing Duplicate Frame. Duplicating the frames will place a copy of any objects on the selected frame, with all their properties intact, onto new frames as specified in the Duplicate Frames dialog box. Place four new frames after the current frame by adjusting the settings in the Duplicate Frames dialog box.

Tip

An object or group of objects that are selected in one frame can also be copied onto other frames by choosing the Copy To Frames option.

14. You can now return to the Frames panel and Property Inspector, and working between the two, adjust the opacity setting of the eight objects. The fade-in effect will appear much smoother now that the document has eight frames, but you should note that the file size has increased as well. You must find the balance between file weight and image quality when designing animations.

15. Modifying Live Effects that are applied to objects can be another useful way to create animations. To create text that has an alternating glow effect takes only two frames, for instance, and can do a great job of drawing attention to your animation. To see this effect in action and learn another technique for duplicating frames, create a new file and name it *frames_practice3.png*. Type any text in the middle of the canvas and drag the name of the frame in the Frames panel (Frame 1) onto the New/Duplicate Frames button to make one new frame with a copy of the text in the same position on the canvas.

8

16. On Frame 2, select the text and open the Effects panel. Simply apply a small glow effect to the object and adjust the color, and your new animation will appear with a flashing glow effect. This is a very quick and easy way to use an animation to draw attention, with the added benefit of maintaining a small file size.

17. In addition to naming and organizing frames, the Frames panel is also the place where you can adjust the amount of time that each frame displays as the animation runs and how many times it will run, or loop.

18. Locate the Frame Delay setting at the far right of the Frames panel for any of the sample animations you have done. Double-clicking this area will open a small window at the bottom of the Frames panel, shown in Figure 8-4, where you can adjust the timing for each individual frame, in increments of 1/100 second. By default, frames play at 7/100 second, but you can just as easily set them to display for one quarter of a second by changing the setting to 25/100 second, for example, or for three full seconds by making the setting 300/100 second. As you experiment with animations, you will find that you often need to adjust the frame timing so that important items don't disappear too quickly.

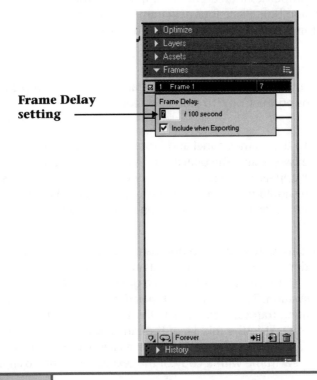

Figure 8-4 Frame timing is adjusted in the Frame Delay portion of the Frames panel.

┤*Note* ───────────────

Don't expect your animation timings to be perfectly exact when seen in a browser. Both the version of the browser in use and the speed of the viewer's Internet connection can affect how the animation will replay. Often, a happy medium is the best that can be achieved.

19. Looping determines how many times an animation will run, and you should give it careful consideration when you design your animations. Large animations in particular should be set to run only a few times because the constant animation will undoubtedly distract (and possibly annoy) your viewer. To set looping, click the Looping button, shown here, in the bottom part of the Frames panel. Set the number of loops to one of the available values.

8

┤*Note* ───────────────

Looping describes the number of times an animation will play after it has gone through its initial playback. An animation set to loop once will actually play twice— one initial run and one loop.

20. Spend some time experimenting with frame-by-frame animation techniques by creating your own practice files. Try different effects by drawing objects and applying different settings in successive frames. Create a line of text and apply a glow effect in the second frame or use the Polygon tool to design a star that spins by applying the transform options found in the Modify menu. The variations are almost limitless, and you are sure to find exciting ways to animate your images as you grow more comfortable with Fireworks.

Project Summary

In this exercise, you've been introduced to just how much fun creating animations in this way can be. For every change that you want to take place in your document, create a new frame in the Frames panel and add, position, or modify the object in the manner you desire. In the end, you will have created an animation by subtly changing objects on each frame and will have discovered one of the most enjoyable aspects of graphic design—seeing an image that you have created come to life.

Note

You'll find sample files with different kinds of animations at www.dw-fw- beginners .com. Explore the files, paying close attention to how frames are used in conjunction with different settings on the objects within them.

1-Minute Drill

● How can you create animations?

● What feature of Fireworks enables you to see and modify multiple objects on different frames?

● How can you use the Distribute To Frames feature?

Animation Techniques with Symbols, Tweening, and Layers

The first project in this module introduced you to the basics of frame-by-frame animation; in many cases, creating images this way will be perfectly acceptable. Simply create a new file, add objects and frames, and create the illusion of animation by modifying objects on succeeding frames.

As you would expect, Fireworks has additional tools to help in the animation process that enable you to make more complex images than the samples you've seen so far and further assist by letting you work more efficiently. Symbols, tweens, and layers all work together to make you a more productive designer.

As Module 6 discusses, layers are particularly useful as an organizational tool because they allow you to stack virtual transparencies, one on top of another, within a document. Layers are most often used when you want to create a static background that remains in place while the animated objects do their thing. Layers that are to appear in every frame in this way are said to be *shared,* and making this happen is simply a matter of creating the layer that holds the

---

● Animations are created when a series of images is placed on separate canvases, called frames, and then played back in rapid succession.

● Onion Skinning creates semitransparent versions of each object in the animation sequence and allows you to position or modify them as you wish.

● The Distribute To Frames feature takes individual objects and places one copy of each into a new frame, removing some of the labor from the animation process.

background by using the Layers panel and then choosing Share This Layer from the expansion arrow options in the Layers panel. Objects on this shared layer will appear in every frame of your animation.

One of the real challenges to working with animations is the issue of file weight. Every frame is essentially a separate canvas, so each one will contain its own images and will add file weight to the document. Organizing your animations carefully is an important part of creating a successful animation. The use of Symbols and shared layers helps animations load quickly and play smoothly.

Project 8-2: Animating with Symbols and Layers

Using an object, or a Symbol, you can define important elements of an animation, such as the Symbol's position in a particular frame, and the program will add and fill in additional frames to create the animation. This great way to automate some of the animation process is called tweening. In this project, you'll learn not only how to apply tweening to animations but also more ways Symbols and layers can be used to further refine your images.

Step-by-Step

8

1. To begin, create a new file that is 300 pixels wide by 300 pixels high with a white canvas. Name this file *symbols_practice.png*.

2. As you learned in the last module, Symbols are a great way to automate some of the work that you do when creating graphics. With animated graphics, Symbols become even more powerful because placing a Symbol into a new frame can be much easier than using the duplicating or copying methods you used previously. Furthermore, with Symbols, if you need to make a change to an animated object at any time in the future, the process becomes infinitely easier if you have to modify only the Symbol and not every object in your animation. Choose Edit | Insert | New Symbol and set the New Symbol dialog box to create a new graphic Symbol called **smiley**.

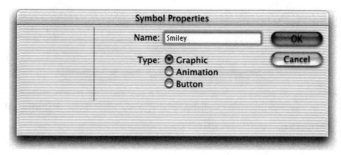

3. Clicking OK opens the Symbol Editor, which you will use to create an object to be placed on the canvas in the main document. In the center of the Symbol Editor are crosshairs that help you to center objects on the canvas and serve as a visual reminder that you are working in the Symbol Editor, and not in the main Document window.

Tip

You can convert any existing object to a Symbol by selecting it and choosing Insert | Convert To Symbol.

4. Using your drawing tools, draw a smiley face in the middle of the Symbol Editor, as shown in Figure 8-5. When you are finished, use the Close button in the upper right-hand corner of the Symbol Editor (Windows) or upper left-hand corner (Macintosh) to close the window and return to the main Document window.

5. When you return to the Document window, a copy of your image will automatically appear with a special indicator of its status that Fireworks provides. The curved arrow in the lower left-hand corner of the window lets

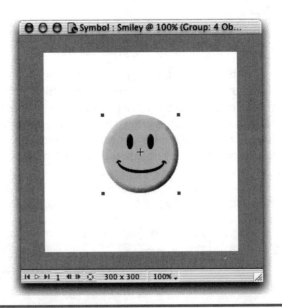

Figure 8-5   You can create new Symbols in the Symbol Editor using all of the usual Fireworks tools and effects.

you know that this is a Symbol, as you see here. As Module 7 discusses, every time a Symbol is placed into a document, it is known as an *instance* of the Symbol, or simply as an instance.

6. Now that a Symbol is linked to this file, it will appear in the Library panel for this document. Remember that Fireworks Symbols are specific to the document and can be shared only if they are imported or exported through the Library panel's options, shown in Figure 8-6. Fireworks provides a preview of the Symbol at the top of the panel, with its description displayed below.

7. Tweening in animated files is done in the same way that Module 7 describes—two instances of a Symbol are placed onto the canvas, and Fireworks completes the process of creating the animation through the magic of tweening. To see this feature in action, drag another instance of the smiley face Symbol onto the

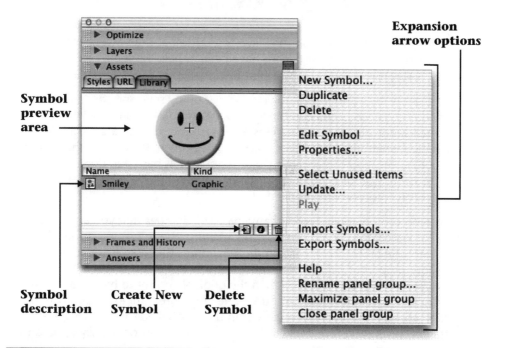

Figure 8-6 The Library panel stores and displays Symbols for each document that contains them.

canvas and position the two instances in opposite corners, like you see here. Be sure that both instances of the Symbol are selected.

8. Choose Modify I Symbol I Tween Instances to animate the movement of the two objects on the canvas by providing information in the Tween Instances dialog box. Fireworks will create as many new frames as you specify and, if the Distribute To Frames check box is selected, will place each instance on a separate frame. Set your options like those in the illustration and click OK.

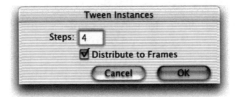

9. Try the animation by clicking the Play/Stop button at the bottom of the Document window. If your tweens have been applied correctly, the smiley face will slide across the canvas—a complete animation in just a few easy steps!

10. Add more tweens and frames to your animation by selecting the last frame and adding a new instance of the Symbol. With both instances selected, use the Modify I Symbol I Tween Instances command to create a complete animation where the smiley face makes one complete lap around the border of your canvas. You can also use Onion Skinning, as has been done in Figure 8-7, to see how your animated object will move around the stage, and then apply further adjustments as needed.

11. Tweening can be applied to the same types of changes that you animated by hand in Project 8-1. The trick to using tweening, though, is to decide what you want the object to look like in the key frames that you are defining and set those properties *before* you create the tween. In this example, the Symbol was first scaled to a smaller size than the original and set to tween after the modifications were in place. Of course, one of the great things about Symbols is that you can modify their properties in the Symbol Editor and have every instance, including those created through tweening, automatically updated

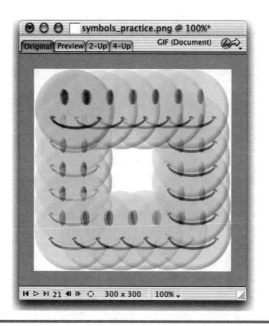

Figure 8-7 Tweening takes much of the work out of animating Symbols, and Onion Skinning makes working with multiple objects easier.

in the file. You can see this for yourself by opening the smiley face Symbol from the Library panel and adjusting its size, for instance. Once the Symbol Editor is closed, the new size will be reflected in every instance of the Symbol, even those created by tweening.

Tip

Tweening works best for animations that change the position, scale, or opacity of an object or modify a Live Effect. Xtras cannot be tweened without breaking the link that the symbol has to its original in the library. In addition, you cannot tween from one color to another.

12. The last item to discuss in this project is how layers can be shared among frames in a document. Try this now by opening the Layers panel and adding a new layer to your file. Click on the Layer name and change it to **Background**. As you do so, you will see a check box that allows the layer to be shared, as has been done here. This technique cannot be applied to layers that already contain images, so Fireworks will remind you with a quick warning box that objects may be deleted if they are not on the current layer. You should always limit objects on shared layers to those that are not animated, so you can simply click OK to go on.

13. To apply an object to this shared layer, just draw the objects that you'd like to appear in every frame. For this example, draw a rectangle that covers the canvas and set the properties the way you would like. This single object will now appear in every frame.

Tip

Remember that you can move layers by dragging them up or down in the stack. To make this background layer appear at the bottom, or in the background, just drag it to a position below the layer that holds your animation.

Project Summary

As you become a more accomplished animator, you will undoubtedly return to Symbols and tweening as two of your primary tools for creating and modifying dynamic images. Add the ability to make a background once and then share it across your entire animation, and you will understand how efficiently Fireworks creates animations for the Web. For now, you can save or discard your practice files as this project draws to a close.

1-Minute Drill

● Which tool can you use to create new Symbols?

● How is tweening accomplished?

● List three ways that an object can be tweened.

● The Symbol Editor is used for creating new Symbols.
● Tweening is accomplished when two Symbols are selected on a canvas and Fireworks is instructed to create frames and modified Symbols that fill in the areas between the two key frames.
● Objects can be tweened for position, size (scale), and opacity.

Animated Symbols

Prior to their introduction in version 4 of Fireworks, Symbols were a useful tool primarily for making graphical objects that were reused throughout a web site. Symbols could be easily modified, and changing a Symbol automatically modified every instance of the Symbol in use in a document. As a result, Symbols were used primarily as a labor-saving device for creating common objects and as a way to do tweening. With the revisions included in Fireworks 4, the use of Symbols for animated effects took a giant leap forward.

Fireworks MX also allows you to work with these special Symbols that can be created to behave as though they were actors on a stage. Animated Symbols can be used for a variety of animation techniques, including having each of these actors moving independently as an animation unfolds. Consider a situation in which you want an animated star to glow in one corner of the image while your company's logo fades in from the background. Using animated Symbols, you can create both the star and the logo as independent Symbols with each placed into the document and set to animate in the sequence you choose.

Symbols are also helpful in maintaining smaller file sizes and in managing the overall look of your file. In many instances, the files you create will only need to download instances of Symbols that actually change. If you use these techniques, animated GIF files can help you achieve optimal file weights. Furthermore, you can edit Symbols independently without changing the look of the rest of your document.

Project 8-3: Working with Animated Symbols

The capabilities that Fireworks MX provides through animated Symbols can tremendously reduce the amount of effort required for creating complex animations. The Property Inspector makes it much easier to modify the properties of your animated Symbols once you have created them.

Be forewarned, though. There is a bit of a learning curve involved with using animated Symbols because designing them requires a fair amount of bouncing back and forth between different Fireworks panels and the Property Inspector and because some special considerations have to be made in the way animations are created. Still, with a little bit of practice, you will be able to create animations that move, fade, spin, and provide the sort of visual impact that these types of files are known for.

8

Step-by-Step

1. Animated Symbols can be created in one of two ways—either from scratch or by converting an existing animation to an animated Symbol. To use the Symbol Editor to create an original animation, first create a new 300 pixel by 300 pixel document with a white canvas. Name this new file *animate_practice.png*.

Note

Although most animated files are much smaller than this one, a larger canvas size is used here for ease of illustration.

2. From the Menu bar, choose Edit I Insert I New Symbol to open the Symbol Properties dialog box. Name the new Symbol **animated star** and be sure that the Animation radio button is selected. When your settings are correct, click OK to close the dialog box.

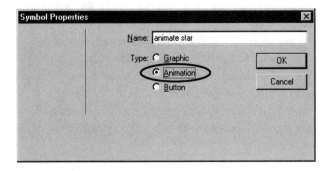

3. You'll recall from previous projects that all operations that you can perform in a regular Fireworks Document window can be done in the Symbol Editor, and this is true for animated Symbols as well.

4. In the Symbol Editor, draw a small star in the center of the canvas, centering it on the crosshairs.

5. Animating this Symbol begins as an easy enough process. With the star still selected, choose Modify I Animate I Animate Selection to open the Animate dialog box, shown in Figure 8-8. What makes this a little intimidating is the sheer number of ways that a Symbol can be animated. You can expect to spend a little experimentation time with this dialog box as you become familiar with its capabilities.

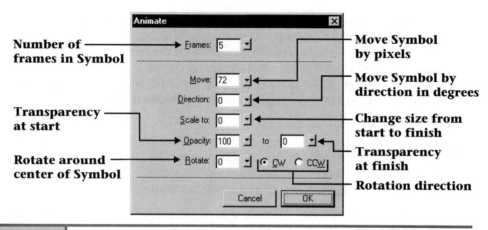

Figure 8-8   The Animate dialog box can be used to set multiple animation effects at once.

6. In this case, the goal is to have the star remain in place and fade from 100 percent opacity to complete transparency. Apply the settings shown in Figure 8-8 to your Symbol and click OK.

7. Creating an animated Symbol requires that more frames be added to the Symbol Editor so that the animation can take place. Fireworks will present a warning that this operation is about to take place. Click OK to allow the automatic creation of the additional frames that the Symbol requires. Once you do so, you will see the animated Symbol with some special handles to denote the beginning point (green handle on your screen) and ending point (red handle on your screen) of your animation, with the other tweened points along the way indicated (by blue handles on your screen). In the example here, the handles have been separated to make their appearance clearer, but you may want to experiment with this process by clicking and dragging the handles to change the positions of the objects in your animation. Even after you've applied settings in the Animate Symbol dialog box, you can make further adjustments as needed by changing the positions of these handles.

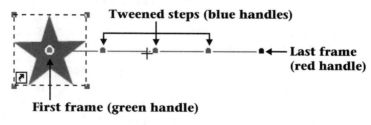

8. Now that the animation effects are set for this Symbol, you can preview them directly in the Symbol Editor by using the Play/Stop button at the bottom of the window. To add frames or otherwise change the settings for the animation, select the Symbol from the Symbol Editor and choose Modify | Animate | Settings to reopen the Animate dialog box. Try changing the opacity setting so that the object no longer fades, or experiment with the Scale To option.

9. You'll also note that the positions of individual objects in the Symbol Editor are listed in the Property Inspector as well. To see how to apply effects with the Property Inspector, change the rotation setting for the Symbol from zero to 360-degree rotation. With that setting applied directly in the Property Inspector, your object will spin as it moves and fades.

10. Closing the Symbol Editor causes a rather curious effect. Rather than place a copy of the animated Symbol on your canvas, an instance of a new Symbol is placed on the canvas as an indication that an animated Symbol is associated with the document. However, this is not the animated Symbol you just created, which must be accessed from the Library panel. The "shortcut" instance that initially appears on the canvas can be deleted or positioned as you choose without affecting the animated Symbol that you bring onto the canvas manually. However, it is not animated, and a quick look at the Library panel will reveal that this Symbol is listed by the generic Symbol name, while your Symbol labeled **animated star** is also listed. This process can be a bit confusing at first, but if you remember to name your Symbols as you create them, then this feature shouldn't be a major stumbling block. For this project, simply delete the Symbol shortcut from your canvas by pressing DELETE.

11. Access the animated Symbol by first finding it by name in the Library panel and then dragging it onto the canvas. Once again, if the document does not have enough frames to support the animation, new frames will be added automatically, as you saw when you first created the animated Symbol. Drag the animated star onto the canvas and allow Fireworks to add frames as necessary now.

12. Once in the Document window, the animated Symbol can be modified not only in terms of its initial position but also in terms of how it moves across the canvas. The same handles that are found in the Symbol Editor reappear here, allowing you to change the position of each instance of the Symbol by adjusting the start and end points.

13. Animated Symbols like this one are most useful when you are creating common objects that you may want to reuse either in a single document or in other projects. If you need a logo that fades in from the background or want to create a spotlight effect by combining Symbols on different layers, and these elements are some that you might expect to use or modify in the future, then taking the time to create them as Symbols is definitely worth the effort.

14. Access animated and graphic Symbols either by exporting the file to a location that you establish as an archive area for your Symbols or by importing them from an existing file. The value in choosing the export method is that you will always know where to find a Symbol when you want to use it later on.

15. From the Library panel, open the expansion arrow options and choose Export Symbols to display the Export Symbols dialog box. In this panel, you can choose to export the Symbol to an existing PNG file or place Symbols in a custom library file that holds all the Symbols you may want to reuse in the future.

Tip

Hold SHIFT down while making your selections to choose multiple Symbols.

16. Click the Export button to export the Symbols you have selected into a special Fireworks PNG file that contains the Symbol and any others that you choose to store there. Using the standard Save As dialog box for your system, you can accept the default Custom Symbols name that Fireworks assigns to the file or name it as you wish. This technique is useful primarily for saving and accessing common objects that you will want to find sometime in the future; give the file a name that will be helpful to you three months down the road when you might not remember where you put that perfect spinning star, for instance. Names like *animated_basic_shapes*, *animated_buttons*, or *animated_logos* are examples of archive filenames that might make your life easier later on.

8

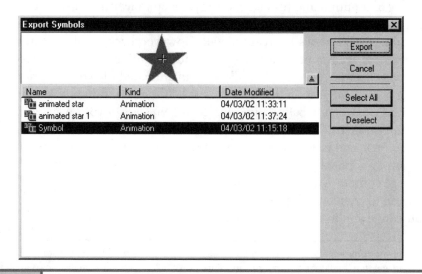

Figure 8-9   Exporting Symbols to custom library files allows you to reuse them in multiple documents.

17. Importing a file into a document works in much the same way. Open the Library panel, choose Import Symbols, and browse to the Fireworks PNG file that contains the Symbol you want to use. Select the Symbol from the list that Fireworks provides in the Import Symbol dialog box, and it will be added to the library for the current document. A terrific technique for saving time and labor!

Project Summary

Using animated Symbols has its drawbacks, and, as with many new technologies, this feature has a few quirks to it. However, if your work requires the repetitive use of the same animated objects, then animated Symbols are definitely worth looking into. With the ability to create Symbols and export them to an archive or to reuse them from existing documents, you may find that using animated Symbols becomes one of your favorite design tools.

1-Minute Drill

● Which dialog box enables you to set multiple animation effects at once?

● What devices can you use to position an animated Symbol on the canvas?

● What steps must you take to make an animated Symbol available in other documents?

Exporting Animated GIFs

Exporting and optimizing files is an essential step in learning how to convert your creations from Fireworks into a format suitable for the Web—a process that Module 10 discusses in greater detail. However, because of their unique characteristics, it's a good idea to have an understanding of how animated files are optimized and exported. After all, with an animated file you have not only multiple objects but also multiple canvases. Without careful optimization, animations can quickly balloon in size, forcing viewers of your web page to wait for the appearance of the other elements on your pages. In addition, because animated files tend to load first in many browsers, a page that contains an overly large animated file may display your clever animation—and none of the other page content—while the viewer waits. If all that the viewer sees before moving on to someone else's web site is your animation, then your image has actually done you more harm than good.

● The Animate dialog box allows you to set options for positioning, opacity, rotation, and scale.

● The start and stop handles that appear with an animated Symbol are positioned on the canvas to change the movement of the animation.

● You can access animated Symbols (and other Symbols as well) either from an existing document or from a special archive file that you create by choosing the Export option from the Library panel.

Setting File Optimization in the Optimize Panel

Optimization, or the process of setting a file's characteristics to attain the smallest file weight, is done in the Optimize panel. If you've saved the animated file created in Project 8-2, you should open it now to see how these settings are applied. Alternatively, you can open the file called *animated_smiley.png* that you'll find in this module's exercise files. You'll note that the Optimize panel is where you set the file's file format. In the case of animations, the animated GIF format is the proper one to choose. With the Optimize panel open, take a few minutes to familiarize yourself with its features by referring to Figure 8-10.

The Optimize panel is contextual in that its settings will change based on the file format chosen. You can see this effect for yourself by changing the file format for your practice file to one of the supported formats. As you use the drop-down menu for file formats to change this setting, you will note that the available optimization settings will change based on the format selected. These formats and the way they are applied to achieve the smallest possible file weights will be covered in detail in Module 10. After you have experimented with the appearance of the Optimize panel, be sure to change the file format for your animated file to the Animated GIF format. For a file produced in Fireworks, this is the only format that supports animated files for the Web.

8

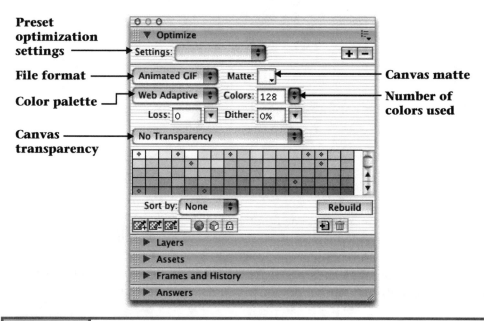

Figure 8-10 File format and optimization settings are applied in the Optimize panel.

Reducing File Weight

Both the standard GIF format and the animated GIF format are constrained by a palette of 256 total colors. You can smooth images somewhat by dithering, a process in which the standard 256 colors are mixed with others to provide a broader range of colors. However, this basic limitation to the GIF format is one you should keep in the back of your mind as you create your images.

To reduce file weight, the standard approach is to reduce the number of colors contained in the image, striking a balance between file weight and image quality. In the *animated_smile.png* file being used for this section, the best quality for the image is obtained by setting the number of colors to the full 256 available. However, that setting produces a file that is a whopping 168 KB in file weight—nearly 3 times larger than the recommended file weight for an entire web page!

The trick then, is to reduce the number of colors in use to the smallest number possible that still maintains an acceptable image quality. Fireworks makes this process easy by allowing you to simply choose the number of colors you want to use and then see a preview of the new setting's effects. As you see here, standard settings are available from a drop-down menu. Alternatively, you can apply the color number directly by typing the value in.

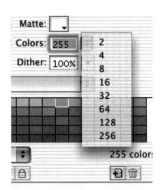

As you apply new settings, you'll notice that the appearance of your image doesn't really change. Remember that when you are working in an original document, Fireworks is applying some settings behind the scenes. To see the effects of your optimization changes, you need to use the 2-Up panel to note the effect not only on your image's quality but on its file weight as well.

Previewing in the Document Window

Figure 8-11 displays the format for previewing optimization settings directly in the document window. This is an especially helpful tool when it comes to animated files because file weight can quickly become a major issue. (Of course, you may use this tool for any file you are working on, regardless of its format.) Fireworks allows you to see your original and optimized files in a side-by-side comparison and even includes a snapshot of the optimization settings you've applied as well as the estimated time in which your file would download to a viewer's computer. To see how this works, click the 2-Up tab at the top of the Document window and change the settings for this file's optimization. As you do so, Fireworks takes a few moments to render your new settings and display both the appearance of the file and its new file weight.

Change view tabs   **Original image**   **Optimized image**

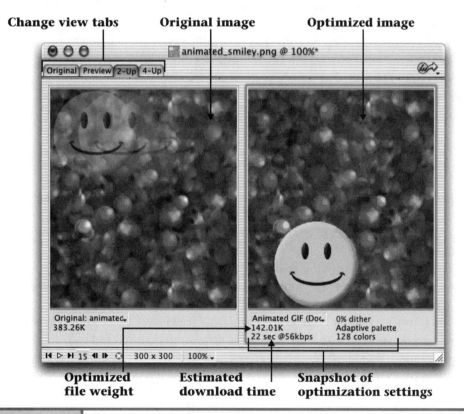

8

Optimized   Estimated   Snapshot of
file weight   download time   optimization settings

Figure 8-11   The 2-Up panel allows you to preview optimization settings.

You may find that you would prefer to see your image in a larger format for applying optimization settings. In that case, you need only select the preview tab to see a full size rendering of your image. Alternatively, you can use the 4-Up panel to apply three different levels of optimization to your file. For a complete description of this function, turn to Module 10.

Previewing Animations in a Browser

One consideration to keep in mind when creating animated GIFs is their inconsistent playback when seen in a browser. Many things can affect the playback speed of an animated GIF, from the operating system on the viewer's computer to the browser in use to how the viewer connects to the Web.

For the truest and most accurate look at how your animated creation will appear, previewing in a browser is the best option. For both the Macintosh and Windows OS, this means simply pressing F12 to open your default browser. Alternatively, you can choose File | Preview in Browser to open your primary browser or even add browsers to the list by selecting File | Preview in Browser | Set Secondary Browser if you haven't done so already. As with most things related to the Web, it's always a good idea to test in at least the two most popular browsers to see how the majority of people will view your image.

What to Take Away

Animations are a terrific way to add movement and excitement to a web page. In this module, you have been introduced to creating animations by placing a series of images on frames that, when replayed in succession, create the illusion of movement. With the tools that Fireworks provides, you can animate objects by modifying their position, opacity, and rotation and can even employ Live Effects in animations by using glows and other techniques. You have also seen that many animated effects can be automated by using tweening, in which you define key frames and Fireworks fills in the in-between frames as you specify. You have also seen how animated Symbols allow you to create small, animated objects that you can use in other animations by accessing them from an archive file.

In all, no program handles the creation and optimization of animated files with the same ease that Fireworks does. However, just because you now know how to create animations doesn't mean that your web site will be best served by having numerous spinning, fading, and galloping animations on every page. Animations, because of their inherently larger file sizes, should be used in small doses and only in ways that meet the overall goals of your site. If you have a need for a graphic that draws your viewer's attention with an animation, then by all means use one. If, however, your goals can be met by a static image, or even by standard HTML elements, then always stay with the method that produces the fastest download time. Ultimately, your audience will appreciate quick downloads more than clever animations.

✓ *Mastery Check*

1. Why is the animated GIF format used so widely on the Web?

_____

_____

2. What tool enables you to "see" multiple frames of an object at the same time?

_____

_____

3. What technique takes multiple objects in a document and places each one in an individual frame?

_____

_____

4. Where are frame timings adjusted?

_____

_____

8

☑ *Mastery Check*

5. How is a new animated Symbol created?

_____

_____

6. What process is required to be able to use an animated Symbol in other documents?

_____

_____

7. What devices can you use for positioning an animated Symbol on a canvas?

_____

_____

8. How can you change settings for animated Symbols in Fireworks MX?

_____

_____

9. What is the only file format appropriate for animated files created in Fireworks?

_____

_____

10. What feature of Fireworks allows you to preview file optimization settings?

_____

_____

Module 9

Creative Tips for Getting the Most Out of Fireworks

The Goals of This Module

- Explore various creative techniques for use with Fireworks MX
- Use photo imaging tools for editing photographs
- Understand how to adjust and edit colors in Fireworks documents
- Use Combine commands to create original artwork
- Use the Scale and Skew tools for creating perspective images
- Understand how to apply light and shadow effects to create 3-D effects
- Explore other creative possibilities with Fireworks MX tools

If you have worked through the exercises in this book, you have spent a considerable amount of time with Fireworks MX and, at this point in your education, you're ready to take the next step. The techniques discussed in this book so far have been fairly sophisticated, but this module will allow you to explore the creative possibilities in Fireworks in greater detail.

This module will take a slightly different approach to the presentation of its content. Instead of going step-by-step through exercises intended to teach you the fundamentals of using Fireworks' tools, here you'll find the material organized along a series of themes. In each section, you'll find a number of different tips and tricks for getting the most out of Fireworks and will have the opportunity to practice using the tools that this fabulous software program provides.

Note

You can download the images used in the exercises in this module at www.osborne.com or at www.dw-fw-beginners.com.

Photographic Techniques

In the world of digital photo processing, Adobe Photoshop is the 800-pound gorilla. With its longer product life, its larger user base, and the very sophisticated features that it includes, Photoshop is considered by most to be the leading software product when it comes to photo processing for print. Of course, it is also much more expensive than Fireworks, and because you will need to use a second program that comes included with Photoshop to process images for the Web, ImageReady, you may find that Fireworks is a better choice for your photo processing needs.

Fireworks' photo processing features may not be as extensive as those found in Photoshop. However, for all but a very few techniques that require filters that are built into Photoshop, Fireworks certainly holds its own when it comes to applying special effects to pictures. In this section, you'll have the opportunity to explore some of the ways that Fireworks allows you to work with photographs and see its tools in action.

Creating Old-Fashioned Photos

One popular technique is to take a photograph and make it look like an antique picture. Fireworks provides a Command that quickly accomplishes this goal by converting an image to sepia tones (that is, brown and white). Follow these steps:

1. Open your image in Fireworks and save the picture. Although this technique could be applied directly to the JPEG file, it is always a good idea to preserve your original file. Saving in the Fireworks PNG format ensures that the original is left unmodified. I started out with the file *fisherman3.jpg* for an example, available in the Module 9 files at www .osborne.com or www.dw-fw-beginners.com.

2. From the Menu bar, choose Commands | Creative | Convert to Sepia Tone.

3. Once the effect is applied, click on the Info icon in the Effects area of the Property Inspector to adjust the Hue, Saturation, and Lightness levels of the applied effect. You will need to experiment with the settings to get just the look you want because the colors in the original image will affect those you see. To view a finished photo, see the file *fisherman4.jpg* in the example files for this module.

Applying Textures to Images

Textures that are applied to filled objects and then placed above an image can add an additional level of interest. In the example shown in Figure 9-1, a pattern gives the image the appearance of being on a heavy canvas. In this example, the same image used in the previous exercise has been used. Open any picture and adjust the color as you see fit. The technique works equally well for pictures in sepia tones, full-color pictures, or images converted to grayscale or black and white.

To duplicate an image like this, take the following steps:

1. With your picture open, draw a rectangle above the image.

2. Set the Fill type in the Property Inspector to Pattern. In this case, the fill has been set to Cloth-Blue, but you can use any pattern you'd like.

3. For an antique effect, convert the color in the rectangle to a sepia tone by choosing Commands | Creative | Convert to Sepia Tone.

4. In the Property Inspector (or the Layers panel), set the transparency of the filled rectangle to a level that allows a desirable amount of the underlying image to show through. In the example in Figure 9-1, the fill transparency was set to 60 percent.

9

Figure 9-1 Applying patterns to objects above an image and adjusting the transparency of the object can add another level of interest to the image.

5. Achieve finer control of the effect by adjusting the angle and distance of the applied pattern. To do this, select the rectangle and, when the control handles appear, as you see here, adjust the position to achieve the desired result. For a streaky look, for instance, you can adjust the location of the square handles so they are closer to the center of the pattern (round handle). The end result can be quite striking.

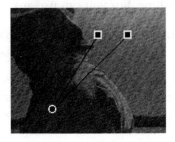

Creating a Picture Frame

Fireworks has always included an automatic procedure for creating picture frames, but in Fireworks MX the power of its new extensibility feature makes this easier. In the past, you were limited to how the picture frame appeared when the automatic command was run; now you can choose the type of fill

9

| **Figure 9-2** | Generate frames for photographs automatically by using the built-in tools in Fireworks. |

you'd like to apply before the picture frame is applied. Here's how to duplicate a frame like the one you see in Figure 9-2:

1. This command does not require that any object on the canvas be selected. Simply open a document, and you're ready to go.

2. Select Commands | Creative | Add Picture Frame.

3. In the window that appears, choose the type of pattern you'd like to use for your image and click OK.

4. Fireworks will automatically apply the image at a width of 10 pixels around your image.

5. To change the pattern, first unlock the frame, listed as Composite Path, by clicking the lock icon in the Layers panel.

6. To mat the picture like the example shown in Figure 9-2, create a second frame by selecting Commands | Creative | Add Picture Frame again.

7. Unlock the object, change the fill from a pattern to a solid fill, and apply the color you'd like to use.

Creating an Oval Picture Frame

The automatic picture frame function found in Fireworks is a handy way to apply a rectangle-shaped frame to an object, but there may be times when you'd like to use another shape instead. To duplicate the picture frame effect that you see in Figure 9-3, follow these steps:

1. This example uses the *woman1.jpg* image you'll find in the exercise files for this module. Open the image and draw an oval shape above the picture to use as a mask.

2. To capture the oval shape to use in following steps, select Edit | Clone followed by Edit | Cut. You will now have a copy of the oval on your computer's clipboard.

3. Set the fill color of the original oval to white and choose Modify | Mask | Group as Mask to crop out unwanted portions of the picture. You may want to experiment with the edge settings for the oval before applying the mask, as previous exercises teach you to do.

| Figure 9-3 | Create custom shapes for frames by using the Combine commands to punch out areas of an image. |

4. Choose Edit | Paste to put the copy of the oval back over the top of your picture. Set the fill color to a pattern of your choosing. This example uses the Wood 1 pattern, but you can use any pattern, gradient, or solid fill color of your choice.

5. Select Edit | Paste to place yet another copy of the oval above your picture. You will need to change this oval to make it smaller than the oval that will act as the frame. Choose Modify | Transform | Scale and reduce the size of this object to approximately 90 percent of the original.

6. In the Layers panel hold SHIFT down and select both objects. Choose Modify | Combine Paths | Punch to punch the oval shape on top of the picture frame and allow the picture to show through.

7. Finish up by applying effects to give the frame added realism. In this example, an inner bevel and drop shadow were applied.

9

Combining Images

In the previous example, you may have noticed that although the woman in the picture is very pretty, the background of the picture includes some unwanted elements. To improve the overall quality of a picture such as this, you can use masking techniques to eliminate unwanted objects in the background of your image. Figure 9-4 displays the results of cropping an image with masking techniques and combining one picture with another for a more pleasing effect. You can do this yourself by following these steps:

1. This example uses the pictures labeled *woman1.jpg* and *floral.jpg* to demonstrate this technique. Open *woman1.jpg* or a picture of your own.

2. Use the Pen tool to "stitch" an outline around the picture of the woman in the picture. The goal is to capture as much of the picture while cropping out as much of the background as possible, so click and release with the Pen tool as close as you can to the image you want to retain. Remember to

| **Figure 9-4** | Combining a masking technique and pasting one picture onto another allows you to improve the quality of your images. |

look for the small circle that appears below the Pen tool as you approach the starting point for your outline that lets you know that you are about to close the shape. When your shape is complete, set the fill color to white.

3. Set the edge of the shape to the feather setting with a width of 3 pixels to blend the edges of your outline. As you've done with masking procedures before, select both the outline shape and the picture and choose Modify | Mask | Group as Mask to crop out the background of the picture.

4. Select Edit | Copy to place a copy of the masked picture on your computer's clipboard.

5. Finish by opening the picture that you want to paste into. In this case, *floral.jpg* has been opened and the cropped picture has been added by selecting Edit | Paste. Your beautiful woman now has a much more appealing background behind her.

6. Remember that you can control the edges of your mask by selecting the masking object in the Layers panel and adjusting the edge settings in the Property Inspector. This may be necessary to help the object blend seamlessly into the background.

7. To complete the effect, blur the background image by selecting Filters | Blur | Blur or Blur More. You may find that you need to apply this effect several times to get the out-of-focus effect that makes the background appear realistic.

8. In addition to the method described above, you can combine images by using other selection tools. For instance, use the Lasso tool to outline the woman in the sample file. Choose Modify Mask | Reveal Selection. Clean up your image by erasing any extra background and then choose Import to import the *floral.jpg* right over the cutout of the woman. Then choose Modify | Arrange | Move Backward to complete your composition.

9

Lightening Images

Not every image you have access to or picture you take will have perfect levels of darkness and lightness. For example, a photograph taken in shadows can be improved by setting the color curves to allow more of the light colors to show through. You can adjust lightness in a picture by following these steps:

1. Open the image. In this case, the example file named *woman2.jpg* is being used.

2. From the Menu bar, select Filters | Adjust Color | Curves.

3. Adjust color curves by defining a point along the diagonal line pictured in Figure 9-5. Note that as your mouse pointer approaches the line, a plus sign appears next to the arrow. To define a point, click on the diagonal line.

4. To select darker colors to adjust, select a point near the top of the diagonal line. To adjust lighter colors, choose a point near the bottom of the line.

5. Drag the point to the left to adjust colors to a lighter range. Drag right to make those colors darker.

6. It is easy to adjust colors with curves, and you will find that you have a greater control over the final output of the modified image.

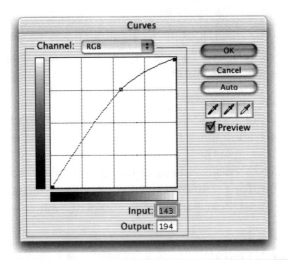

Figure 9-5 Adjusting Curves allows for the fine control of light levels within an image.

Tinting Images

You may have seen pictures in which an artificial color tint has been applied to achieve a dramatic visual effect. You can combine colored objects with photographs to create those types of effects very easily by adjusting an image's hue. Here are the steps to apply a tint to a photograph:

1. Open the file and draw a rectangle that completely covers the image. Choose a solid fill color.

2. Select both the original picture and the rectangle by choosing Select | Select All or by selecting them in the Layers panel. Remember to hold down SHIFT while selecting multiple objects in the panel.

3. In the Property Inspector, locate the Blend Mode settings that you see pictured here. The Blend Mode can also be set at the top of the Layers panel.

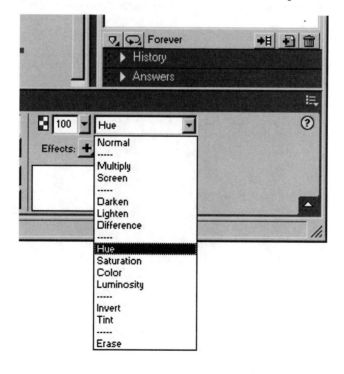

9

4. Select Hue from the options in the Blend mode. As the blend is applied, a colored tint will appear over the photograph.

5. Note that not all fill colors will blend as you might expect. To experiment, simply change the Blend Mode back to Normal and change the color of the colored object. Note that you can use this technique to tint an entire picture or just portions of a picture and that you can create blends with any vector object that you draw.

Special Effects with the Difference Mode

The final photographic technique for this section takes advantage of the use of Difference settings that can be applied in the Blend Mode section of the Property Inspector or the Layers panel. Just as you can tint images, you can apply the Difference Mode to fundamentally change the appearance of an object. This enables you to generate some striking effects, such as those seen in Figure 9-6.

Figure 9-6   Applying a Difference Blend Mode setting allows you to distort image colors.

As with applying a tint, this technique will take some practice, but the basic steps to follow are these:

1. With an image file open, draw an object above the picture and position it where you would like. You can apply this setting to just a portion of an image or to the entire picture. In the example, the file called *hibiscus.jpg* has been opened and a circle has been drawn over the flower in the picture.

2. Set the fill color for the object you have drawn. Applying the Difference Mode causes the color applied to the object above the image to be removed from the photograph. Experimenting with this technique is the best way to see its effect. Choose a solid color and select both the picture and the drawn object.

3. Locate the Blend Mode settings in either the Property Inspector or the Layers panel and choose Difference from the options. The colors in your image will be transformed to create some startling results.

4. You can use Difference Mode in conjunction with patterns, gradients, or textures for even more interesting effects.

Summary—Photographic Techniques

Fireworks is an excellent program for manipulating and working with photographic images, a role that many people tend to overlook. Because it is not as well known as that other program used for working with photographs, and because many of the effects that you can create in Fireworks are not done as automatically as those used in Photoshop, the capabilities of Fireworks as a photo effects tool are not often fully utilized.

Fireworks MX has added tools to make working with your photographs even easier. The new Blur, Sharpen, Dodge, Burn, and Smudge tools have improved Fireworks' capabilities as a tool for working with photographic images in a big way. It will be up to you to experiment with the kinds of special effects that Fireworks allows, but for most operations involving the editing of photographs for use on the Web, the program is certainly up to the task.

9

1-Minute Drill:

- What command gives an image an old-fashioned look?
- What steps should you take to make the background of an image appear to be out of focus?
- What is the advantage to using color curves for adjusting the colors in an image?

Creative Text Effects

Many times, the best way to get a message across is through the simple use of the printed word. Whether you're writing in HTML in a web editor such as Dreamweaver or using Fireworks' tools to create text, simply spelling things out will meet your needs in many cases.

To add a little zing to your text, though, you will need to explore the capabilities that Fireworks provides for combining text with other objects to generate more interesting effects. In this section, you learn some of the ways that Fireworks can be used to give the printed word more appeal in order to grab your viewer's attention.

Two-Tone Text

By manipulating gradients, you can easily create text that uses two colors as a fill. This technique not only enables you to create the kinds of effects you see here but also allows for some interesting combinations when you use your text

---

- To apply a sepia tone that simulates the look of an old-fashioned picture, select Commands I Creative I Convert to Sepia Tone.
- Applying a blur through the Effects area of the Property Inspector will make a background appear to be out of focus.
- Color curves allow greater control over the correction of colors in an image and do a better job of retaining color tones.

as a mask or in conjunction with other filled objects. To create two-tone text like that in the following illustration, follow these steps:

1. Create a new practice document and select the Text tool to add text to the canvas. For this type of effect, a heavier font will generally work better. Click off the text box when you are done typing to close the on-canvas editor.

2. In the Property Inspector, select the Fill button. From the pop-up window, choose the Fill Options button at the bottom. Set the fill type to a linear gradient.

3. To edit the gradient so that there is sharp definition between the two colors in your text, and to set the colors, click on the edit button that appears once the option to use a gradient has been selected.

4. Choose the colors for the gradient by clicking the Color tabs in the bottom portion of the Gradient Editor window. Once you select your colors, slide the tabs together so they are directly on top of each other, as you see here.

9

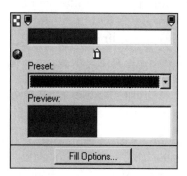

5. Finish by adjusting the gradient fill handles so that the center of the gradient (round handle) is at the top of the text and the square handles are at the bottom, as you saw in the first illustration in this section.

6. If you have chosen a color for your fill that is the same as your canvas color, you will need to apply a stroke to create an outline.

Joining Text with Vector Objects

Joining text with a vector object is a very easy way to create the kinds of effects that you often see on company logos. This technique is easy to achieve by following these steps:

1. Draw an object on the canvas using any of the Vector drawing tools. In the example you see here, a simple rectangle has been used, but this technique will work with any vector object.

2. Use the Text tool to create your text. When you finish typing, reselect the text box and position it as you'd like over the top of your shape. Remember that you can drag a text box from the corner handles to resize the box and separate words or lines of text.

3. With the text box still selected, choose Text | Convert to Paths.

4. Marquee both objects with the Pointer tool so that both the text and the shape are selected.

5. Choose Modify | Combine Paths | Join. Your text will in effect punch out those areas of the object where the text overlays the object below, and the text outside the object will take on the attributes of the shape.

6. Once the objects are joined in this way, you can continue to work with this new vector shape by applying strokes or changing the fill settings to meet your needs.

Joining Text with Text

In the same way that you can join text with vector shapes, you can also join one text object with another. This technique demonstrates how text can be converted to vectors and then joined together to create an interesting visual effect. Here's how to get it done:

1. Use the Text tool to enter a line of text on your canvas. Note that this effect is more successful with heavy font types.

2. With the text box selected, choose Text | Convert to Paths.

3. Your text is now a vector object, but it is still grouped together. To ungroup the individual letters choose Modify | Ungroup.

4. Each individual letter is now a vector object and can be manipulated as you choose. In the example shown here, the letters ABC were scaled to a larger size by selecting them and then using the Scale tool to increase their size.

5. The individual letters can also be moved closer together, as was done in this example. Just select each letter and use either your mouse or the arrow keys on the keyboard to move the letters or groups of letters into place. Remember that by holding down SHIFT you can select multiple objects on the canvas and move or scale them as a group.

6. Once you have positioned the objects on your canvas as you'd like, finish by selecting Modify | Combine Paths | Join. Your letters will now be joined as single vector object.

9

Text with a 3-D Shadow

One of the most important ways to achieve the illusion that an object on a computer screen is three-dimensional is to provide lighting and shadow effects that appear realistic. To make a line of text appear as if it has a light shining behind it, follow these procedures:

1. Create a line of text on your canvas with the Text tool. With the text box still selected, create a duplicate by choosing Edit | Duplicate.

2. Achieve the initial mirror image effect by flipping this duplicated text box. To do so, select Modify | Transform | Flip Vertical.

3. To stretch and distort the text that will act as the shadow, choose the Distort tool from the Tools panel and stretch the corners of the box that appears. Keep the top and bottoms of the bounding box parallel to the bottom of the text to make it easier to align the two text objects together and achieve the shadow effect you want.

4. Once your shadow text is stretched, use either the mouse or the arrow keys to nudge it into place so that the bottom edges of the text meet.

5. Finish up by adjusting the fill color of the shadow text. You may want to try a linear fill, or apply a blur to this object to make it look more shadowy. In the end, you should have no problem duplicating the cool effect you see here.

Windy and Zippy Text

Prior to the introduction of the Smudge tool in Fireworks MX, creating text that had streaks applied to it to make it appear to be affected by the wind, or to be moving, required the use of streaked textures that were applied as masks.

The Smudge tool now makes it much easier for you to generate the kinds of effects you see here.

Follow these steps:

1. Create your line of text on your canvas by using the Text tool.

2. To use the Smudge tool, you must first convert vector objects to bitmaps. A quick way to do that is to apply a filter. Chose Filters | Blur to convert your text to a bitmap image and make using the Smudge tool possible.

3. Select the Smudge tool from the Tools panel and note its settings in the Property Inspector. To duplicate the effect you see in the example, set the width of the tool to 5 pixels and use a rounded tip.

4. Apply the smudges to your text in a random manner—making some strokes short while smudging through the entire line of text with other strokes. Applying smudges to the tips of your letters will help improve the effect.

5. Finish up by using the Distort tool to skew the text in the direction you want. For an object being affected by the wind, skew the text in the same direction as the smudges. For the illusion that an object is accelerating, skew the text in the opposite direction of the smudges.

Creating Brushed Metal Text

One of the most often asked questions at the Fireworks online forum regards how a brushed-metal look can be achieved with text. You can do this in a number of ways, but the one detailed here is fast and easy to achieve.

Brushed Metal

9

1. Create a line of text on your canvas. Set the fill for the text to a linear gradient and use the default Silver color setting. This example creates a brushed silver look using a Fireworks preset gradient, but you can achieve similar results for other metals by adjusting the colors you use in the gradient.

2. Position the center of the gradient above the text by moving the round handle. Shorten the gradient and change its direction by moving the square handle perpendicular to the text and locate it at the bottom of the text, as you see here.

3. Achieve greater control of the look of the gradient by adjusting the colors in the gradient itself. Open the Gradient Editor by clicking the color button in the Property Inspector. As you see here, the two center gradient tabs have been moved closer together and set to a white color, and the other gradient colors have been set to match their counterparts on the opposite side of the gradient.

4. Finish up by applying an inner bevel effect to the text with the bevel set to a smooth setting. Your final results depend on how carefully you position the gradients, but you should be able to easily achieve this effect with a

little practice. Adding a narrow stroke to the text as has been done in the example will allow you to further refine this look.

Fun with Wingdings and Webdings

Many people have a difficult time trying to generate icons and other common shapes and spend a great deal of time and energy searching for free clip art that contains the images they need—without ever realizing that they already have access to an entire library of icons right on their computers.

Both the Wingding and Webding fonts that come installed on most computers already contain many common images suitable for use as button icons or for any number of other images that you may need. With Fireworks' powerful ability to convert text to vector paths, these images can be typed directly onto your canvas and then converted to vector shapes that can be manipulated as if you had painstakingly drawn them yourself. Here's how to create your own icons and begin having fun with these fonts:

1. The real trick to using these fonts is in determining what keys to press to get the image that you want. With the large number of operating systems available these days, it isn't possible to list each method for gaining access to a map of fonts. In writing this book, I found the character maps for Macintosh OS X by looking in the Utilities folder and opening the Key Caps program. For Windows 98, I found the character map by choosing Start | Programs | Accessories | System Tools | Character Map. You may need to consult the Help files for other systems to see how each keystroke is used for the Webding or Wingding fonts.

2. Once you determine which keys you'll need to type to get the characters you want, simply use the Text tool to create your objects directly on the canvas. In this example, the font was set to Webdings, and the keystrokes of SHIFT-Q, SHIFT-Y, and SHIFT-1 were used to create the objects you see here.

9

3. Once the text object is on the canvas, select Text | Convert to Paths to change it from a font character to a vector object. After you have completed this step, you will be able to resize the object and apply any modification to the objects that you want, including changing its fill, setting effects, and adding strokes.

4. The miniature drawings that come as part of these fonts may be just what you're looking for when you need an icon or drawing to add to one of your compositions. Take the time to look at the characters and then use the power of Fireworks to convert the text to a vector object for even more fun.

1-Minute Drill

● What technique joins text with vector objects?

● What tool applies streaks to text to give the illusion of movement?

● What font types contain miniature pictures?

Summary—Creative Text Effects

You have seen in these examples just a few of the ways you can use Fireworks to generate interesting effects with your text. There are, of course, many other ways to modify text with the fabulous and comprehensive set of tools that Fireworks provides. This section introduced you to some techniques that you may want to explore further on your own, or you can visit the many Fireworks web sites to learn more about how to create these and other kinds of effects with your text.

● Join text to other vector objects by first converting the text to vectors (Text | Convert to Paths) and then selecting Modify | Transform Paths | Join to combine the objects.

● In Fireworks MX, the Smudge tool may be used to add streaks to text to give the illusion of movement.

● The Webding and Wingding fonts contain miniature images that you can convert to vectors for use in your compositions.

Creative Techniques with Vector Objects

Fireworks MX contains such an impressive and comprehensive set of tools that it's often a little difficult to find just the right tool for creating the kind of image you want. In this section, you learn some of the ways that the vector drawing tools in Fireworks can generate effects that take you beyond the beginner's stage. With the techniques and tips introduced here, you not only learn how to duplicate the effects that are demonstrated but also hopefully see how to apply similar techniques when you have your own ideas for a new graphic design.

Creating Custom Brush Strokes—the Dashed Line

Many people wonder why Fireworks doesn't include a facility for creating dashed lines. One method often used is to simply type a series of dashes with the Text tool and then convert the text object to a vector path. However, by following these steps you will learn how to draw a dashed line with a custom brush stroke that you design.

1. On a practice canvas, draw a line with either the Pen or Vector Path tool. Use the Stroke category drop-down arrow in the Property Inspector to open the settings for the stroke and apply a Random | Dots stroke to your line.

2. Before creating your custom stroke, click the Stroke category drop-down arrow and, in the window that appears, click the plus sign icon in the lower left-hand corner to create a custom stroke. Name the stroke Dashed Line.

3. To access the custom settings for strokes, click on the Stroke category drop-down menu again and look for the Advanced button at the bottom of the pop-up window. Click the button to open the Edit Stroke dialog box that you see in Figure 9-7.

4. Select the Options tab, set the spacing to 303 percent, and uncheck the Build-up check box. Leave the other settings as they are.

9

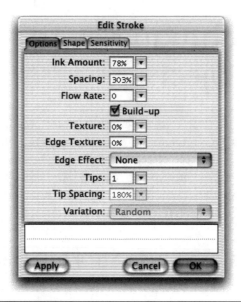

Figure 9-7 Custom strokes are designed in the Edit Stroke dialog box.

5. Click the Shape tab and change the size of the stroke to 10. Leave the other settings as they are.

6. Click the Sensitivity tab, and change every field that you see in the Size category to zero. Repeat this process for the other options in the Sensitivity window, setting all fields to zero for Angle, Ink Amount, Scatter, Hue, Lightness, and Saturation. Note that as you complete this process, the preview in the bottom of the Edit Stroke dialog box will eventually look like a dashed line.

7. To make this custom stroke available as a Command, finish this exercise by selecting the final Stroke listing in the History panel. Use the Options flyout to save the Command and name it something like "Make Dashed Line." You will be able to create a dashed line at any time in the future by choosing your named Command in the Commands menu.

Experimenting with custom brush strokes can lead to some fabulous results. You can not only generate a simple stroke like the one you just designed for making a dashed line but also design your own custom strokes and save them as Commands for application in other instances. Perhaps you'd like to have a custom stroke composed of three separate colors, or one that applies a consistent color scheme to the outlines of letters. All of these things and many more can be done when you combine the power of custom brush strokes with Fireworks' capability to save them as Commands.

Creating 3-D Shapes—the Box

Part of the magic of using a program like Fireworks is learning how to create common shapes on a computer screen. It is often easier to turn to special plug-ins and other helper applications to apply special techniques, but it can be equally satisfying to learn how to create a particular shape all on your own. In this exercise, you will create a box by combining simple shapes to generate a 3-D effect.

1. Begin by drawing the three rectangles that represent the front, top, and side of the box. In the following example, the three objects have been decorated by adding some labels to the box to simulate a box of cold tablets. Use the Info area of the Property Inspector to set the width of the front and top to the same value and the side and the front to equal values.

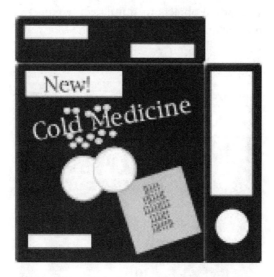

2. To create the edges of your rectangles, apply an outer bevel and set the width of the bevel to a small width. In this case, a value of 3 pixels has been used.

9

3. Once your rectangles are in place and the widths and heights set correctly, add some decoration to the rectangles to simulate the labels and text you might find on a box. Finish by grouping the decorations with the rectangle they are on by selecting Modify | Group. Be sure to group only the individual rectangles and their respective decorative objects.

4. Generate the 3-D effect by scaling and skewing the top and side rectangles carefully to fold them in as you'd see with an actual box. The best tool to get this done with is the Distort tool because it allows you to freely manipulate the corners of your rectangle. As you fold these objects in on themselves so that the corners meet, keep the lines of the rectangles parallel for a more realistic effect. When you are finished, group the entire image, and your finished project should appear similar to the one you see in Figure 9-8.

Scaling and Skewing to Create Perspective Objects

In the same way that you can skew objects to give them a three-dimensional look, you can skew individual objects to simulate a perspective view. By carefully arranging objects on a rectangle and then using the Skew and Distort tools, you

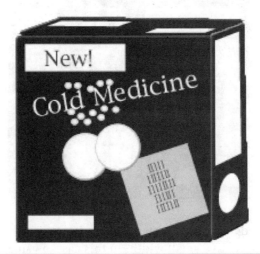

Figure 9-8 By skewing three rectangles, you can create a simple box shape that simulates an object in three dimensions.

will be able to create the illusion that an object is receding into the distance. Here's how to apply that technique:

1. This effect will be more realistic if the objects are arranged on a flat surface. Draw a rectangle and apply a 2-pixel wide stroke setting.

2. On the rectangle, add some decoration or the text that you want to appear.

3. Once the rectangle is prepared to your liking, select all of the objects by marqueeing them with the Pointer tool and group them by choosing Modify | Group.

4. Finish by using the Distort tool to move the corners of the object to generate a sense of perspective. Collapse the corners on one side of the rectangle and expand the corners on the opposite side. When you finish, your perspective object should appear as you see in this example.

Using Symbols with Multiple Objects

When a particular graphic project facing you requires a number of duplicates of the same shape, the most efficient approach is to create a symbol and then use multiple instances to generate your graphic. In this case, the goal is to create an image of candy-coated chocolates. Utilizing the power of symbols, this project becomes manageable and easy to duplicate when you follow this procedure.

1. Begin by starting a new practice document. Choose Edit | Insert | New Symbol to open the Symbol Editor.

2. Name the new symbol **Candy** and set the symbol type to graphic. Click OK to accept these settings and open the editor.

9

3. Draw a circle in the center of the Symbol Editor's canvas, with a size of approximately 25 pixels by 25 pixels. Apply an inner bevel effect with a smooth setting to the circle. Once your circle appears similar to a piece of candy, close the Symbol Editor.

4. Drag the number of copies of the Symbol onto your canvas from the Library panel to create the effect you want. Although this may seem a little tedious, it is still more efficient than using copy and paste to duplicate an object and then position it on your canvas. With Symbols, you need only drag from the Library and drop the Symbol where you want it.

5. To change the color of the candies, hold SHIFT down and select a number of instances of the Symbol with the Pointer tool. In the Effects area of the Property Inspector, select Adjust Color | Hue | Saturation.

6. In the dialog box that appears once this option has been selected, check the Colorize check box and begin moving the sliders that set the values for hue, saturation, and lightness. Watch the objects on the canvas as they change color and, when they appear as you'd like, click OK and move on to the next group of candies.

7. In this way, you can quickly create multiple shapes with different color characteristics and duplicate the example of scattered candies that you see here.

Punching Multiple Shapes

Many times as you are working with Fireworks, you may come across a situation that requires multiple objects with differing characteristics. As the previous example shows, this situation can often be handled by using Symbols.

However, in some cases, similar objects not only must have different colors but also may have to be placed in different positions or orientations to meet your needs.

In this example, you will create a shape similar to a peace sign using a technique that punches shapes and then rearranges them to meet your needs. You may not need to create too many symbols like this in the course of your work, but the technique that you apply here can be used for similar situations where you need to create objects with varying attributes. Here's how to get it done:

1. On a practice document, start by drawing a circle. Hold down SHIFT as you drag with the Ellipse tool to create your circle. Don't worry about the fill colors at this point.

2. Select the Polygon tool and, in the Options area of the Property Inspector, set the shape type as Star and the number of points to 3. Set the number of sides to 3 and the angle of the star to 1.

3. Draw a three-pointed star while holding down SHIFT and dragging straight down the canvas.

4. This star is upside-down, so choose Modify | Transform | Rotate 180° to turn it to its correct orientation. Select Edit | Copy to place a copy of the star on your computer's clipboard for a future step.

5. Place the star above the circle and position it so that the center of the star is in the center of the circle. Choose Modify | Combine Paths | Punch to separate the circle into thirds. This illustration displays how the star and circle should appear after you've competed this step.

6. To make the separate pieces of the circle editable, choose Modify | Transform Paths | Split to break this circle apart. Use the Pointer tool to choose each one individually and change the fill color.

9

7. To clean up a little, use the Subselection tool to move the center points of the broken circle back together in order to close any gaps in the middle.

8. You can add some additional definition to this image if you wish by pasting the original three-pointed star back onto the canvas, drawing a circle above it, and joining the objects together to make an overlay to go above the symbol. Use inner bevels and strokes to define the edges of the overlay, and set the fill to none.

9. When you are finished, you should have a nicely drawn circle divided into separate regions like you see here, or at least a good appreciation of how this technique can be applied for images of your own.

Summary—Creative Techniques with Vector Objects

The exercises in this section have been designed to expose you to techniques that use the basic Vector drawing tools provided by Fireworks to generate special effects. This has certainly not been a comprehensive look at all that Fireworks can do but merely a way for you to see some techniques that you may wish to apply in your own graphic design work in the future. By drawing basic shapes and modifying them through the use of tools such as the Distort and Skew tool, or by creating basic vector shapes as Symbols, you have seen a few ways that Fireworks can let you put your own creativity to use. As you become more comfortable with the use of these tools, you will undoubtedly find new ways to apply these techniques or will develop entirely new ones that use the software in ways that others have not attempted yet.

Ask the Expert

Question: How can I find additional creative techniques to use with Fireworks?

Answer: The first place to look for tutorials and techniques for using Fireworks is at the web sites devoted to the use of this wonderful program. As the number of sites continues to grow, check often at the Macromedia Fireworks web page for a listing of sites currently online that cover Fireworks tools and tips. You can find that listing at www.macromedia.com/go/13187.

Many additional tips and techniques can be learned by examining the ways that other programs are used for creating the kinds of special effects you are after. The trick to applying techniques written for other programs is to decipher how the effect is applied and then translate the terms that the other program uses for describing its techniques into comparable terms in Fireworks. Programs such as Adobe Photoshop and Illustrator or CorelDraw may have different names for the tools that they use, but many times it is a simple matter of determining which tool corresponds in Fireworks in order to duplicate the technique used by the other program. Searches on the Internet for tutorial pages that cover techniques with these other programs will show you that there is a vast store of knowledge available for you to take advantage of.

9

Project 9-1: Combining Creative Techniques

This module has been dedicated to an exploration of just some of the creative techniques that can be used with Fireworks MX. As you have seen, Fireworks' tools for generating special effects, for editing photographs, and for taking the simplest object and transforming it into an entirely new creation are rich and varied.

In this project, you will have the opportunity to take a step-by-step look at how these tools might be used in combination to create a graphic. You are certainly not limited to this single example as you explore what Fireworks is able to do. As with any software program, the more time you can spend experimenting and working with your own creations, the more adept you will become at harnessing the power of Fireworks.

Your goal in this exercise is to duplicate the image you see displayed in Figure 9-9. The picture in black and white may not do justice to your final creation, but your goal is to create a picture frame that contains a portrait that has been modified and combined with other images to achieve a totally new look. When you use the techniques you have learned here, this operation is a great deal of fun and is another example of how Fireworks allows you to reach your creative potential.

Figure 9-9   Fireworks allows you to create unique graphics by combining various techniques in one image.

Step-by-Step

1. Locate the file called *creative_sample.png* in the exercise files for this module and open it. Take a few minutes to examine how the layers have been named and organized. As you do, you'll note that the image contains five distinct areas, each on its own layer—*Buttons, Text, Matte, Pictures,* and *Outer Frame.* Each of those layers will be addressed separately here. Create your own 500 pixel by 500 pixel file to begin.

2. To frame in the canvas, start by naming the first layer in the document **Outer Frame**. Using the Rectangle tool, draw a rectangle approximately 50 pixels high and exactly 500 pixels long. Position this rectangle at the top edge of the canvas. Clone the first rectangle (Edit I Clone) and align the copy to the bottom edge of the canvas.

3. Clone a third copy and use the command Modify I Transform I Rotate 90° CW to reorient the object for use on the left edge of the canvas. Position the rectangle, clone a copy, and place this last object on the right side of the canvas. Set the fill on all four rectangles to a brushed chrome fill using a linear gradient set to the Silver preset as you learned to do previously.

4. With the first part of your frame in place and the fill applied, select all four objects and choose Modify I Group to combine them into one object. Finish this first element by applying an inner bevel effect set to the Smooth option, and apply an inner glow effect with a black color.

5. To create the four decorative appliqués in each corner, create a 25-pixel-square object and set an inner bevel effect. Apply a Copper gradient fill and make copies for each corner. Once each square is in position, click on the Pencil icon in the Layers panel next to this layer's name to lock the layer.

6. Create a new layer and rename the layer **Matte**. This layer will contain the canvas and the border that is inside the frame. On this layer, draw a rectangle that is 475 pixels square and center it in your document by choosing Modify I Align I Center Horizontal followed by Modify I Align I Center Vertical. In the example, a solid fill with a texture has been applied to the rectangle as well as an airbrush stroke type. Experiment with those settings until you achieve an effect you like.

9

7. To complete the matte, use the Text tool to create decorative symbols using the Webdings font type. For the beveled stars in the example, a lowercase **I** was typed in repeatedly until the required number of symbols were present. As with the pieces of the frame, these text objects were cloned and rotated to achieve a border effect. Once these objects are in place, lock this layer by clicking the Pencil icon in the Layers panel.

Note

The Matte layer must be at the bottom of the stacked layers in the Layers panel. To move the layer, select it and drag it to the bottom of the stack. As new layers are added, be sure that this layer remains at the bottom.

8. Create a new layer and name it **Pictures**. Locate the two files called *bougainvillea.jpg* and *bougainvillea2.jpg* in the exercise files for this module. Using the creative techniques discussed in this module, mask these images and arrange them on the canvas as you see in the example.

9. Locate the file called *woman1.jpg* in the exercise files and create an oval picture-frame effect as you learned to do in the photographic technique section of this module. Apply a sepia tone effect to the image to give it an antique look. You may wish to refer back to the photographic portion of this module to review both those techniques. When you are finished, use the Modify | Arrange commands to place the woman's picture on top of the picture of the flowers that you created earlier. Finish by locking this layer.

Tip

When composing complicated graphics such as this, you may want to open a second canvas to do your work on and copy completed graphics from this working canvas onto your final canvas.

10. Create a new layer and name it **Text**. To create the three-dimensional text objects, choose Edit | Insert | New Symbol and set the Symbol type as Graphic. In the Symbol Editor, choose a font and type in the text **Poinciana Beach**. In the sample file, a pink fill was used with a 1-pixel purple stroke to give the text further definition. Drag a second instance of the Symbol onto the canvas and position it above and slightly to the left of the first instance. Choose Modify | Symbol | Tween Instances to create text with a three-dimensional look as you learned to do in the section on text effects.

11. Create a second graphical Symbol with the text **Tropical Deco Days 2002** and repeat the process of generating three-dimensional text by bringing a second instance of the Symbol onto the canvas and tweening the instances. Use the Distort tool to enlarge the first part of this text string and to rotate it on the canvas. When you are finished, lock this layer.

12. Create a final new layer and name it **Buttons**. This layer will contain the three circles, the text, and the icons created with the Webdings font. Start by holding SHIFT down while dragging with the Ellipse tool to create a circle. Give the circle an inner bevel effect with a Smooth setting and set the fill color to your liking. When this object is complete, make two copies and position them as you see in the sample.

13. Select the Text tool and set the font type to Webdings. For the home icon, type a capital letter **H**. Set a fill color that will stand out from the button color. Repeat the process for the announcement button by using a capital letter **V**, and, for the questions button, use a lowercase **s**. Position each of these icons on their respective buttons.

14. Complete this project by typing regular text in a font of your choice to label the buttons **Home**, **Announcements**, and **Questions**. Your very complex image is now complete.

Project Summary

This project has been designed to let you put into play some of the creative techniques that you learned in this module. Although not every example of the power of Fireworks has been used here, you have just completed a very complicated image by working with some simple objects and sample photographs. The power of this software as a creative tool is often overlooked as it is employed for building simple graphics for use on the Web. As you have just seen, Fireworks can do much more than build basic buttons; with some exploration of your own, you will be able to compose images far more creative than the example provided for you here.

9

What to Take Away

As a graphics production tool for the Web, Fireworks certainly has no rivals. When looking for a graphics-creation and photo-editing software title, you have many programs to choose from, including some that contain more sophisticated tools for creating images than Fireworks does. However, by gaining an understanding of the different ways that Fireworks can be employed in the creative process, you should be able to extend your abilities with this highly capable program.

In this module you have seen not only how Fireworks can be used for simple digital photo-editing tasks (such as adjusting colors and lightness in photographs), but also how the program enables you to crop and rearrange images, apply tints, and even completely change the look of a photograph taken yesterday so that it looks like one taken many years ago.

You have also seen how to use text tools that come with Fireworks for generating interesting and unique text effects, from creating shadows that simulate the look of light shining behind a line of letters to using Wingding and Webding fonts for making icons and clip art of your own. You have wide latitude in determining the look of text in your graphics when you combine the text and vector-editing tools that come with Fireworks.

Finally, you have used some of the fundamental tools for creating and modifying vector objects to generate custom brush strokes and combine multiple objects to make entirely new creations that began as simple rectangles, stars, and circles.

In all, the kinds of creative techniques that Fireworks affords you are quite extensive. As one person has said, Fireworks can quickly become your favorite computer game. As you continue to develop your skills in this incredibly robust application, you will come to appreciate just how much fun you can have making your own creations come to life on your canvas.

✓Mastery Check

1. How can you apply textures to images?

_____

_____

2. What technique tints images?

_____

_____

3. What steps do you need to take to have Fireworks automatically create a picture frame?

_____

_____

4. What command enables you to flip text over for use in a shadow effect?

_____

_____

5. What type of fill can you use to create a brushed metal effect?

_____

_____

6. Which tool can you use to skew objects so they appear to be receding into the distance?

_____

_____

7. Where are the settings for custom brush strokes found?

_____

_____

9

☑ Mastery Check

8. What timesaving device should you use when you need to create multiple copies of the same object?

_____

_____

9. How can you split a circle into three equal slices?

_____

_____

10. Where can you find a listing of web sites devoted to the use of Fireworks?

_____

_____

Module 10

Optimizing and Exporting Files

The Goals of This Module

- Understand the importance of file optimization
- Explore file export options
- Review appropriate file formats for use on the Web and in print
- Explore options for previewing optimized files
- Apply optimization techniques to GIF and JPEG images
- Understand the features of Export Preview and document previews
- Apply image-slicing techniques to large graphics

Module 2 teaches how images affect web design and describes some of the challenges presented by their use. In summary, images are read universally by browsers only when they are in the GIF or JPEG formats that all common browsers support. GIF images are superior when a project requires a limited range of colors, as do the simple styles found in many vector shapes and text. Photographs and vector-based images that have fine differences among colors, such as gradients, are more suitable when converted to the JPEG format.

All of the files you have created to this point have been in the Fireworks PNG format. Recognizing that converting these files to web-friendly GIFs and JPEGs would be a major component of a program designed from the ground up to create graphics for the Web, the developers at Macromedia have equipped Fireworks with a number of ways to fine-tune images so they maintain quality while achieving the smallest file sizes possible. This is no mean feat; until Fireworks came along, most designers working on graphics intended for publication to the Web had to wade through multiple complicated steps to do both. Fireworks takes all of those steps and contains them in the compact panels and dialog boxes that you are familiar with, allowing you to quickly minimize the download time of a graphic and convert it to the proper format.

In this module, in addition to learning standard methods for file optimization, you will learn a technique often used when large graphics are required on a web page, called *slicing*. When large images are sliced, they are broken into several smaller graphics that are then reassembled in an HTML table that is inserted into a web page. Before Fireworks, this was an incredibly tedious task that didn't always work out just right. With the slicing tools in Fireworks, optimizing large files so that they download as quickly as possible is a relatively painless operation.

Note

Be sure that you have downloaded the exercise files for this module from www.osborne.com or from www.dw-fw-beginners.com.

Performing Image Optimization

Optimizing and exporting Fireworks PNG files is a four-step process. Every time that you need to prepare an image for use in another program, whether for the Web or for print, you will need to complete these four tasks:

- Choose the best file format for the image based on how many colors the image contains and how you will use the image.

- Specify the optimization settings for the image by choosing the amount of file compression that most closely maintains the quality of the original image.

- Adjust the number of colors used in the image or its quality setting.

- Establish specific export options based on how you will use the graphic.

With the many ways that Fireworks modifies and applies effects to images, you cannot always assume that every vector-based image is best exported in the GIF format or that every photograph or scanned image should become a JPEG. In addition to examining how the image looks, you must decide how it will be used. GIFs, for instance, enable part of an image to be transparent so that you can blend the image more seamlessly into the background of a web page. JPEGs, on the other hand, can contain millions of colors; for those images in which you need more than the maximum 256 colors that GIFs allow, a JPEG is the appropriate choice.

For a quick look at how file formats are chosen, open two files from the exercise files for this module—*girls_text.png* and *girls_photo.png*. Both images are in the native Fireworks format and must be optimized before you export the files in a format for the Web.

Take a good look at the images on your computer and as they are represented in Figure 10-1. You'll notice on your computer that *girls_text.png*, although colorful, contains a limited number of colors, and the image overall is relatively flat—making this file suitable for the GIF format. The photograph of the girls, on the other hand, has fine differences in the amount of colors that are displayed, especially soft tones such as the girls' skin and hair colors. The photograph should be exported in a JPEG format.

In the File menu, you have two choices for optimizing and exporting your file: either the Export Wizard, which will hold your hand while you decide which file format to choose, or Export Preview, which takes you directly to the Export Preview dialog box, shown in Figure 10-2. Before moving on, take a few minutes to orient yourself to the major features of the Export Preview dialog box. The Export Wizard ultimately leads you to the Export Preview dialog box, so that option will be bypassed.

10

Figure 10-1 By closely examining the number of colors and the amount of color gradation in an image, you should be able to decide between the GIF and JPEG formats.

On the left side of the Export Preview dialog box are three tabbed panels that control the settings for file optimization—File, Options, and Animation. The options available in each of those panels are summarized here:

- The File panel is used to apply final settings for size and numeric cropping of the image. This panel is useful if you have one master graphic that you then use in different images by cropping or resizing the master graphic.

- The Options panel contains those parameters that control how the file is compressed—depending on the format—and additional choices for limiting the number of colors used in the image. Most of your optimization work will take place in this panel.

- The Animation panel contains specific information related to an animated GIF file. As Module 8 discusses, options such as the amount of time each frame in an animation plays (frame delay) and looping properties for animated files can all be adjusted.

On the right side of the Export Preview dialog box, you'll find information about the file's estimated download time and total file weight based on its optimization. You will also find controls that allow you to view different

Dither check box

Format selected

Optimization settings

Tabbed panels

Exported
file size

Estimated
download time

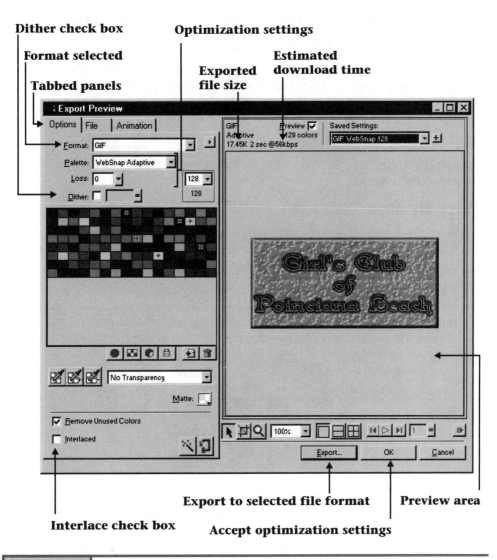

Export to selected file format

Preview area

Interlace check box

Accept optimization settings

Figure 10-2 | The Export Preview dialog box provides multiple options for controlling file sizes and quality.

optimization settings, play animations, and a preview area that shows how each file will appear as optimization settings are changed. The first project in this module explores these options.

Project 10-1: Optimizing Files with the Export Preview Feature

In this first exercise, you will work through the process of exporting an optimized file using a special dialog box called Export Preview, where you will be able to apply all of your optimization settings and see a live representation of how your image will look once converted to a GIF or JPEG format.

Fireworks' ability to accomplish optimization and export tasks so easily and consistently is part of the program's appeal for web designers and is a big reason that it has become the leading software application for designing web-specific graphics.

Step-by-Step

1. Select the *girls_text.png* image that you opened previously. Based on the number of colors in this graphic, you need to optimize it for the GIF format.

2. The primary means of optimizing a GIF file is to adjust the number of colors that are used in the graphic. Changing the color palette is a simple matter of clicking the expansion arrow and choosing a new set of colors based on the number that will be available, as you see in the following illustration. As you do this, watch the file and download sizes change above the preview area.

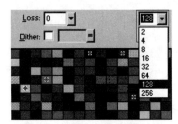

3. In this example, a small file size of 3.24K has been achieved by setting the number of colors used to only 8, but you'll notice that the quality of the image has suffered as a result. As colors are removed, effects such as bevels and textured fills lose their crisp appearance and the edges of the text become blocky.

4. Here, the quality of the image has been improved by adjusting the number of colors in the palette to 128, but the file size has grown to 11.43K as a result.

5. This is the crucial part of optimizing the file—deciding what carries more weight for you and for the goals of your site. If this graphic is one of only a few you plan to insert into an HTML page, then a larger file size with better quality should not be a problem. On the other hand, if the web page will have many similar, or larger, graphics, then you may need to sacrifice quality to gain download time. Ultimately, you must decide where the right balance is for your site's needs and choose the optimization settings that best meet them.

10

Tip

Open a web editor such as Dreamweaver and insert the image into a blank page to see the total effect of the graphic on estimated download times. Remember that Dreamweaver also tracks file sizes and displays an estimate of how long it will take a page to load in the toolbar area at the bottom of the Dreamweaver Document window.

6. The Export Preview dialog box includes the ability to change to different file formats and quickly compare file sizes. Try this now by changing the export file type to JPEG. Although the image quality improves, the file size jumps to 15.21K. Try the TIF format, which is recommended for files that will be used in desktop publishing applications, and the size balloons to 60.68K. By using the Format drop-down box, you can quickly switch between the available image formats of GIF, JPEG, BMP, PNG, or TIF and compare the results.

7. Beyond simply limiting the colors available in the GIF color palette, you can also do some fine-tuning to your image in the Export Preview dialog box. Dithering, for instance, automatically replaces one color for another so that colors outside the basic 256-color palette are simulated. Dithering will improve the look of GIFs that have more than 256 colors in their source file but will increase the file size as a result. Dithering is applied by checking the Dither check box, located near the middle of the dialog box. Once the box is checked, you can set the amount of dithering to be applied by using the slider. Try this technique now and note the effect on your image's quality and file weight.

8. Interlacing, accessed at the bottom of the panel, divides an image into component parts that download more quickly in a browser. The viewer's browser will display a low-resolution version of the graphic almost as soon as the page opens and then fill in the details as more information is received at the viewer's computer. Interlacing can be a good way to keep viewers interested in how a large image will ultimately display once the entire image is downloaded from the server. To set this option, simply check the Interlaced box. Once again, apply this setting and note how the file weight is affected.

Note

When optimizing a GIF or JPEG that has a transparent element, be sure that the Transparency options have been set. For most images with a transparent canvas or transparent elements, you will want to set this option to Index Transparency. Alpha Transparency gives you more precise options and allows you to set a transparent element within an image without affecting the transparency of the canvas. Working with transparencies carries some additional considerations, so that option will be dealt with separately in a later exercise.

9. Fireworks provides a super option that allows you to compare optimization settings in one location. At the bottom of the Export Preview panel, locate the buttons for displaying two or four versions of the same image at once. By choosing these options, you can click in each panel, change the optimization settings, and compare it with other images with different settings applied.

Figure 10-3 displays the appearance of the Export Preview dialog box when the 4-Up button has been selected.

10. At the bottom of the Export Preview dialog box, you will find two buttons that will complete the process of optimizing this image. To accept the optimization settings for this file and return to the Fireworks Document window, just click OK button. You will need to select File | Export Preview to return to the dialog box to make more adjustments, but you will be able to convert the file to its new format by choosing File | Export.

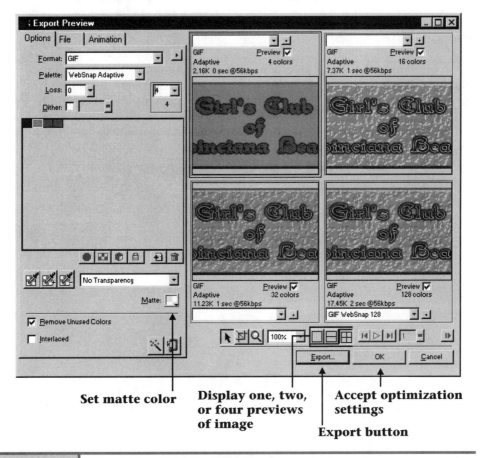

Set matte color | Display one, two, or four previews of image | Accept optimization settings

Export button

Figure 10-3 Previewing images with different optimization settings can help you to decide which best meets your needs.

11. Clicking the Export button takes you directly to the Export dialog box, shown in Figure 10-4. For a standard GIF or JPEG format, accept the file type as Images Only, browse to the location on your hard drive where you want the file to be saved, give the file a name, and click OK. You've optimized and exported a Fireworks file for the first time!

12. Remember that once you export a file, you actually have two images saved— the original Fireworks PNG format with all the original colors and the optimization settings you have chosen, and a second GIF version of the same image that has been optimized. Close *girls_text.png* and save the original file when Fireworks prompts you to do so. Saving the file preserves any optimization and export choices you have applied to the source document.

Tip

Keep your original Fireworks PNG files in folders that mirror the file structure of your web site but contain unique names that identify them as the originals, such as *png_originals*. This will make it easier to find the original when you need to make an adjustment to an optimized file.

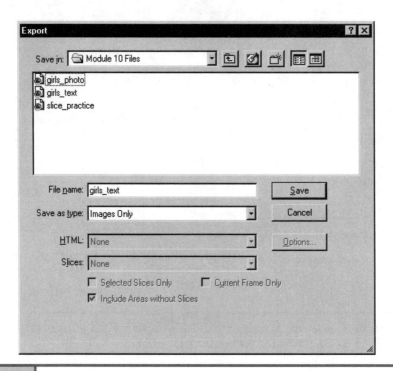

Figure 10-4 Set filenames, file types, and file locations for an exported file in the Export dialog box.

13. With the file *girls_photo.png* open, choose File | Export Preview and refer
to Figure 10-5 during the following discussion of how JPEG images are
optimized for export.

14. In the same way that the color palette is restricted for files exported in GIF
format, JPEG file optimization limits the colors available for an image. JPEGs,
however, use a setting known as Quality that removes colors through a
mathematical process. Two standard quality settings are available from the
drop-down box above the preview area: Better Quality and Smaller File. Try
both of these settings while paying close attention to the file size and image
quality that results.

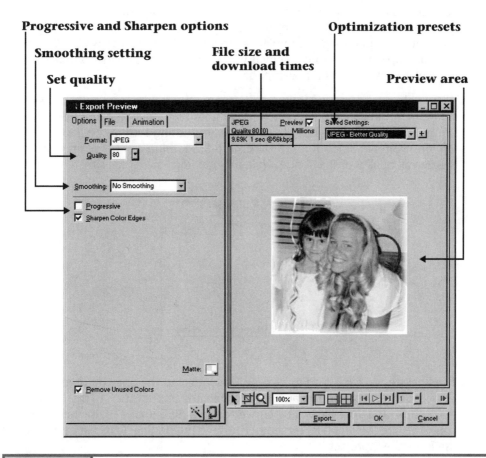

Progressive and Sharpen options

Smoothing setting

Set quality

File size and
download times

Optimization presets

Preview area

| **Figure 10-5** | Preparing files for export in the JPEG format requires setting options for file quality and smoothing. |

15. You can also fine-tune image quality settings in the Options panel by choosing the slider next to the Quality box. You probably noticed that this image gets very fuzzy when set to the Smaller File option. Instead of using the value of 60 that this preset gives you, try setting the value between 60 and 80 and see whether you can find a balance between small file sizes and image quality. Just as with GIFs, choosing between optimal download times and an acceptable image quality is a delicate balancing act.

16. Choosing the Quality setting is the primary way to optimize JPEG files, just as limiting the color palette allows you to optimize GIFs. In addition to that choice, you can also use the Progressive option, which works the way that interlacing works with GIFs—producing a low-resolution image when the page opens and then adding detail as the viewer's computer receives more information. You may also want to experiment with sharpening color edges to produce crisper images, but with a sacrifice in file size. Just as with GIFs, you can apply a matte to the canvas when you need the image to match a particular background on a web page.

17. When colors are removed from a JPEG image, the results may look "blocky" if a range of similar colors is removed. To fine-tune the image and blend similar colors together, choose one of the Smoothing settings available. Options from No Smoothing to Maximum Smoothing can help improve the overall quality of the image while maintaining smaller file sizes.

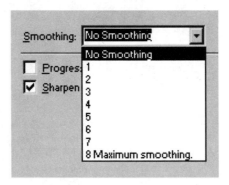

18. The final step to exporting this image is identical to the one you used in step 11. Click the Export button and set the filename and location in the Export dialog box, and your file will be converted to a JPEG image ready for use on your web site. Meanwhile, remember to save the original PNG file for further use in the next project.

Tip

If you're not sure what the correct format is for an image you are working on, Fireworks will provide assistance with the Export Wizard. Choose File | Export Wizard to open a step-by-step process that will lead you through questions about choosing the correct format and help you find ways to minimize file weight.

Project Summary

In this project, you have seen one of the most common uses of Fireworks in action—optimizing files for the smallest file weight possible. Fireworks is so efficient at this process that many people who use Photoshop actually import their artwork into Fireworks for final file optimization.

As you continue working on your files, remember that this final export process is nearly as crucial as the creation of the graphic itself. Without a program such as Fireworks to modify the output of your graphics into a format suitable for the Web, many of your viewers would never see your creations, opting instead to leave your page rather than continue to wait for an unoptimized file to download.

1-Minute Drill

- What is the first step in optimizing and exporting Fireworks PNG files?
- What is the primary method for limiting file sizes for the GIF format?
- What is the primary method for limiting file sizes for the JPEG format?

10

- The first step in optimizing and exporting Fireworks files is to choose the appropriate export file format.
- The primary method for reducing file size in a GIF format is to limit the number of colors used in the color palette.
- The primary method for reducing file size in a JPEG format is to limit the number of colors used by adjusting the Quality setting.

Working from the Document Window

Although the Export Preview option puts all the tools you need for optimizing and exporting your files in one easy-to-access location, many designers choose to take advantage of the other method for previewing, optimizing, and exporting files that Fireworks provides—working directly in the Document window itself, where optimized versions of files will display "live" while you work on the original. Access this option by using the tabs located at the top of the Document window that allow you to switch between your original image on the working canvas and a preview of the image as it will appear once it is optimized. Figure 10-6 displays a typical arrangement where the 2-Up preview tab has been selected.

One of the primary reasons to operate directly within the Document window is that you will see any changes you make to the original image automatically applied to the preview. This can be a real time-saver when you want to try out new settings or just tweak an image for either better quality or better download time. You can switch between the original and the optimized file simply by clicking in either window and looking for the black border that appears around the active window. In 2-Up preview, the original file will display on the left.

Even more previews are available when the 4-Up tab is selected. In this mode, you can set optimization for three versions of the original and can even switch between GIF and JPEG formats so that you can examine the results of your choices.

Whether you are working in the single, 2-Up, or 4-Up previews, optimization settings are available while you are working in the Document window in the Optimize panel. Locate the Optimize panel in the docked panel group and note the features shown in Figure 10-7.

Working between the previews in the Document window and the settings applied in the Optimize panel allows you to quickly apply optimization settings and go directly to the Export dialog box, bypassing the Export Preview dialog

Original image   **Active window border**   **Optimized image**

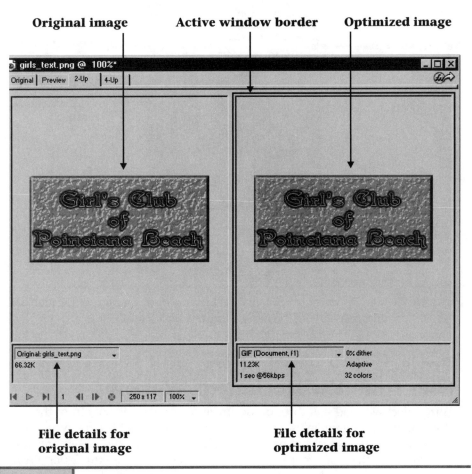

File details for   **File details for**
original image   **optimized image**

Figure 10-6 | The 2-Up preview displays original and optimized images side by side.

box entirely. You'll often find that this method works perfectly well for your needs with a particular graphic, and you may even use this as your primary means of exporting and optimizing files.

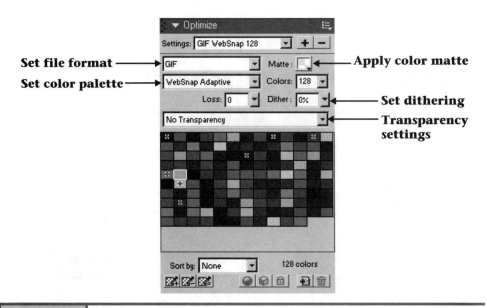

Figure 10-7	The Optimize panel contains the same optimization settings for GIF files available in the Export Preview dialog box.

Project 10-2: Optimizing and Exporting Files from the Document Window

This project will lead you through optimizing your files directly from the Document window while using the Optimize panel to set the file type and optimization settings for your document. Ultimately, your own preferences will determine whether you work in the Document window or use the Export Preview option. Regardless of which option you use, you retain complete control over the appearance of your image and the weight of the file when it is exported.

Step-by-Step

1. Open the original copy of *girls_text.png* that you used in the last project and take note of the four tabs across the top of the Document window—Original, Preview, 2-Up, and 4-Up.

2. Click the Preview tab and you will see a GIF version of this image, based on any previously saved export and optimization settings. If you completed the last project and optimized this file, you would see those settings applied in the preview. Fireworks tracks and saves all optimization settings applied to your files and, by default, returns to the settings that were last used when the file was exported.

3. In addition to a single preview, you can also see the original and the optimized version of the file in the preview called 2-Up. Click this tab and your Document window will appear as you saw in Figure 10-6.

4. Set the optimization parameters for a GIF file in the Optimize panel the same way you did when working with the Export Preview dialog box. Start by limiting the number of colors available and then fine-tune the image by using options such as dithering, transparency, and background mattes. The primary advantage here is that you can see a live preview of how the optimized file will appear as you make changes to the original. Try this now by changing the colors used in this sample image and watching as the preview displays your changes.

5. In the 4-Up preview mode, you can apply three different optimization settings and see all three displayed. Simply click anywhere in the window of the image that you want to optimize and then change the settings with the Optimize panel. By using this option, you can compare three entirely different sets of optimized images, as shown here. Take note of the information provided at the bottom of the Document window for each image where Fireworks displays the file size and estimated download time for each version of the graphic. Experiment with this method now by changing the optimization settings on the three versions of *girls_text.png*.

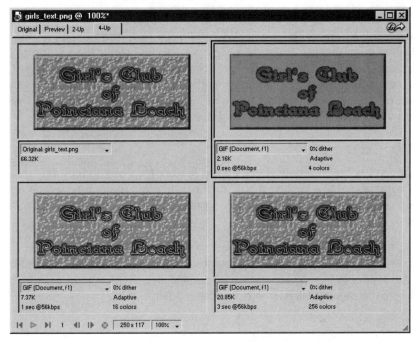

10

6. Open *girls_photo.png* now and choose the 2-Up option in the Document window. The Optimize panel changes to the JPEG options shown here.

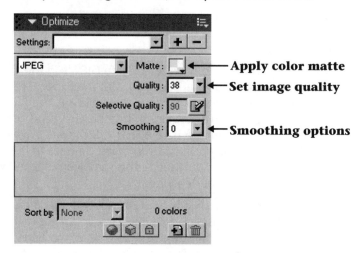

7. Just as with the Export Preview dialog box, the Quality setting for a JPEG image is the primary way to adjust the file size. The higher the Quality setting, the more colors will be used and the larger the file size will be. Adjust the Quality setting for this sample file and note how your changes affect the preview of the image.

8. Once you have optimized either a GIF or JPEG (or PNG, BMP, or TIF) file, you are ready to export the image. You could return to the Export Preview dialog box at this time, but the easiest method is to first select the version of the image that you wish to export by clicking anywhere in its window and then choose File | Export to go directly to the Export dialog box. Just as with Export Preview, set the filename and location and click OK to have Fireworks convert the file to the format you have selected.

Note

Fireworks MX contains a new Quick Export feature for sending files directly to other programs for use in special applications, such as navigation bars prepared for use in Dreamweaver. The Quick Export feature will be covered in upcoming modules.

9. To complete this project, experiment with the optimization settings for both of the sample files. You can save or discard any changes you make to these files because you will not be using them again here.

Chicago Public Library
Harold Washington - HWLC
11/26/2008 4:21:02 PM

- PATRON RECEIPT -
- CHARGES -

1: Item Number: R0179551786
    Title: Fireworks MX : a beginne
    Due Date: 12/17/2008

------ Please keep this slip ------

Project Summary

Ultimately, you will either find working directly in the Document window to be a great choice for you or will feel restricted by the smaller window size and prefer to use Export Preview. However, to really appreciate the advantages of working in this mode, try creating a new image while working in the 2-Up preview mode. Notice which effects translate well to the GIF format. Do glows, for instance, take a great deal of file size to display properly? Do they look better in a JPEG format? The real plus here is being able to try out new things in a document and then see immediately the effect they have on your image. Can you afford the additional file size and download time that the cool effect you're fond of costs you? Working in the preview mode can help you make that kind of decision and more.

Fireworks makes it possible to work in the manner most comfortable for you and allows you the most efficient workflow. If you prefer to work on a full-size canvas and preview and optimize your images at a larger size, then you will want to use the Export Preview feature. If, on the other hand, you are working on smaller graphical objects and can work in an environment where the images are smaller, then you'll want to explore optimizing your files in the Optimize panel and using the 2-Up or 4-Up panels to preview your work. Either method enables you to achieve the smallest file weight possible while maintaining image quality. The choice of which working environment to use is up to you.

1-Minute Drill

● Which Fireworks panel can you use to change file optimization settings?

● Which preview panel displays the original version next to a single optimized version of the same graphic?

● How can the preview panels assist you in choosing appropriate effects and colors for use in a graphic?

● The Optimize panel applies the same settings available in the Export Preview dialog box.
● The 2-Up panel displays a copy of the original Fireworks PNG file alongside the optimized version of the graphic.
● Any work done with the original Fireworks PNG file will automatically display estimated download times in a preview panel, so this method is useful for gauging the effect a change will have on overall file size.

Slicing Large Images

There may be times when your web site requires a particularly large graphic for insertion into a web page. Perhaps you want to create an image map (which Module 11 discusses) so that hyperlinks can be embedded in a graphic. Perhaps you need a large image that simply won't have the necessary impact if set at a smaller size. Slicing, in which an image is literally cut into rectangular pieces like pieces of a puzzle and then reassembled in an HTML table, can greatly improve the download time of an image. In addition, when an image is sliced, the individual slices can have properties of their own, including different file types for export, hotspots that contain hyperlinks, and even rollovers that function inside the image. Slicing has some very sophisticated uses, and in the next project you get an introduction to how slices are created and to some special considerations when you export them.

Fireworks contains a great feature that has not been covered at this point. Guides are special layout tools that are placed on top of an image to assist you in either aligning objects or, as in this case, slicing a large graphic into smaller rectangular images. You can use these special lines, which are simply layout tools and will not become a part of the graphics in your document, for slicing images as well as for positioning objects on the canvas.

Project 10-3: Slicing Large Graphics with Guides

Guides are special layout tools that allow you to divide an image into separate areas that are then cut by Fireworks and reassembled in an HTML table for insertion into a web page. In a case such as the one presented in this project, where the image is large, this technique helps the file download quickly to the viewer's computer. Each image will download separately, which means that your viewers will begin to see portions of an image appear almost instantly rather than having to wait for the entire file to appear. Although the total download time for the image is the same, the viewer sees something happening on the page and is more likely to stay on your site and wait for the page to load rather than clicking off to some other Internet destination.

Step-by-Step

1. From the exercise files for this module, locate the file named *guides_practice.png* and open it.

2. To create a guide, you must first enable the rulers for your document, which Fireworks will place above and to the left side of your canvas. To turn rulers on, choose View | Rulers.

3. To create a guide, place your pointer anywhere within one of the ruler areas and simply click and drag to "pull" a guide away from the ruler. As your pointer moves away from the ruler, a green line will appear. This is your guide, which can now be positioned anywhere you choose on the canvas with the Pointer tool. Multiple guides can be created, but to keep this project simple, drag one horizontal guide and one vertical guide onto the canvas and position them so they intersect near the center of the image. When you are finished, your image with its two guides should appear as you see here.

Rulers

Vertical guide   Horizontal guide

4. With just these two simple guides, you can now create four separate documents that Fireworks will put into an HTML document, which in turn can be inserted into a web page. To begin the process, choose File | Export Preview. As you would do with any image, adjust the optimization settings for the image and preview your optimized settings. When you are satisfied that you have achieved the correct balance between file weight and image quality, click the Export button.

5. The Export dialog box is where all the real action for a sliced image takes place. As you can see here, there are a number of settings that are different from those you used with the GIF and JPEG images exported previously.

File name and file extension

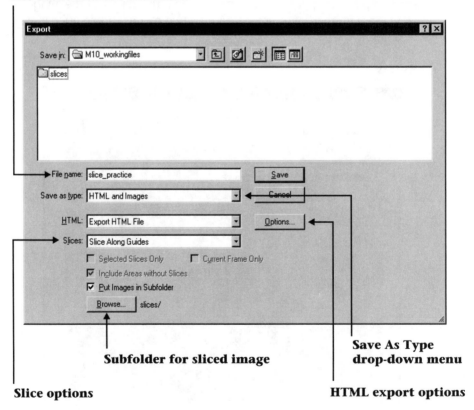

Subfolder for sliced image

Save As Type drop-down menu

Slice options

HTML export options

Tip

Although this image displays the Export dialog box in Windows, the options available for Macintosh users are the same.

6. Fireworks is about to create an HTML table that will hold the four rectangular pieces of the image together. Just a few years ago, designers had to do this by hand, but Fireworks makes the process simple as long as you get the export settings correct. Start by using the Save As Type drop-down box to change from Images Only to HTML and Images.

7. In the HTML options, choose Export HTML File so that Fireworks will automatically create the table to hold the images and save them to your hard drive. Alternately, for an image like this that does not contain any web objects, you could choose to export only the images and rebuild the graphic by placing the separate image files into a table you build in your HTML editor yourself.

8. Finally, in the Slices area, use the setting Slice Along Guides so that Fireworks will use the guides you placed on the image to slice it into separate rectangles. Your file is almost ready for export now.

9. With image slices, managing the files that are created is a prime consideration. In this simple exercise, you will be creating five separate documents—the four pieces of the original image plus the HTML file that holds the image together. Although five files may not seem like a large number to deal with, it is best to create a new subfolder to hold the images in one place. Fireworks will automatically name the five files for you (unless you choose to do it manually), and having them in a separate subfolder will make them easier to find and modify later on. Create a new subfolder called *slices* by using your computer's system tools for creating folders.

10

Note

You must be careful at this point to scrupulously follow the file-naming guidelines for the Web—use only lowercase letters and do not use spaces in your file or folder names. In this case, the name *slices* has been used, but in actual practice, use a subfolder name that identifies the file and its use.

10. Use the Browse button to locate the folder you just created and select it as the location for saving your images. Once this is done, click the Save button, and Fireworks will generate the files for you. If you check your files, you will see that one HTML file and four image files have been created from the one image. You are now ready to insert the image into a web page.

slice_practic...   slice_practic...   slice_practic...   slice_practic...

Note

Dreamweaver and Fireworks are built to work together, so you will find a button in the Objects panel of Dreamweaver (Insert panel in Dreamweaver MX) that will allow you to insert the HTML file created during the export process directly into a web page. Not only does this make the insertion of a large image like this much easier, but you can also select the table created by Fireworks while working in Dreamweaver, launch Fireworks automatically, revise your image, and have Dreamweaver automatically update the image in your web page. This is just one example of how well the two programs work together.

11. To insert the HTML file, browse to the subfolder where you stored it with the image slices in steps 9 and 10. Remember, the HTML file is what needs to be inserted, not the images. Select the file and click OK to insert it into your practice web page. Almost magically, the image is reassembled and appears in your page as if it had never been cut apart. Preview the completed image in a browser and you'll be able to see for yourself how efficiently Fireworks has accomplished the task of slicing and reassembling this image.

Project Summary

Image slicing is a great tool for dealing with large images and improving the download time of a large graphic. However, because of the number of images this creates, you should think about file management before you use this technique. For now, you can save or discard the practice images you have been working on, as you conclude this project.

1-Minute Drill

- What objects must be visible in the Document window before you can create a guide?
- Which dialog box can you use for setting the options necessary to create sliced images?
- What kind of file is inserted into a web page when you use a sliced image?

Using Slices for Image Exports

Slices are powerful tools for controlling the appearance and function of your images. They are categorized as *web objects* because they are intended for use in a web page and can have special HTML and JavaScript functions attached to them. Part 2 deals with applying these functions to slices.

Slices are also useful for applying optimization settings. Fireworks enables you to apply different optimization settings to slices so that you optimize a portion of your image as a GIF file, another as a JPEG, and a third as an animated GIF. Many web designers prefer to use the procedure you are about to learn when they have large images that they need to divide into separate pieces for reassembly in an HTML table.

- To create guides, you must first make rulers visible in the Document window.
- Use the Export dialog box to instruct Fireworks to slice along guides and create an HTML table to hold the image together.
- To reassemble a sliced image, an HTML file (created when images are sliced) is inserted into a web page.

10

Project 10-4: Exporting Graphics with Selected Slices

Some people want to use Fireworks to optimize their images but prefer to build their own HTML tables to control each image's appearance once it is reassembled in Dreamweaver (or some other web-authoring software). Fireworks enables them to slice an image and export the individual slices with their own optimization settings applied.

Once again, this technique may or may not become your preferred method of working with Fireworks. This project is presented to acquaint you with the method of exporting selected slices. The final decision as to which export option you choose is left to you.

Step-by-Step

1. From the exercise files for this module, locate and open the file called *slice_practice.png*. This file is the same one you worked with in the previous exercise, but you'll be using a different export and optimization technique here.

2. You can place slices on a Fireworks canvas in one of two ways—either by inserting them over an existing object or by drawing them with the Slice tool. In this case, because of the complexity of the image, drawing the slices manually is the best choice. Locate the Slice tool in the Tools panel and begin in the upper right-hand corner of the image, drawing a slice that covers the "For Visitors" button and extending about halfway to the top of the boat. This illustration shows how your first slice should appear.

3. When you draw slices on a canvas, a green overlay appears, the slice is labeled with its optimization setting, and a small behavior target appears in the center of the slice, as you see in the illustration. These objects are layout tools placed over the image for your use and will not appear in the

completed image. In fact, you can turn off the view of the slices altogether by clicking the Hide Hotspots and Slices button in the Tools panel, seen here.

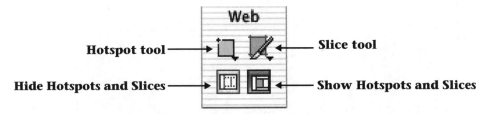

Note

Hotspots are another kind of web object that can be used to add interactive elements to an image, but they do not divide the image in the way that a slice does.

4. Fireworks MX has improved the creation of slices by making it easier to snap these objects together as you draw them. Draw two more slices now by selecting the Slice tool and drawing a slice over the second and third buttons on the top row, noting how the slice edges snap to each other and to the red slice guides that appear over the top of your image. If you do not see the slice guides, be sure this option is selected by choosing View | Slice Guides and looking for the check mark that indicates the option is selected.

5. The trick to making effective use of slices is to lay these objects out carefully on your document. In Figure 10-8, you see a fully sliced image. Note that the slices are neatly placed over the top of the image and that only single slice guides appear—indicating that the slices are properly joined to each other and that no small slices are left behind.

6. One of the most useful benefits of slicing an image like this is Fireworks' capability to apply different optimization settings for each slice. Note in Figure 10-8 that the slices for the areas of the image containing the buttons have been optimized in the GIF format, and the areas of the image containing the photographs have been set to the JPEG file type. This powerful Fireworks feature gives you the ultimate in flexibility in optimizing complex images.

7. Now that this image has been sliced, it could be exported in the same manner you used in the previous exercise, by choosing File | Export and saving the file as an HTML file with its supporting images. To see a different approach, right-click (CTRL-click on the Macintosh) one of the slices and note the option to export the selected slice at the top of the menu that appears. Select that option now.

10

Optimization settings   Slice Guides

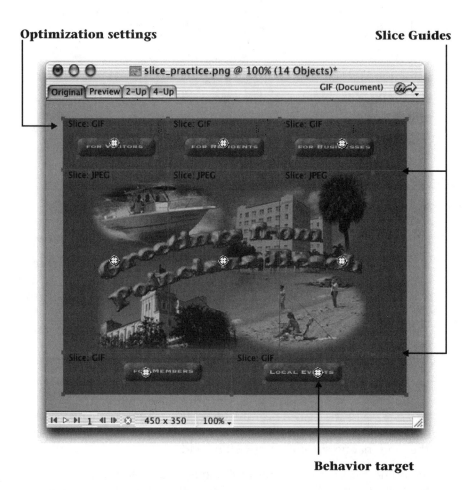

Behavior target

Figure 10-8 Success with slicing an image for use in a web page begins with the careful positioning of the slice objects.

8. Fireworks will present the same Export dialog box that you have seen previously, with a small twist. The basic filename will have additional information added; in this case an "r1_c1" has been appended to the file name, indicating that this is the upper right slice in the image—Row 1, Column 1. You can accept this default filename or change it to one of your own. Figure 10-9 shows you the appearance of the Export dialog box when slices have been selected for export.

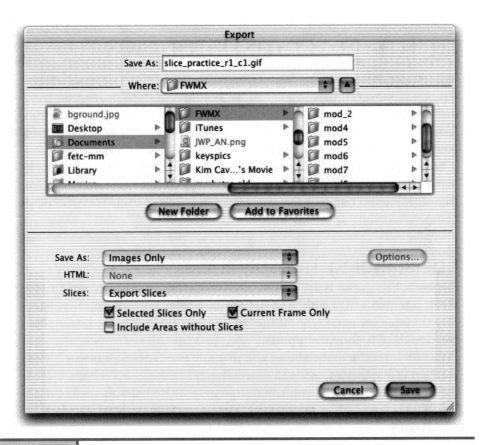

Figure 10-9   When you export slices, Fireworks names the file based on its position on the canvas.

9. You can continue to export the remainder of your slices to get comfortable with this process. Note that when the Images Only option is selected, you will not be able to export to subfolders automatically.

Project Summary

Although this method lacks some of the automatic features you have worked with before, many web professionals prefer this method of exporting larger images because it gives the designer ultimate control over the entire process, from optimizing slices individually to naming sliced graphics to finally building the HTML table that will hold the slices together. If this workflow seems more appropriate to you, then slicing and exporting selected slices may be your best choice for preparing images for insertion into web pages.

10

About Image Transparencies

All computer graphics are, by definition, contained within a rectangular box. If that is true, how is it that you see so many round buttons or irregularly shaped images on the Web? The effect is achieved either by creating a graphic with a canvas color that matches the page background or by using transparent backgrounds that make the image appear to float above the page.

The concept seems simple enough but, in practice, applying transparent backgrounds can be a very frustrating experience because of the irregularities that often occur. This section will give you a brief overview of using transparencies and some tips on how to use them.

Understanding Transparencies

Transparent backgrounds are only supported by the GIF format, and any image that you want to display without a background color must be optimized and exported in that format. Right off the bat, this fact limits you to the number of colors that the GIF format supports.

The GIF format actually allows you to apply two types of transparencies: an index transparency or an alpha transparency.

In *index transparencies*, you can designate a single color as the color that will not appear when the image is exported. This is the proper format to use with GIFs.

Alpha transparencies, on the other hand, allow one color to appear transparent while others may appear as semitransparent. Alpha transparencies allow for greater control of the image's transparent areas, but they are only supported by the Portable Network Graphics (PNG) file format—a format that is still not widely supported by web browsers.

Practical Considerations When Working with Transparencies

If transparencies are limited, how is it that so many web pages are able to achieve the effect seamlessly?

The key to applying transparencies lies in the planning that goes into the entire design process. Whenever possible, the best approach is to know the precise color that will be used as the web page's background and then choose that as the color to be transparent. By setting the precise matte color in the Export Preview dialog box or the Optimize panel, you will achieve optimal results.

In some cases, such as those in which the page has a patterned background, the choice is not so clear. In those situations, you will often be forced to strike a balance between colors to come up with the best compromise. If, for instance, your page background has a gray and white background, then choosing a matte color somewhere between the two may give you the best results. It would be great to give you concrete advice in this area, but the simple truth is that applying transparencies involves trial and error. In many cases, the simplest approach is the best—merely set your graphic's canvas color to match the page color and leave transparencies out of the equation altogether.

Tip

For an excellent tutorial on transparencies and color theory, visit Thomas Niemann's web site at www.epaperpress.com/fireworks.

What to Take Away

Optimizing and exporting graphics files is a key component of Fireworks, and as software that was designed as a web-specific graphics tool, it contains a huge number of options for creating files that download as quickly as possible while maintaining image quality. This optimization is always necessary for images that are exported for use in other applications and is especially true when working with images for the Web.

Through either the Export Preview dialog box or the preview tabs in the Document window, you now know how to prepare both GIF and JPEG images for export. You know how to limit the number of colors they use and to adjust other settings that affect the quality and download time of the graphic. In addition, you have seen how large images can be sliced automatically into separate pieces that Fireworks and Dreamweaver reassemble into a web page. The variety of drawing and composing tools that Fireworks includes, coupled with its many file-optimization options, makes it easy to see why this program has become a favorite of web designers all over the world.

10

☑ *Mastery Check*

1. What is your primary goal when optimizing Fireworks PNG files?

_____

_____

2. What is your primary goal when exporting Fireworks PNG files?

_____

_____

3. What two methods does Fireworks provide for viewing and adjusting optimization settings?

_____

_____

4. Describe an image that is best exported in the GIF format.

_____

_____

5. Describe an image that is best exported in the JPEG format.

_____

_____

6. How does the number of colors present in an image affect file size? How can you apply this in file optimization?

_____

_____

7. How can you use guides to slice an image into smaller pieces?

_____

_____

☑ *Mastery Check*

8. How does Fireworks append filenames when slices are exported?

_____

_____

9. What common file format used on the Web supports transparencies?

_____

_____

10. What two types of transparency formats can you apply to a
computer graphic?

_____

_____

10

Part 2

Fireworks MX
and the
World Wide Web

Module 11

Creating Image Maps and Buttons

The Goals of This Module

- Understand the use of web objects
- Apply hotspots to an image to create an image map
- Use slices for attaching behaviors to images
- Understand the function of the Button Editor
- Create buttons for use in a web page
- Understand how to preview interactive images in a web browser
- Understand how to edit button instances
- Explore the uses of the URL panel
- Understand the methods used for exporting interactive images

Throughout the course of this book, you have heard the almost mantra-like statement over and over: "Fireworks MX is a web graphics production tool, Fireworks MX is a web graphics production tool." You might be a little tired of hearing that statement, but Fireworks' capability to create graphics for use on the Web is what the program is all about. In this module, you'll begin working with the tools that enable Fireworks to accomplish its basic mission—creating images designed for the Web. Although many of the graphics you've produced up to this point have been web-ready due to the outstanding file-optimization features found in Fireworks, the focus has been primarily on creative tools. This section of the book discusses how to transform those images into interactive elements for the Web by adding links to web pages, by creating image effects to help viewers navigate your site, and by adding additional features that enhance the effectiveness of your web presence.

As companion products, Dreamweaver and Fireworks work together seamlessly to make the use of interactive images possible. New product features in both programs have further extended what was already an excellent working relationship; with both Fireworks MX and Dreamweaver MX at your disposal, you have a powerful combination of tools for creating engaging and sophisticated content for your site. Even if you don't have the latest version of Dreamweaver, or you use another method for generating your web pages, you'll find that the new features built into Fireworks MX make working with images intended for the Web a fabulous experience.

Understanding Web Objects

Recall from Module 6 that Fireworks refers to interactive areas defined above an image as *web objects* and displays the location of the objects in a special layer all their own. Web objects are simply special instructions written either in HTML or JavaScript that add interactivity to an image or, as you saw in Module 10, enable an image to be sliced into separate regions for reassembly into an HTML table. You will work with two types of web objects in Fireworks.

Hotspots

As the name implies, *hotspots* are special areas that are added above an image that make a defined region clickable when viewed in a browser. With hotspots you can create an *image map*—an image that contains many areas that a viewer can click on to be taken to an assigned URL or to generate special effects such as displaying a message in the status bar of the viewer's browser. Hotspots are simple to use because they are limited in their scope and do not change the basic construction of the image. They are simply special coding that lies on top of an image and provides an area for assigning JavaScript behaviors.

Slices

The term *slice* is also fairly self-explanatory. Slices are regions to which behaviors can be attached. Unlike hotspots, however, slices break an image into different areas like pieces of a puzzle. Slices are the more robust of the two web objects because, in addition to enabling the functions that hotspots perform, they can serve as tools for optimizing and exporting files. You can even use them to construct entire navigation bars and you may employ them to trigger an image on one part of the canvas to display a second image in another slice. You'll find as you work in Fireworks that using slices for creating interactive images will be a large part of your workflow.

Fireworks' Web Object Tools

Fireworks provides the tools for working with web objects in the same thoughtful ways that you have already seen when working with its graphics creation tools. Access the web tools you need for creating interactive images primarily in the Web area of the Tools panel, as seen here in both the Windows and Macintosh versions. You may also wish to refer to Table 1-4 back in Module 1 for an overview of these tools.

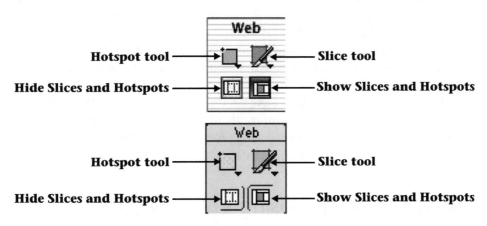

You can make hotspots in rectangular, round, or irregular shapes through the Tools panel by accessing the different tool options available from the flyout menu. Just like the other drawing tools, these options enable you to draw a hotspot directly above the canvas.

Slices also contain an option for creating varied shapes by choosing the Polygon slice option from the flyout menu for that tool. Note that you cannot create slices in a round shape.

In addition to drawing slices or hotspots, you can add these objects to your images by inserting them directly above a selected object. You may find this option especially useful when you want to ensure that an object is completely covered without any overlap. To use this feature, select the graphic or text where you want to create the web object, choose Edit | Insert and choose either Hotspot or Slice from the options presented. Note that when a slice is inserted using this technique, it will only be created in a rectangular shape, whereas hotspots will be drawn to conform exactly to the shape and size of the object below them when they are inserted.

As you create hotspots or slices on top of an image, Fireworks provides a visual reference for the web object's size, shape, and location. By default, hotspots are defined with a light blue overlay, and slices are displayed in green. When you don't want to be distracted by these overlays, use the button on the Tools panel that enables you to hide them from view. When you need to work with them again, simply click the same button and the overlays will become visible again. These overlays will not appear when your image is exported, when you view it through the preview tabs in the Document window, or when you preview it in a browser. They exist only as a visual reference of the code that Fireworks uses to create slices and hotspots.

Finally, you can move or resize both hotspots and slices by using the Pointer tool to grab the selection handle to resize the object or by clicking and dragging to move the object into a new location. Fireworks will display the name of a selected slice and display a symbol that enables behaviors to be attached to both types of web objects. Figure 11-1 displays both a hotspot and a slice and provides labels for these modification tools. Take a moment to acquaint yourself with their location and use as you prepare to utilize them in upcoming exercises. In addition to observing these basic tools, notice that Fireworks provides slice guides that define how the HTML table will be created when the file is exported.

Considerations for Using Image Maps

All images add file weight to a web page, so using images as interactive elements is not a decision you should make lightly. If, for instance, you find that your page can be visually appealing and easy to navigate through the use of simple HTML links, or even HTML links formatted with Cascading Style Sheets (CSS),

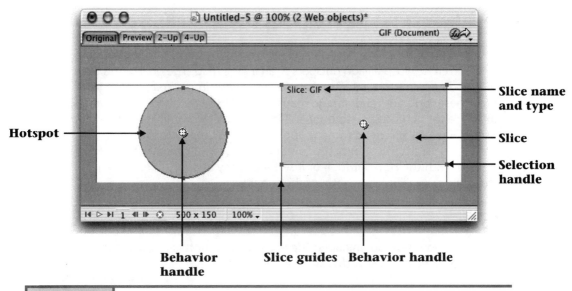

Hotspot

Slice name and type

Slice

Selection handle

Behavior handle

Slice guides   Behavior handle

Figure 11-1   Hotspots and slices both contain special labels and modification tools for altering their size, location, and function.

then you may be better off using a method with less impact on download time. As always, web designers must find a delicate balance between providing engaging visual content and creating pages that load quickly.

In addition to considering file weight and download times, it is important to realize that the use of images in place of standard HTML has an impact in other aspects of web design as well. Search engines will primarily look for textual references on a page and, when faced with an interface almost entirely composed of images, may fail to index your pages as you might wish.

Accessibility is also affected by the use of images for navigational elements. If your page is accessed by people who are visually impaired and use special devices to navigate the Web, they may have difficulty finding their way around your site. The federal government of the United States requires that all sites posted by government agencies be fully accessible, and many other local and national governments have issued similar mandates. As you delve into all the possibilities that image maps and interactive images provide, keep in mind that, at the very least, you should plan for alternative text-based navigation features on your site and be sure to provide alternate textual references for images as you are including these objects.

11

Project 11-1: Creating Image Maps with Hotspots

In this exercise, you will add hotspots to an image map. The goal of this exercise is to introduce you to the interface for creating a basic image map and so you can see how these tools are used. Image maps are fairly simple objects to create; the interface for getting the job done in Fireworks is uncomplicated but incredibly useful when all you need to do is apply links to defined areas of an image.

To create a hotspot over the top of an image you can either draw the hotspot with the Hotspot tool, or insert it directly above a selected object on the canvas. You'll explore both methods here.

Note

Be sure that you have downloaded the exercise files for this module either from www.osborne.com or www.dw-fw-beginners.com.

Step-by-Step

1. Start by opening the Fireworks PNG file named *pbresort_main.png* from the exercise files for this module. Alternatively, if you'd like additional practice, create your own file and use the images provided for Module 6 to prepare an image similar to the one you see in Figure 11-2. Take a minute to open the Layers panel and investigate how this image has been composed.

2. Begin by selecting the Hotspot tool and drawing a rectangular hotspot above the text "Information" that you find in the Navigation bar. Draw additional rectangular hotspots above the words "Rooms and rates," "Facilities," and "Attractions." As you see in Figure 11-2, Fireworks applies an overlay over this part of the canvas as you add hotspots to the image.

3. For the final text link, select the text "Contact" with the Pointer tool and choose Edit | Insert | Hotspot. Notice that when this hotspot is created, it is much smaller than those you drew with the Hotspot tool but conforms neatly to the selected text. For constraining hotspots to the smallest possible size, this method is often preferable to manually drawing these web objects.

4. Web objects that you create are organized into their own special layer in the Layers panel. Each of the hotspots you have created are stored in the panel, making this a very handy tool to use when you need to select individual web objects in a complicated graphic. Take a moment to note how web objects

Figure 11-2 Fireworks applies an overlay to an image as hotspots are created.

are organized in the Web layer by opening that panel and examining the order in which the objects are listed.

5. To create a circular hotspot, choose the Circle Hotspot tool by clicking and holding down your mouse pointer over the Hotspot button in the Tools panel. Select the Circular Hotspot tool and draw this new type of object above the picture in the image's upper left-hand corner. Notice that you can draw circular hotspots only as circles and not as irregular ellipses.

6. To draw an irregularly shaped hotspot, choose the Polygon Hotspot tool from the options in the Tools panel. Use this much in the way that you would the Pen tool or Polygon Lasso tool: Click and release repeatedly around an area you want to define as a hotspot. As you stitch this object together, be sure to complete the shape by clicking on the first point you defined to close things up. Try this by stitching an irregular hotspot around the picture of the cabin in the lower left-hand portion of the image.

7. Now that your hotspots are in place, you can begin attaching links and behaviors to these web objects. Just as with other items you've defined in the past, the Property Inspector lists information for individual hotspots. To create your first link, select the hotpot above the word "Information" by using the Pointer tool (or selecting it in the Layers panel) and note the appearance of the Property Inspector, shown here.

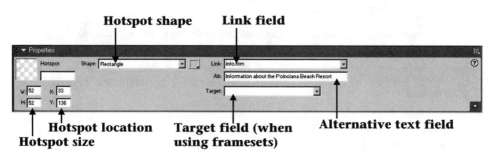

Hotspot shape   **Link field**

Hotspot location   **Target field (when**   **Alternative text field**
Hotspot size   **using framesets)**

8. In this case, to attach a link that will be in the same folder as the page where this image will be displayed, simply type the name of the HTML file. You'll be looking at more advanced methods for obtaining this information in later projects, but for now type **info.htm** into the Link field.

9. Alternative text will display in a web page even if the viewer has turned off the capability to view images. More importantly, it will appear if the image itself fails to load or if the viewer is visually impaired and is using an assistive device to see your pages. Any time you are using images as navigation elements, it is important to enter this alternative text information. In this case, type **Information about the Poinciana Beach Resort** into the Alt field of the Property Inspector.

Tip

Many browsers will also display this alternative text in a box that appears on users' screens when they float their mouse pointers over the hotspot. Although this is not a foolproof method for adding tool tips, it does work in many modern browsers.

---

10. Complete this exercise by adding URLs in the Link field and alternative text for each hotspot in the image by creating your own link and alternative text. These links won't really function, so the name you give them isn't important. What is important is that you name them properly, adding the .htm or .html file extension to the URL.

Project Summary

In this exercise, you have seen how to create the simplest web object of all, the hotspot. No additional behaviors have been assigned to these new objects, so they will perform only one function—provide a link to a separate file within your web site or to another destination on the World Wide Web. Even though they are simple links in this case, Fireworks makes the creation of this type of interactive image very simple, and you may find yourself returning to the Hotspot tool in the future when all you need is to attach a link to an image.

1-Minute Drill:

● What shapes can hotspots be?

● What two methods can you use for inserting hotspots and slices into a document?

● Where is URL information added to create links with hotspots or slices?

Previewing Interactive Images in a Web Browser

11

As you build interactive images, one of the essential steps will be previewing the image in a web browser. You can still use the Preview tab directly in the

---

● Hotspots may be created either as rectangles or as circles, or you may use the Polygon Hotspot tool to create them in irregular shapes.
● Hotspots and slices can be drawn over an image with the hotspot and slice drawing tools found in the Tools panel, or they can be inserted directly above a selected object by choosing Edit | Insert and selecting Hotspot or Slice from the options presented.
● URL information is entered in the Link field of the Property Inspector.

Document window to check the appearance of your interactive graphics, but only a browser gives you a true indication of how it will both appear and function once you've included the image in a web page.

Fireworks makes checking your images in a browser quite simple. Right out of the box, the program will determine which program is set as the default browser for your computer and will display your image by choosing File | Preview in Browser and selecting the name of your primary browser. For an even quicker look, simply press F12, and your browser will load a temporary file that Fireworks generates. You should use one of these methods to test each image's functionality whenever you create interactive images.

You can also add browsers to the list of programs that you can use for testing your image maps. Select File | Preview in Browser | Set Primary Browser to choose which program will open when you press F12, and set browsers other than your default program by choosing File | Preview in Browser | Set Secondary Browser. Once you have designated these browsers, you will be able to check in multiple browser programs—a real necessity in the world of web design, where a page or a graphic may appear decidedly different when viewed in Netscape Navigator or Internet Explorer.

Note

In the Windows operating system, you can only have one version of Internet Explorer installed at one time. Netscape enables you to install multiple versions, and on my PC I regularly test in the latest version of Internet Explorer and both Netscape versions 4.7 and 6.2.

Project 11-2: Creating Rollover Effects with Slices

One of the most common visual effects used in conjunction with links on web pages is the *rollover*. When you create a rollover, one image on the page is replaced by another when the viewer passes a mouse over the graphic. This type of effect is everywhere you look on the Web, and it adds an important visual clue to a viewer that an image is a link to another page. If you think of any button or link that you've seen on a page that changed when your mouse passed over it, then you have seen a rollover in action.

In Fireworks, there are any number of ways to create this effect, including some that you'll explore in more detail as you do future exercises. In this example, you will use a slice to create a rollover on a navigation bar that changes the appearance of a text object in one frame by replacing it with a text object in a second frame. This effect is being created manually here, but you could just as easily create this effect with the Button Editor as you'll learn to do in the next project of this module.

Step-by-Step

1. From the exercise files for this module, open the file called *slice_practice.png*. Much of the work that you would normally do to create an image such as this has been done for you, including the creation of the button graphics and the initial text labels for the buttons.

2. Organizing the image itself is an important consideration for creating a rollover. In this case, open the Layers panel and note that there are two layers present, labeled *text* and *buttons*. When you create your own rollovers, a little advance planning and organization will greatly assist you. The goal is to replace only the text when the viewer rolls over the hotspot, so the button graphics are on their own layer, and need not change. Open the Layers panel and examine how the objects in this image have been organized.

3. To maintain the look of the button, you must designate the layer where these graphics are found as one that will be shared across frames. To do this, select the buttons layer by clicking its name in the Layers panel and open the options for the Layers panel. Locate the option labeled Share This Layer, as you see here, and select it. Sharing a layer in this way ensures that the images on this layer will not change as the rollover takes place. With that bit of housekeeping out of the way, it's time to actually create the rollover effect itself.

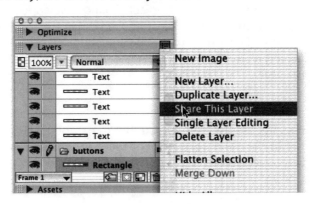

4. The images that will be exchanged to create the rollover effect will be organized onto two different frames using the Frames panel. With the Pointer, select all of the text on the text layer and copy the objects by selecting Edit | Copy.

5. New frames can be created easily by locating and clicking the New/Duplicate Frame button at the bottom of the Frames panel, illustrated here. Click this button to add one new frame at this time.

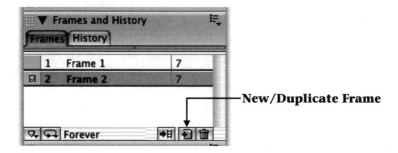

New/Duplicate Frame

6. The text that you copied earlier is now ready to be placed onto this new frame. Select Frame 2 in the Frames panel and choose Edit I Paste to drop a copy of the text onto the button graphics. Remember: The buttons are n a shared layer, so they will appear in every frame of this image.

7. When a rollover is created, the images on Frame 1 will be replaced by those found on Frame 2. In order for the viewer to see the effect, you will need to change the objects on the second frame. You'll note as you look at the example file on your computer that the color of the text on Frame 2 has been changed to white, but you can make any change you would like to these objects, including adding glow effects, shadows, or even changing the font or the location of the text object. Change the appearance of all your text objects at this time by selecting Frame 2 in the Frames panel and modifying the text. Remember that you can change all of the objects at once by selecting all the text objects and changing their attributes in the Property Inspector.

Tip

The choice of what effect to use is up to you, but remember: a little goes a long way when it comes to the use of rollovers. You want to provide viewers with a visual cue that the button is a link, not assault and distract them with movement and flashing graphics.

8. The final steps for creating your rollovers involve inserting the slices and attaching the behavior. Start by selecting the buttons and inserting the slice above each by selecting Edit I Insert I Slice. In a situation such as this, when you want to precisely control the location and size of the web object, inserting the slice will give you better results than drawing one with the Slice tool.

9. To complete the rollover, you need only attach the behavior to the slice and let Fireworks do the work of generating the JavaScript that makes the effect happen. Locate the Behavior handle, represented by a small white target-shaped symbol in the center of the slice. As you see here, selecting the Behavior handle causes a pop-up window to appear. Select Simple Rollover Behavior from the options presented, and your first rollover image will be complete.

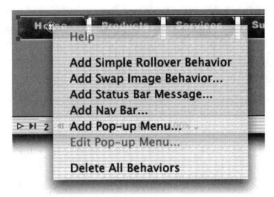

10. Press F12 to preview this image in your primary browser, and you will see that the text objects on Frame 1 in your image are now swapped with the text objects on Frame 2. Notice also that the button images themselves remain intact as the rollover effect takes place.

11. To finish up, return to the Fireworks file and select each slice, applying a link by entering a filename in the Link field of the Property Inspector and alternative text in the Alt field. Your work on this document is now done.

Project Summary

You have seen just one of the ways that slice objects can spice up the visual appeal of your web page. Rollovers may be one of the most common visual effects found on the Web, but creating them only became truly easy when Fireworks was introduced. This project shows how to make simple objects more interesting through some careful planning and the use of the tools that Fireworks provides.

11

1-Minute Drill:

- What method for previewing images gives the best indication of how they will appear and function on the Web?

- Define the term rollover.
- What type of web object is required to use the simple rollover behavior?

File Formats and Interactive Images

New users of Fireworks are often confused about how to optimize interactive images for use on the Web. It's easy to make the mistake of assuming that images that contain more than one frame should be designated as animated GIFs and exported in that format.

Doing so will produce some highly unusual results though. The rollover effect that you created in the last exercise is triggered by a JavaScript behavior, so the images themselves should be optimized in either the standard GIF or JPEG format. As you saw in Module 10, once you apply a slice over an object, you can set its optimization in the Optimize panel, a very handy shortcut when using slices that are present to control and trigger behaviors.

For the exercise that you just completed, a quick trip to the Optimize panel to set the number of colors to use in a GIF format would be the appropriate choice. Just as with other optimization choices, deciding which file format to use requires an examination of the image itself to determine which format is most appropriate. For images such as those found in the last project, in which limited colors are being used, the GIF format is the correct choice to make. If, however, your image includes a photograph or gradients with subtle shifts in tone and color, then the JPEG format would be appropriate. The actual image effect is created through the code generated during export (which you'll learn to do in the last project in this module), so you optimize interactive images the same way you do standard graphics.

- Previewing in a web browser gives the best indication of how an image will look and how the JavaScript behaviors will function when an interactive image is seen on the Web.
- When a rollover is created, one image is replaced by another when the viewer passes a mouse over a trigger on the page.
- Simple rollover behaviors can only be attached to slices.

Project 11-3: Using the Button Editor

In the last project, you saw how to use slices and frames in conjunction to create simple rollovers. Fireworks certainly makes this easier than building the images by hand and coding them separately, but the method described in Project 11-2 still requires a fair amount of planning and setup.

Fireworks makes it possible for you to do much of this work in an easier manner by using a special editor that combines the automatic placement of slices with separate panels that let you preview how the button will appear when the viewer passes a mouse over it. In addition, with the Button Editor, you can decide how a button will appear when the viewer clicks on it and can provide up to four different looks for an individual button. You will learn how the appearance of buttons is defined by the use of button *states* in the next project.

The Button Editor gives you the greatest amount of control over the appearance of a button and provides an easy-to-use format for making your buttons come to life. In addition, in Fireworks MX, buttons that you create as Symbols are now easier to edit, making the process of using this important design tool even more effective.

Step-by-Step

1. Start this exercise by creating a new Fireworks document with a size of 500 pixels by 50 pixels. Set the canvas to white and save the file as *buttons_practice.png.*

2. To open the Button Editor, select Edit | Insert | New Button.

3. Once you have done so, a new window will appear in which all of your work for creating this button will be done. Take a few moments to familiarize yourself with the features of the Button Editor by referring to Figure 11-3.

4. The Button Editor uses a series of tabs across the top of the window enabling you to access separate canvases where you define the appearance of the button based on how a viewer will interact with it. For the definition of these buttons states, refer to the instructions at the bottom of each panel and to this list:

   ● **Up**   The appearance of a button when it is first loaded into a web page.

   ● **Over**   The appearance of the button when a viewer passes over it with the mouse pointer.

11

Button states   **Set slice location and size**

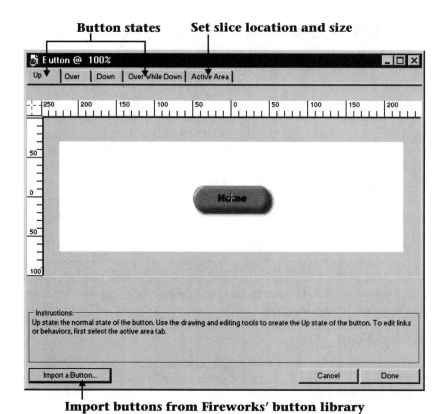

Import buttons from Fireworks' button library

Figure 11-3   The Button Editor provides an easy-to-use format for quickly designing button Symbols.

- **Down**   Used when a navigation bar is designed to display a button as it might look if it were pressed down. This button state can be used to help viewers orient themselves to their location within your web site.

- **Over While Down**   When a button displays in the Down state, you can still change its appearance by using this option. A button already displaying its down appearance can change again when a viewer passes a mouse over it.

5. Using the standard drawing tools, create a button in the Button Editor and apply a bevel to the button. You have complete control over how objects appear in the Button Editor, but, for the purposes of this exercise, refer to Figure 11-3 and create a basic shape. In the Effects area of the Property Inspector, apply a bevel to the object. Add the word **Home** to your button

after the shape has been created and centered on the crosshair in the middle of the canvas.

6. Switching to the next canvas in the Button Editor is as easy as choosing the Over tab at the top of the window. You will find yourself with a new blank canvas, with the added button at the bottom of the panel, thus enabling you to automatically copy the button you created on the Up canvas onto this new one. Locate the Copy Up Graphic button that you see displayed here, and select it to copy your first button.

7. Just as with the manual method (in which you modified the appearance of an object in Frame 2 when using the simple rollover technique), the process of defining button states requires that you make a change to the appearance of the button on the Over canvas to give your viewer a visual clue that the object is a link to another web page. Again, although you have complete freedom in modifying this image, for this exercise select the button graphic and return to the Effects area of the Property Inspector.

8. Fireworks has a number of predefined effects that you can apply to bevels to help define them as buttons. To see this in action, click on the Information icon next to the Inner Bevel listing in the Effects area of the Property Inspector, indicated by a lowercase *i* in a blue circle. The properties for the bevel will appear and can be changed at this time. Locate the options at the bottom of this pop-up window and change the Button Preset from Raised to Highlighted. The appearance of this window is shown here. When this option is selected, the button will take on a lighter appearance.

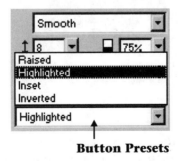

Button Presets

9. Continue on to the Down state canvas by clicking its tab in the Button Editor. As you did in the steps above, locate the button in the panel that enables you to copy the graphic from the previous canvas onto this new blank one.

11

Return to the Effects area of the Property Inspector and choose the Inset option from the Button Presets for the bevel effect. Your button will now appear as if it has been pressed in, as shown here.

Note

The check box found in the Down state window enables you to automatically cause this image to load when the page with the button is presented to the viewer of the web page. Module 12 discusses the use of this feature.

10. To finish defining the appearance of this button, switch to the Over While Down tab and copy the graphic from the Down canvas. Once again, modify the appearance of the bevel by selecting the bevel effect and using the preset to change the appearance to the Inverted setting. You are now finished with the visual part of this image.

11. The final tab in the Button Editor enables you to fine-tune the size and location of the slice that is automatically placed above the graphic. Fireworks can take only an educated guess at how this slice should be defined, so be sure to select the Active Area tab and check that the slice completely covers the button and is in the correct position. As you see here, the slice has been centered over the button and covers an area large enough to include the shadow effect. Reposition the slice the same way you've done in the past, by using the Pointer tool to position it or resize it with the selection handles.

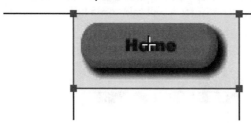

Tip

Be especially careful when using drop-shadow effects that the slice covers the button plus any areas added outside the button that include the shadow itself.

12. Your button is now done, and it's time to return to the main Document window. Locate the Done button at the bottom of the panel and select it. Once you return to the main document, you'll see, as you do in the following

illustration, that Fireworks has placed a copy (or instance)of this Symbol onto the canvas. It has the shortcut marking in the lower left-hand corner denoting its status as a Symbol. Note that a slice with the usual slice labels automatically covers the button.

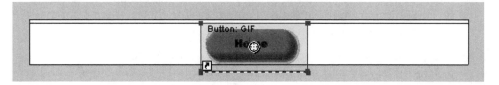

13. The button you just created is a Symbol and you will find it listed in the Library panel so that additional instances can be dragged onto the canvas. Locate the Library panel by opening the Assets group and clicking the Library tab. For this exercise, drag three additional instances of the button onto the canvas. As you drop each instance onto the canvas, you may find that positioning it with the arrow keys on your keyboard is easier. The goal is to get the Symbols as close to each other as possible without having them overlap. Overlapping slices can cause serious problems in some browsers and must be avoided.

14. As you are positioning your symbols, you should take note of the appearance of the slice guides as well, the red lines that will appear as you work with sliced objects. Once again, the key to having a successful Navigation bar with multiple buttons is to get each slice as close as possible to its neighbors without overlapping. Slice guides provide an important visual clue for getting this done. This illustration shows a document with proper positioning of sliced objects.

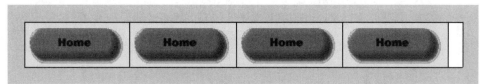

On the following canvas, the buttons are not properly aligned and have multiple slice guides visible and empty spaces between instances of the Symbol.

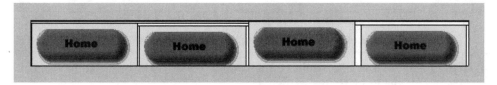

11

15. In previous versions of Fireworks, the fact that all of the buttons are labeled "Home" would have presented a problem. The label was part of the Symbol, so you could not edit or change it without changing the Symbol itself. Fireworks MX makes it possible to edit each instance of the Symbol without breaking its connection to the Symbol library for this document. Select the second button from the left and orient yourself to the appearance of the Property Inspector that you see in Figure 11-4.

16. In the Text field of the Property Inspector, change the text for this button to **Products.** As you do so, note that, although the text changes, no other properties of the button are affected. Continue in this way, changing the text for the additional buttons to **Services** and **Content.**

17. To complete this Navigation bar, you would use the same procedures for applying the links to the buttons that you have used in the past. Enter a filename for a page in your site, or a complete URL for a page outside your site, into the Text field. Add your alternative text in the Alt field, and your Navigation bar is ready to go. Preview your new Navigation bar in a browser by pressing F12.

Project Summary

In this project, you have seen how you can use the Button Editor to create symbols that can contain up to four different appearances and can interact with viewers of your web page to give them visual clues for navigating your site. You have also seen how button instances are editable even after you have created them, which is one of the great new features of Fireworks MX.

In this exercise, you have used buttons that look rather traditional, but remember that using the Button Editor does not confine you to making buttons that look like, well, buttons. Each canvas of the Button Editor is a fully functioning Fireworks canvas, so you can use this tool to create any kind of graphical object that you want to use to interact with your viewers. A good place to begin is the library of symbols that Fireworks includes. Look at the buttons that have been

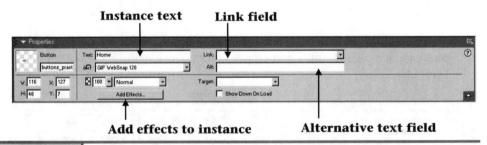

Figure 11-4   You can edit Symbol instances in Fireworks MX by using the tools in the Property Inspector.

designed there and let your imagination take those objects in entirely new directions. How your buttons appear is up to you—Fireworks merely provides the tools to enable you to put your own creativity into play.

1-Minute Drill

● What is the proper file format for an interactive image?

● What button state is displayed when a viewer's browser first loads a web page?

● Where can you find predefined bevel effects that you can use when creating buttons with beveled edges?

Using the URL Panel

Managing all of the links in your web site can often be a daunting job. Although Dreamweaver and Fireworks are excellent tools for making the work flow in your site-production more efficient, simply listing the links that you'll need to access as you create interactive images can often be a great deal of work. Luckily, Fireworks provides an additional panel that enables you to work even more efficiently by importing URLs from an existing web page for use in your images and to track all of the URLs that you add to your images.

Figure 11-5 shows the URL panel, which is organized as part of the Assets panel group. With this handy tool, links that you've used in a document can be stored in a central location for use in other Fireworks files. You can even import web pages that include links for use as a custom URL library.

Importing URLs

One of the most effective uses of this panel is to import links from a web page that you've created in Dreamweaver or another HTML editor and add the complete listing of URLs to the library. You'll find two sample files in the exercise files for this module that will enable you to practice this technique— *urls_practice.png* and *links.htm*. Follow these procedures for importing a listing of links for use in a Fireworks document.

11

● Interactive images should be set in either the standard GIF or JPEG file formats appropriate for the appearance of the image. The behaviors that are created using JavaScript are set during the final export process for the image when an HTML file is generated.

● When a web page is first loaded, the Up state of the button will be displayed.

● Predefined bevel effects are applied by accessing the bevel settings found in the Effects area of the Property Inspector.

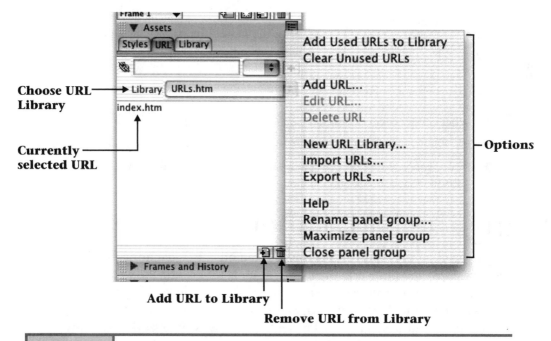

- Open the image where you want to use the links. In this case, open *urls_practice.png*. Once URLs are added to any document, they will be available to all documents through the URL panel.

- In the URL panel, click the arrow to access the panel's options. Select Import URLs. You will be able to browse to any HTML document containing links that you want to import.

- Browse to the location where you saved *links.htm* and select the file. Click Open to add the URLs in the selected document to the listing in the URL panel.

- To add a URL to a slice, you need only select the slice or hotspot where you want it applied and click the appropriate link as it is listed in the URL panel. This offers a quick and simple way to apply links, without the worry of mistyping the link into the Property Inspector.

- Practice this technique now by attaching the links in the listing to the slices in the image. Save this file, and you'll have a ready reference to the best Fireworks web sites on the Web by simply previewing the file in a browser.

About Links and URLs

In the examples so far in this module, you have seen both types of URLs that you will use when working with interactive images—*relative* URLs that link to your own files by listing their file name and extension, and *absolute* URLs that are specified by listing the full web address of the page you wish to display.

Absolute URLs are often the easiest to work with because they do not require any knowledge of the relationship of the files within a site. Simply type in the full address, such as http://www.osborne.com, and your browser will be directed to that page when the link is selected.

Note

To create a link you must include the full address, *including* the protocol (which is the *http://* that precedes the address to the page). Although it is acceptable for users of browsers to type in an abbreviated address, such as www.osborne.com, you must specify the entire address to create a link.

Relative URLs require that you know not only the name of the file you are linking to but also its location within your site structure. You'll learn some new tips for managing this issue when you explore the integration with Dreamweaver in Module 13, but you should also have a working understanding of the way that relative URLs are written. Figure 11-6 displays a simplified web site structure to help you understand how relative URLs are created.

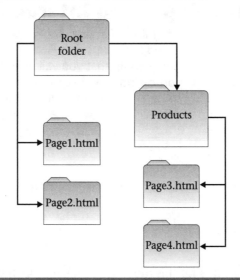

11

Figure 11-6 Using relative URLs requires that you understand the structure of your site and the folders and subfolders it contains.

When a link is created between two files within the same folder, you need only list the filename. To link from *page1.htm* to *page2.htm* in the example shown in Figure 11-6, you would only need to enter the name of the file and its extension in the Link field of the Property Inspector.

To create a link to a page that is one level below the file where the link will be located, you must add information about the *path* that the browser should take to locate the file. To link from *page1.htm* to *page3.htm* for instance, the correct path would be *products/page3.htm*, indicating that the folder where the page is located is one level below *page1.htm*.

When you create links that move up in the site structure, add two dots and one slash in front of the filename to indicate that the browser should search up to find the file. To link from *page3.htm* to *page1.htm*, then, the correct URL to enter in the Link field would be *../page1.htm*.

By having a clear understanding of the site structure you are working with, you should be able to specify relative URLs with some ease. To move down two or more levels of site folders and their names, add the folder names separated by slashes in front of the filename you are linking to.

To move up multiple levels, add the symbol sequence of two dots and one slash for every level of folders that the browser must navigate to find the specified file.

Project 11-4: Exporting Interactive Images

Now that you have created a number of interactive images, it's time to see how those graphics and the HTML and JavaScript that Fireworks creates should be exported. This process is only different in that you will need to choose a different set of options in the final Export dialog box that specifies the types of files and the location where they are to be exported. In addition, Fireworks contains options that you'll want to be familiar with when exporting images that contain hotspots or slices.

Note

Fireworks MX also contains a new Quick Export feature that you will explore in upcoming modules.

Step-by-Step

1. From the exercise files for this module, locate and open the file named *slice_complete.png*. Alternatively, if you prefer, use one of the files that you've created yourself.

2. Any file that contains either slices or hotspots will need to be converted to a series of files: one that contains the code, and all of the additional files that contain the images themselves. Fireworks accomplishes these tasks automatically through the export process. With your file open, select File | Export preview.

3. In the Export preview dialog box, you will have the opportunity to finalize any optimization settings that you want to apply to the graphics contained in the file. As you saw in Module 10, the Export Preview dialog box is used for applying the settings that allow you to get the best quality for the appearance of your images while achieving the smallest file weight. Once you have set the optimization for your images and selected either the GIF or JPEG file format based on the appearance of your graphics, click the Export button.

Tip

Remember that you can also optimize any graphic contained by a slice by accessing the Optimize panel.

4. Fireworks will automatically sense the presence of code in your image and open the Export dialog box with the settings you see in Figure 11-7. Take a moment to orient yourself to the features you will encounter when exporting interactive images.

5. You can certainly choose the default settings that Fireworks presents. However, you'll find that a little advance planning and understanding how Fireworks generates files that enable interactive images to function properly will be worth your time. Begin by looking at the options you can use for creating the HTML file and its supporting image files by clicking on the Options button. When you do so, you will see the HTML setup dialog box presented in Figure 11-8.

6. By choosing the tabs at the top of this dialog box you, will be able to change the way that Fireworks exports any interactive image you create. By default, Fireworks is set to work best with its sister program, Dreamweaver, but you can also change the HTML style so that the images work more effectively with Microsoft FrontPage or Adobe GoLive. You can even output generic HTML that can be used with a text editor. These settings are found in the General tab. For now, leave them as they are.

7. Choosing the Table tab allows you to specify how Fireworks will build the HTML table to hold your slices. Using transparent spacer images, Fireworks by default will create a table that contains these special shims that hold the table together and keep it from collapsing.

11

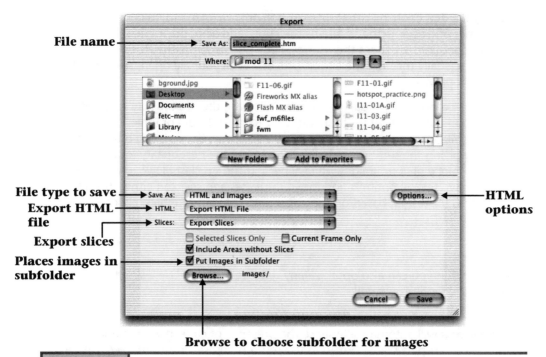

File name

File type to save

Export HTML file

Export slices

Places images in subfolder

HTML options

Browse to choose subfolder for images

Figure 11-7 Special export settings are present in the Export dialog box when hotspots or slices are found in an image.

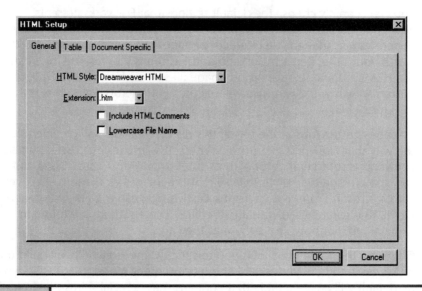

Figure 11-8 Set options for exporting interactive images in the HTML Setup dialog box.

Often, however, you may find that changing to an option such as using nested tables without spacers will give you better results. This is an important area of the HTML interface that you should be aware of, but for now, leave the settings as they are.

8. Finally, the Document Specific tab contains information about how Fireworks should name the graphics files that it outputs when the export process is complete. Again, the default settings are appropriate for this exercise, but you should know that you have control over the filenames that Fireworks creates by returning to this dialog box in the future. Click OK to return to the Export dialog box.

9. The final option that you should be aware of allows you to place the image files that are generated during the export process into a separate subfolder. This is an important option to consider because there will be a large number of files created when the export process begins. Check the option and then browse to the location on your hard drive where you want to save this file and its supporting graphics. Create a new folder named *sliced_images* and be sure that this folder is listed when you return to the Export dialog box.

Note

It is essential that these folders be named properly. Be sure that these folders do not contain capital letters or spaces. JavaScript is involved in making the rollovers and other image effects take place. JavaScript functions will break down, especially in Netscape Navigator, if any spaces are found in filenames or folder names.

10. With all of this groundwork done, it is now time to click the Save button to generate an HTML file and all of the supporting graphics files that your web authoring program, and ultimately the browser, will need to display the image with its effects.

11. The final process is to insert the HTML file that you just created in your web-authoring program. Fireworks was built to work seamlessly with Dreamweaver, but you can use the HTML file with other programs as well. You'll be exploring these options in the final two modules of this book.

11

Project Summary

This project has demonstrated the essential process that you must complete any time you create images that contain web objects. This additional step of selecting the kind of HTML file you want to generate and specifying a location for holding the images that Fireworks will create during the export process adds to the work you will need to do when working with interactive images. However, when compared to the amount of time required to create these images by manually slicing and exporting graphics, rebuilding the image in an HTML table, and applying the JavaScript behaviors to each image, this kind of export is quite efficient.

What to Take Away

As a web production tool, Fireworks simply has no equal among its competitors.

You have seen in this module that image maps containing hotspots can be easily created either by drawing the hotspot directly above the canvas or by inserting it on top of a selected object. Hotspots provide the ability to add links to an image and can be used for simple JavaScript functions.

Slices are the more robust of the two web objects that Fireworks allows you to create. With these powerful objects, you can break an image into separate parts for later reassembly in an HTML table, add rollover behaviors, and add other behaviors that you'll explore in the next module.

You have also been introduced to the way that the Button Editor can be used for creating navigational objects that can contain as many as four separate states, with the appearance of each controlled by JavaScript that Fireworks automatically creates. In Fireworks MX, you can even modify separate instances of the same button Symbol to make working with these special Symbols more efficient.

You have been also been introduced to how the URL panel can be used for organizing and importing links to add to your interactive images so that viewers can use these objects to navigate within your web site or to other locations on the World Wide Web.

Finally, in the last exercise of this module, you have seen how image maps and other interactive images are exported as HTML files with supporting graphics and explored the ways that you can control those options to produce exported files that meet your needs.

☑ Mastery Check

1. What special term is applied to both hotspots and slices?

_____

_____

2. How do hotspots and slices differ?

_____

_____

3. What visual reference is provided to show the location, shape, and size of hotspots and slices?

_____

_____

4. What is the advantage to using shared layers when creating images that contain rollovers?

_____

_____

5. What method for previewing images gives the best indication of how they will appear and function on the Web?

_____

_____

6. What tool enables you to create buttons that can contain up to four different sets of attributes?

_____

_____

7. Which Fireworks panel helps you organize and manage links in your interactive images?

_____

_____

11

☑ Mastery Check

8. Define a relative URL.

_____

_____

9. Define an absolute URL.

_____

_____

10. What is the appropriate file format for exporting a Fireworks file that contains web objects?

_____

_____

Module 12

Creating Advanced Navigation Elements

The Goals of This Module

- Examine options for page navigation elements
- Learn to create disjoint rollovers
- Explore the use of the Behaviors panel
- Create navigation bars
- Export multiple navigation bars for use in site navigation
- Understand the pop-up menu feature in Fireworks MX
- Create advanced graphics with the pop-up menu feature
- Employ interactive images with pop-up menus in a web site

The title of this module states that the techniques covered here are considered advanced, but creating the sophisticated navigational elements that you'll work with here is not beyond the skills of someone just starting out with Fireworks. If you've worked your way through the previous modules of this book, you are already beyond the beginner's stage and ready to try some more complicated projects.

Fireworks excels at creating these advanced navigational elements. Many designers prefer to use the program only for creating and optimizing their graphics, completing all of the coding in Dreamweaver or another web-authoring program. Working in Dreamweaver, however, often means that you must navigate through a series of dialog boxes to apply JavaScript behaviors that won't be visible until you test the page. In Fireworks, on the other hand, you work in a visual setting and can see your creation come to life and test it in a browser as you're working.

Fireworks provides the best of both worlds—the ability to create clean HTML and JavaScript code that is compatible with Dreamweaver and other web design programs, and the ability to see what you are doing as you work. Personally, I find this a major advantage over the methods used to create the same effects in Dreamweaver. In this module, you'll have the opportunity to create some very sophisticated programming and see how Fireworks makes this possible through its excellent user interface.

Disjoint Rollovers

If you think of what happens when you flip a light switch (an event), causing a light to come on (an action), then you'll have a basic understanding of how disjoint rollovers work. In Fireworks, you define where the actions and events take place by using slices with attached JavaScript behaviors.

You can create disjoint rollovers for simple effects, such as having an additional explanation appear when a button is rolled over. You can also design an entire web page based on disjoint rollovers. This is a good example of how Fireworks enables you to work in a visual environment. Were you to create the same effect in Dreamweaver, you would have to work in a dialog box that applies the behaviors to the areas of the page where the actions and events take place, and you wouldn't see the effect until you tested your web page in a browser. Fireworks creates identical behavior, but in a manner that many people find easier to use.

The explanation of how disjoint rollovers work may be a bit confusing, but composing your images, slices, and behaviors in Fireworks is relatively easy. Once you get the hang of it, disjoints are lots of fun to make, and they can add a great look to a web page.

Project 12-1: Creating a Disjoint Rollover

In this exercise, you'll build a fairly simple disjoint rollover using three buttons that will make text appear in the center of the document when the mouse pointer rolls over the appropriate button. This is just one example of how these kinds of interactive elements can add to your web page. As you see the effect in action, you'll undoubtedly think of other ways that you can use these special effects in your own projects.

Step-by-Step

1. To begin this project, create a new Fireworks document that is 400 pixels wide by 120 pixels high. Save your document with the name *disjoint_practice.png*.

2. In the document, create three rectangles, each 100 pixels wide by 40 pixels high, as you see in the illustration. In the sample file, the Info area of the Property Inspector has been used as a way of controlling the size of the buttons precisely. To create a bevel effect, a Style has been selected from the Styles panel and applied to each rectangle.

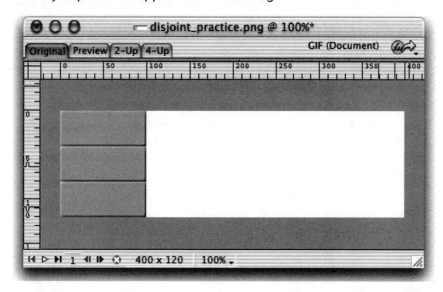

12

3. Rename the layer where these objects reside by opening the Layers panel and clicking on the Layer 1 label to change the layer's name. Name this layer **Buttons** and check the box that enables the images to be shared across frames. Add a second layer and name it **Text**.

4. Next, add the following text to the buttons: **Products**, **Services**, and **Contact**. You can position the text by eye or drag a guide from the ruler area to align the text properly. In the following example, Verdana has been set as the font type, with a size of 12 and a bold style applied. This provides the first part of the disjoint rollover—the three trigger areas that will activate the image in the blank part of the canvas.

─┼─*Tip* ──────────────────────────────────
SHIFT-click to select all of the text boxes and choose Modify I Align I Distribute Heights to line up your text boxes equally from top to bottom.

5. This image will contain a rollover effect, so the text objects in Frame 1 need to be copied to Frame 2. Fireworks makes this easy. Just open the Options menu in the Frames panel by clicking the arrow in the upper right-hand corner of the panel, and choose Duplicate Frame. Set the number of frames to be duplicated to 1 in the pop-up window that appears. The objects on Frame 1 will be duplicated to Frame 2, ready for some modification to create the rollover effect.

6. Choose Frame 2 in the Frames panel and modify the appearance of the text. In this example, a text style has been applied from the Styles panel to the text objects, just to keep things simple. You could just as easily add a glow effect, change from bold to normal text, or even change the color of the font.

7. The next task is to add some frames to the document. This time, the frames will be empty because these frames will be used to display the text that will appear in the blank area of the canvas when the viewer rolls the mouse over the trigger. There are three buttons, so you need three additional frames. Click the arrow in the upper right-hand corner of the Frames panel once again and, this time, choose Add Frames, which will add blank frames to the document. Set the number of frames to three and add them at the end of the set of existing frames. When you're finished, you will have a total of five frames: two for the buttons and three for the text objects that will appear.

8. The final steps for creating the objects for this image require some bouncing around between the frames in the image. If you're not sure how to do this, just click on the frame by name and see how your canvas appears. Frame 1 has your "Up" buttons, Frame 2 has your buttons as they'll appear when the mouse passes over them, and the final three frames are empty except for the shared rectangles that represent your buttons.

9. To make navigating among the frames easier, take a few moments to name the frames. Click the frame name label in the Frames panel, and name them in order, **Up**, **Over**, **Products**, **Services**, and **Contact**. Figure 12-1 displays how both the objects on the layers and the frames should be organized and named. Although it is not strictly necessary, you'll see in a few minutes how valuable it can be to take a little time to name your frames as you work.

10. Frame 3 (now labeled Products) will hold the text that will appear when the Products button is activated. Select this frame and use the Text tool to add the text you see in the illustration to the blank area of the canvas to the right of your button objects.

For the best in all you need for your home or business our product catalog provides the ultimate in quality and selection.

12

+Tip

Drag a text box with the Text tool to define the area of the canvas where you want the text box to appear. You'll spend less time resizing the text box if you give Fireworks an idea of how large it should be before you start typing.

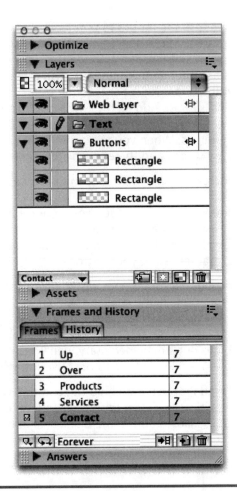

Figure 12-1 Organizing and naming frames and layers is an important step when you are working with advanced behaviors such as disjoint rollovers.

11. Wrap up this portion of the exercise now by adding more text in Frame 4 (Services) and Frame 5 (Contact). You can add your own text or use the examples listed below for adding text objects into these two frames:

● Services frame *Service is our middle name! For expert repairs and consultations, contact one of our service representatives today to schedule an appointment.*

● Contact frame *Contact us by phone at 555-1234 or via e-mail at moreinfo@ ourcompany.com. Sales and service representatives are standing by!*

12. That completes the setup of the document. Now it's time to move on to adding the slices and behaviors that will make this image work.

13. Go to Frame 1 (Up) and select the top button on the canvas, labeled Products. From the Menu bar, choose Edit I Insert I Slice. You will see a green overlay appear over the button and red lines that define the portions of the HTML table that Fireworks is generating. These overlays won't appear in the final document—they are there as a reference only. Continue adding slices to the two additional buttons until all three slices have been applied.

Tip

Use the Layers panel to make it easier to select the different objects on your canvas. Once you begin adding slices, it can become a little tricky when you're trying to select graphics. Just look for the thumbnail of the graphic in the Buttons layer, select it, and insert the slice.

14. The last slice for this image goes immediately to the right of the buttons. Use the Slice tool from the Tools panel to draw this one, being careful not to leave any space between the slices over the buttons and this new slice, and to completely cover the canvas. When all your slices have been added, your document should appear as you see here.

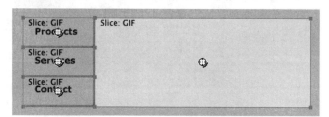

Note

Slices should never overlap. Fireworks MX makes it easier to position your slices by allowing them to snap to the edges of existing slices, but it is important that your slices be positioned properly whenever you add these web objects to a document.

12

15. The first behavior you'll attach is the simple rollover that will allow the buttons to swap from Frame 1 (Up) to Frame 2 (Over). Accomplish this by selecting the slice and then clicking the Behavior handle symbol that appears in the center of the slice. Select each slice over a button in turn and attach the Add Simple Rollover Behavior from the pop-up menu that appears. You may wish to preview the document in a browser to see that the effect has been applied properly.

16. Next comes the behavior to make the text appear as the mouse activates the trigger slice. Select the slice over the Products button and click the Behaviors handle. Select Add Swap Image Behavior from the menu to be taken to the Swap Image dialog box you see in Figure 12-2.

17. Designating how the effect is to be handled is a simple process at this point. To have an image appear in the area you've designated, click the large slice on the right side of the canvas to designate it as the place where the new image is to appear and specify the frame that is to show when the viewer rolls the mouse over the trigger. You've named your frames, so this is even easier. For the Products button, swap the image so the Products frame appears. Click OK to return to the document.

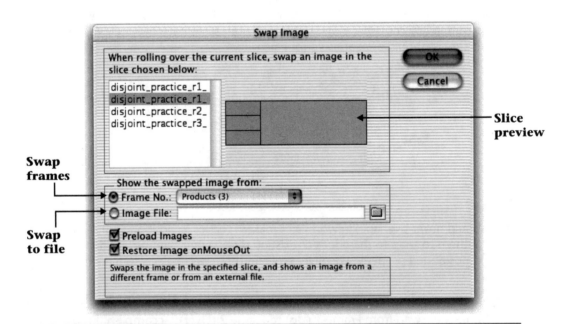

Figure 12-2 Specify image-swapping effects in the Swap Image dialog box.

┼Note

In addition to swapping frames, you can also swap images so that another image file appears in the designated slice. The next project explores this option.

18. Take note of the visual cue that Fireworks presents as the behaviors are attached to your slices. As you see in this illustration, as each slice is linked to another slice, a curved line connects the behavior handle to the adjacent slice to let you know that a behavior has been attached.

19. Finish by applying the swap image behavior to the Services and Contact buttons with their respective frames. You need only save the document and preview in your browser to see what great visual effects disjoint rollovers can produce. If all of the behaviors have been applied properly, rolling over a button in the image will cause the appropriate message to display in the assigned area of the canvas—a great effect to add when you wish to have a message or picture appear based on a viewer's interaction with the image.

Project Summary

This project has demonstrated how you can create an advanced technique such as a disjoint rollover effect in Fireworks. The image you've created here is fairly simple, and a similar combination of slices and behaviors will allow you to produce a wide range of image effects.

You should note that you export this image in the same way that you've exported any image that contains web objects. Many new users mistakenly set the file type for images such as this to an animated GIF format. The correct format to use when exporting is HTML and Images, with the individual slices optimized as you would with any static image in the GIF or JPEG format. The function of the swap image behavior is controlled by the JavaScript that Fireworks creates, so you'll need the HTML file to define the table that you've created by using slices and to attach the JavaScript to the images. Once you export the image, enabling it becomes as simple as inserting the HTML file into your web page.

12

1-Minute Drill

● How are behaviors attached to slices?

● Is it permissible for slices to overlap?

● What two frames are swapped when a simple rollover behavior is applied?

Exploring the Behaviors Panel

In the previous project, you saw how Fireworks enables you to attach prebuilt JavaScript behaviors to slices to create image effects based on an action that a viewer takes. In the case of a disjoint rollover, the action is contact between the viewer's mouse and the triggering slice, and it is followed by the display of a new image in a different slice.

All behaviors that Fireworks applies are summarized in the Behaviors panel. Although not part of the default panel set in Fireworks MX, this panel is an important tool to be aware of because you'll use it to modify or remove behaviors from a slice. Figure 12-3 displays the appearance of the Behaviors panel in Windows. To open the Behaviors panel, select Window | Behaviors.

In most cases, the JavaScript behaviors that Fireworks attaches by default do not need further modification. However, you may wish to do some fine-tuning from time to time to get an effect that differs from the norm. The Behaviors panel is also a great place to check when the effects you're seeing don't match your expectations. Fireworks tracks every behavior you apply, so you can best accomplish troubleshooting with your image effects by opening this panel and checking to see how the behaviors have been applied to your slices.

The organization of the Behaviors panel is quite simple. The panel displays each event that has been defined, the action that is accomplished, and the area of the image affected in the listings area of the panel. To change an action, simply click on the arrow to the right of the selected action, and you'll be able to change from the default *onMouseOver* event to others that match the behavior. For a disjoint rollover, for instance, you could change the action so the event

---

● Behaviors are attached to slices by clicking the Behavior handle and choosing from the behavior options presented.

● No. Slices should never overlap.

● In a simple rollover, objects on Frame 1 are replaced with objects on Frame 2 when the viewer's mouse passes over the trigger.

Add/Delete behaviors

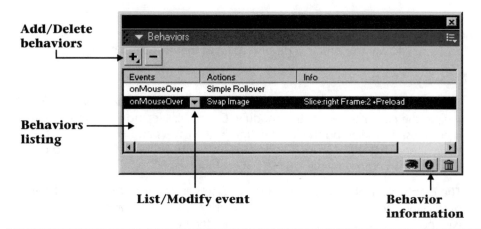

Behaviors listing

List/Modify event

Behavior information

Figure 12-3 | The Behaviors panel summarizes attached behaviors and enables you to modify them.

---

occurs when the viewer's mouse leaves the trigger (*onMouseOut*), when the viewer clicks on the trigger slice (*onClick*), or when the web page first loads (*onLoad*). Note that for the simple rollover effect, this arrow will not appear because the action cannot be modified from the default *onMouseOver* event.

To modify the actions and how they are applied, all you need do is double-click on the name of the action in the listings area. This will lead you back to a dialog box where the action can be modified as needed. You can also see specifics of how the actions are applied by clicking the Information icon in the lower right-hand corner of the panel. This ability to view and modify the behaviors you've attached to objects in your images will become more important as your images become more complex.

Project 12-2: Disjoint Rollovers with Animations

Fireworks is such a fun program to use for making animated GIFs that you'll undoubtedly want to include at least a few of these types of images in your web pages as you continue to develop your skills. As fun as they can be, though, controlling them can be a bit problematic. By default, an animated GIF will simply load into your page and play as soon as the browser is able to display it. That's fine in some cases. However, for more precise control over an animation, you'll want to explore how you can attach an action that calls the animation into play when the viewer interacts with a trigger. In other words, you will want to create a disjoint rollover that displays an animated file.

Step-by-Step

1. To make this project a little easier, you'll find a file called *animated_ disjoint .png* in the exercise files for this module. Open this file and note how the file is composed by viewing the information in the Layers and Frames panels. You will see that this document contains four buttons with slices placed over them with an empty slice to the left of each button.

2. The graphics are already provided for you, so you can lock the *Objects* layer by clicking the pencil icon next to the layer's name in the Layers panel. This will make it easier to select the slices in the document as you work.

3. The goal with this project is to create an image effect that will cause a small animated star to appear when the viewer rolls the mouse over a button. This is a very simple example, but you can easily use this technique for creating much larger and more involved disjoint rollovers with animations. To begin creating this effect, select the slice over the top of the button labeled *Home*.

4. Click on the Behaviors handle and choose Add Swap Image Behavior from the menu that appears. This will open the dialog box seen in Figure 12-4. You have two tasks to perform in this panel—selecting the slice where the animated file is to appear and selecting the file itself. Click the small slice in the upper left-hand corner of the slice preview area to specify that location as the place for the animation to appear.

5. In contrast to the way that you performed image swapping in the previous project, when using an animation you should swap a file into the slice and not a frame. Click the radio button next to the label *Image File* to enable this option and then click the folder icon to the right of the dialog box to browse to the file that is to appear. In this case, a small file has been provided for you called *star_rotate.gif*. Locate that file and select it. Once the file is selected and its name appears in the Swap Image dialog box, simply click OK to accept the application of this behavior.

6. Preview this file now in a browser, and you'll see that once you roll your mouse over the Home button, the star will appear to the left and will rotate around its axis. As long as your mouse pointer remains over the trigger area, the star will continue to rotate.

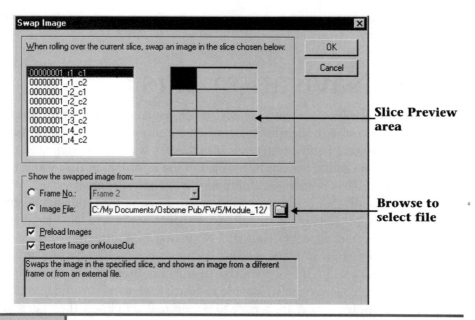

Figure 12-4 The Swap Image dialog box is used for swapping both images to frames and images to files.

7. Complete this simple exercise by repeating the steps for attaching the swap image behavior to the remaining slices over the buttons in the practice file. When you're done, rolling over each of the buttons will cause the animated star to appear on screen, and you will have gotten a good introduction to how this effect is created.

Project Summary

This simple project has introduced you to a very sophisticated technique that you can easily create in Fireworks. The example you've been provided with may not be the most artistic expression of all that Fireworks can do, but you now know how to attach a swap image behavior to a slice that causes a file to open. In this case, an animated image has been used; you could easily apply the same technique to static images, as well.

The same cautions apply with this technique as with any animated GIF. The images are composed of multiple frames, so you should keep a close eye on the file weight of the page as the objects are inserted. As always, your enthusiasm for using animated files should be tempered with the realization that a viewer of your web page will typically wait no longer than ten seconds for the page to download. If you've filled your page with animated files that cause the page's

12

download time to exceed this guideline, your audience may simply leave your site before they ever see just how artistic and clever you are.

Creating Navigation Bars

A web site that is difficult to navigate isn't much use to the site's owner or to its visitors. Even if you've thoughtfully constructed a site structure and carefully designed your pages, if you haven't provided an easy way for the audience to see where they are and figure out how to get to the information they want, then the entire exercise has been a waste of time. Navigation bars are special interactive elements that can assist you in meeting one of the fundamental goals of good web design—making your site easy to use. *Usability*, in fact, may be the single most important aspect of your site. No matter how attractive or filled with useful information your site may be, if visitors can't find their way around your site, then you will not be as effective in reaching them as you wish. A navigation bar can be extremely valuable to your viewers by providing them with a way not only to move from page to page but also to know their current location.

Any collection of links to pages within your own site can technically be called a navigation bar, but a true navigation bar adds some JavaScript wizardry to allow buttons to interact with each other in ways that aren't possible with text links, simple rollovers, or simple buttons.

Navigation bars are created by defining buttons with at least three button states—Up, Over, and Down—and may include a fourth, Over While Down. Module 11 teaches just how easy it is to define these objects using the Button editor. The states of each button are defined as follows:

- **Up** The appearance of a button when it is first loaded into a web page.

- **Over** The appearance of the button when a viewer passes over it with the mouse pointer.

- **Down** Used when navigation bars are designed to display a button as it might look if it were pressed down. This button state can be used to help viewers orient themselves to their location within your web site and does not have to look like an actual button to do so.

- **Over While Down** When a button displays in the Down state, you can still change its appearance by using this option. A button already displaying its down appearance can change again when a viewer passes the mouse over it.

Fireworks writes a tiny bit of code to let each button in a navigation bar determine the state of adjacent buttons. With this technology in place, only one button at a time will display the Down state, giving your visitors a visual signal of which page they are on. Fireworks MX has improved this process by automating the creation of the JavaScript that controls the appearance and functionality of your buttons.

Using navigation bars in this manner requires some extra work on your part. You must specify which button state to load when the page first appears on the viewer's screen, so you need to plan ahead if you want to use these elements. Fireworks makes it possible to automate the output of the code that makes the images appear correctly, and a little work on your part enables you to implement the code more easily once it is exported. You'll learn some tips for more successfully implementing navigation bars in the next project.

1-Minute Drill

- Which panel summarizes behaviors attached to web objects?
- What option should you use when you wish to display an animated file as a disjoint rollover?
- How do navigation bars benefit the usability of a web site?

Project 12-3: Creating a Navigation Bar with Multiple Down States

One of the more popular navigation features on the Web is the tabbed interface that simulates the appearance of file folder tabs for site navigation. Most people are quite familiar with file folders, so this simple interface can create a comfortable experience for viewers and allow them to quickly find your site's navigation features and begin moving through the site.

In this project, you'll learn not only how to create the graphical interface that uses tabs as the primary means of navigation but also how you can add to your site's usability by employing multiple instances of a navigation bar.

12

- The Behaviors panel summarizes all behaviors attached to a web object.
- Checking the swap file option in the Swap Image dialog box enables a file to display in a selected slice of your document.
- Navigation bars can assist viewers of your site by providing a consistent scheme for navigating the site as well as a visual clue for where they are.

This is a rather lengthy and involved project, so you may wish to complete the exercise in a series of steps rather than taking it on all at once. Steps 1 through 9 explain how to create the graphical interface for the navigation bar using the Button Editor. In Steps 10 through 14 you compose the navigation bar and set its properties. The project concludes in Steps 15 through 19 as you learn how the navigation bar is exported for use in your web site. If you decide to work in steps, be sure to save your file as you move along.

Step-by-Step

1. Start by creating a new document with a canvas size of 500 pixels wide by 40 pixels high. Set the canvas color to white and save the file as *navbar_ practice.png.* In addition to creating this file, use your computer's Explorer or Finder controls to create a new folder named *navbar* somewhere on your hard drive.

2. Creating the tabs is a relatively easy process. Start by selecting Edit | Insert | New Button to open the Button Editor. Using the Rounded Rectangle tool, draw a rectangle with a corner roundness of 35 pixels. Remember that to change this setting, you'll need to look in the Property Inspector for the roundness setting. Using the Info area of the Property Inspector, set the size of the rectangle to 100 pixels wide by 50 pixels high.

3. To remove the bottom part of the rectangle, select the rectangle and use the Knife tool to cut the lower portion of the rectangle. Hold down SHIFT while dragging the Knife tool across the object to draw a straight horizontal line. Once the rectangle is cut, click once on the canvas to deselect the rectangle and then use the Pointer tool to drag away the lower portion of the object, as you see in this illustration. With this lower portion selected, you need only press DELETE to remove it from the Button Editor's canvas.

4. Return to the Property Inspector once you have performed this bit of minor surgery and set the height of the object to 40 pixels. You should also set any fill color you'd like to use at this point and set a stroke, if you'd like. In the examples you'll see here, a 1-pixel soft rounded stroke has been applied.

5. The next step to complete is the insertion of text to label the button. You may recall from the last module that Fireworks MX enables you to modify the text of each button without breaking the link to the Symbol. You'll see this operation in action in a bit. For now, add the text **Home** above your button. Apply a drop-shadow effect to the text in the Property Inspector to give it a little more definition.

Tip

When entering text in a button, set the text to a center alignment. You can change the text itself when you modify an instance of the button, but you cannot change its alignment. Centering the text will ensure that longer or shorter text will still be positioned correctly when you modify a button instance.

6. Click the Over tab at the top of the Button Editor and click the button you find that enables you to copy the Up state onto this canvas. Modify the text's appearance by removing the drop shadow in the Property Inspector.

7. Move on to the Down state tab, and once again copy over the previous graphic. This is the button that will appear when a viewer is on the web page associated with it. Change the fill color of the tab graphic so your viewers will be able to clearly see where they are on your site. So that this button will still retain an appearance similar to its neighbors', reapply the drop-shadow effect to the text object.

8. To finish the graphical portion of this project, copy the Down state graphic to the Over While Down canvas. Leave the color as you set it in the Down state, but remove the drop-shadow effect from the text.

9. The final tab to select is the Active Area tab where the slice for the button will be displayed. Select the slice and check its size in the Info area of the Property Inspector. The slice size should match the rectangle and be set at 100 pixels wide by 40 pixels high. When everything is set as you'd like, click the Done button in the Button Editor to be returned to the document canvas.

12

Tip

You can return to one of the other button states and check the size and position of the rectangle in the Property Inspector. Return to the Active Area tab to change the properties of the slice to match the rectangle precisely by entering the values in the Info area of the Property Inspector.

10. With your Symbol created, you need only open the Assets panel and choose the Library tab to gain access to the Symbol. Move the first instance of the Symbol to the left edge of the canvas and use the Pointer tool to drag additional instances from the library. For this project, you will need five total instances of the button arranged on your canvas. As you position these objects, keep an eye on the Info area of the Property Inspector to help in positioning the objects. For this type of positioning, it is often best to drag the instance onto the canvas and use the arrow keys on your keyboard to move them into place.

Note

Creating multiple instances of a navigation bar requires that you follow some rules in naming the objects and linking them to your web pages. The next steps will explain exactly what you must do for this technique to work properly.

11. For multiple navigation bars to be generated automatically, each button must have a particular name applied to it that matches the name of the file it is linked to. Select the slice over the left-most button on the canvas. This button will take the viewer to the home page of this imaginary web site, so the file it will link to is called *index.htm*. Note that for multiple navigation bars, only the .htm extension may be used. In the link field of the Property Inspector, type **index.htm**. Figure 12-5 displays the correct setting for the link.

12. In addition to naming the file, you must also name each instance of the button to match. In the case of the Home button, set the button name to **index** in the Property Inspector, leaving off the .htm file extension. Refer to Figure 12-5 for the location of the field to name the button.

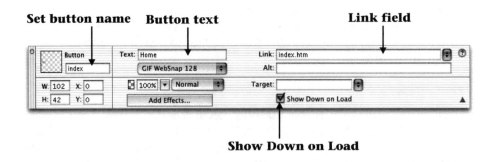

Figure 12-5 Exporting multiple navigation bars requires you to name the button to match the file that it is linked to

Button Name	Button Text	Link
products	Products	products.htm
catalog	Catalog	catalog.htm
services	Services	services.htm
contact	Contact	contact.htm

Table 12-1   Use the Property Inspector to apply the changes to each instance of the button as you see in this table.

13. Your final bit of housekeeping is to check the option in the lower portion of the Property Inspector that will enable the down state of the button to show when the page loads.

14. To complete the navigation bar, move to the other four buttons and set the properties of each to match the values found in Table 12-1. Note that, in addition to changing the name of each button and the file it is linked to, you must change the text for each button in the Text field of the Property Inspector.

15. With all of the button instances set, it's time to move on to the actual export of the file for use in your web site. You have only one more special step to take before this file is ready for use. Check the optimization settings of your file in the Optimize panel to ensure that the image type is set to GIF. Choose File I Export to open the Export dialog box.

16. Fireworks enables you to export multiple HTML files based on the settings that you've already applied in the Property Inspector. To do so, click the Options button in the Export dialog box and go to the HTML Setup dialog box. Locate the Document Specific tab at the top of the window and find the check box, labeled Multiple Nav Bar HTML Pages, seen here, that enables this automated process to take place. Check the option and click OK to return to the Export dialog box.

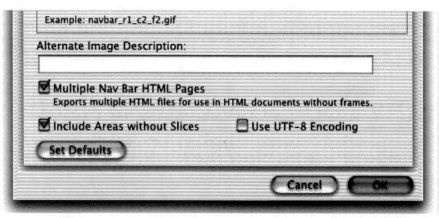

12

17. You have just one more step to take and your navigation bar will be complete. As you've seen in previous exercises, exporting buttons with multiple states will generate a huge number of files. To make these files manageable, choose the option at the bottom of the Export dialog box that enables you to browse to designate a subfolder for storing these image files. Locate the *navbar* folder that you created in Step 1 of this project and create a new subfolder called *nav_images*. Designate this folder as the location for your images to be placed in and set the main files to be stored in the *navbar* folder. Do not change any of the file-naming defaults that Fireworks has applied to the image.

18. Click the Save button, and all of the separate navigation bars for your site will be generated at once. The next module discusses how these HTML files would be inserted into a Dreamweaver document, but for now you can preview your document in a browser to see whether it appears as you see in this illustration.

19. Take a minute also to open the folder where you stored the HTML files during export. If you've followed all of the steps properly, you'll find a separate HTML page that Fireworks created for each of your buttons. To display a navigation bar in the down state for the appropriate button, you need only locate the correct file by name and insert it into your web page.

Project Summary

This project has been fairly lengthy, but the time you've spent learning how to create multiple navigation bars automatically will actually save you a great deal of effort down the road. Had you been using a competing product, for instance, you not only would not have been able to name and apply behaviors automatically, as you've done here, but also would have had to create separate documents for every individual navigation bar that you wanted to show a different down state. Fireworks helps you make your web site more usable by making this valuable navigation feature a relatively easy and automatic process.

Creating Pop-Up Menu Navigation

Often when a site contains a large number of pages and the designer needs to create a simple and intuitive navigation system, one of the best choices is a pop-up menu navigation scheme. This navigation type has become popular recently as designers emulate the simple navigation style found in most modern operating systems, in which the menu bar is used to select from a variety of options. A pop-up menu works in the same way; when a button is selected, a box appears with a menu of options. In the case of pop-up menus, the options lead to other pages within the web site. Almost anyone who uses a computer knows how to access options through a menu bar, so a pop-up menu system can make site navigation quite easy for a viewer.

The style of these menus is simple, but the technology that creates them is quite complex. Version 4 of Fireworks introduced this new feature with somewhat mixed success. Macromedia intended the menus to mimic the appearance and function of simple menu bars, but people almost immediately wanted their pop-up menus to do more than drop straight down from a horizontal menu. Fireworks MX addresses this with advanced methods for controlling the appearance and function of pop-up menus. In addition, Dreamweaver MX makes using pop-up menus easier than in previous versions.

Employing pop-up menus as a navigation scheme for a web site requires some forethought. These advanced objects have certain limitations; you should be aware of these factors before you decide to use pop-up menus in your site.

- Active content such as HTML forms, Flash movie files, and Java applets will obscure a menu generated with JavaScript. If you anticipate using any of these objects in your web page, you must design the page carefully so that menus and active content do not conflict with each other.

- The menus generated with the pop-up menu feature cannot cross frame boundaries. If you use a framed interface for your web site, the menus will need to be contained within one frame.

- The JavaScript that Fireworks and Dreamweaver use to generate these effects is rather large because it has been written for maximum compatibility with different browsers and operating systems. The JavaScript alone can be as large as 25K, half of the recommended file weight for a web page, so you should give strong consideration to using other methods for navigating your site if file weight is an issue.

12

With those considerations in mind, Fireworks' pop-up menus enable you to do some incredibly sophisticated programming in a visual environment using some simple dialog boxes to define the position and appearance of your menus.

Project 12-4: Designing Pop-Up Menu Navigation

Fireworks 4 introduced web designers to a simple yet effective method for designing pop-up menu navigation. Fireworks MX improves those methods by simplifying the control of the menus that appear when a viewer passes the mouse over a triggering slice. In this project, you will go through the design process involved in creating and exporting a pop-up menu from Fireworks MX.

Step-by-Step

1. To speed up the process of learning how to design pop-up menus, find a file named *popnav_practice.png* in the exercise files for this module. Open that file and note the location of the navigation bar with the button objects already prepared with their respective slices.

2. Note how the picture and the resort logo have been incorporated into the top portion of this document. You could certainly compose a web page in Dreamweaver that matches the layout you see in Figure 12-6. However, because pop-up menus will be applied to the navigation bar on the page, these images are designed in Fireworks so that the menus will appear in the correct location.

Figure 12-6   Using pop-up menus often means that you must compose the upper portion of the web page entirely in Fireworks.

3. The goal for this project is to produce a series of menus that appear when the triggers in the navigation bar are activated. To begin, select the slice located over the *Rooms* text in the navigation bar. Click once to select the slice and a second time to open the behaviors options for the slice. Once the slice is selected, you will see blue outlines on the screen denoting the location of the menus that are attached to this slice.

Tip

For small slices, you can select the slice and open the Behaviors panel. Clicking the plus sign button will allow you to add behaviors to the selected slice. You may also find it easier to select the slices by choosing them in the Web Objects layer of the Layers panel.

4. Choosing Edit Pop-up Menu from the options presented will take you to the Pop-up Menu Editor seen in Figure 12-7. This editor is where you will apply all of the settings you need to make your menus function and to determine their appearance. Take a few minutes to familiarize yourself with the interface by examining Figure 12-7. This first slice already has the pop-up menus applied for convenience, so you will see that the menu items are already included. To add your own menus, choose Add Pop-up Menu when the behavior handle is selected. These options are also available by selecting Modify I Pop-up Menu when a slice is selected on the canvas.

5. As you examine the settings that have already been applied for this first slice in the Content window, note that adding text as it will appear in the menu and the links to your web pages is a very simple process. Type in the text as you wish it to appear and add the name and path to the web page. Click the plus sign to add a new space below the existing menu or simply double-click below the last menu item to add a blank space. Note that you can change the order of the menu objects by dragging a menu item up or down in the stack. Try this now by moving the menu item *Key Largo Room* to the top of the list.

6. You'll also note that menu items can be indented or outdented by clicking the appropriate buttons at the top of this first dialog box. Again, experiment with the currently indented listings found under the *Cabins* listing. When you're done, indent the two cabin listings to their original position. To see how these settings are applied once the page is loaded in a browser, select Edit I Preview in Browser to see the effects of any changes you've made.

12

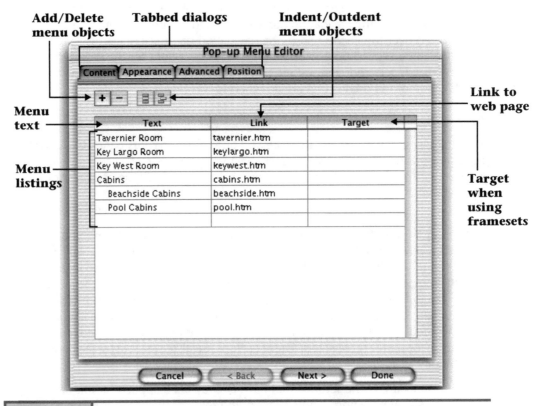

Add/Delete menu objects

Tabbed dialogs

Indent/Outdent menu objects

Menu text

Menu listings

Link to web page

Target when using framesets

Pop-up Menu Editor

Content | Appearance | Advanced | Position

Text	Link	Target
Tavernier Room	tavernier.htm	
Key Largo Room	keylargo.htm	
Key West Room	keywest.htm	
Cabins	cabins.htm	
Beachside Cabins	beachside.htm	
Pool Cabins	pool.htm	

Cancel   < Back   Next >   Done

Figure 12-7   Fireworks uses a tabbed interface to navigate the dialogs for attaching the pop-up menu behavior.

7. With the content of your menus determined in this first dialog box, it's time to move on to the Appearance dialog box. Click the Next button to move on and review the settings for this new window found in Figure 12-8.

8. Fireworks enables you to apply two different types of styles to your pop-up menus—either an HTML style that will display a basic table cell with the properties you apply or a table cell filled with an image set to display the choices found in your saved Styles. Deciding which to use depends on the look you want to present and how much file weight you are willing to invest in your menus. Choosing between the two is a simple matter of clicking inside the radio buttons at the top of the window. As you do so, you will see a live preview of how the menus will appear as each Style is selected and

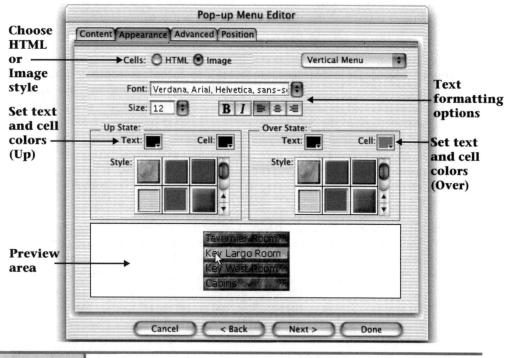

Figure 12-8   Set the appearance of pop-up menus in the Appearance window of the Pop-up Menu editor.

styling choices are made. Spend some time now changing the settings applied to the sample file, noting how each change affects the image you see in the Preview area.

9. Pop-up menus use dynamically generated HTML to display the text that appears in each menu item, so you are limited to the basic five families of fonts that all browsers can display. You can change the font to any listed in the drop-down menu and modify size and alignment or apply bold or italic styles, but you cannot use fonts other than those listed. Again, experiment by changing the font types and sizes on the menus provided.

10. The final area of this window enables you to set the appearance of both the Up and Over states of the menu items as they will appear. For images, you have a large number of options and can even create your own custom Styles for use in your menus. For now, try applying both an HTML style and an

12

image style to the menus and try the different settings that are possible. You'll quickly see that the number of options is extensive. Click the Next button to move on to the Advanced window when you are finished.

11. The Advanced window enables you to fine-tune the appearance of your menus, giving you options to change from an automatic width and height to a fixed width or height that you apply to your menus and to make other modifications such as changing the amount of time that the menu remains on the screen. All of these options have been added to Fireworks MX because of input from the users of this feature in Fireworks 4. You can now make very precise changes to the appearance and function of your menus—an operation that previously required revising the JavaScript manually. For most operations, the default settings are adequate, so you can either experiment with these settings now or click the Next button to move to the final window.

12. The final window in the Pop-up Menu Editor is also a new feature of Fireworks MX. The Position menu enables you to change the location of the pop-up menus relative to both the slice and indented submenus. You'll note that in the sample file, the menus have been placed to the left of the slice, represented by the –32 pixel value, and set to display 12 pixels below the bottom edge of the slice. These values have been used so that the menus do not obscure the bottom edge of the navigation bar in the sample file and so that the submenus will display flush with the right side of the menus that trigger them. Once again, you can easily change these values as you experiment with the effect that their properties have on the appearance of your menus.

13. Click the Done button once you have completed your first examination of the way that Fireworks pop-up menus are designed and modified. If you preview the file in a browser, the menus should appear as you see in Figure 12-9.

14. Returning to the Document window on your screen, you'll note the blue outlines of the menus that appear below the selected slice over the Rooms button. In addition to positioning your menu with the editor, you can drag these outlines into position on your canvas freely, placing them by eye where you wish. You may also wish to create a guide for positioning your menus by dragging one from the ruler area of the Document window. Menus will snap to guides in the same way that other items will snap to guides.

15. Your final chore for this project is to apply the pop-up menu behavior to the remaining slices on the navigation bar and fill in the information needed for

| **Figure 12-9** | Fireworks pop-up menus can make a complicated navigation scheme easy for the viewer to follow. |

the Content window. Fireworks will remember the settings for the appearance of your menus. Once the information is in place, position the menus and continue to experiment with how these objects are designed. You'll find a summary of the information that should be entered in those slices in the following table.

Button Name	**Button Text**	**Link**
Rates	Summer	summer.htm
	Fall	fall.htm
	Winter	winter.htm
	Spring	spring.htm
Facilities	Recreation	recreation.htm
	Relaxation	relaxation.htm
Attractions	Fishing	fishing.htm
	Snorkeling	snorkeling.htm
	Sight-Seeing	sights.htm
	Shopping	shopping.htm
Contact	Phone Listing	phones.htm
	E-mail	email.htm

12

16. As with any Fireworks document that contains HTML, the correct format for exporting files containing pop-up menus is HTML and Images. Once the HTML file and all its supporting images are exported, your final task is to insert the Fireworks HTML document into your web page. Once you have done so and tested your web page in a browser, you will see the cascading menus appear as each button in the navigation bar is activated.

Project Summary

In this project, you have had the opportunity to examine the interface that Fireworks MX uses for the design of the sophisticated pop-up menu navigation system. You have also seen how the changes to the interface in Fireworks MX make controlling these complex menus more manageable and give you greater control over the final output of the menu items.

Here is one final note of caution regarding pop-up menus. The JavaScript that is written during the export process must make certain assumptions about how the pages and images are structured in your site, so any page that uses Fireworks pop-up menus must be located in the same folder on your site as the JavaScript file itself. You will note that not only is an HTML file generated during export, but an additional file named *mm_menu.js* is created as well. This file controls the function and appearance of all of the menus in your document. Locating a web page that uses pop-up menus in a folder other than the one where this file is located will cause the pop-up function to fail. There are solutions for revising the script to make the location of your pages within your site more flexible, but they all require significant hand-editing of the JavaScript found in the *mm_menu.js* file. They should not be undertaken unless you have experience in working at the code level.

Although pop-up menus are a fascinating navigation system, you should also come away from this project understanding their limitations. Fireworks makes it possible to design the menu system in a graphical environment, but these menus are not suitable for every application. If you find that you need even greater control over the location or appearance of your pop-up menus than Fireworks provides, your best option is often to look for alternative sources of similar available menus. One company in particular—Project VII found at www.projectseven.com—has alternative forms of cascading menus that do not contain some of the limitations of Fireworks pop-ups. The solutions that Project VII provides do not allow you to work in a visual design environment, but you may find them to be a better choice than trying to manipulate the Fireworks JavaScript yourself.

1-Minute Drill

- How do pop-up menus and active content such as form objects and Flash movies interact?

- Where do you apply settings for pop-up menus?

- What improvements have been made in Fireworks MX to the pop-up menu interface?

What to Take Away

In this module, you have had the opportunity to see some of the more complex interactive images that can be designed in Fireworks MX. From the relatively simple disjoint rollovers to the very complex pop-up menus, in every instance Fireworks gives you the opportunity to work in a visual design environment that lets you test and view your creations every step of the way. Creating these kinds of interactive images is possible by manually writing code and attaching it to images, but Fireworks enables someone with no programming experience to make very advanced navigation systems with just a little practice.

Fireworks provides the best of both worlds—the ability to create clean HTML and JavaScript code that is compatible with Dreamweaver and other web design programs and the ability to see what you're doing as you work. The examples you've seen in this module only begin to show how Fireworks excels as a graphics editor with superior capabilities for creating advanced interactive images for use on the Web.

- Active content will always appear above pop-up menu objects. Using both items in a web page requires you to design the page so that they do not conflict.
- Apply settings for pop-up menus in the Pop-up Menu Editor.
- Fireworks MX has added advanced controls for determining the position of menu items and for modifying their appearance.

12

✓ *Mastery Check*

1. How do you create disjoint rollovers?

_____

_____

2. What is the advantage of creating disjoint rollovers in Fireworks rather than in Dreamweaver?

_____

_____

3. What four button states can you create with the Button Editor?

_____

_____

4. What technology controls the appearance of buttons in a navigation bar?

_____

_____

5. How must you name buttons when the multiple navigation bar export option will be used?

_____

_____

6. What reference point should you use to define the location of pop-up menus?

_____

_____

✓ *Mastery Check*

7. What limitation of pop-up menus must you consider when designing web sites with frames?

_____

_____

8. What method does Fireworks provide for designing pop-up menus?

_____

_____

9. What two styles of pop-up menus may you create in Fireworks?

_____

_____

10. What is the proper format for exporting a Fireworks document containing pop-up menus?

_____

_____

12

Module 13

Integrating Fireworks with Dreamweaver

The Goals of This Module

- Understand the integration features of Fireworks and Dreamweaver
- Insert interactive images in Dreamweaver
- Optimize Fireworks graphics from within Dreamweaver
- Edit Fireworks documents from within Dreamweaver
- Compose web pages for use in Dreamweaver
- Explore the Quick Export feature in Fireworks MX
- Work with Dreamweaver libraries and templates
- Explore additional integration features of the software suite

Fireworks is a terrific graphic design tool for the Web that enables you to create some truly fascinating images quickly and easily. The real strength of Fireworks, though, has always been its ability to work as a graphic design tool for images especially targeted for publication to the Web. You can certainly use Fireworks in conjunction with other web authoring tools or even with a simple text editing tool when hand coding web pages. However, the program really stands out when used in conjunction with the other half of the Macromedia web design studio—Dreamweaver.

You have already seen how, when you create images in Fireworks, apply optimization settings, and even include JavaScript behaviors, the program will output all the code you need to insert the image into a Dreamweaver document. In this module, you learn a little more about how to use the two programs together to maximize your work and allow you to make modifications to images from directly within Dreamweaver's web-authoring environment. As you become a more experienced designer, and your pages become more complex and rich with images, you will quickly come to appreciate how closely integrated the two programs are and how easily you can move between one program and the other to accomplish your design tasks.

In the MX versions of both Fireworks and Dreamweaver, the integration between the two programs is stronger and more full-featured. In addition to seeing these programs' similarities in appearance, you'll find that having both Fireworks MX and Dreamweaver MX at your disposal will make your work more efficient.

Note

You should have a basic understanding of the uses of Dreamweaver to successfully complete the exercises in this module. This includes understanding how a web site is defined, the location and function of the Dreamweaver Property Inspector, the Insert panel, and the insertion of images and interactive images. All of these features are covered thoroughly in the Dreamweaver Help files, which you may wish to review before proceeding.

Understanding Dreamweaver/ Fireworks Integration

Installing both Dreamweaver and Fireworks links the two programs together in ways that enable them to assist you in working in both the web design and image design environments. Dreamweaver is programmed to recognize images and code that are imported from Fireworks as being uniquely editable. Fireworks is able to read HTML tables and code generated in Dreamweaver and open, for instance, an image that has been placed into a table. Fireworks MX will even allow you to reconstitute an HTML table with all of its images intact when the source files are not available. Working between the two programs gives you an incredible amount of flexibility when working with images for the Web.

Preparing Fireworks and Dreamweaver Editing Preferences

No other software combination features the tight integration that Dreamweaver and Fireworks possess for creating and optimizing graphics for use on the Web. As previous modules discuss, creating graphics that are exported to an image or HTML file for insertion into a Dreamweaver document is an essential part of what Fireworks does. However, what about those times when you just need to make a small adjustment to a graphic, such as resizing it or tweaking the optimization settings so that the file size is reduced? In those cases, Dreamweaver can launch Fireworks while you are working on a web page, saving you the time and effort that might normally be required to open Fireworks, access the image, modify it as you need, export the image, and reinsert the modified version into your page. Dreamweaver and Fireworks save you all of those additional steps by working closely together to make minor modifications a breeze.

Setting Dreamweaver Editing Preferences

When both Dreamweaver and Fireworks are installed on your computer, the two programs search for each other and make modifications to the preference files for each program that allow them to work together. To be certain that this integration will take place, you should check the preferences for both programs to see that these settings are correct.

To set image editing preferences, start by opening Dreamweaver and, from any open window, choose Edit | Preferences (or Dreamweaver MX | Preferences in Mac OS X). In the Preferences dialog box, select the File Types/Editors category, as you see in Figure 13-1, and check the Extensions area at the bottom of the window. For PNG, GIF, and JPEG file extensions, be sure that Fireworks is set as the primary editor by finding its name in the Editors listing. If Fireworks is not listed, click the plus sign in the Editors area and browse to the main program file for Fireworks and select it. Use the Make Primary button to set Fireworks as the default editor for those three file types.

13

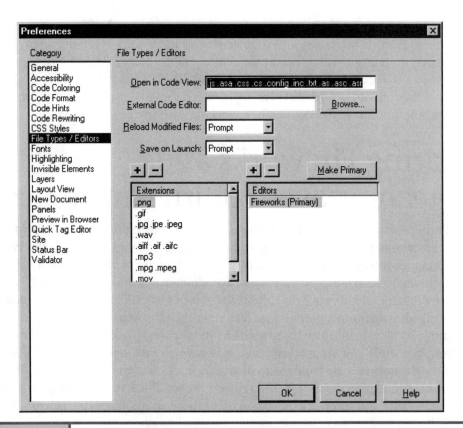

Figure 13-1 Use the Preferences dialog box in Dreamweaver to designate Fireworks as the primary editor for PNG, GIF, and JPEG files.

Setting Fireworks Preferences

Fireworks also has preferences that you can set to determine how files will be handled when you're working in both programs. As you'll recall, almost all images you will use begin as Fireworks PNG files that are optimized and exported to either the GIF or JPEG format. Any time you export a file from Fireworks, information about the original source file is stored in a Design Note that Dreamweaver can access when the file needs modification. Fireworks will allow you to either work on the original source file or work on the exported version when making modifications from within Dreamweaver. By default, Fireworks will always ask whether you want to work on the source PNG file or only on the exported version when you edit an image from within Dreamweaver. You can change the settings so that you always edit the source file or never edit the source by selecting Edit | Preferences in Fireworks (Fireworks | Preferences in Mac OS X) and making adjustments in the Launch and Edit preference category.

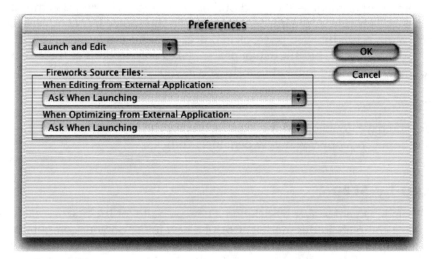

The best approach is to always edit the source PNG document and let Dreamweaver and Fireworks work together to export the revised files. By maintaining the integrity of the source file, you'll avoid problems down the road when you may wish to edit the original file again.

In addition to setting your editing preferences, you should also be sure to check the HTML Setup preferences found by selecting File | HTML Setup. In the General tab, be sure that the HTML style is set to Dreamweaver and that the File Creator lists Dreamweaver as well. Note that you will need to have a document open for this menu item to be available. Taking this step ensures that both programs properly maintain any specific references used in the creation of JavaScript effects.

Project 13-1: Editing Fireworks Graphics from Within Dreamweaver

There are any number of reasons why you might want to optimize or a revise an image when you begin working in Dreamweaver. From the simple correction of an obvious error to improving file weight of a graphic by changing its optimization settings to resizing an image to meet your page design needs, all are common tasks that face a web designer. The tight integration of Dreamweaver and Fireworks makes these chores much easier. No matter what changes you need to make to an image (or even to a file that contains both

13

HTML and images), having Dreamweaver and Fireworks working together makes the task easy. In this next exercise, you'll go through the steps required for some simple image editing and optimization steps, allowing Dreamweaver to call up Fireworks as the image editor, launch the source file, complete the edits, and update the web page, all in one easy round-trip fashion. Those steps may sound lengthy, but the actual process takes only seconds as these two programs work hand in hand to assist you in your image editing tasks.

Note

Be sure you have downloaded the exercise files for this module from www.osborne.com or www.dw-fw-beginners.com.

Step-by-Step

1. Begin in Dreamweaver by defining a new web site for the practice exercises you'll complete in this module. Create a new folder on your computer's desktop and name the Folder *practice.* Define the new site in Dreamweaver using this folder as the root folder for the site. For further instructions in defining a web site, choose Using Dreamweaver from Dreamweaver's Help menu.

Note

To avoid seeing error messages from Dreamweaver that the image files you'll use in this exercise are outside the defined root folder, be sure to copy the exercise files for this module into the root folder you've designated.

2. Create a new document in Dreamweaver, name it *page_practice.htm,* and place it in the root folder of your practice site. Dreamweaver will not allow you to perform optimization and editing work in Fireworks unless the web page is saved.

3. Choose the Insert Fireworks HTML button from the Common tab of the Insert panel in Dreamweaver MX, or choose Insert | Interactive Images | Fireworks HTML. In the exercise files for this module, browse to the folder called *header* and find the HTML file named *header_practice.htm.* Remember that for any file you create in Fireworks containing slices or hotspots, the correct file to insert into a Dreamweaver document will be the Fireworks HTML created during export.

4. The original source file for this interactive image includes slices, so the file that you have just inserted into your web page is actually an HTML table

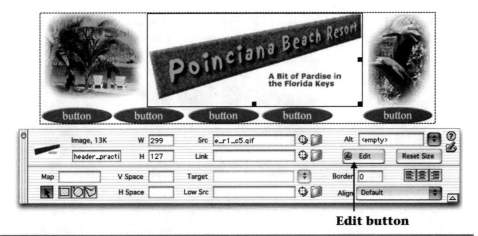

Edit button

Figure 13-2 Dreamweaver displays information about each cell of a Fireworks table as it would for any other HTML table.

composed of the individual cells. To see the position of the cells, click once anywhere within the image on your web page and note how the cell is outlined and its properties displayed in the Dreamweaver Property Inspector. Figure 13-2 displays the appearance of a Fireworks table and the Dreamweaver Property Inspector where the cell containing the resort logo has been selected. Note the location of the Edit button in the Property Inspector. Although you can edit the individual images as they are located in the table cells, this is not the recommended method.

5. In order to maintain the integrity of the Fireworks table, the best method for modifying individual images is to modify the entire table. With any cell of the table selected, locate the Quick Tag Selector in the lower left-hand corner of the Document window in Dreamweaver and find the first table tag to the left of the other tags that are displayed, as seen in this illustration. When you click the table tag, you will see that the entire table is selected in the Dreamweaver document.

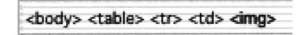

13

6. When a Fireworks table is selected, the Property Inspector will change to reflect the fact that the source for the table has come from Fireworks. Note in the following illustration that the Edit button is in a new location and that the border that designates the active selection now encloses the entire

Fireworks table. Dreamweaver will also list the Fireworks source file when the image has been associated with its original Fireworks PNG file.

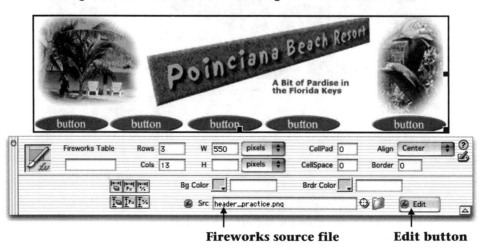

Fireworks source file   Edit button

7. With the Fireworks table selected, click the Edit button in the Property Inspector. If your system preferences are set to ask before launching a source file, Dreamweaver will present a dialog box asking whether you want to edit the source file and will allow you to browse to the file's location. Click Yes to open your system's Open file dialog box and browse to the original PNG file for this exercise—*header_practice.png*. Fireworks will launch, and a special Document window will appear. Note the presence of the button in the upper left-hand corner of this window as you see illustrated here.

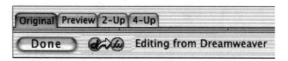

Note

The Document window that you see when editing from Dreamweaver has two primary differences from a standard Fireworks document—the presence of the Done button that takes you back to Dreamweaver when you are finished editing and the lack of the Quick Export button that standard Fireworks Document windows contain. Other than those two changes, this window is exactly the same as any Fireworks document, and all of the tools and panels that you would normally find in Fireworks are present and functional.

8. Your first chore here is to align the buttons in the image. Using the Pointer tool, SHIFT-click to select all the buttons in the image. Choose Modify | Align | Distribute Widths to change the alignment of the buttons so they are equidistantly spaced. You may want to turn off the view of the slices to make selecting these objects easier by clicking on the Hide Slices and Hotspots button in the Tools panel.

9. Obviously, leaving these buttons with their current *buttons* text does nothing for the appearance of this page, so select each button in turn and change the entry in the Text field of the Property Inspector to read **Home**, **Rooms**, **Rates**, **Facilities**, and **Contact**. When you are finished, your buttons should appear as you see in this illustration.

10. The next modification to make to this image is to adjust the optimization of the slices over the photographs. In your original sample file, these have been set to 100 percent. To save some file weight, select the slice over the picture of the beach and the picture of the dolphin statue and, using the Optimize panel, change the quality setting from 100 percent to 80 percent. If you have turned off the view of the slices, turn that view back on by selecting the Show Slices and Hotspots button in the Tools panel so that you can select the slices that are placed over those pictures.

11. To finish up, change the text block under the logo by adjusting the properties of the text. Try a new font, change the color, or make the font size larger. The goal here is to see how the modifications will be applied, so feel free to make any changes you wish.

12. Once the image has been modified, you can finish updating your web page. Nothing could be simpler than what Fireworks requires you to do at this point—just click the Done button at the top of the Document window. Your web page will instantly be updated to reflect the changes you've made in the source file, Fireworks will close, and you will find yourself back in Dreamweaver with all the changes applied. It's hard to imagine this being any easier!

Project Summary

Modifying images that are intended for publication on the Web is a common chore that faces web designers. Whether you need to change the layout of a series of objects, change the file optimization settings, or just tweak color combinations or effects that you've applied in Fireworks, you need only launch Fireworks while you're working in Dreamweaver, edit the source file, and return to Dreamweaver when you're done. The process is seamless, quick, and unparalleled by any combination of software tools in the world of web design.

13

1-Minute Drill

● How can you establish preferences that allow Dreamweaver and Fireworks to communicate properly when editing files?

● How are graphics that have been sliced in Fireworks labeled when the image is selected in Dreamweaver?

● What are the two differences between a standard Fireworks Document window and a window that opens when you are editing from Dreamweaver?

Integrating Web Page Design with Fireworks and Dreamweaver

Often, new users of Fireworks wonder why they shouldn't simply build their web pages as Fireworks documents, slice the pages, and post their new creations to a web server. The idea is tempting because (unlike Dreamweaver, in which you often have to spend considerable time composing your pages around tables or layers) Fireworks allows you to do everything on one canvas, export as HTML and Images, and have a complete web page ready to go in a fraction of the time.

There are several problems with that approach. First, you are limiting yourself to a page that is composed entirely of images—one that will undoubtedly be significantly larger in file weight than a comparable page that is made up of a combination of standard HTML elements and some images to add visual interest. As a result, your viewers will be penalized by having to wait much longer for the page to appear.

Second, you will be limited in the kinds of things that you'll be able to do with this method. Standard web pages built in Dreamweaver allow you to use Cascading Styles Sheets (CSS) for page presentation, forms for adding interactivity, or Flash elements for animations and interactivity, but a page built in Fireworks will not allow you to do any of those things. In fact, if you build your page in Fireworks and then modify it so that those elements can be added in Dreamweaver, you will lose the ability to do the kind of round-trip editing you saw in the last project.

● Both Dreamweaver and Fireworks contain preference settings that can be set by choosing Edit | Preferences (Dreamweaver MX/Fireworks | Preferences for the Macintosh).

● When an entire graphic composed of slices is selected in a Dreamweaver page, the Property Inspector labels it as a Fireworks table.

● When you edit from Dreamweaver, the Document window in Fireworks contains a Done button and lacks the Quick Export button.

Finally, web pages that lack standard HTML objects will almost certainly be passed over by search engines as they index pages for inclusion in their databases. You will have a page that not only takes a long time to download and is difficult to manage but you will also reduce the chances that people searching for a page with a topic you cover will ever find your site.

The proper method for using Fireworks as a page design tool, then, is to think about the discrete areas of the page and how each one will function. In many cases, you'll find that examining what you want to do with your page will lead you to a solution for its construction. Because you can use slices for defining the various elements on your page and for exporting, you can in fact do an entire mock-up in Fireworks, design the various elements you want to use, and then ship the parts off to Dreamweaver for final assembly in a fully functional web page. The next project in this module introduces you to this approach.

Project 13-1: Designing a Web Page Interface in Fireworks

You may often wish to do all of your design work in Fireworks before exporting the completed project to Dreamweaver. After all, Fireworks makes it so easy to generate the graphics and place your objects on the page—without the annoyance of having to control how browsers will display your content—that it is simply easier to do the page design in a graphics program and export the various parts for use in Dreamweaver. With some careful forethought about how you will compose the page, you can define your Fireworks image so that some areas of the page can be formatted with standard HTML. Other areas of the page where you do not need to apply HTML formatting can then be composed of images. This project leads you through an example of how that process might be completed.

This is a lengthy project you may wish to complete in stages. Steps 1 through 9 lead you through the process of preparing a Fireworks document for export to Dreamweaver, including the export of the individual slices in the image. Steps 10 through 19 show how the exported images are reassembled in Dreamweaver. Finally, in Steps 20 through 26, you learn how you can create some portions of a web page so that images are used as the background of a table cell, allowing HTML elements and images to exist in the same area of the page. If you choose to complete the project in stages, be sure to save both the Fireworks and Dreamweaver documents as you work.

13

Step-by-Step

1. As with any web project, planning plays a critical role in designing a successful page layout. For the sample that will be used for this project, a basic design of the various parts of the page has been created. The goal here is to determine how to put all the pieces of the graphic back together again in Dreamweaver, so it is essential that you understand how the various areas of the page will function. Figure 13-3 shows the initial page layout developed for this page.

2. The next goal is to begin creating the graphics that will match the page design. In the sample file for this project, called *interface_practice.png*, the sketch that you saw in Figure 13-3 has been placed in its own layer, labeled *Layout*, so that the different regions of the page can be clearly seen. Open this file now and note how the graphical elements of the page match the page layout decided on during the planning of the page. When you are done examining the Layout layer, turn off the view of the layout by clicking the eyeball icon next to its label in the Layers panel.

3. Transferring this graphic to a Dreamweaver document involves some tricks to allow some slices to be inserted into HTML table cells while others are used as cell backgrounds. Take a close look at how the slices have been arranged in the sample file as you prepare to export the individual slices.

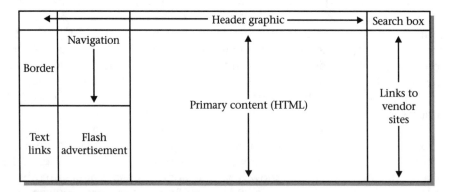

Figure 13-3   Defining the separate areas of a web page based on appearance and function will make page layout much easier.

Note

The buttons already contain slices by definition, so the process of adding slices over the rest of the page that contains graphical elements involves adding the slices and positioning these new slices as neatly as possible next to the existing slices in the buttons. Slicing carefully and ensuring that no gaps exist between slices is critical to the success of this technique. This has been done for you already in the sample file, but you should spend some time practicing on your own to get comfortable with the process of drawing and positioning slices.

4. Prior to exporting these slices, name and optimize each slice. You can name slices in the Property Inspector by changing the default name that Fireworks automatically applies as slices are added to a document. Select each slice in the sample file and note how it has been named so that you can identify the slice more easily once you begin inserting the images into your Dreamweaver table. You will find that each slice has been named to match its position on the page and its function.

5. The final step in preparing to export the slice is to optimize the areas of the Fireworks document based on their appearance. The header and border graphics are created using gradients, so you should export these slices as JPEG images to avoid the banding effect that the GIF format often produces with gradients. Set the remaining portions of the image, including the buttons, to the GIF format. Check the optimization settings for each slice to be sure that the export settings are correct before you move on.

Tip

Once the optimization settings are correct, check the appearance of the image by previewing in a browser. Carefully examining the appearance of a file as it will look in a browser before exporting saves you much time and effort later.

6. To prepare your web site for these files, return to Dreamweaver and create a new folder in the practice site you defined previously in Dreamweaver so that you'll have a convenient spot in which to save the slices. In the examples you'll see here, a folder called *page_images* has been created to hold the exported slices.

7. Exporting the slices as you've prepared them involves selecting each slice in turn, right-clicking (CTRL-clicking in Macintosh) the slice, and choosing Export Selected Slice from the Context menu that appears. Try this now by

13

selecting the corner slice in the upper left-hand corner of the document, labeled *corner,* and export the slice. When you do so, you will see the Export dialog box as it appears in Figure 13-4. Note that the name of the slice applied in the Property Inspector becomes the name of the exported file and that the check box at the bottom of the dialog box is set so that only the selected slice will be exported.

8. Continue exporting the remaining image slices in the practice file now but do not export the buttons at this point. When you are finished, you should have completed the export of seven individual image files into the folder that you prepared for these images in your site.

9. Because the buttons in the page contain JavaScript that creates the rollover effect, the buttons cannot be exported with the same technique. For images

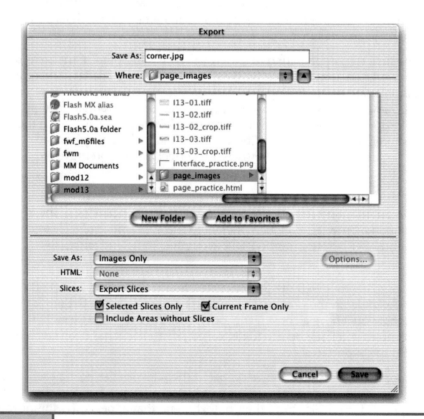

Figure 13-4   Exporting slices leads to the standard Fireworks Export dialog box.

containing HTML or other code, you must first select the button slice and choose File | Export. In the Export dialog box for each button, be sure that the check box that lets you export only the selected slice is checked and the file type is set to HTML and Images. In addition, even though the buttons are named in the Property Inspector, you must give a filename to the buttons as they are exported. Finish the export process now by exporting all of the buttons, naming them *sales_button*, *services_button*, *dockage_button*, and *store_button* as you work through the export of the four buttons.

10. Now for the challenging part! In Dreamweaver, create a new document in the practice site that you've defined and save it as *pbmarina.htm*. It is essential when working in Dreamweaver that you name all files before working with interactive images.

11. Refer back to Figure 13-3 for a look at the sketch that was used to define the layout for this page. As you can see in the sketch, the page is composed of a table containing 3 rows and 4 columns. In Dreamweaver, insert a table with those characteristics, leaving the table borders set to 1 pixel for now until the page layout is complete. Be sure that the width of the table has been set to 760 pixels so that it matches the width of the Fireworks canvas. Your Insert Table dialog box should appear as you see here before you click OK.

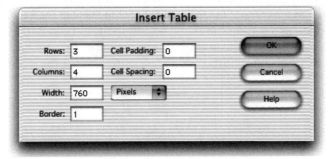

12. Controlling how a page will display requires that you give some thought to how HTML tables function. Table cells will always collapse around any content found in them, so using images to maintain the width of individual cells is an essential skill when designing your web pages. With that in mind, you can begin to establish the layout of this page by inserting the simple graphics that compose the header at the top of the page. Locate the file called *corner.jpg* and insert it in the upper left-hand corner of the table using the Insert Image button from Dreamweaver's Insert panel, or simply choose Insert | Image. Insert *header_left.jpg* in the cell to the right, followed

13

by *header_center.jpg*. Once the three images are inserted, your web page should appear as you see in this illustration.

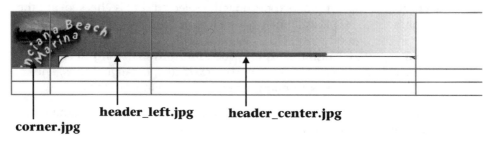

corner.jpg   **header_left.jpg**   **header_center.jpg**

Note

The final cell in the header will contain both the exported image and some HTML, so don't insert the image in the upper-right table cell at this time. You'll be returning to that task in a few minutes.

13. Now that the width of the page is established, you can begin defining the table's height. Table and cell height properties are not valid HTML and will often fail to display properly, so you will use the exported images to define the cell heights for you. Start by clicking inside the cell directly below the corner image and setting the vertical alignment of the cell to Top in the Dreamweaver Property Inspector, as you see here. This will ensure that the image you are about to insert will snug tightly against the image above it.

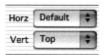

14. Once you have set the alignment, insert the image called *border_left.jpg* into the cell. When you insert this image, the table will be forced into the correct height and be prepared for the buttons. Click inside the cell immediately to the right to prepare for the placement of the buttons onto the page.

15. One of the frustrating parts of dealing with page alignment is the effect that changes in one cell of a table row have on other table cells in the same row. The large central area of this page may need to expand to accommodate additional page content, so the appearance of the buttons as they are stacked in their own cells may change. To avoid this problem, the buttons will be placed in a table that will be nested into cells where they belong. Set the vertical alignment of this cell to Top and choose Insert I Table or the Insert

Table button on the Insert panel. This new table only needs one row and one column to accommodate the buttons and should be set to a width of 100 percent so that it fills the entire cell. Check your settings against the illustration of the Insert Table dialog box that you see here and click OK to insert the table.

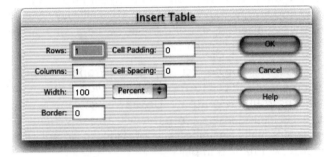

16. Click inside the new table and once again set the vertical alignment to Top. Inserting the buttons themselves now becomes a simple process of using the Insert Fireworks HTML button on the Insert panel or choosing Insert I Interactive Images I Fireworks HTML. The first button to insert is called *sales_button.htm*. Browse to the file in the Insert Fireworks HTML dialog box, select it, and click OK to insert the file into your page. Be sure to select the file with the .htm extension and not one of the image files that you'll see with the same filename.

17. With this button inserted into the page, note how the images begin to align with each other based on how they were sliced. To insert the next button, press the down arrow on your keyboard one time to drop to the next available location in the table. Do not press ENTER or RETURN because that will break the structure of the table by inserting a new paragraph. Simply press the down arrow, and you'll be all set for the next button.

18. Complete the navigation bar portion of the page by inserting the files named *services_button.htm*, *dockage_button.htm*, and *store_button.htm*. Note that inserting these objects may create a gap in the table cell to the right of the buttons. Don't be too concerned about this space at the moment because previewing your work in a browser will reveal that the table is in fact constructed properly. You'll fix the gap in the next few steps.

19. As you look closely at your web page, you'll note that the right-most column in the main table has collapsed because no content has been inserted into any cells in that column. However, you'll recall from the layout plan for this page that this column is intended for HTML content such as the search box that will be placed in the upper right-hand corner. To accomplish this and

13

maintain the design for the page, a special transparent GIF file, called a spacer or *shim*, will be placed into the cell to prop it open. You will find this file, called *spacer.gif* in the exercise files for this module.

20. Click inside the top row of the table and use your arrow keys to position the cursor in the upper right-hand corner cell. The cell may have collapsed when your buttons were inserted, so using the arrow keys will make navigating to the correct insertion point much easier.

21. Once your cursor is in the correct cell, use the Property Inspector to set the vertical alignment of the cell to Top. With the alignment set, choose Insert | Image or the Insert Image button in Dreamweaver's Insert panel. Locate the file called *spacer.gif* and insert it into the cell. This tiny image can be difficult to select in Design view once it is on your page, so do not click anywhere on the page once the image is in place.

Note

You may be prompted by Dreamweaver to copy the file into your site. Choose Yes when prompted to do so and save the file into the *page_images* folder.

22. The key to using shims to assist in page layout is to change the image's width in the Dreamweaver Property Inspector. This is not something you would do with a regular image, but using a transparent GIF in this way will prop open the cell to the desired width and allow you to use the exported image as a background for the cell. With the spacer file still selected, use Dreamweaver's Property Inspector to change the width to 137 pixels, matching the width of the image that will be placed in the cell as a background in the next step. This illustration displays how the width property of the image should be set in the Property Inspector.

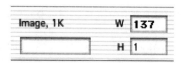

23. With the shim in place, the background image for this cell can now be inserted. Setting images as cell backgrounds allows HTML elements to appear in the same cell as the image. Press the down arrow one time to drop to the insertion point for this cell and click the Browse to File button in the Property Inspector next to the background image field. Browse to the file called *header_right.gif* and choose it as the background image to display in the cell. When your image is properly inserted, the Property Inspector for this cell will appear as you see here.

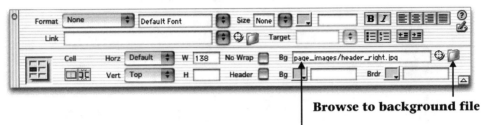

Browse to background file

Background filename

24. The cell below the header must also be propped open with a shim in order accept the file called *border_right.gif* as the background image. Again, click inside this cell and set the vertical alignment to top. Insert the *spacer.gif* file and use the Property Inspector to set its height attribute to 337 pixels to match the background image's size. Once the spacer is in place, set the background image property so that *border_right.gif* is selected for the background.

25. You have only one additional image to set as the background for this page before your visual design will be complete. Click inside the cell below the buttons and set the file called *button_border.gif* as the cell background. The table is already stretched to the correct proportions, so you do not need a spacer for this cell.

26. The final step in this project is to select the table and change the cell border property in the Property Inspector to zero. This will allow the borders to disappear and the images to snap into place. If all of your images are neatly displayed in your new web page and match the design that was originally configured in Fireworks, you should pat yourself on the back and take a break!

Project Summary

By carefully inserting images to define the structure of your page and mixing them with images that are used as cell backgrounds, you can develop a complete web interface working between Fireworks and Dreamweaver. This has been a lengthy project, but the steps and techniques you have learned here are ones that you will return to when you want to take full advantage of the strengths of both programs. By designing in Fireworks and exporting sliced elements of the page, you can complete an entire interface like the one displayed in Figure 13-5 in a much more efficient manner than would be possible without these two programs working together.

13

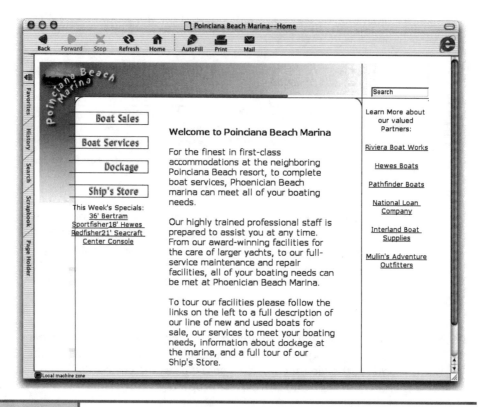

Figure 13-5 This completed web interface uses sliced images and elements from Fireworks to make up an entire web page in Dreamweaver.

Continuing on with this web page might entail additional layout changes that are beyond the scope of this book. For instance, you might choose to insert other nested tables into the existing table cells to further define the look and function of the page. Once those elements are in place, you could easily save the page as a Dreamweaver template and use the design throughout your entire site. Working together, Fireworks and Dreamweaver make it possible for you to quickly return to the source file for additional updates to the individual objects in the page.

1-Minute Drill

- How do search engines react to web pages composed entirely of images?
- How do you name individual slices in Fireworks?
- What technique is used during the layout process when a table cell needs to be set to a precise size?

Automating Workflow with Dreamweaver Library Elements

In the last exercise, you saw how an entire page can be designed in Fireworks and then pieced back together in Dreamweaver by exporting individual slices. This is a common way to put together a web interface, but there will be times when creating an entire page such as this is more than you really need from Fireworks. In many cases, all you really require are the various graphical parts of the page for insertion into your project. If those pieces are items that you may wish to update from time to time, such as a navigation bar, then Dreamweaver library items can save you a substantial amount of work.

Library items are common elements that Dreamweaver tracks and maintains in the Assets panel. Library items in particular can save you a great deal of work; Dreamweaver tracks their use and allows you to update changes to the library item so that all changes to the object automatically apply to every instance of the item in your web site. Imagine a site made up of dozens or even hundreds of pages that all share the same graphical object, such as a navigation bar. You can appreciate what an incredible chore you would be faced with if you needed to change the navigation bar.

- Search engines often ignore pages that are composed entirely of images and that contain no HTML elements.
- Name slices in a Fireworks file by filling in the name field in the Property Inspector.
- When a table cell height or width needs to be set during layout, a transparent GIF file, called a spacer or shim, is inserted into the cell and stretched to the desired size.

Using Fireworks and Dreamweaver together, though, you can export an image directly out of Fireworks as a Library item and insert it into your pages as you wish. Once you need to change the object, all you must do is update the image in Fireworks, save the changes in Dreamweaver, and let the magic of automatically updating every page that uses the Library item take place. Once the updates are done, your only remaining task would be sending your revised files to your web server. Instead of taking hours and hours to update your site, you can accomplish the same process in a fraction of the time by letting Fireworks and Dreamweaver work together.

Project 13-3: Creating Dreamweaver Library Items

Dreamweaver library items save you countless hours of work through their capability to automatically update all pages that use the object. The updating is done in Dreamweaver, but the actual creation and modification of library items that are graphical objects is done in Fireworks. In this next project, you will go through the steps required to create a navigation bar, export it as a Dreamweaver library item, and modify and update the object while working in Fireworks. This is a great timesaving feature and another example of how well the two programs work together.

Step-by-Step

1. Before working with library items in Dreamweaver, you must have a folder in your defined site named *Library*, and this folder must be located one level below the main folder, or root folder, for the site. Dreamweaver will insert this folder automatically when it is used for creating a library item, but when you work from Fireworks the folder must be in place before you can save a Fireworks file as a library item. To create a new folder in Dreamweaver, open the Site window and right-click (CTRL-click on the Macintosh) the folder at the top for the defined site you are working in. Choose New Folder from the Context menu that appears and name the folder **Library**. Be sure the folder name is capitalized. This illustration displays the proper site structure as it should appear in the Site window when you are done.

2. Locate the practice file for this project named *library_practice.png* in the exercise files for this module. Open the file in Fireworks and note that the file consists of four buttons arranged as you might find them in a navigation bar. Unfortunately, the top button also contains a spelling error, but you'll be correcting that in a few minutes.

3. Exporting the file as a Dreamweaver library item is quite simple, involving only a minor change in the export properties for the Fireworks document. Choose File | Export to open the Export dialog box as seen in Figure 13-6.

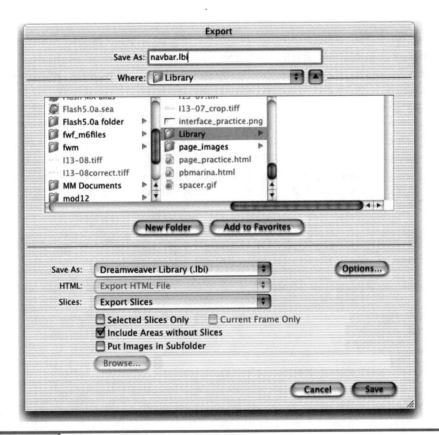

Figure 13-6 Exporting Fireworks files as Dreamweaver library items requires that each file be saved to a defined Library folder and set as a Dreamweaver library item.

4. Your first task is to simplify the name of the file and to make it more descriptive. In the Save As field, change the filename to **navbar**. In the Save In field (Where on the Macintosh), set the location for the file to be saved as the *Library* folder you created in Step 1. In order for Dreamweaver library items to maintain their capabilities, they must be located in this special folder. Finally, change the Save as Type field (Save As for Macintosh) to Dreamweaver Library (.lbi) by dropping the arrow in the menu down and selecting that option. Your final export settings should appear as you see in Figure 13-6. Once all the settings are correct, click the Save button.

Note

To put the images generated during export into a separate subfolder, check the Put Images in Subfolder check box at the bottom of the Export dialog box. You can browse to a folder that you've already selected for holding these images or create a new folder within your site using your system's standard methods for making a folder.

5. Dreamweaver will place the new object into your site's Assets panel, but you will need to click the Refresh button at the bottom of the panel to update the library. With the panel open and the assets for the site refreshed, the *navbar* library item that you created will appear in your site's listings, as you see here.

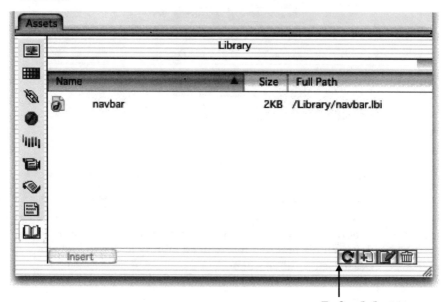

Refresh button

6. Create and save several new practice web page files in Dreamweaver to see how easily you can employ and modify library items. You might want to save these pages with names such as *test1.htm*, *test2.htm*, and *test3.htm* just to keep things simple.

Tip

Create new pages in Dreamweaver by right-clicking (CTRL-clicking in Macintosh) the folder in the Site window and selecting New File from the Context menu. This assures that any new files you create will be properly associated with the current web site and all of its assets, including the library item you just created.

7. Open each of the new web pages you created and drag an instance of the *navbar* library item onto the page. Save each page after the navigation bar is in place and leave these files open in Dreamweaver. Click on top of one of the navigation bar images you just inserted and note how the Property Inspector, seen here, defines the object as a library item. The object is only editable by changing the main library item itself, so you will not see the usual properties displayed for this image.

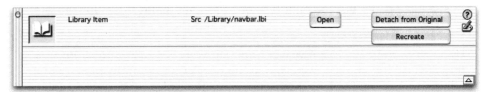

8. You'll recall that the top button in this navigation bar contains a spelling error and needs to be changed. To access the file that Dreamweaver uses to track this item, click the Open button on the Property Inspector. When you do so, a special web page will open that Dreamweaver uses for tracking this object and the Property Inspector will revert to its usual appearance. As you did in the first exercise of this module, select the table that contains images and note that the Property Inspector now lists the object as a Fireworks table and includes the Edit button. Click the Edit button now to launch Fireworks and return to the source file for the library item.

Note

In the event that Dreamweaver does not recognize the source file used for the creation of the library item, you will receive a warning that the source file was not found. Click OK, and you will be able to browse to the location where *library_practice.png* is found. Choose the image as the source file, and Fireworks will open the file for editing.

13

9. Just as with the first exercise in this module, the new canvas that you see will contain the Done button that will close Fireworks and automatically update your pages. Select the top button in the navigation bar and use Fireworks' Property Inspector to change the text from *Boat Sails* to *Boat Sales* and press ENTER or RETURN to accept the changes. Click Done once you have made your changes. Fireworks will close and you will return to the library item Document window in Dreamweaver.

10. With the library item modified, all you need to do at this point is save the document in Dreamweaver and allow the software to update all of the pages that use it. Choose File | Save, and Dreamweaver will ask whether you wish to update all the files that use the library item. Click the Update button to automatically apply the changes. Once the update is complete, you will receive a report on the screen listing the pages that were updated. Click the Done button and close the library item file.

11. Return to the test pages that you created and note how the changes to all of the navigation bars in each has been applied. As you see how quickly this has been done, you should also be able to appreciate how important having a tool like this at your disposal might be if your spelling error appeared in not just three pages but the hundreds of pages that might make up your site!

Project Summary

Using Fireworks and Dreamweaver together, you can make corrections to a mistake (like the simple misspelling in this project) or do more fundamental editing such as adding a new button, changing a link, or modifying a color scheme throughout an entire site by combining the power of library items with the editing capabilities of Fireworks. In all, the process greatly reduces the amount of work that might be required were these two programs not capable of working together so efficiently. The end result is less work for you, a better experience for the viewers of your site, and increased productivity as the software programs complete much of the work for this common web design task automatically.

1-Minute Drill

- What is the primary advantage of using library items in Dreamweaver?
- What special storage location must you designate when a library item is exported from Fireworks?
- How are library items placed into a Dreamweaver page?

- Library items enable you to automatically update an element throughout the site whenever you modify and save the original object.
- Library items must be stored in a folder called *Library* directly below the root folder for the web site.
- Place library items into a page in Dreamweaver by dragging an instance of the item from the Assets panel onto the page.

Exploring Additional Integration Features

The discussions in this module so far have focused on the most common tasks that a web designer might face when working between Fireworks and Dreamweaver. From updating graphics from within Dreamweaver by launching Fireworks, to designing an entire page in Fireworks and exporting the parts you need for your page, to using Dreamweaver library items, you have now seen examples of the kinds of things that these two programs can do together.

As part of the Macromedia MX Studio, the integration between these two programs extends further than the examples you have explored in this module. Macromedia has added enhancements in the latest versions of both Fireworks and Dreamweaver that allow you to work in an even more integrated environment, making you a more productive designer. These additional features are summarized here.

Quick Export

Every Fireworks canvas now contains the Quick Export button located in the upper right-hand corner of the Document window, as shown in Figure 13-7. With the Quick Export feature, you can not only go directly to the Export dialog box by selecting Export HTML, but you can also update HTML files previously exported from Fireworks, copy HTML to your computer's clipboard so that it can be pasted into the Code view of Dreamweaver or

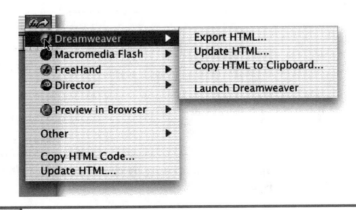

13

Figure 13-7   The Quick Export button in each Fireworks Document window gives you quick access to the most common export functions.

another HTML editor, or even launch Dreamweaver while you are working in Fireworks. You may find that using this feature is more efficient for you than selecting File | Export to export your files or even exporting selected slices.

Image Placeholders

One of the many new features added in Dreamweaver MX is the capability to insert image placeholders into a web page as you are designing. This terrific new tool allows the page designer to insert images into the page so that the appearance and layout of the page can be tested before images are created rather than by trying to fit the images to the page structure. In the world of web design, in which the exact location and size of even a single image can break an entire page's structure, the capability to precisely control the size of the images that will compose the page is incredibly important.

Dreamweaver couples this ability with the power of Fireworks by letting you set the image placeholders and then launch Fireworks to create a replacement file of the exact size to fit your layout needs. Simply insert the image placeholder, select it once the layout of the page is finalized, and click the Create button found in the Dreamweaver Property Inspector to create the image in Fireworks. Figure 13-8 displays a typical Dreamweaver table used for a simple page layout with the Property Inspector set to replace an image placeholder.

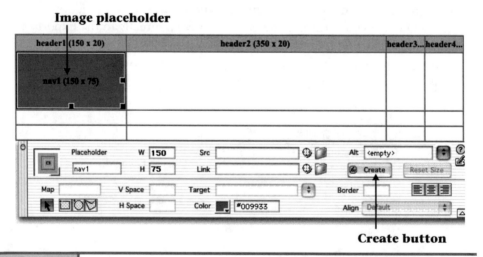

Image placeholder

Create button

| **Figure 13-8** | Replace image placeholders easily by clicking the Create button in the Property Inspector. |

Enhanced Pop-up Menu Editing

Prior to Dreamweaver MX, the pop-up menus created by Fireworks were often frustrating to use because Dreamweaver did not recognize the code that Fireworks used as a native behavior. This meant countless hours of hand-editing web pages that used the feature, as designers discovered that revising the Fireworks source file and reinserting the revised HTML into a Dreamweaver document did not produce the desired results.

Dreamweaver MX and Fireworks MX now share a common naming scheme for their JavaScript, making editing a file that uses pop-up menus much easier. Now, when you need to change a file that has pop-up menus, you need only launch Fireworks from within Dreamweaver, edit the file, and update the page as you would with any Fireworks HTML document. This makes the entire process much more manageable and lets the software, rather than you, do the grunt work of rewriting the code.

Reconstitute HTML Tables Command

One lesson that this book emphasizes is the importance of maintaining your Fireworks source files. Without these critical files and all the information they contain such as the positioning of vector objects, effects that have been applied, and optimization settings, your work as a designer would be much more difficult. As you've seen in the earlier parts of this book, working with vectors is infinitely easier than working with the kinds of bitmap images that are created when the source file is exported.

Unfortunately, not everyone saves his or her source files, and there may come a time when you need to rebuild a web page that someone else has created or for a site where the original PNG files have been lost.

Fireworks MX now has the capability to restore a web page built from a standard table into a PNG document with all of the behaviors and structure of the page intact. To create a PNG file from a web page, you need only choose File | Reconstitute Table and work through some simple dialog boxes to create a PNG file from a standard HTML table. This feature alone will be extremely popular with professional designers who often take over a web site where the previous designer has not maintained site files properly.

13

What to Take Away

In this module, you have learned about several of the most common ways that Fireworks and Dreamweaver work together in the creation and modification of images for the Web. With the capability to open a Fireworks file directly from within Dreamweaver, you can quickly optimize or modify images as you need. Using Fireworks and Dreamweaver together saves you many unnecessary and tedious steps in getting your images to look as you would like, while maintaining the smallest file weights possible.

You have also learned how Fireworks enables you to design an entire page and use sliced areas of the page for the creation of an interface for the Web. By carefully reconstructing a page that you've laid out in Fireworks into a Dreamweaver table, you can combine the graphic capabilities of Fireworks with the design flexibility that Dreamweaver gives you to design beautiful web pages.

Finally, this module has introduced you to the power of Dreamweaver library items. These special tools make it possible to take an object that you use repeatedly throughout your web site and update it automatically. For graphical objects such as navigation bars, the power of library items combined with the ability to edit and update in Fireworks makes this a powerful one-two punch for your design productivity.

As stated before, no other web-authoring and graphic design software combination is as closely integrated as Fireworks and Dreamweaver, and the capabilities that the two programs provide when used together keep the designer in mind when it comes to ease of use. It's no wonder, then, that the Macromedia MX is likely to remain the most popular software available on the market for designing high-impact web sites.

☑ *Mastery Check*

1. How can you access preference settings for Dreamweaver and Fireworks?

2. How can you optimize images from within Dreamweaver?

3. What is the correct file type to insert into a Dreamweaver page where the file contains hotspots, slices, or behaviors?

4. What are the two differences between a standard Fireworks Document window and a window that opens when you are editing from Dreamweaver?

5. What technique can you use during layout when a table cell needs to be set to a precise size?

6. What is the primary advantage of using library items in Dreamweaver?

7. Where are Dreamweaver library items stored?

13

☑ Mastery Check

8. What new feature allows for the quick export of slices or files from Fireworks MX?

_____

_____

9. What options exist in the new Quick Export feature for sending files to Dreamweaver?

_____

_____

10. How can image placeholders be replaced by the actual images you wish to use in a Dreamweaver page?

_____

_____

Module 14

Integrating Fireworks with Other Applications

The Goals of This Module

- Explore the advantages of using Fireworks as your primary graphics program
- Understand proper formats for export to other applications
- Explore the export options when using Fireworks graphics in Flash MX
- Understand editing options when working between Flash and Fireworks
- Import and export graphics between Fireworks and FreeHand
- Understand export options when working with Director and Homesite
- Explore the use of Fireworks graphics for use in Microsoft FrontPage
- Examine the capabilities of Fireworks when working with Adobe Photoshop documents

As you become more comfortable with the drawing and graphics tools that Fireworks MX possesses, you will undoubtedly come to appreciate what an elegantly simple program it is. With the refined user interface that puts all of the design tools you need within easy reach and its other powerful capabilities, Fireworks could easily become your favorite computer program, as it has for me.

Fireworks can do so much to accomplish all of your design needs that you will undoubtedly wish to explore its use in conjunction with programs other than web-authoring tools. Even though it was originally designed as a complement to Dreamweaver and excels at integrating with Macromedia's primary web-authoring program, it is also tightly integrated with the other products in the Macromedia MX Studio. This module teaches how to use Fireworks in conjunction with Flash MX to create objects that enhance that program's drawing capabilities when animations and rich web content are your goal.

Fireworks also works well with Macromedia's primary print tool, FreeHand, and allows you to move between the two programs when you need to produce graphics that will be published both on the Web and with more traditional printing methods. For more advanced interactive elements, Fireworks allows you to work just as easily with Director to generate graphics, enhancing that product's capabilities for creating highly complex interactive Shockwave movies.

Finally, Fireworks can be used with products outside the Macromedia family. Many users, in fact, work with Fireworks to create their images for export into Microsoft's FrontPage web-authoring program. Some users choose to create their artwork in Adobe Photoshop and use Fireworks to add interactive elements or simply take advantage of Fireworks' more effective optimization techniques when they're ready to prepare their images for the Web.

Regardless of how you work, Fireworks will be ready to assist in the creation of the images you need for the Web or to allow you to work with other software programs when your requirements go beyond its capabilities.

Fireworks MX and Flash MX Integration

Macromedia's Flash animation and scripting program is one of the most fascinating software releases of the last few years. Many people believe that this one software program will revolutionize how designers create content for the Web and how consumers of Internet content interact with the companies that supply the content.

With the release of the Macromedia MX Studio, Flash MX has become a tightly integrated part of the company's strategy of allowing designers and developers to work closely to create rich active content for the Web.

Fireworks plays its part in the integration of the MX product line by providing graphics capabilities that Flash does not possess. The drawing tools in Flash are quite effective for many uses, but their reliance on the vector method for generating graphics results in limited choices when creating effects such as bevels, glows, shadows, and other effects that Fireworks excels at. In addition, without any way of modifying and editing JPEG or GIF images, Flash does not allow you to work with existing artwork such as clip art or photographs. Enter Fireworks.

With Fireworks, you can easily create simple objects like buttons with glows and bevels or complex interfaces that are designed in Fireworks and imported into Flash. The possibilities are almost limitless as these two programs are designed to work hand-in-glove in the same way that Fireworks integrates with Dreamweaver.

Note

If you do not currently own a copy of Flash MX, you can download a fully functional trial version that gives you thirty days to experiment with the program. All Macromedia products are available as trial downloads at www.macromedia.com/software.

Export and Import Options for Flash MX

Flash is capable of reading entire Fireworks PNG files, including information stored in separate layers and frames, in such a way that the entire Fireworks PNG file can be utilized in Flash. Design your complete graphical object in Fireworks and simply import the image into Flash, or copy and paste, and the complete graphic will be displayed and ready for use.

The two programs use different methods for creating images, so Flash will ask what features of an imported Fireworks PNG file are most important to you. You will have the option of maintaining the image's appearance or maintaining the vector paths that the Fireworks file contains so you may modify them in Flash. When text objects are present in the document, you will also have the option of maintaining text editability or maintaining the appearance of the text. Figure 14-1 displays the dialog box that Flash uses to help you decide which properties are

14

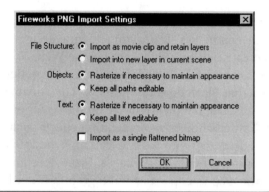

Figure 14-1 A simple dialog box allows you to import Fireworks PNG files with the proper attributes for use in Flash.

most critical for your image as it is brought into Flash. You will have the opportunity to see the effects of choosing different options in Project 14-1.

Fireworks PNG files give you the greatest number of options for importing your images directly into Flash; additionally, you can easily export a graphic from Fireworks as a standard GIF or JPEG file and insert it directly into your Flash movie or choose to insert an animated GIF file as a movie symbol. Finally, Fireworks also allows you to export images in the file format native to Flash— Shockwave Flash Format (SWF)—allowing you the freedom to create a graphical object that you can then manipulate further using Flash's own editing tools.

There are five different ways that Fireworks files are commonly exported to Flash:

- **Copy and Paste** Using the Quick Export feature, you can copy a Fireworks object and paste it directly into a Flash movie.

- **Import Bitmap Images (GIF or JPEG)** Flash will accept images exported from Fireworks in the GIF or JPEG format with all applied effects intact. This is similar to the way that images are imported into Dreamweaver.

- **Export Animated GIFs** Images that are exported from Fireworks in the animated GIF format can be used as movie symbols or other miniature movies within a Flash movie. For special effects, or to use animated clip art, importing an animated GIF file into Flash is a great choice.

- **Import Fireworks PNG**   Flash will accept importing an entire Fireworks PNG file, including maintaining any transparency settings applied to the object and exporting objects on separate layers as separate objects in the Flash movie. Importing Fireworks PNG files is a great way to bring an image composed of multiple objects into Flash for use as buttons or other interface objects.

- **Export SWF Files from Fireworks**   Fireworks can export images in the format native to Flash (SWF). Doing so enables you to preserve animations as well as the objects' editability. This is a good choice when you want to export an image that is difficult to draw in Flash, such as a star, but is quite easy to do in Fireworks.

Regardless of the choice you make, these two programs work together exceedingly well, and as you begin to explore the dynamic capabilities of Flash, you will want to use Fireworks in many instances to extend your design capabilities.

Note

You should have a basic understanding of the Flash interface before starting the next project. The example provided here does not delve into advanced properties of using Flash, but topics such as layers, frames, symbols, and tweening of objects in Flash will be discussed.

Project 14-1: Importing Fireworks Files to Flash MX

Fireworks and Flash are an unbeatable combination when you want a way to combine the vector animation capabilities of Flash with the bitmap and special effects options of Fireworks. With so many options to choose from for exporting graphics from Fireworks to Flash, understanding which method is most appropriate for your desired effect is a large part of successfully integrating the two programs.

In this project, you will develop a simple animation that has interactive control buttons created in Fireworks. All of the graphics that you use here are found in the sample files for this module. When you are finished, you will have exported these graphics into Flash and built a complete movie with interactive objects without ever using the drawing tools in Flash at all.

14

Note

You will find the completed project in the exercise files for this module at www.osborne.com or www.dw-fw-beginners.com. Open the file named *fireworks_completed.swf* to see how your movie will look once you have completed this project.

Step-by-Step

1. Open a new file in Flash and save the file as *fireworks_movie.fla*. Choose Modify | Document and change the default document dimensions to 500 pixels by 400 pixels.

2. From the exercise files for this module, locate and open the file named *movie_text.png*. This file has been prepared using the techniques covered in Module 9 to give the text a three-dimensional look by stacking text objects on top of one another and applying a drop-shadow effect—effects that are difficult to create in Flash. For the first objects in the movie, select the top text object and click the Quick Export button in the upper right-hand corner of the Fireworks Document window. Choose Flash | Copy. Figure 14-2 displays how the document and the Quick Export button will appear once you have made the correct choices.

3. Once you return to Flash, inserting the text is as simple as choosing Edit | Paste. The complete object will be pasted into your Flash document. Note how the drop shadow and other effects have been preserved from the

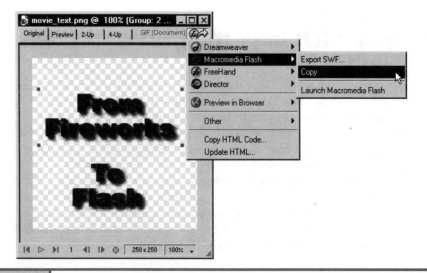

Figure 14-2 The Quick Export feature found in Fireworks MX enables selected objects to be copied for insertion into a Flash movie.

original file in Fireworks. Insert a keyframe in Flash at Frame 10 and create a simple motion tween that brings this text object from off the stage to the center of the stage.

4. Complete this section of your animation by adding keyframes at Frames 20 and 30. Leave the frames between 20 and 30 set as static and set a motion tween that takes this first text object off the stage in Frame 30. When this, sequence is complete, add a new layer to your Flash movie.

5. Add a blank keyframe at Frame 15 of your new layer and return to Fireworks. For the next sequence, use the Quick Export button to copy the bottom text object in the Fireworks document. Paste this object into Frame 15 of Layer 2 in your Flash movie and create a new animated sequence that brings this text object onto the stage, leaves it in place for ten frames and then removes the object as the animation concludes. Return to Fireworks and close this first file.

6. The next object to bring into Flash is the viewport that the movie will be seen through. In this case, the entire Fireworks PNG file will be imported so that the transparency settings and the bevel and gradient effects for the images can be maintained. In Flash, choose File | Import and navigate to the file called *viewport_movie.png*. Once you select this file to open, you will see the dialog box in the following illustration. Flash and Fireworks give you several options as to how the image should be imported. The goal here is to maintain the appearance of the bevels and other effects applied to this image, so be sure the settings match those seen in the illustration and click OK to import the movie. Flash will import the movie and place it in a new layer that is automatically created for the Fireworks object.

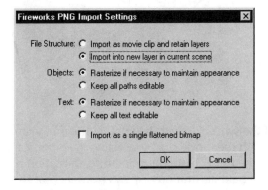

7. For the movie's control buttons, you will need to create two Symbols in Flash: a basic button Symbol that allows an action to be applied to the controller for the movie and a movie clip Symbol that lets the button animate as the viewer clicks on it. Both Symbols will use the same imported graphic from Fireworks, *movie_button.png*. Begin in Flash by choosing Insert | New Symbol

14

and setting the Symbol type as a movie clip. Name this button **Animated Button** and click OK in the Create New Symbol dialog box, seen here, to go to Flash's Symbol Editor.

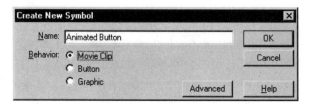

8. This Fireworks file has been prepared by placing the control knob and the background for the switch into separate layers. By doing so, you can import the objects separately into Flash, allowing for their modification while still maintaining their appearance. Choose File | Import and locate the file called *movie_button.png* and click Open so that it can be imported into the Symbol Editor. In the Fireworks PNG Import Settings dialog box, be sure that you set the File Structure option so that the Fireworks layers are maintained by creating new layers in Flash. Set both of the Rasterize options to keep the appearance of the image as it is. Once you have set the import properties, click OK to import the Fireworks graphic.

9. As you see in this illustration where all the objects in the image have been selected, the button graphic has been separated into its component parts. This allows for some quick animation so that the knob can slide to the right when the viewer activates the button. For the simple effect that is your goal here, add two additional keyframes to the movie clip Symbol.

10. In Frame 2 of the symbol, select the knob in the image and move it to halfway to the right. Finish the movie clip by selecting in Frame 3 and moving the knob completely to the right. Test your miniature animation by choosing Control | Test Scene. The next illustration displays how each of the Symbols should appear in Frames 1 through 3.

Frame 1   Frame 2   Frame 3

11. The next step is to add a second Symbol to this movie. Select Insert I New Symbol and for this Symbol set the Symbol type as a button. Name the button **Control** and select File I Import to bring another copy of the Fireworks *movie_button.png* file into Flash. For this file, retaining layers is not important because the movie clip Symbol has already been prepared. Set the import parameters so that this file is imported as a single flattened bitmap by checking that option in the bottom of the dialog box. Note as the image appears in the Up state frame of the Symbol Editor that it is a single image and no longer retains its editability. Continue preparing the button by inserting keyframes in the Over, Down, and Hit states of the Symbol Editor.

12. To generate a little motion for this button, add a new layer and insert a blank keyframe into the Down state of the button. Open the Library and locate the *Animated Button* symbol that you created previously. Drag an instance of this movie clip onto the stage and use the Flash Property Inspector to match the X and Y coordinates of the static button that appears in Layer 1. When your symbol is ready, check its appearance by choosing Control I Test Scene and return to Scene 1 of the movie.

13. With the buttons now constructed, you need only drag two instances of the *Control* symbol from the Library onto the stage and position them next to the text that is found on the viewport graphic that you inserted earlier. You are now prepared to attach actions to the movie to control the playback.

14. Select the button next to the word *Play* and open the Actions Inspector. Locate the Movie Control category and assign a Play action so that the button begins playing the movie. Select the instance of the button next to the Replay text and assign a Go To and Play action so that Frame 2 of the current scene is played when that button is selected.

15. Your final step to create the actions that you need to control this movie is to apply frame actions that cause the looping of the movie to stop. Select any keyframe in Frame 1 of the movie and use the Action Inspector to set a simple Stop action. Select the final keyframe and apply a Stop action to that frame as well.

16. To give the movie a little color and more interest, you will now add one additional Fireworks file to this document, and your work will be complete. The file called *movie_led.png* consists of a series of beveled rectangles that have been placed into frames and animated in Fireworks so that the colors of the buttons change as the animation plays. Once again, it is easier to import this file into a Flash symbol for later insertion into the movie. Chose Insert I New Symbol and set the Symbol type to Movie Clip. Name it *LED Lights*.

14

Tip

Animated files can also be exported from Fireworks as SWF files using the Quick Export feature. If you do not need to retain effects such as bevels for the exported animation, that option will result in a smaller file size than an animated PNG file.

17. Once the Symbol Editor opens, choose File | Import and navigate to the *movie_led.png* file and insert it into the editor. For this file, choose the top option in the Import Fireworks PNG dialog box so that the animated file is converted to a movie clip. Close the editor and return to the main movie.

18. From the Library, drag an instance of this movie clip Symbol onto the stage and position it in the lower right-hand corner of the movie. Your work with this file is now complete. Test your movie and, if all has gone well, it should appear as you see in Figure 14-3 (where onion-skinning has been enabled), with moving control buttons that allow you to start and reset the movie. You can also preview the movie by opening the file called *fireworks_completed.swf* from the exercise files for this module.

Figure 14-3 Using graphics created in Fireworks enables you to assemble a complete movie in Flash.

Project Summary

In this project, you have seen how to use Fireworks to augment the drawing capabilities that are included in Flash. Flash creates only vector images that cannot generate effects such as bevels and drop shadows; using Fireworks for making those graphics and importing the completed Fireworks files into a Flash movie is a great way to have the best of both worlds. Flash and Fireworks work so well together that often you will find that you create most of the graphics for your movie in Fireworks and use Flash only for applying actions and generating the movie's animations.

You should also now have an appreciation for the different ways that Fireworks files can be imported into Flash. The key to getting the most out of the interaction between the two programs is to understand how you intend to use your Fireworks graphics once they are brought into Flash. For simple objects, you may simply copy and paste Fireworks files into Flash using the Quick Export feature. For more complicated images requiring additional work in Flash to generate the effects you desire, Fireworks PNG files can be imported with their layers intact so that separate objects on the canvas can be modified. Finally, for Fireworks files containing animations, a file can be imported as a self-contained movie clip that is simply inserted from the Flash Library onto the stage. This project did not cover every method for integrating the two programs, but the examples you have seen here provide you with a solid understanding of how the programs work together and how different import settings affect the use of Fireworks images in Flash.

1-Minute Drill

● What import format is best when you want to preserve object transparency for a Fireworks file imported to Flash?

● How should images containing effects such as bevels, glows, and shadows be prepared for import to Flash?

● What export option allows vector objects to be edited once they are imported into Flash but loses all bitmap effects that have been applied?

● Where the preservation of image transparency is important, Fireworks files should be imported into Flash in the native Fireworks PNG format.
● Images containing effects such as glows, bevels, and shadows should be exported from Fireworks in the GIF or JPEG format before you insert them into a Flash movie.
● Fireworks objects exported in the SWF format remain fully editable in Flash but lose all bitmaps effects applied to them.

Integrating with Other Macromedia Products

The release of Macromedia's MX family of products is more than simply a marketing ploy. As the company defined its goals and evaluated how its customers work, they found just how often people used their products together. As a result of this market research, Macromedia set out to design its latest product line with the goal of creating a seamless integration that allows users to work more efficiently. Dreamweaver, Fireworks, and Flash were the primary benefactors of this philosophy, but other products such as FreeHand, Director, and even Homesite benefited as well. In Fireworks, the primary evidence of the integration that Macromedia intended is the inclusion of the new Quick Export feature that enables you to more easily export files to these applications.

As with Flash, the best approach to take when preparing Fireworks files for export to other applications is to examine how those files will be used in the program. As there are a number of methods for importing graphics into these software products, the following sections will summarize how each pair of programs may be used together and will look at some of the advantages and disadvantages of these methods.

Working with Macromedia FreeHand

FreeHand is Macromedia's vector-based illustration program that contains a much richer set of features for creating drawings and complex multiple-page layouts than does Fireworks. Although FreeHand is usually thought of as a print application, it also has terrific capabilities for integrating with Flash, allowing images to be blended, rotated, and traced in ways that far exceed Flash's graphic capabilities. In addition to these tools, FreeHand also can apply special effects such as perspectives and lenses that let a skilled designer create rich and varied images.

Importing Fireworks Images to FreeHand

Fireworks' ability to print images is very limited, so one of the most common uses for integrating the two programs arises when a graphic designed in Fireworks needs to be placed into a print format. Perhaps you've created a company logo for use on a web site and wish to use the same image for company letterheads and brochures. Being able to export directly into FreeHand for the final page composition enables you to use a single graphic not only for web design work but also for other output formats.

There are a number of methods at your disposal for exporting Fireworks files to FreeHand. FreeHand imports Fireworks PNG files directly into a document, so often the simplest method to use is to choose File | Import while in FreeHand and navigate to the original Fireworks file. When a Fireworks PNG file is imported into FreeHand, it will be imported as if it were a regular bitmap image and lose any editability. Still, for a simple graphic like the one you see in Figure 14-4, simply importing directly into FreeHand is often the best option. In addition to importing in this way, you can also drag a Fireworks graphic from an open window in Fireworks and drop it into a FreeHand page. The key to remember is that this method will cause the object to lose editability.

For more advanced operations in which you may wish to edit the text placed in a Fireworks graphic, change the fill of objects, or make use of FreeHand's capabilities for creating special effects with FreeHand lenses and blends, the correct export method is to convert the file into a format that FreeHand and other vector drawing programs recognize. The current default file type for vector drawing tools is the *.ai* format associated with Adobe Illustrator. Fireworks files can be converted to the Illustrator 7 format by choosing File | Export and choosing Illustrator 7 from the options available in the File Type field. In addition, you can use the Quick Export button in Fireworks MX to save the file directly as

Lorem ipsum dolor sit amet, consetetur sadipscing elitr, sed diam nonumy eirmod tempor invidunt ut labore et dolore magna aliquyam erat, sed diam voluptua.

At vero eos et accusam et justo duo dolores et ea rebum. Stet clita kasd gubergren, no sea takimata sanctus est Lorem ipsum dolor sit amet. Lorem ipsum dolor sit amet, consetetur sadipscing elitr, sed diam nonumy eirmod tempor invidunt ut labore

Figure 14-4   Fireworks graphics imported into FreeHand allow for more advanced page layout tools to be combined with images originally designed for the Web.

14

an Illustrator 7 file by selecting the FreeHand button and choosing Export to FreeHand, as you see here.

Once the Fireworks file is exported to the Illustrator 7 format, you can open it directly in FreeHand or import it into an existing FreeHand document. With the powerful tools available in FreeHand for working with the vectors originally designed in Fireworks, you can produce some great effects that wouldn't have been possible in Fireworks. For example, the following illustration was created in FreeHand by placing the imported object into an envelope, creating the illusion that the original text has been wrapped around a sphere. In addition to this example, a Fireworks file imported as a vector illustration can have the full range of effects applied to it, including modification of fills and strokes.

The final method for importing a Fireworks file into FreeHand is to copy the vector outlines of the objects you have drawn and paste these simple objects into a FreeHand document. With this technique, you can paste an object such as a simple drawing created with the Pen tool (or one of the other vector drawing tools) directly into FreeHand for further modification. It should be noted that this is the most limited option because only the vector points and paths will appear in FreeHand when the objects are pasted onto the page, and all fills, strokes and effects will be removed. This may still be a viable option, though, when the scope of your work is limited and you need only capture a particular shape for use in FreeHand.

Note

You'll find copies of the original Fireworks files used in this section in the exercise files for this module. For working with the original Fireworks files, open *fireworks2freehand.png*. For practicing with the same file in the Illustrator 7 format, open *fireworks2freehand.ai*.

Importing FreeHand Files to Fireworks

FreeHand contains many vector drawing features not found in Fireworks, so there may be times when you want to take advantage of the program's superior illustration capabilities to create images for the Web. This is another case in which the two programs work extremely well together. Images created in FreeHand can be dragged from a FreeHand window and dropped on a Fireworks canvas or copied in FreeHand and pasted into Fireworks. This simple transfer of images allows you to quickly move an image into Fireworks so that it can become part of a page composition for the Web.

When this method is used, Fireworks will employ its default settings for converting the vector image into a format that can be worked with in Fireworks. Both programs use vectors for defining objects on the canvas, but the underlying technology is different, and Fireworks will convert the FreeHand image into Fireworks' native format so that objects can be edited. You should be aware that there is often some degradation in image quality when this technique is used. The following example takes advantage of FreeHand's ability to create envelopes for curving text. An image with some text was placed on a circle with a gradient fill.

14

The text objects retained their shape, but the quality of the gradient degraded during the transfer to Fireworks.

You can attain more precise control of images imported from FreeHand by choosing File | Import in Fireworks and setting the exact attributes that you want applied to the FreeHand file. As you see in Figure 14-5, there are a large number of options for determining the quality of the FreeHand file before you bring it into Fireworks. By using this option, you can change the size of the image, set the resolution, and determine how multiple objects in the FreeHand

Figure 14-5 Use the Vector File Options dialog box when importing complex images from FreeHand

document are to be converted for use in Fireworks. For complex images containing multiple layers, this method is preferred.

Note

You will find a file labeled *freehand2fireworks.fh10* in the exercise file for this module to practice with.

Working with Macromedia Director

Director is the program that designers turn to when they want to develop interactive games and training applications for delivery over the Web or through CDs. This incredibly powerful and complex program enables you to design content that allows for intricate interactions with viewers in ways far too numerous to detail here. Director has its own drawing tools, but they are similar to those in Flash in that there are limitations to the types of images that can be created directly in the Director authoring environment.

Exporting Fireworks Files to Director

In cases where you wish to complete your design work in Fireworks and import images into Director, you have a wide range of options. For simple images, you can create your graphics in Fireworks and export them as GIFs or JPEGs for insertion into Director. Director will maintain the appearance of these objects exactly as they look when exported.

Director also allows for the import of Fireworks files that have been exported to the 32-bit PNG format. This option is useful when your image contains transparencies that you wish to maintain. For that option, either use the Optimize panel to set the file format to PNG32 and export the image as you normally would or choose File | Export Preview and change the file format in the preview window before completing the export process. In both cases, assuming you wish to export the canvas with a transparent setting, be sure to change the matte color to the transparent option.

Director also enables you to import interactive images from Fireworks. This means that you can slice your image and apply behaviors to the slices such as rollover effects and buttons that will be active once imported into Director. To prepare a Fireworks file containing slices and behaviors for export to Director, choose File | Export and set the file type to Director. You will also need to determine how the slices are to be treated by Director by choosing the correct option from the Source menu. For Fireworks files containing multiple layers and animations, set the option to Fireworks Layers. For files containing behaviors attached to slices, the correct format is Fireworks Slices. These two options also

14

appear in the options available for Director when the Quick Export button is selected.

Importing Fireworks Images to Director

The process of importing graphics created in Fireworks is determined by the way that the files were exported. For simple GIF, JPEG or PNG32 images, you need only select File | Import and navigate to the location where the file has been saved. Once the file is selected, Director will present a simple dialog box asking how the image's color depth should be set. Once these settings are determined, the image will be imported into the Cast window and be available for insertion into the Director movie.

To import a Fireworks file containing behaviors, choose Insert | Fireworks | Images from Fireworks HTML. Director will again present a dialog box asking how the image's colors are to be preserved and will allow you to convert the behaviors to Director's native scripting language, known as Lingo. Once these options are determined, the HTML file and its associated images become part of the Director cast and are available for insertion into the movie.

Working with Macromedia Homesite

For working directly in a code-authoring environment, Macromedia offers the program called Homesite. This application is used for writing HTML code so that web pages can be built by creating and editing the source code directly, without working in a visual design environment as you would with Dreamweaver. Homesite is also used for the creation of scripts that use interactive languages such as Cold Fusion and Active Server pages.

Fireworks images exported in the standard web formats such as GIF or JPEG can be inserted into Homesite quite easily. In most cases, this is accomplished by simply dragging the image file from Homesite's Resource window directly into the Edit window. Homesite requires that you save the file you are working on before inserting images so that the proper paths to the image's location can be maintained.

Fireworks files that contain behaviors or slices can also be imported into Homesite page quite easily. The process of exporting an interactive Fireworks file for use in Homesite is identical to the one used for Dreamweaver, except that the HTML format must be set to the Generic HTML category. To export an interactive image, choose File | Export after the file has been optimized and choose a location for the file within the current Homesite project folder. Click the Options button and change the HTML style to Generic HTML and export the HTML file with its supporting graphics.

Note

If you work extensively in Homesite rather than in Dreamweaver, you will want to change the default HTML style from Dreamweaver to Generic. Make this change by choosing File I HTML Setup and setting the style in the dialog box that appears.

In addition to this method, you can also choose to export the images separately and copy and paste the HTML code into a Homesite document. For this approach, export the images using the Images Only option in the Export dialog box into your Homesite project folder. Follow by clicking the Quick Export button and choosing the Copy HTML Code option. Fireworks will present two dialog boxes that allow you to set the HTML style and apply a base name for the slices used in the code.

As with Dreamweaver, Fireworks files inserted into a Homesite document can be edited in Fireworks by using the launch and edit capabilities of the software. In the Homesite Resources window, locate the file you wish to edit and right-click the filename. From the options that appear, select Edit in Macromedia Fireworks. Fireworks will launch with a special Document window that contains a Done button at the top of the window. You need only modify the image as you like and click the Done button, and Fireworks and Homesite will work together to update both the source file and the Homesite document.

1-Minute Drill

- What file format enables a Fireworks file to maintain editability of vector objects after it is exported to FreeHand?

- What file format allows a Fireworks file to maintain transparency and effects settings when imported into Director?

- What action is required before Fireworks HTML can be used within Homesite?

- Exporting Fireworks files in the Adobe Illustrator 7 format allows vectors to be edited in FreeHand.
- To maintain transparency and effects settings, export a Fireworks file in the 32-bit PNG format for use in Director.
- Before Fireworks HTML can be used in Homesite, the HTML style must be set to the Generic style.

14

Integrating with Other Applications

Fireworks MX works well with programs other than its siblings from Macromedia. These programs do not feature the common user interface and tight integration that exists between products in the MX product line, but they are still used by many people. Recognizing this, Macromedia has made it possible to work efficiently even when you choose to use one of its competitors' products—Microsoft FrontPage or Adobe Photoshop.

Working with Microsoft FrontPage

Many fans of Macromedia products would never consider using an HTML editor other than Dreamweaver, but the fact is that a huge number of web designers use FrontPage. With an easy-to-use interface and automated features that Dreamweaver lacks, many people find designing for the Web in FrontPage to be easier than working in Dreamweaver with its stricter compliance with Web standards. Regardless of your reasons for choosing FrontPage as your HTML editor, Fireworks MX has been designed so that all of your images can be designed just as if the final output were intended for Dreamweaver, including the same launch and edit feature found in Dreamweaver.

You must keep a few special considerations in mind when you intend to use Fireworks files in FrontPage; the most important is the HTML style that Fireworks exports. Dreamweaver and FrontPage use different naming conventions, especially for creating JavaScript behaviors, so you must set the HTML style for exporting images containing behaviors before exporting this kind of image. To change the default HTML style to FrontPage, select File | HTML Setup and set the style to FrontPage. Figure 14-6 displays the appearance of the HTML Setup dialog box when FrontPage has been specified as the style for export.

For images containing behaviors, the best approach for working with the JavaScript associated with the interactions is to open the Fireworks HTML document and copy and paste the sections required for the interactive elements to function directly into another FrontPage document. FrontPage does not allow the HTML to be inserted directly into a web page with its behaviors intact; this method allows you to modify the scripts as required so they function correctly within the FrontPage environment.

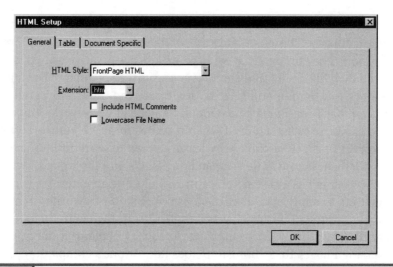

Figure 14-6   Preparing interactive images for export to FrontPage requires changing the HTML style to one compatible with FrontPage.

For images without interactive behaviors, the process of inserting graphics is much simpler. For files exported as simple GIFs or JPEGs, you need only choose Insert | Image in FrontPage to put the image onto the page. For images that have been sliced, you can export the images separately and then copy and paste the HTML that contains instructions for reassembling the images directly into the code in FrontPage.

Fireworks MX has also added the ability to edit images from within FrontPage. Similar to the way that Dreamweaver launches Fireworks when an image needs to be modified, FrontPage will open Fireworks when you need to edit a graphic. To do so, simply click the button that FrontPage provides labeled Launch and Edit Selected Graphic in Fireworks. Fireworks will ask whether you wish to edit the source PNG file and open that image if that option is selected. Once you have finished editing the image, simply click the Done button and Fireworks will return you to FrontPage with the edits in place.

Working with Adobe Photoshop

It may seem unusual that two fiercely competitive companies such as Adobe and Macromedia would actually produce products that are compatible with each other. However, because both companies understand the reality of how people buy and use software, it has been to the advantage of both companies to make it

14

possible for one product to support another even though they are not produced by the same company. This is certainly true of the relationship between Fireworks and Photoshop. The companies have become less cooperative as this is being written, including filing suits and countersuits against each other regarding patent infringements, but there is still relative peace between the two programs.

Photoshop has been in existence much longer than Fireworks and is recognized as the de facto standard when it comes to photo editing software, so many designers begin their careers by learning how to work in Photoshop and then stay with the program as they expand their skills into the world of web design. Photoshop certainly has a rich set of features, including an extensive set of filters that allow users to apply special effects not possible in Fireworks.

Fireworks, on the other hand, was designed from the beginning as a tool for working with images intended for the Web. As such, it contains features for slicing and optimizing images that Photoshop does not. Adobe's companion product to Photoshop, ImageReady, performs many of the same functions as Fireworks, including slicing and attaching behaviors; however, it is a common practice for designers to create their images in Photoshop and prepare the image for output to a Web format in Fireworks. Fireworks contains options that allow retention of many objects in a Photoshop document, so the two programs work very well together.

Importing Photoshop Files to Fireworks

If you choose to work in Photoshop and optimize in Fireworks, you will need to be aware of the options for importing Photoshop files into Fireworks. You can simply open a file created in Photoshop or drag and drop an image from a Photoshop document to a Fireworks canvas, but you will have the greatest control over the appearance of the image by checking and setting the import preferences for your files. To set the preferences for importing Photoshop files, choose Edit | Preferences (Fireworks | Preferences in Mac OS X). The dialog box displayed in Figure 14-7 shows the appearance of the Import Preferences dialog box and points to the primary settings that affect how Fireworks will convert a Photoshop file.

At the top of the dialog box, you see the options for importing existing layers from a Photoshop file. Most Photoshop images are composed of multiple layers, so this is an important setting to consider when bringing a file into Fireworks. These settings can be changed to create the following options:

● **Convert to Fireworks Objects**   Each layer in the Photoshop file will be converted to an object that appears in a single Fireworks layer. In most cases this will be the appropriate choice to make.

- **Share Layers Between Frames** All layers are visible in separate frames in the Fireworks document. This option allows you to use a Photoshop image as a background where animations occur in other frames.

- **Convert to Frames** Each layer in the Photoshop document is placed in a separate Fireworks frame. For Photoshop images that will be converted to an animated GIF format, this would be the appropriate import setting to use.

In addition to working with graphical objects, you can also work with text created in Photoshop, with some limitations. You'll recall the brief discussion of how competitive these two companies are, and part of the fallout of that competition has been the refusal by Adobe to provide documentation so that text objects created in newer versions of Photoshop can be edited in Fireworks. Text created in Photoshop 5.5 and earlier can be edited in Fireworks as long as the font type used is present, but text from documents created in Photoshop 6 and later can no longer be edited in Fireworks. If you anticipate a need to edit your text once you import the file into Fireworks, you must save the file in a Photoshop 5.5 format.

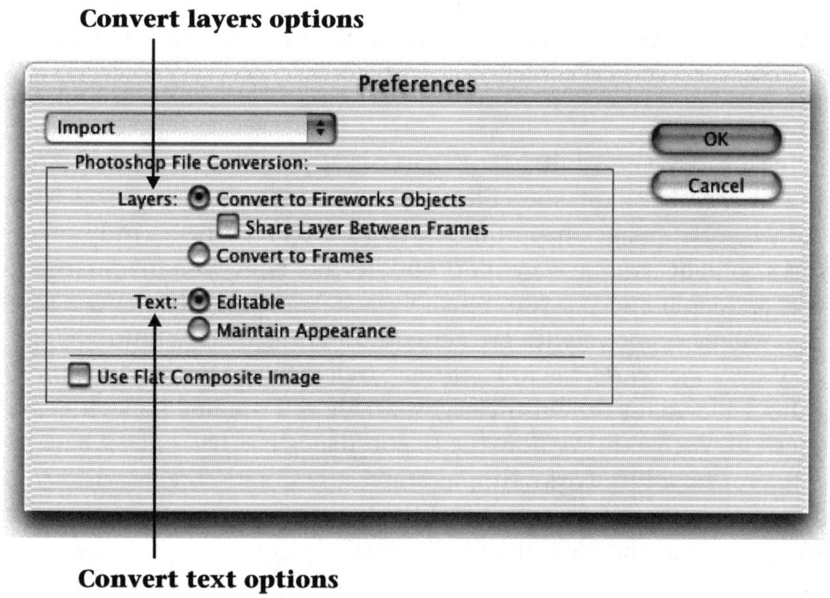

Convert layers options

Convert text options

Figure 14-7 Settings applied in the Import Preferences dialog box control how Fireworks converts Photoshop files.

14

With that said, Fireworks contains additional preferences for how Fireworks will treat text imported from Photoshop. To set these options, choose one of the two available choices in the Import Preferences dialog box:

- **Editable** Use this option if you wish to change the appearance of text by using the Fireworks Text tool or Property Inspector. By keeping text editable, you will be able to change fonts, font size, and styles. You'll also be able to apply fills, strokes, and effects as if you had created the text in Fireworks.

- **Maintain Appearance** For those instances in which it is more important that the text maintains its appearance than its editability, choose this option.

The final option in the Import Preference dialog box converts the Photoshop image to a flattened bitmap image with no editable regions. Select the check box labeled Use Flat Composite Image if you do not need to work with individual layers or text. This option has the effect of converting the image to a simple JPEG or GIF image.

Note

You will find a file labeled *photoshop2fireworks.psd* in the exercise files for this module to practice using the different import settings for bringing a Photoshop file into Fireworks. Special thanks go to my local Photoshop guru, Anthony Asci, for preparing this composite image for use here.

Exporting Fireworks Files to Photoshop

In the same way that Photoshop files can be imported into Fireworks, you can export Fireworks images from Fireworks for further editing in Photoshop. Fireworks contains two preset export options that allow you to specify a range of export options at once, or you can apply custom settings that let you determine how files will be exported with greater control of the final output.

To export a Fireworks file to Photoshop, select File | Export or use the Quick Export button to access the Other category where you will find the option to Export to Photoshop. With either option, the Export dialog box will open where further controls over how Fireworks should convert text and objects will be found. Figure 14-8 displays the appearance of the Export dialog box where Photoshop PSD has been set as the file format for export.

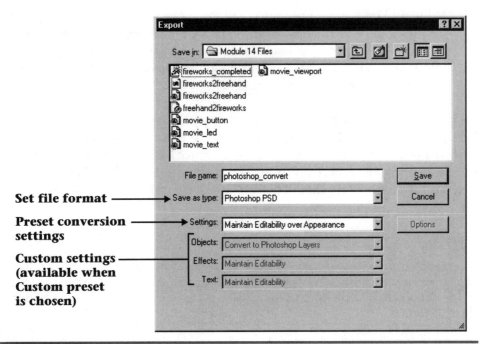

Set file format

Preset conversion settings

Custom settings (available when Custom preset is chosen)

Figure 14-8 Converting a Fireworks file to the Photoshop format is controlled by settings applied in the Export dialog box.

─┤Note─────

When File I Export is selected, you will need to change the Save As field to Photoshop PSD to access these options. Using the Quick Export option will take you to the Export dialog box with the Photoshop PSD file format already selected.

In most cases, one of the two primary conversion presets will be adequate for transferring a Fireworks file for further use in Photoshop. The two available presets for file conversion are summarized here:

● **Maintain Editability Over Appearance**   This option converts separate objects on the Fireworks canvas to separate layers in Photoshop. Where the ability to change and modify an image is more important than keeping the exact appearance intact, this is the appropriate choice.

14

● **Maintain Fireworks Appearance** In those cases where you wish to keep the appearance of an object exactly the same as it appears in Fireworks, this option removes editability of the Fireworks objects by placing them into a single Photoshop layer. This option will keep effects, strokes, and fills you've set in Fireworks in place.

In addition to these presets, you can choose the Custom setting and specify exactly which attributes are most important to maintain and which may be rendered in a state that maintains their appearance but loses editability. When the Custom setting is chosen, you can specify how individual graphical objects, text, and applied effects should be converted when the file is exported to Photoshop.

Tip

To experiment with these options, create a simple Fireworks document with graphical objects and text on the canvas. Apply simple effects such as bevels and drop shadows to see how changing the export settings affects the image when it is converted to the PSD format.

1 Minute-Drill

● What step must you take before exporting Fireworks HTML for use in FrontPage?

● Where can you find import options that will enable you to change the way that Fireworks converts Photoshop files when they are imported?

● Where can you find export options that will enable you to change how Fireworks converts images when exported for use in Photoshop?

What to Take Away

In this module, you have had the opportunity to explore just a few of the ways that Fireworks can be used as an image editor to export files for use in programs other than Dreamweaver. Fireworks was originally intended as

---

● Before exporting Fireworks HTML for use in FrontPage, you must set the HTML style to FrontPage by choosing File I HTML Setup.

● Preferences for converting Photoshop files are found in the Import Preferences dialog box, accessed by selecting Edit IPreferences (Fireworks I Preferences in Mac OS X).

● Export settings for converting Fireworks files for use in Photoshop are found in the Export dialog box when Photoshop PSD has been set as the export file type.

a graphics program for exporting images for use on the Web, and it features a tight integration with its sister web design program. However, it is not restricted to exporting images solely for Dreamweaver.

You have seen in a lengthy but instructive project how to construct an entire interface for a Flash movie in Fireworks and then, by choosing import and export options, complete the interface for an animated movie in Flash. The combination of Fireworks and Flash opens a world of possibilities to the designer as both vectors and bitmaps are combined in Flash movies and in Flash interfaces. As more designers and application developers work between these two programs, you can expect to see even greater interactions between the two programs as people discover just how seamlessly the two can be used together.

You have also had the opportunity to explore how FreeHand can be used for its superior printing capabilities when a graphic originally created in Fireworks for use on the Web needs to be printed. FreeHand contains a wide range of options for creating vector graphics with special effects such as lenses and blends, so you have also been introduced to ways to import a FreeHand file into Fireworks for optimization and use in a web document.

In the final section on integrating Macromedia products, you have learned how Fireworks files can be used in both Director and Homesite for adding graphics to these programs. In the case of Director, you now know that Fireworks files containing interactive elements can be imported and Director will convert the JavaScript behaviors into its native Lingo programming language.

In the final section of this module, you have seen how Fireworks can be used with two of the most popular web and graphics editors—Microsoft FrontPage and Adobe Photoshop. Even though these programs come from two of Macromedia's fiercest rivals, Fireworks still contains many features that allow you to work seamlessly between these programs when you need to create web pages in FrontPage or work with images in Photoshop. Fireworks makes it easy to work with these competing products by providing the Quick Export feature that enables you to immediately set the proper file formats when you need to leave the world of Macromedia and work in another company's program.

Finally, as this book concludes, I hope that you leave it with an appreciation for the many ways that the fabulous program known as Fireworks MX can be used to create graphics that add a level of sophistication and beauty to your work for the Web. As the Macromedia slogan says, Fireworks adds a great deal to "What the Web Can Be," and as you leave the beginner label behind, it is my sincere hope that this book has helped you discover what you can be as well.

14

☑ Mastery Check

1. What file format allows all objects in a Fireworks file to be read when it is imported into Flash?

_____

_____

2. Under what conditions would the Export as SWF feature be useful when working with Fireworks and Flash?

_____

_____

3. What file format allows both frames and effects to be preserved when imported into Flash?

_____

_____

4. What is Macromedia's primary application for working with documents that will be printed?

_____

_____

5. What is the simplest method for importing a Fireworks file into FreeHand?

_____

_____

6. Which file format allows for the greatest control over an image's appearance when imported into Director?

_____

_____

7. How are images files in Homesite opened for editing in Fireworks?

_____

_____

☑ *Mastery Check*

8. What new features in Fireworks MX make the integration between FrontPage and Fireworks more efficient?

_____

_____

9. What limitations exist when working with text created in Photoshop?

_____

_____

10. Where are export settings found that enable you to change the way that Fireworks prepares images for export to Photoshop?

_____

_____

14

Part 3

Appendixes

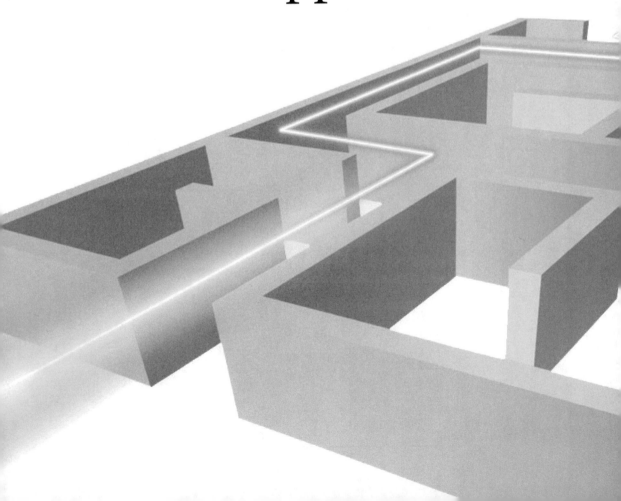

Appendix A

Answers to
Mastery Checks

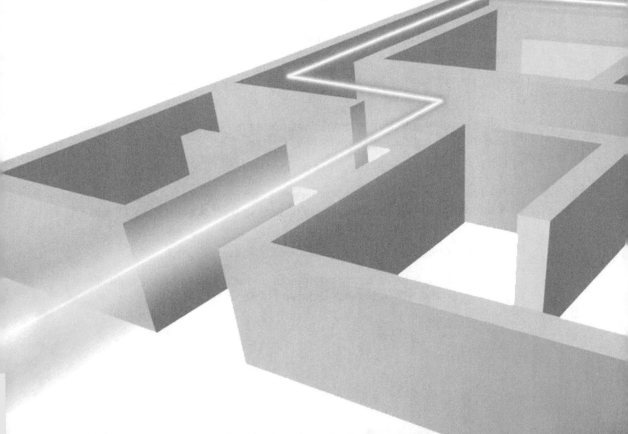

Module 1: An Introduction to Fireworks MX

1. What is the primary function of Fireworks?

Fireworks was created with one mission in mind—to produce the best possible images available for use on the Web while maintaining small file sizes for faster downloads.

2. Why are files created in Fireworks exported to another image format?

In their native PNG format, Fireworks files contain additional information embedded in the image to make it easier to modify them. This creates larger file sizes that need to be optimized and exported to a standard web format before inserting them in a web page.

3. How are the different tools in the Tools panel organized?

The tools in the Tools panel are grouped into function categories: selection, drawing, editing, hotspot/slice, panning/zooming, and color.

4. What is the primary tool used for selecting and moving objects on the canvas?

The Pointer tool is used for selecting objects on the canvas and changing their location.

5. Why should caution be exercised when selecting colors from your system Color Chooser options?

Colors selected with the system Color Chooser may not be web-safe, in which case they will not display properly in a browser.

6. What is the function of the Property Inspector?

The Property Inspector is used for viewing and modifying basic information about objects in a Fireworks document such as their size, location, fill and stroke color, and applied effects.

7. How are panels and inspectors grouped in Fireworks MX?

Panels and inspectors are now arranged in a docking area on the right side of the Fireworks MX Integrated Desktop Environment.

8. Where are common commands for operations such as saving, printing, modifying, copying, and pasting found?

As with most computer programs, common commands for changing objects are found in the menu bar. Windows users may also access many of the most common, such as copy and paste, in the Main toolbar.

9. What is the purpose of "slicing" an image?

Slices are used when a large image is divided into separate smaller images that are reconstructed by the browser.

10. What types of commands area available through the Context Menu, accessed by right-clicking (CONTROL-clicking with a Macintosh) an object?

Fireworks places many of the most common operations into the Context menu, including Help, editing commands, magnification options, and transforming commands.

Module 2: Creating Original Artwork with Vectors

1. How are bitmap images created?

Bitmaps are created by devising a grid and then filling each square of the grid with a color.

2. List three rules for naming files that will be used on the Web.

Files that will be used on the Web should not have any spaces in the file name, should not contain any special characters other than the underscore or dash, and should not begin with a number.

3. What visual aid does Fireworks use to let you know that an object is available for selection?

As the pointer passes over an object on the canvas, the object becomes outlined in red, letting you know that it is now available to be selected.

4. How are vector-based drawings created?

Vector-based objects are composed of a series of points that are connected by strokes, known as paths.

5. What basic shapes can be drawn using the tools provided in the Tools panel?

The Tools panel allows you to draw: rectangles, rectangles with rounded corners, circles and ellipses, and polygons and stars.

6. What does the term "marqueeing" refer to?

Marqueeing is a method of selecting multiple objects on the canvas by using the Pointer tool to draw a box around them.

7. Which tool is used for selecting and modifying a single point on a path?

The Subselection tool is used for selecting and manipulating individual points on a path.

8. How are objects freely rotated on the canvas?

To rotate an object on the canvas, select the object and then use the Scale, Skew, or Distort buttons to rotate an object by hand.

9. How is the SHIFT key used for the selection of multiple objects on the canvas?

Multiple objects are selected by holding down the SHIFT key and using the Pointer tool to select the objects.

10. How is the magnification of an area of the canvas increased?

Use the Zoom tool (magnifying glass icon) to zoom in on a portion of a drawing by dragging a box around the place on the canvas you wish to magnify.

Module 3: Working with Bitmap Images

1. What three settings do you determine each time a new Fireworks file is created?

The New Document dialog box is used to determine the size, color, and resolution of a new canvas.

2. What is the purpose of having a negative area around the edges of a canvas in a Fireworks Document window?

The negative area around a canvas can be used when you want to drag images off the canvas so you can rearrange them. In addition, when an object is selected on the canvas, a handy way to deselect it is to click in the negative area of the Document window.

3. What options are available for edge settings when using bitmap selection tools?

When working with bitmap selection tools, use the Options panel to set edges to Hard, Anti-Alias, or Feathered.

4. How does anti-aliasing affect the edge of a bitmap?

Anti-aliasing makes the edges of bitmaps appear smoother by adding pixels and modifying the colors along the edge so they blend more smoothly with the canvas or a background color.

5. How does the Eraser tool create the effect of erasing part of an image?

The eraser works by painting an area of new pixels onto the canvas. If this is set to be transparent, or if the color is the same as the canvas, the replacement colors appear to erase part of an image.

6. How can bitmap lines, shapes, or brush strokes be removed from a bitmap image?

Lines, shapes, brush strokes, and areas that have been "erased" must be changed by using the Undo function.

7. Which bitmap painting tool provides the greatest flexibility for adding colored lines and shapes to an image?

The Brush tool has the greatest number of options available for adding strokes and objects to the canvas. Options available in the Stroke panel allow brush sizes and shapes to be changed, as well as line colors and special effects.

8. What new photo retouching tools have been added in Fireworks MX?

Fireworks MX has added the Blur, Sharpen, Dodge, Burn, and Smudge tools specifically for photo retouching.

9. What is a mask?

A mask is produced by combining two objects on a canvas, using one object to obscure or define another.

10. What special color does Fireworks use to mark a selected area when a mask is applied?

Fireworks changes the color of a selected area to yellow when a mask is applied.

A

Module 4: Working with Text and Text Effects

1. What is the major advantage to using text that is converted to graphical images?

The major advantage to using text converted to graphical images is that all major browsers will be able to display the images once they are converted to a bitmap format.

2. What is the major disadvantage to using text that is converted to graphical images?

The major disadvantage to using text converted to graphical images is that their file weight is greater than that of HTML files, and they increase the download time of web pages.

3. What font types are available for use in Fireworks?

Fireworks displays all of the fonts that are installed on your computer.

4. What is the difference between proportional and monospaced fonts?

Proportional fonts allocate space for each letter based on the amount needed for the letter to display properly. Monospaced fonts allocate the same space to each letter.

5. How are stroke options applied to text?

Stroke options may be applied to text in the Property Inspector.

6. How are effects options applied to text?

Effects options are assigned in the Property Inspector.

7. Can text that has been converted to a path be edited? Can font types be changed once text is converted to a path?

No. Once text is converted to a path, the ability to change basic characteristics such as font type is lost. Fireworks treats it as it would any other vector object once it has been converted.

8. What step must you take to use text that has been converted to a vector object in combination with other vector shapes, as in punching letters through another object?

Once text has been converted to a path, you must ungroup it in order to combine the text objects with other shapes.

9. What kinds of shapes can you attach text to?

Text can be attached to any vector shape, including lines, curves, rectangles, ellipses, or polygons.

10. How can you modify the orientation of text after it has been attached to a path?

You can modify the orientation of text attached to a path by choosing Text | Orientation.

Module 5: Exploring Strokes, Fills, and Effects

1. Define open and closed vector paths.

Closed vector paths have beginning and end points in the same location on the canvas. In open paths, the beginning and end points do not meet.

2. What unique approach does Fireworks use for the application of strokes, fills, and effects?

Fireworks uses a method that enables vector paths to define an object's structure and its location, size, and shape. Applying strokes, fills, and effects applies a coating of bitmaps on top of that basic structure that enables you to modify the appearance of the graphic.

3. What does the "Snap to Web Safe" option accomplish?

When you select colors, the "Snap to Web Safe" option enables Fireworks to find the color nearest the one you are using that will appear the same regardless of the browser or operating system being used to view the image on the Web.

4. How do you access and modify settings for an applied effect?

Effect settings are accessed and modified by clicking the Info button next to the effect's name in the Effects area of the Property Inspector.

5. How do inner bevels and outer bevels differ?

Inner bevels are contained within the outline of an object or text. Outer bevels are applied outside the borders of objects or text.

6. How are filter options accessed?

Filter options are accessed by choosing the Filters command on the Menu bar.

A

7. Where are third-party filters found once they are installed in Fireworks?

Third-party filters are found in the Filters area of the Menu bar once the plug-in has been installed in Fireworks.

8. What are Styles?

Styles are used to record one of two types of object properties—fills, colors, strokes, and stroke colors as applied to objects; or fonts, font sizes, font styles, and other text properties when applied to text objects.

9. What kinds of settings can be saved as Styles when used with vector objects?

Styles for vector objects can contain information about the graphic's fill type and color, stroke type and color, and applied effects.

10. What kinds of settings can be saved as Styles when used with text?

Styles for text can save information about a text object's font type, size, style, or other settings such as stroke and fill.

Module 6: Creating and Organizing Complex Graphics

1. What is the primary advantage of using vector objects for masking?

Because of the ease with which vector objects can be modified and the fact that masking with vectors is a nondestructive process, masking with vectors is a far superior technique to masking with bitmaps.

2. How does Fireworks list objects in the Layers panel?

Objects in the Layers panel are listed with a thumbnail of the object and the object's type.

3. What tool would you use to hide an object on the canvas?

Clicking the Show/Hide icon in the Layers panel enables you to hide individual objects. You may also hide entire layers.

4. Define grouping.

Grouping is the process of combining multiple graphical objects into a single object.

5. Define masking.

Masking is the process of using one image to partially hide an underlying graphical object.

6. What is a grayscale mask?

A grayscale mask uses a gradient that changes from black to white to define areas of a masked object from fully transparent to fully opaque.

7. How do the color properties of an image used as a mask affect transparency when the mask is applied?

In Fireworks MX, lighter colors allow more of the underlying object to appear more opaque, and darker colors cause areas of greater transparency when a mask is applied.

8. How can you select multiple objects using the Layers panel?

You may select multiple objects in the Layers panel by holding down SHIFT and clicking the object by name.

9. How can you use the Layers panel to modify a mask after the mask has been applied?

Selecting the object in the Layers panel marked with the Pen icon enables you to modify the individual control points along an object's path.

10. How can you use the Layers panel for deleting objects from a document?

Selecting an object by name in the Layers panel and clicking the trash can icon removes the object from the document.

Module 7: Tools for Creating Consistent Content

1. What primary features does Fireworks contain for the creation of consistent content?

Fireworks uses Symbols, Commands, batch processing, and the Find and Replace function to assist you in designing consistent content for a web site.

2. How can you access Symbols?

You can access Symbols from the Library panel.

A

3. Are Symbols available in all Fireworks documents?

Symbols exist only in the document in which they are created. Unless you export them to a custom library, they are not available to other documents.

4. What attributes of Symbol instances can be safely tweened?

Symbol instances that change size, opacity, or location can be safely tweened.

5. What panel tracks changes made in a Fireworks document?

The History panel tracks changes made in a Fireworks document.

6. How can you apply custom Commands to objects or documents?

Once a custom Command is saved, you can access it at any time by choosing its name from the Commands menu.

7. What is the first step in applying a batch process?

The first step in the batch process is to select the files that are to be processed.

8. How can you use the Find and Replace feature?

The Find and Replace feature is used by deciding which files are to be searched and which attributes are to be sought and then designating the new settings that are to be applied.

9. What kinds of objects can you search for using the Find and Replace feature?

You can use Find and Replace to search for colors, text, fonts, web addresses, or patterns of text called regular expressions.

10. How is the process of finding and replacing colors completed?

To Find and Replace colors, first select the color to be found and then choose the color that is to replace it.

Module 8: Creating Animated Files

1. Why is the animated GIF format used so widely on the Web?

The animated GIF format is the most widely used file format for animations because of its (almost) universal acceptance by web browsers.

2. What tool enables you to "see" multiple frames of an object at the same time?

Onion Skinning allows multiple frames to display at the same time, and is enabled in the Frames panel.

3. What technique takes multiple objects in a document and places each one in an individual frame?

The Distribute to Frames option found at the bottom half of the Frames panel takes multiple objects on a document's canvas and places them in separate frames.

4. Where are frame timings adjusted?

Frame timings can be adjusted directly in the Frames panel or by making final adjustments in the Export Preview dialog box.

5. How is a new animated Symbol created?

A new animated Symbol is created by choosing Insert | New Symbol, setting the Symbol type to animation, and using the Animate dialog box while in the Symbol Editor to animate the object.

6. What process is required to be able to use an animated Symbol in other documents?

Animated Symbols that you wish to use in other documents must be exported to a custom library and then imported into a new document.

7. What devices can you use for positioning an animated Symbol on a canvas?

Handles are provided for positioning instances of animated Symbols on the canvas—green for the beginning frame, and red for the final frame.

8. How can you change settings for animated Symbols in Fireworks MX?

In Fireworks MX, settings for animated Symbols can be accessed both by choosing Modify | Animate | Settings or by using the Property Inspector.

9. What is the only file format appropriate for animated files created in Fireworks?

Animated files created in Fireworks must be exported in the animated GIF format for use on the Web.

A

10. What feature of Fireworks allows you to preview file optimization settings?

File optimization settings can be previewed by using the Preview, 2-Up, or 4-Up tabs in the Document window.

Module 9: Creative Tips for Getting the Most Out of Fireworks

1. How can you apply textures to images?

Textures are applied to images by placing an object with a textured fill above the original picture and adjusting the transparency of the object so that the picture appears.

2. What technique tints images?

Images may be tinted by changing to the Blend Mode and adjusting the hue of the image.

3. What steps do you need to take to have Fireworks automatically create a picture frame?

To automatically create a picture frame, choose Commands | Creative | Add Picture Frame.

4. What command enables you to flip text over for use in a shadow effect?

Text that needs to be rotated may be changed by selecting the text and choosing Modify | Transform | Rotate 180°.

5. What type of fill can you use to create a brushed metal effect?

Brushed metal effects can be achieved by applying a linear gradient fill to an object and using the preset Silver color scheme.

6. Which tool can you use to skew objects so they appear to be receding into the distance?

To skew an object so that it appears to be receding into the distance, choose the Distort tool.

7. Where are the settings for custom brush strokes found?

Settings for creating a custom brush stroke may be found by selecting the Advanced button in the Stroke Type field of the Property Inspector.

8. What timesaving device should you use when you need to create multiple copies of the same object?

When a graphic calls for the use of multiple copies of the same image, it is best to create a Symbol and use multiple instances of the Symbol to achieve the effect you want.

9. How can you split a circle into three equal slices?

A circle can be split into three equal slices by placing a three-pointed star above it and selecting Modify I Combine Paths I Punch.

10. Where can you find a listing of web sites devoted to the use of Fireworks?

Macromedia maintains a listing of web sites that cover the use of Fireworks at www.macromedia.com/go/13187.

Module 10: Optimizing and Exporting Files

1. What is your primary goal when optimizing Fireworks PNG files?

The primary goal when optimizing Fireworks PNG files is to minimize the file's download time by adjusting the quality of the graphic. Optimization entails maintaining image quality while limiting file size.

2. What is your primary goal when exporting Fireworks PNG files?

The primary goal when exporting Fireworks PNG files is to choose the appropriate format that maintains image quality while limiting file size.

3. What two methods does Fireworks provide for viewing and adjusting optimization settings?

You can preview and optimize Fireworks PNG files either in the Export Preview dialog box or by using the preview tabs in the Document window.

4. Describe an image that is best exported in the GIF format.

Images suitable for the GIF format are those files that contain a limited number of primarily solid colors, with few subtle differences between colors.

5. Describe an image that is best exported in the JPEG format.

Images suitable for the JPEG format are those files that contain many different colors, with subtle shades and variations of colors.

A

6. How does the number of colors present in an image affect file size? How can you apply this in file optimization?

Fewer colors in an image mean a smaller file size. GIF files are optimized by limiting the available colors in the color palette. JPEG images are optimized with the Quality setting, which limits the available colors for that file format.

7. How can you use guides to slice an image into smaller pieces?

Guides are used to slice images into smaller pieces when the Slice along Guides option is selected in the Export dialog box.

8. How does Fireworks append filenames when slices are exported?

When slices are exported, Fireworks appends the filename with the slice's position in the table that is created, using the letter r for rows and the letter c for columns.

9. What common file format used on the Web supports transparencies?

The GIF file format is the only commonly used file format on the Web that supports transparencies.

10. What two types of transparency formats can you apply to a computer graphic?

Computer graphics that have transparent areas are set either to an alpha transparency or an index transparency.

Module 11: Creating Image Maps and Buttons

1. What special term is applied to both hotspots and slices?

Both hotspots and slices are referred to as web objects.

2. How do hotspots and slices differ?

Hotspots are primarily used to add an interactive area to an image that contains a link to a URL. Slices add the ability to create simple or advanced JavaScript behaviors or attach a link, allow for the application of different optimization settings, and function by breaking the image into separate areas that are reassembled in an HTML table.

3. What visual reference is provided to show the location, shape, and size of hotspots and slices?

The location, size, and shape of web objects are indicated by a colored overlay that Fireworks adds above an image—light blue for hotspots and light green for slices.

4. What is the advantage to using shared layers when creating images that contain rollovers?

By using a shared layer in an image with rollovers, you can determine which graphical object will remain fixed in each frame and which will change when the viewer mouses over an image.

5. What method for previewing images gives the best indication of how they will appear and function on the Web?

Previewing in a web browser gives the best indication of how interactive images will appear and function on the Web.

6. What tool enables you to create buttons that can contain up to four different sets of attributes?

The Button Editor enables the creation of graphics that can contain up to four different sets of attributes.

7. Which Fireworks panel helps you organize and manage links in your interactive images?

The URL panel is used for organizing and managing links in your interactive images.

8. Define a relative URL.

A relative URL is a link to a web page or document within your own web site and is specified by entering the file's path and name.

9. Define an absolute URL.

An absolute URL is a link to a web page or document outside your web site and is listed by its full web address, such as http://www.dw-fw-beginners.com.

10. What is the appropriate file format for exporting a Fireworks file that contains web objects?

A Fireworks file that contains web objects is exported as HTML with all of the supporting graphics files that comprise the image in either the GIF or JPEG format.

Module 12: Creating Advanced Navigational Elements

1. How do you create disjoint rollovers?

Disjoint rollovers are created when one object, the trigger, is designed in such a way as to make another object, the target, appear.

2. What is the advantage of creating disjoint rollovers in Fireworks rather than in Dreamweaver?

Fireworks enables you to work in a visual editing environment; creating a similar effect in Dreamweaver requires you to work in dialog boxes that do not display your results until you preview the page in a browser.

3. What four button states can you create with the Button Editor?

The Button Editor enables you to define button states as Up, Over, Down, and Over While Down.

4. What technology controls the appearance of buttons in a navigation bar?

The appearance of the buttons in a navigation bar is controlled using cookies.

5. How must you name buttons when the multiple navigation bar export option will be used?

When you export multiple navigation bars, you must name each button with the same name as the page being linked to, without the file extension.

6. What reference point should you use to define the location of pop-up menus?

Fireworks pop-up menus are positioned using the top left corner of the canvas as a reference point.

7. What limitation of pop-up menus must you consider when designing web sites with frames?

When designing with frames, you must consider the fact that pop-up menus cannot cross frame boundaries.

8. What method does Fireworks provide for designing pop-up menus?

The design of pop-up menus in Fireworks is done in Pop-up Menu Editor.

9. What two styles of pop-up menus may you create in Fireworks?

Pop-up menus may be designed in either an HTML style or a style that uses images.

10. What is the proper format for exporting a Fireworks document containing pop-up menus?

Fireworks pop-up menus must be exported in the HTML and Images format.

Module 13: Integrating Fireworks with Dreamweaver

1. How can you access preference settings for Dreamweaver and Fireworks?

Access preferences for Dreamweaver and Fireworks by choosing Edit | Preferences.

2. How can you optimize images from within Dreamweaver?

To optimize an image, right-click the image and choose Optimize With Fireworks to be taken to the Export Preview dialog box, in which optimization settings can be changed.

3. What is the correct file type to insert into a Dreamweaver page where the file contains hotspots, slices, or behaviors?

When a file contains hotspots, slices, or behaviors, the correct file to insert into a web page is the Fireworks HTML file.

4. What are the two differences between a standard Fireworks Document window and a window that opens when you are editing from Dreamweaver?

A

When editing from Dreamweaver, the Document window in Fireworks contains a Done button and lacks the Quick Export button.

5. What technique can you use during layout when a table cell needs to be set to a precise size?

When a table cell height or width needs to be set during layout, a transparent GIF file, called a spacer or shim, is inserted into the cell and stretched to the desired size.

6. What is the primary advantage of using library items in Dreamweaver?

Library items enable you to automatically update the element throughout the site by simply changing the library item itself and then letting Dreamweaver do the work of finding every instance of the library item and making the changes as necessary.

7. Where are Dreamweaver library items stored?

Library items are stored in a folder called *Library*, located in the same root folder as the files for the web site where it will be used.

8. What new feature allows for the quick export of slices or files from Fireworks MX?

The Quick Export button found in the upper left-hand corner of the Fireworks MX Document window allows for the quick export of slices or files for use in Dreamweaver.

9. What options exist in the new Quick Export feature for sending files to Dreamweaver?

The Quick Export button enables you to export files or slices, to update existing Fireworks HTML files, or to copy HTML to your computer's clipboard for use in Dreamweaver.

10. How can image placeholders be replaced by the actual images you wish to use in a Dreamweaver page?

Replace image placeholders by selecting the placeholder and clicking the Create button in the Property Inspector to launch a Fireworks file that matches the placeholder's exact size.

Module 14: Integrating Fireworks with Other Applications

1. What file format allows all objects in a Fireworks file to be read when it is imported into Flash?

Importing images in the Fireworks PNG format enables all of the objects in the image to be used when working in Flash.

2. Under what conditions would the Export as SWF feature be useful when working with Fireworks and Flash?

Exporting an object in the SWF format is useful when you want to edit a complex shape, such as a star, that is difficult to create in Flash.

3. What file format allows both frames and effects to be preserved when imported into Flash?

The animated GIF format enables you to use frames and effects in an image imported into a Flash movie.

4. What is Macromedia's primary application for working with documents that will be printed?

FreeHand is Macromedia's primary application for working with documents that will be printed.

5. What is the simplest method for importing a Fireworks file into FreeHand?

The simplest method for importing a Fireworks file into FreeHand is to simply copy in Fireworks and paste in FreeHand.

6. Which file format allows for the greatest control over an image's appearance when imported into Director?

The 32-bit PNG format allows for the greatest control of an image's appearance when imported into Director.

7. How are images files in Homesite opened for editing in Fireworks?

In the Homesite Resources window, locate the file you wish to edit and right-click the filename. From the options that appear, select Edit in Macromedia Fireworks.

A

8. What new features in Fireworks MX make the integration between FrontPage and Fireworks more efficient?

Fireworks files can now be prepared for export to FrontPage by using the Quick Export button in the Document window. FrontPage will also allow you to open a Fireworks file for editing using the Launch and Edit feature.

9. What limitations exist when working with text created in Photoshop?

To edit text created in Photoshop, the file must be saved in the Photoshop 5.5 format or an earlier version.

10. Where are export settings found that enable you to change the way that Fireworks prepares images for export to Photoshop?

Export settings for converting Fireworks files for use in Photoshop are found in the Export dialog box when Photoshop PSD has been set as the export file type.

Appendix B

Working with Fireworks Extensions

One of the breakthrough improvements in the latest edition of Fireworks is the ability to extend the capabilities of the program by adding additional functions known as *extensions*. Extensions add powerful capabilities to Fireworks MX by enabling developers to create panels and Commands in Macromedia Flash so that Fireworks can perform additional creative and automated operations.

Fireworks MX ships with a number of extensions that allow the software to go beyond its basic functionality. This appendix will introduce you to many of the extensions that are included with Fireworks MX and explain how additional extensions are installed to the program as they become available.

Working with Included Extensions

Right out of the box, Fireworks MX includes some important new additions to the program's creative tools. You can think of extensions as tool sets that work to automate the manipulation of images in much the same way that Fireworks Commands work. Extensions differ from Commands in that the interface for the Commands has been developed by using Flash, and additional extensions are available either through the Macromedia Exchange or for purchase from third-party developers.

The following sections describe how the extensions included with Fireworks MX are used.

Add Arrowheads Extension

In order to add arrowheads to a vector path, follow these steps:

1. Draw a path on the canvas using one of the vector drawing tools. Arrowheads can be added to a line drawn with the Line tool, Pen tool, or Vector Path tool.

2. Open the Add Arrowhead extension by choosing Commands | Creative | Add Arrowheads.

3. Set the properties for the arrowhead by making selections in the panels you see displayed in Figure B-1.

4. Select the check boxes at the top of the panel to apply the arrowhead to the beginning, end, or both ends of the path.

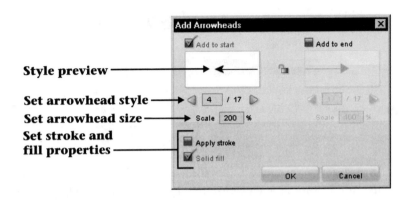

Style preview

Set arrowhead style

Set arrowhead size

Set stroke and
fill properties

Figure B-1 Apply arrowhead styles and sizes in the Add Arrowheads
extension panel.

5. Choose from one of the 17 arrowhead styles by clicking the button to the left or right of the styles listing. Note that different styles can be applied to the beginning and end points of the line.

6. Set the arrowhead size. The size of the arrowhead is measured in relation to the size of the line and can be set from 100 percent to 999 percent.

7. Set the stroke and fill properties for the line and click OK.

8. Once the arrowhead has been created, you can apply or modify stroke and fill properties in the Property Inspector.

Add Picture Frame Extension

The Add Picture Frame command has been available in previous versions of Fireworks, but additional controls have been added in Fireworks MX. To make a picture frame for a document, follow these steps:

1. With any document open, choose Commands | Creative | Add Picture Frame. The panel you see displayed in Figure B-2 will appear.

2. Choose the pattern you would like to use for the frame.

3. Set the width of the frame in pixels and click OK to create the frame.

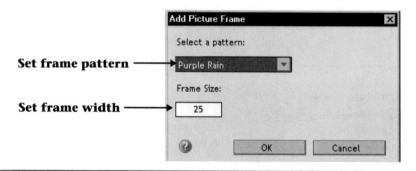

Figure B-2   Use the Add Picture Frame extension to add a border around a document's canvas.

4. Fireworks will apply a frame of the width you specify around the outside border of your document, inset from the canvas edge, in the Add Picture Frame panel.

5. To modify the panel, unlock the object labeled Composite Path in the Layers panel by clicking on the lock icon.

6. Modify the picture frame if needed once the path is unlocked.

Fade Image Extension

The Fade Image command works by automatically applying a mask to an image you select on the canvas. Much quicker and easier than creating a fade effect by manually drawing the masking object and applying the mask, this extension is an excellent example of the power of Fireworks extensions. To use the Fade Image extension, complete these steps:

1. Select an object on the canvas. The Fade Image extension will work with both vector objects and bitmap images.

2. Select Commands | Creative | Fade Image. The Fade Image panel you see in Figure B-3 will appear.

3. Select the fade effect you wish to apply by examining the thumbnail examples provided. Click on the thumbnail that most closely resembles the fade effect you wish to create.

4. Click OK to apply the fade effect.

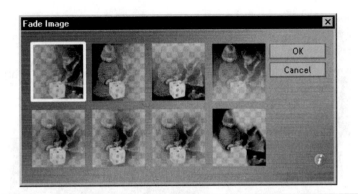

Figure B-3 | The Fade Image extension, developed by Joseph Lowery, automatically applies a fade effect in a set pattern.

Twist and Fade Extension

One of the most fascinating and complex new extensions included with Fireworks MX is the Twist and Fade extension developed by Steven Grosvenor and Stephen Voisey. As the name implies, this extension automatically rotates a selected object while modifying its transparency. With Twist and Fade, you can create fascinating graphics that would be extremely tedious to duplicate manually. Although the creative possibilities of the extension may not immediately come to mind, experimenting with the command will give you a good understanding of its capabilities. In addition, you can find a complete tutorial about this extension on the developer's web site at www.phireworx.com.

To use the Twist and Fade extension, follow these steps:

1. Create an object or set of objects on the canvas.

2. Select the objects that you want to apply the Command to.

3. Select Commands | Creative | Twist and Fade to open the Twist and Fade panel you see in Figure B-4.

4. Before experimenting with the settings that modify how the Command is applied, try the default settings on some sample objects. Note how the preview area appears as the Command is selected.

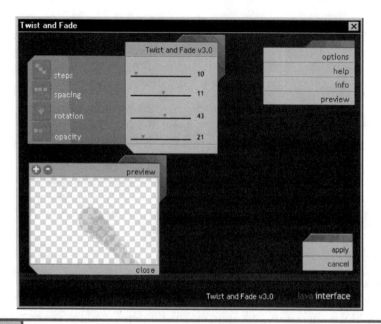

Figure B-4 The Twist and Fade panel allows objects to be multiplied on the canvas while they are also twisted into new positions.

5. To change the number of objects that are copied onto the canvas, increase or decrease the Steps setting by moving the slider. Note that as you apply more steps, the command will take longer to process and the file weight will increase.

6. The Spacing setting determines how far apart the objects will be from each other as they are copied onto the canvas.

7. To change the amount each object is rotated as it is copied, move the slider either left or right in the Rotation setting.

8. To adjust the opacity of the object, change the Opacity slider to the desired setting. An opacity setting of zero will result in a transparent object, and a setting of 100 will create an object that is completely opaque.

9. Additional settings that allow the object to be converted to a Symbol or to fade completely are available by selecting the Options button.

B

Resize Selected Objects Extension

One of the most elegantly simple extensions available in Fireworks MX is the Resize Selected Objects extension. With this simple-to-use panel, you can change the size of an object that you've selected on the canvas in increments of 1 or 10 pixels with the simple click of the mouse. Developed by John Dunning, an expert in the design of user interfaces, the Resize Selected Objects extension is another outstanding example of the direction that Fireworks extensions may take in the future.

To use this extension, follow these steps:

1. Select an object or multiple objects that you've drawn on the canvas. The Command can be applied to both vector and bitmap objects.

2. Open the extension by choosing Commands | Resize Selected Objects. The panel you see in Figure B-5 will appear.

3. Use the blue arrows to change the size of the selection in the direction you want. Selecting the arrows outside the box will increase the size of the object. Selecting arrows inside the box will decrease its size.

4. Use the large arrows to change the object in increments of 10 pixels. Use the small arrows to change the object in 1-pixel increments.

5. Click the check mark to accept the changes. Click the X to reject the changes you've made. Selecting either option returns you to the canvas where you can continue your work.

Align Extension

One of the less functional aspects of Fireworks is its ability to align objects on the canvas. Although you can perform some alignment operations by choosing the commands available through the Modify | Align menu, these functions have always been limited and somewhat difficult to implement.

The new Align panel, developed by Kleanthis Economou, addresses this problem by providing a graphical interface for aligning objects on the canvas. The Align extension makes it simple to position objects by providing buttons that demonstrate how the operations will be performed and allows objects to be aligned either relative to the canvas or to a selected point on the canvas. The

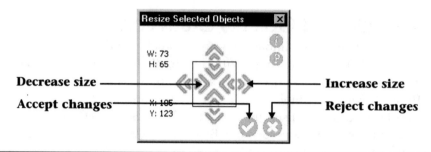

Decrease size ——————— Increase size
Accept changes ——————— Reject changes

Figure B-5 The elegant Resize Selected Objects extension allows for the quick adjustment of an object's dimensions.

appearance and function of the extension differs based on how you choose to set alignment, so this brief description of its capabilities will detail both options.

You can find additional information about this extension and others that the developer has created on his web site at www.projectfireworks.com.

Align to Canvas

To align objects relative to the canvas, follow these steps:

1. Select the object or objects you wish to align on the canvas.

2. Open the Align panel by choosing Windows | Align. This panel may be left open while you are working on the document. The panel can also be docked with the other panels in the panel group. The panel as it appears when it is not docked is seen in Figure B-6.

3. To align horizontally, choose the horizontal alignment buttons to align the object to the left edge, center, or right edge of the canvas.

4. To align vertically, choose the vertical alignment buttons and align the selected object to the top, center, or bottom of the canvas.

5. To center an object on the canvas, select both the center vertical and center horizontal buttons.

6. To distribute multiple objects on the canvas, choose the options in the second row of buttons. Objects can be distributed equally to the edges of the canvas as referenced on the buttons.

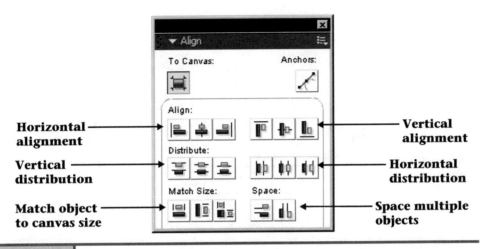

Horizontal alignment
Vertical distribution
Match object to canvas size
Vertical alignment
Horizontal distribution
Space multiple objects

Figure B-6   The Align panel contains multiple options for aligning, spacing, and resizing selected objects.

7. To change the size of an object so it matches the width or height of the canvas, choose the options in the Match Size category.

8. To space multiple objects on the canvas, choose the options in the Space category.

Align to Anchors

The second option in the Align panel allows selected anchor points on a path to be aligned to another vector path. This feature allows objects that have been drawn with the Line or Pen tool to be positioned relative to another path or to transform closed paths such as circles and rectangles. To align paths to selected anchors, follow these steps:

1. Open the Align panel by choosing Windows | Align. Click the Anchors button at the top of the panel to switch to that alignment mode. The features of this panel are displayed in Figure B-7.

2. Use the Subselection tool (white arrow) to select an individual anchor point on a path drawn with any vector drawing tool. To use this option, the control handles for the anchor point must be visible.

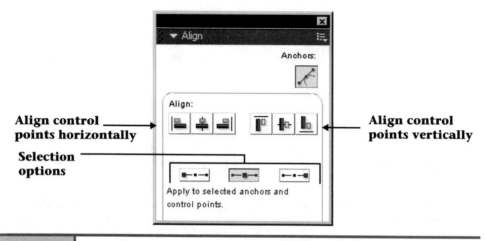

Align control points horizontally

Align control points vertically

Selection options

Figure B-7 | The Align to Anchors feature of the Align extension enables control points to snap to locations relative to one another.

3. For operations with selected control points, use the center button at the bottom of the panel. This option allows the greatest control over how the alignment features will be applied.

4. To align a selected anchor to the left, center, or right relative to a second selected anchor, use the row of buttons on the left.

5. To align a selected anchor to the top, center, or bottom of a second selected anchor, use the row of buttons on the right of the panel.

6. For operations that transform a closed path, draw the shape and choose Modify | Ungroup to make the individual control points in the shape available for selection with the Subselection tool.

Additional Extensions

In addition to the extensions covered here, other automated tools for making use of the power of Fireworks extensions are included with the software, and more are sure to follow as this new feature in Fireworks MX is developed further by Macromedia and private developers. You can expect to see additional extensions for the control of creative tools as well as extensions that will allow for further integration with the MX family of products.

One important extension that will not be covered here due to lack of space is the Data Driven Graphics Wizard. With this powerful tool, it is now possible to set a list of variables in a Fireworks document that connect to a remote database so that images can be inserted based on any number of parameters that you determine. This extension is just one example of the kinds of tight integration that Fireworks extensions now allow and offers a peek at what the future holds for Fireworks and the other programs from Macromedia.

As new extensions become available, you will need to know how to import the tools into Fireworks and manage your extensions. These operations are covered in the next section.

Managing Extensions

Extensions can enable you to automate repetitive tasks, or you can use them to apply filters, modify objects, or to use creative tools that change the appearance of both bitmaps and vector art. By combining JavaScript commands with the tools found in Fireworks MX, you can develop your own extensions or make use of those created by others.

Extensions that are available for Fireworks MX are found online at the Macromedia Exchange at www.macromedia.com/exchange. Through the exchange, you can locate new extensions as they become available and download them for installation in Fireworks MX. Fireworks MX uses the same Extension Manager to install, remove, and manage extensions that is used by both Dreamweaver MX and Flash MX. Figure B-8 displays the appearance of the Extension Manager in Windows. To open it, select Commands | Manage Extensions.

When you locate an extension that you would like to add to Fireworks, you must first download it and save the file to a folder called *Configurations/ Commands*. Alternately, if your browser supports this option, you may be asked whether you prefer to open the extension or save it to your hard drive. If you choose to open the extension, the Extension Manager will automatically open and install it. Fireworks provides multiple user support through Mac OS X and Windows XP, so the exact location of your configuration folder will depend on which operating system you are using. For assistance in locating this folder, see Help files in the category labeled Preferences and Keyboard Shortcuts. You'll also find instructions for downloading and installing extensions at the Macromedia Exchange.

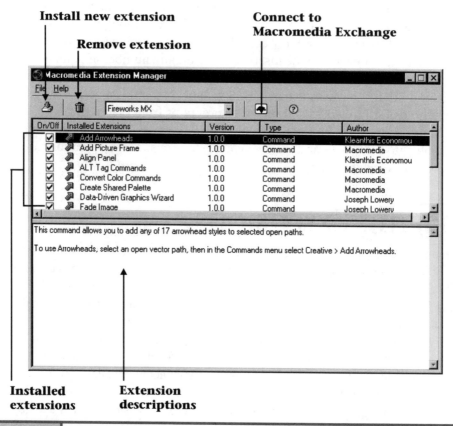

Install new extension

Remove extension

Connect to Macromedia Exchange

Installed extensions

Extension descriptions

Figure B-8 The Extension Manager is used for installing and managing Fireworks MX extensions.

Once you install an extension, you will see it listed in the Installed Extensions area of the Extension Manager. You can enable or disable an extension by highlighting its name and clicking in the check box to its left. As an extension is selected, you will also see a brief description of its capabilities in the Descriptions area. To delete an installed extension, highlight its name in the Listings area and click the trash can icon.

Additional information can be found in the Extension Manager's Help files, including detailed instructions on how to download, install, and manage extensions, as well as how you can create your own extensions to share with the Macromedia community.

Glossary

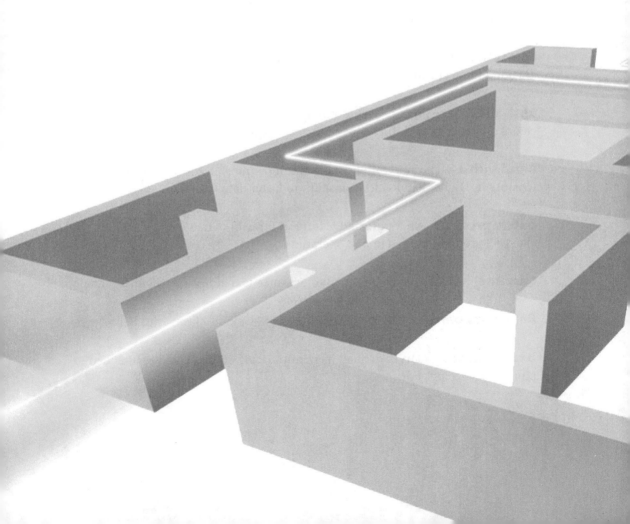

absolute URL   A hyperlink that contains the full web address of a web page, such as http://www.osborne.com.

action   A response triggered by an event that the viewer of a web page initiates, perhaps by rolling the mouse pointer across embedded code.

active link   A hyperlink that is currently selected by a web page viewer.

address   The unique location of an individual web page on the Internet. See **Universal Resource Locator (URL)**.

alt text   Short for *alternative text*. Provides additional information to a viewer of a web page in situations in which the browser is set to not display images or in which the viewer is using a page reading device.

animated GIF   An image file that plays a series of frames, creating the illusion of movement.

anti-alias   The process of smoothing the edges of an image by mixing the colors on the edge with the color of the canvas or background.

bandwidth   The amount of data that can be transferred from one computer to another. Higher bandwidth translates to faster data transfer.

batch process   An automated feature in Fireworks that enables you to change a group of images in one operation.

baseline   An imaginary line used to organize text along a horizontal plane.

Behaviors panel   The panel used to insert or modify JavaScript behaviors.

Bézier curves   Curves defined by manipulating control handles attached to points on a vector path.

bitmap   An image format in which individual elements of the graphic are stored in a grid formation, with each block of the grid filled with a particular color.

browser (web browser)   Program used to access and view web pages stored on the World Wide Web. The two most popular browsers are Internet Explorer and Netscape Navigator.

button   An individual graphic that contains a hyperlink.

Button Editor   The editor used in Fireworks to assign appearance, effects, and hyperlinks to a button.

canvas   The work area in a Fireworks document.

cell   The individual box that is created by the intersection of a row and a column in an HTML table.

closed path   A vector object that has its beginning and end points in the same location; for example, a circle.

Commands   A set of instructions applied to an image and saved for further use.

crop   The process of removing certain portions of an image.

dithering   The process of mixing colors in an image to create the illusion that another color is present.

Document window   The work area in Fireworks.

domain name   A unique name assigned to a company, individual, or organization that identifies its web site, such as www.osborne.com.

download   The act of retrieving information stored on a remote computer and copying it to a local computer.

export   The process of converting a Fireworks working file from its original PNG format to one suitable for use in a web page or other document.

extensions   Enhancements added to Fireworks that add functions to the program. Accessed through the Extensions Manager.

event   An action that occurs within a web page, often triggered by the viewer, such as the "event" of a mouse pointer coming into contact with an object. Coupled with actions to create a particular JavaScript behavior.

fill   Properties such as colors, textures, and gradients applied to a closed shape.

file weight   The total size in bytes of an image or file that is transferred on the Internet.

flyout menu   Used in Fireworks to denote additional tool options in the Tools panel.

font   A text style.

font size   The height of a particular font style. Set in the Property Inspector or Text Editor in Fireworks.

frame   A feature that allows web developers to design separate HTML documents that load into a browser at the same time.

gradient   A type of fill created when two or more colors are blended together.

Graphics Interchange Format (GIF)   Common image file format in use on the Web, popular because of the typically small file size that the format generates. GIFs are limited to 256 colors.

hexadecimal   The 6-digit number and letter code that describes a color.

History panel   The panel that tracks changes made to a document.

hotspot   An overlay applied to an image that contains a hyperlink.

hyperlink   An object in a web page that takes the viewer to another web page, causes a file to download from the web server, or causes some other action to be performed, such as playing a sound file.

Hypertext Markup Language (HTML)   Computer coding language that allows web browsers to read information using tags and attributes that define the document.

Hypertext Transfer Protocol (HTTP)   The standard method for transferring information between a web server and a web browser.

Internet   The worldwide collection of interconnected computers that are capable of passing information in the form of text and images.

image map   An image that contains JavaScript or HTML information that creates hyperlinks or adds functions such as rollovers.

image slicing   A technique used in Fireworks for breaking a large graphic into smaller images to be contained in an HTML table.

JavaScript   Computer coding language that is embedded in an HTML document to add functions to the page. In Dreamweaver, JavaScript functions are added using the Behaviors panel.

Joint Photographic Experts Group (JPEG)   Image file format used for graphics that can display millions of colors and fine distinctions in shading and contrast. Used primarily for photographs.

kerning   The spacing between text characters.

layer   In Fireworks, layers act as transparencies that can be stacked to combine and organize complex objects. Organized and modified through the Layers panel.

leading   The amount of spacing between lines of text.

Library panel   The panel in Fireworks that allows objects such as buttons to be stored and reused.

link   See hyperlink.

Main toolbar   The toolbar in Fireworks that allows access to common operations such as copying and pasting (Windows only).

mask   An effect created by the combination of two images that uses the image on top to partially obscure the image below it.

Modify toolbar   The toolbar in Fireworks that provides access to operations for placing, grouping, and aligning objects on the canvas.

monospaced text   A font style that gives each letter the same amount of space.

navigation bar   A set of hyperlinks organized to improve the viewer's ability to access other portions of a web site. Usually a set of graphical buttons.

opacity   The relative transparency assigned to an object in Fireworks.

open path   A vector object that has beginning and end points that do not meet.

Optimize panel   The panel used in Fireworks to prepare images for conversion to the web-friendly image formats of GIF, JPEG, and PNG.

path   The lines or curves that connect points in a vector-based object.

pixels   The individual dots of light or color that compose a computer-generated graphic.

Portable Network Graphic (PNG)   The native file format used by Fireworks. Fireworks PNG files must be optimized and converted to a GIF, JPEG, or standard PNG format before they are used in a web page.

Property Inspector   The primary tool in Fireworks that displays the selected object's properties and enables them to be modified.

proportional text   A font style that allows a varying amount of space for each letter. For example, the letter *w* receives more space than the letter *i*.

raster   Another term for an image composed of bitmaps such as a GIF or JPEG.

relative URL   A URL that links to a web page or file within a web site.

rollover   A JavaScript behavior that causes an image to change when the viewer passes the mouse pointer over it.

sans-serif   A category of fonts that are without the extra decorative elements attached to individual letters in fonts; for example, Arial is a sans-serif font.

serif   A category of text in which letters have extra decorative strokes applied such as those found in Times New Roman.

slice   A web object applied to an image that creates an HTML table cell when the image is exported. Used for dividing large images into separate pieces and for attaching JavaScript behaviors.

stroke   The lines that define the perimeter of a closed shape such as a rectangle or the simple lines in an open path. Stroke settings are applied and modified in the Property Inspector.

Styles panel   The panel used in Fireworks to display predefined or custom styles that can be applied to objects, such as color, fill, and stroke characteristics.

symbol   An object stored for reuse in the Fireworks library for each document.

table   An element of HTML that organizes information into rows and columns.

Tools panel   The primary panel used in Fireworks for accessing drawing and selection tools.

tweening   An animation technique used in Fireworks to automatically draw images that complete an animation sequence.

typography   The process of styling text for use in a document.

Universal Resource Locator (URL)   The exact address of a web page as it is stored on a web server, such as http://www.osborne.com.

URL panel   The panel in Fireworks where a library of links is stored.

vector graphic   A graphic created by mathematical formulas that describe the position and color of points and lines in an image.

web object   HTML or JavaScript instructions embedded in an image.

web page   A single HTML document, including any supporting files, that displays on a browser.

web-safe colors   Colors that will display correctly when viewed in any browser or in both the Macintosh and Windows operating systems.

web site   A collection of web pages organized and stored under one domain name on a web server.

World Wide Web Consortium (W3C)   The organization responsible for maintaining and creating HTML standards including acceptable image formats for use on the Web.

Index

INTERNATIONAL CONTACT INFORMATION

AUSTRALIA
McGraw-Hill Book Company Australia Pty. Ltd.
TEL +61-2-9417-9899
FAX +61-2-9417-5687
http://www.mcgraw-hill.com.au
books-it_sydney@mcgraw-hill.com

CANADA
McGraw-Hill Ryerson Ltd.
TEL +905-430-5000
FAX +905-430-5020
http://www.mcgrawhill.ca

**GREECE, MIDDLE EAST,
NORTHERN AFRICA**
McGraw-Hill Hellas
TEL +30-1-656-0990-3-4
FAX +30-1-654-5525

MEXICO (Also serving Latin America)
McGraw-Hill Interamericana Editores S.A. de C.V.
TEL +525-117-1583
FAX +525-117-1589
http://www.mcgraw-hill.com.mx
fernando_castellanos@mcgraw-hill.com

SINGAPORE (Serving Asia)
McGraw-Hill Book Company
TEL +65-863-1580
FAX +65-862-3354
http://www.mcgraw-hill.com.sg
mghasia@mcgraw-hill.com

SOUTH AFRICA
McGraw-Hill South Africa
TEL +27-11-622-7512
FAX +27-11-622-9045
robyn_swanepoel@mcgraw-hill.com

**UNITED KINGDOM & EUROPE
(Excluding Southern Europe)**
McGraw-Hill Education Europe
TEL +44-1-628-502500
FAX +44-1-628-770224
http://www.mcgraw-hill.co.uk
computing_neurope@mcgraw-hill.com

ALL OTHER INQUIRIES Contact:
Osborne/McGraw-Hill
TEL +1-510-549-6600
FAX +1-510-883-7600
http://www.osborne.com
omg_international@mcgraw-hill.com

About the Online Files

To get the most out of this book by following along with the exercises, you'll want to download the associated files. These files serve a variety of purposes and are organized into separate bundles for each module of the book.

For example, in the exercises related to bitmap tools, you need digital photographs to experiment with selecting portions of an image for editing and to understand how effects and filters can be applied. All of the digital photographs you need are provided for you in the correct size and resolution to accomplish those exercises.

For some exercises, a Fireworks source file is provided so you can see exactly how effects have been applied and how the images have been composed. In many cases these files will save you considerable time; the basic drawings have been done for you so you can focus on using the tools.

You will also find files in a variety of formats when you begin exploring the integration between Fireworks and other programs. Files for Module 14, for instance, contain sample files in Flash and FreeHand format, as well as files for exploring the interaction between Adobe Photoshop and Fireworks.

To download the exercise files for this book from www.osborne.com or the book's companion web site, www.dw-fw-beginners.com, follow these instructions:

1. Create a new folder on your computer's desktop or in some other convenient location. Name the folder **Exercises**.

2. Right-click on the name of the module's files that you would like to download.

3. In the menu that appears choose either "Save Target As…" (Internet Explorer) or "Save Link As…" (Netscape Navigator).

4. Browse to the Exercises folder that you created in the first step and save the files.

5. You will need an unzipping utility to unzip the files for your use in the exercises—either WinZip (Windows) or StuffIt (Macintosh). Both programs can be downloaded at popular shareware web sites such as www.download.com.